On Wings of Eagles

On Wings of Eagles

The Plight, Exodus, and Homecoming of
Oriental Jewry

By

JOSEPH B. SCHECHTMAN

New York • Thomas Yoseloff • London

To My Wife and Collaborator

Preface

Throughout the ages, "Orient" invariably carried the connotation "static." The 900,000-strong Jewish communities of the area were included in this standard image of immovability. But in the last decade Oriental Jewry has dramatically disproved this commonplace label. It has been, and largely still is, on the move on an almost wholesale scale. And its migrations are not of the ordinary sort, involving merely a sizable section of the communities affected: their "surplus" or certain economic or social strata. They are in the main total transplantations, amounting for all practical purposes to actual liquidation of several communal entities.

Of Iraq's 130,000 Jews, 123,000 were in 1950–51 transferred to Israel by the unprecedented airlift known as "Operation Ali Baba." The "Magic Carpet" airlift of 1949–50 brought to Israel 48,000 Yemenite Jews; subsequent piecemeal emigrations reduced the dwindling remnant to some 600. Emigration, both to Israel and to other countries, has reduced Egypt's Jewry from 75,000 in 1947 to a current low of 4,000 to 5,000. Eighty-eight per cent of Libya's postwar Jewish community of 40,000 are now in Israel, and only 700 of the Aden colony's 7,200 Jews remain. Syria, which had 29,000 Jews in 1943, now has less than 3,000. Studies on religious rights and on discrimination in various countries, prepared for consideration by the February 1960 session of the U.N. Commission on Human Rights in Geneva, estimate that of the 291,000 Jews who in 1948 lived in the Arab states, only 44,000 to 51,000 remain.

Other substantial Jewish centers in the Middle East and North Africa, though not at the stage of liquidation, have during the past decade lost an impressively high percentage of their former numerical strength. Of Turkey's 77,000 Jews, 37,000 have come to Israel. Almost one-half (39,000) of Iran's 80,000 Jews are now in Israel. Over 160,000 Jews have left Morocco, Tunisia and Algeria, reducing by one-third their Jewish population. Further exodus from Morocco, which assumed the character of a stampede, was barred in 1956 by the Government.

Two features of this fateful geopolitical transformation are of major significance.

Eclipse or disappearance of single communities is in itself not a novelty in Jewish annals. Mother Diaspora has always had a multitude of widely scattered pockets and has been repeatedly shifting her wards from one to another. Shimon Dubnov's philosophy of history was based on periodic cycles of emergence and decline of Diaspora centers, vying for supremacy within the iron circle of dispersion. Yet, what has happened during the last twelve years is different. We have witnessed the migration of some 540,000 Jews from a dozen Oriental countries. Of this number, hardly 5 per cent have moved to countries other than Israel, thus perpetuating the pattern of dispersion. Ninety-five per cent came to Israel.

It would be less than candid to claim that all of them have done so merely because of choice. Many went because Israel was the only place where they could go. The fact remains, however, that more than half a million Jews did not exchange one country of dispersion for another, but have left the Diaspora altogether. About 11,600 re-emigrated. Some returned to their former countries; others obtained visas to Australia, Canada, the United States, Latin America. Yet some 500,000 stayed on and have been integrated, or—as in the case of the Yemenites, Iraqis, Syrians, Egyptians and Libyans—had no country to return to.

Another outstanding characteristic of this demographic upheaval is that it is rooted not in the age-old pattern of destruction by external forces, but in a purposeful self-transplantation of entire communities. In the years following the emergence of Israel, Jewish migration has been converted from a movement, however considerable, of individuals or groups into a total transfer of several Jewries of the Orient, intent upon putting an end to their dispersion. These entities had the good fortune of beginning—and some of them completing—the process of liquidation by timely self-evacuation, by homecoming.

For the first time in modern history, a steadily increasing number of countries are becoming *judenrein*, not because their Jewish population has been destroyed or forcibly deported, but in the main because the Jews themselves have taken stock of their position and decided that there was no security and no future for them in those lands. Belonging to various levels of general and Jewish culture and consciousness, living under different regimes, they have independently and often simultaneously reached an identical conclusion: that they were dwelling in the most exposed and explosive world areas and under government systems bent on destroying the very foundations of their economic and spiritual (if not always physical) life, and that they should go while the going was good. Moreover, they found in themselves the vigor and the courage to overcome the natural inertia rooted in their centuries-long residence in the respective home countries.

Necessity was their teacher. But they proved to be alert and willing pupils. They moved out, and did it just in time, thus writing a happy epilogue to their hazardous Diaspora existence.

This does not mean that there are no Jews left in the evacuated lands, or that there will be none in the future. But it does mean that the bulk of the Jews in those lands who wanted to leave have done so. Some residual groups have remained of their own volition and for good. Others have lingered on because of various complications or simply because of indecision, although many of them later joined the exodus.

More complicated, and often pathetic, is the case of those who decided to stay for good. Irrespective of the size (usually minute) of these clusters, their continued presence does not alter the fact that their former mother communities no longer exist as organic and viable entities. The pitiful remnants of Yemen's, Afghanistan's, Iraq's, Libya's, Syria's, or Egypt's Jewries, isolated and cowed, are disintegrating. They are the "lost tribes" in the world balance of Jewish national survival.

Unlike earlier patterns of Jewish displacements, the Oriental Jewish Diaspora, which is again on the move, is this time contracting rather than self-perpetuating, let alone expanding. An ever increasing number of vulnerable and untenable positions in the Moslem countries have been or are being evacuated wholesale and with unprecedented dispatch.

In several cases, it has been a "now or never" emigration opportunity, involving a great deal of hardship, almost total loss of personal and communal property, yet no loss of life. For the first time in the history of Jewish dispersion, mass displacement is not fanning out. It is centripetal, Israel-oriented—partly by choice and partly by necessity.

Outlining the history and the recent plight of the involved Jewish communities of the Orient, this study is intended to elucidate the background of their mass exodus and describe both its actual proceedings and its impact on the countries from which the movement has taken place.

A concluding chapter deals with the arduous and challenging economic, cultural, social, and psychological problems which are facing the integration of the 500,000-strong mass of Oriental immigrants in Israel.

The study is based on extensive published and unpublished source material, made available to the author by major cultural and social service organizations working in the Middle East, North Africa, and Israel.

Joseph B. Schechtman

New York
October, 1960

Contents

Illustrations

Immigrants at Haifa customs

North African Jews in a Ma'abara

Laborer from Kurdistau

Bokhara woman

Girl from Tripoli

En route to Israel

Moroccan Jews in new house

Introduction

The Dhimmi and the Millet Status. The problem of minorities in the Moslem world is as old as Islam itself. When Mohammed's warriors, some 1,300 years ago, began to conquer increasingly large portions of Asia, Africa and Europe, they had to establish some procedure for dealing with the subjugated populations. As codified in the eleventh century, this pattern distinguished between believers in Islam and infidels. Christians and Jews, as "People of the Book," and receivers of some form of divine revelation, were placed between these two groups. They escaped the tragic fate of other non-Moslems who had refused conversion and were either exterminated or enslaved. The "People of the Book" were tolerated under Islamic rule and were permitted to practice their own religions with certain restrictions. Their status was defined as that of *dhimmi*, a person protected by covenant.

The degree of this tolerance has been largely overestimated.

The fundamental Islamic concept is that of government by God, who uses Moslems as his instruments, all others being subject to the Moslems. "Moslems may be very tolerant," aptly said W. Wendell Cleland of the U. S. Department of State, who taught sociology for a time at the Cairo School of Social Work, "but it is the tolerance that comes from a proud conviction of vast superiority."[1] Added Pierre Rondot, Director of the curriculum in the Center of Advanced Moslem Administrative Studies in Paris: "A Moslem who feels and experiences from within the exalted character of his faith, derives from it a calm but profound disdain for those who do not share this faith with him. . . . Almost down to our own days, the Christian communities of the East have survived, among Moslem peoples . . . [as] a lateral group, tolerated, perhaps even prosperous, but excluded from the mainstream . . . relatively secure, but humiliated."[2]

In fact, heavy restrictions have been imposed on *dhimmis*. The victorious Arabs did not, as a general rule, force Islam on the conquered populations, but they did make the non-Moslems citizens of lower class.

Restrictions imposed on minorities were many and diversified. Transgression of some of them meant the withdrawal of protection by covenant, and made capital punishment possible. But even some of the minor rules, transgression of which led only to fines and other penalties, were in their nature both discriminatory and humiliating. *Dhimmis* were required to pay a head tax and land tax and were further taxed for the up-keep of the Arab armies. Cleland believes very realistically that the substantial revenue from these taxes restrained the Moslem rulers from encouraging mass conversion to Islam with a consequent loss of income. While some of the features of this code have fallen into disuse with the passing of centuries and the introduction of Western codes in much of the Islamic world, it still persists in countries where Islam is the religion of the state —in Egypt, Iraq, Jordan, Saudi Arabia, Yemen, and, to a certain extent, in Syria. The U.N.-sponsored new Arab state of Libya has also established Islam as its official religion.

When Arab domination in the Moslem-conquered countries was replaced by Turkish rule, Christian and Jewish minorities in the Ottoman Empire for some 400 years lived under the most remarkable regime of the *Millet*. Each religious group formed a community of its own, within the state and coterminous with it, managing its own affairs autonomously, under the general authority of the Sultan. At the beginning of the century, there were in the Ottoman Empire fifteen such fully autonomous religious communities—fourteen different Christian groups and one Jewish. They had their own schools where the teaching of Turkish was not obligatory, retained their own language and customs, and were free to maintain their identity.

With the dismemberment of the Ottoman Empire and the emergence of a series of independent Arab states, new problems arose for the minority groups who found themselves in the territories of these states. They present a multicolored and complicated variety. Albert Hourani enumerated at least two dozen different religious, linguistic and ethnic minorities in the Arab world, totalling 7.5 million out of a total population in this area of some 28 million. In other words, *every fourth human being in the Arab countries belongs to some minority group.* In 1947, when Hourani's book was published, the main components of this total were:[3]

Christian minorities .... 2.5 million
Various unorthodox Moslem
   religious sects .... 3 million
Various linguistic minorities ...... 1.25 million
Jewish minorities 750,000

The plight of the Jewish minorities is being extensively dealt with throughout this study. Less known is the position of non-Jewish minority groups.

THE CHRISTIAN MINORITIES

Summing up the plight of the Christian minorities, Pierre Rondot says:

In the Arab countries of the East, since they became national states, the Christians are no longer in subjection. The law recognizes them as full-fledged citizens with the same rights as Muslims. On the theoretical plane this is a tremendous advance. But in reality the law does not always succeed in prevailing over the old Islamic sentiment, always so alive in the masses of the populace, and to which the authorities themselves seem to take recourse whenever the state is confronted with a crisis. . . . In the modern East, Christians are nowhere the targets of systematic persecution, but there are few places where they are really safe and not subject to maltreatment if occasion arises; few, too, are the places where they do not suffer, occasionally or permanently, from discrimination, whether it be mere chicanery, or the intermittent effect of a social prejudice deeply rooted in the Muslim masses.[4]

In Iraq. The plight of the Christian minorities is best illustrated by their position in Iraq, Egypt, Syria, and Iran.

Iraq began its statehood under the British mandate with a very liberal declaration by the newly elected King Feisal I: "There is no meaning in the words 'Jews,' 'Moslems' and 'Christians' in the terminology of patriotism. There is simply a country called Iraq, and all are Iraqis." Before Iraq was granted full independence in 1933, the Iraqi Government submitted to the League of Nations a "Declaration of guarantees on matters of international concern." Ten of the sixteen articles of this declaration dealt with minorities and provided for their full equality before the law. But the very first year of Iraq's independence was marred by a wholesale massacre of the small Nestorian (Assyrian)* minority by regular Iraqi troops. Sixty-five villages were burned, 600 persons were murdered. Lieutenant Colonel A. S. Stafford, British Administrative Inspector in Iraq, gives a blood-curdling eye-witness account of the massacre:[5]

Machine gunners set up their guns outside the windows of the houses in which the Assyrians had taken refuge, and fired among them until not a man was left standing in the shambles. Women were ripped open with knives and then made sport of while they were in a state of agony. Little girls of nine were raped and burned alive.

The remnants of the Assyrians repeatedly petitioned the now defunct League of Nations to transfer them to some other country where they could live a secure and constructive life. Decisions to this effect were taken by the League. Projects of resettlement in Syria, Brazil, British Guiana and Tanganyika were studied and abandoned. The Assyrians are still in Iraq, living dangerously, permanently threatened with annihilation. On June 17, 1948, in the British House of Commons, the outspoken Conservative M. P. Skeffington-Lodge said:[6] "They live almost as the Christians of the pre-Christian Roman Empire lived. . . . They are facing virtual annihilation."

* Adherents of Eastern Churches in Iraq, Iran, and Turkey, called by the name of Nestorius, a fifth-century Syrian ecclesiastic. They prefer to be called "Assyrians," though this is also the name of a nation in biblical times.

In Egypt. The most numerous—and till very recently the least known—Christian minority in the Arab world are the 1,085,000 Copts in Egypt, 7 per cent of the country's population. Sizable Coptic groups exist in Ethiopia, the Sudan and Libya.

The Copts are no newcomers to Egyptian soil. Almost 200 years before the Arabs conquered Egypt in the seventh century, the ancestors of the modern Copts had constituted themselves as a Monophysite Christian Church. The Copts, like the Jews, were tolerated as a "protected" minority, subject to various disabilities and liable to special taxes imposed by their Arab rulers. They lived in their own semifortified walled quarters, strictly segregated from the Moslem majority.

British occupation (1882–1922) gradually abolished this segregation. Walls and gates were thrown down or disused. The Copts began to mix and live freely among the Moslems. Their children began to attend the same schools as Arabs. Competent observers assert that the best Arabic in Egypt is now spoken, not by Egyptian Arabs but by the Copts and the Jews. When Zaghlul Pasha launched the revolution of 1919, Copts and Moslems alike responded enthusiastically to his call. One of the most popular slogans of the Wafdist movement was: "Long live the Crescent and the Cross." In fact, more than half the Wafd party were Copts.

In 1922 Egypt became independent. The constitution of 1923 granted the Copts equal rights with all other Egyptian citizens, yet in the third decade of the twentieth century the seemingly united body of Egyptian society was undermined by mounting Moslem religious fanaticism which found its most violent expression in the Moslem Brotherhood. In the next decade disunity was accentuated and strengthened by Egypt's adherence to the Arab League with its racist Pan-Arab policy. Being neither Moslems nor Arabs, the Copts felt themselves reduced to a position of an isolated minority group which is increasingly discriminated against. They feel uneasy, oppressed and without a future in the land of their ancestors. Coptic leaders have been most outspoken in their complaints against the disabilities they are suffering under the Arab rule.

On September 24, 1951, the Cairo Coptic weekly, *Al-*

Manarat Al-Misriat, forcefully summarized the main Coptic grievances:

The Copts are considered foreigners in their own country by the government which fired them from every public civil office and forbade their return. The government ordered the foreign companies doing business in Egypt to employ only Egyptians, and interpreted the word *Egyptian* to mean only the Moslem. The Copts are also forbidden freedom of worship. No new churches can be built and no repairs of existing churches can be made except under impossible conditions that even the most savage barbarian people could not impose.

Concluded the *Al-Manarat Al-Misriat* editorial:

The Copts are determined now to demand security for their rights to life, belief, property and honor. If the country closes its ears to their demands, they must follow another road in order to arrive at a guarantee of their whole existence . . .

What is the "other road" hinted at by the Coptic spokesman? It leads in two different directions.

The first is the traditional way: the most energetic world-wide protest, to organize a special Christian conference to "demonstrate and parade before every embassy, Christian and Moslem. . . . We will go to America, if necessary, to make the Christian world a witness to our fate," said an editorial in the *Al-Manarat Al-Misriat*.

A more pessimistic and radical view was voiced by another editorial which advocated a different solution to the Coptic problem. The editorialist, a dean of the Coptic Church, anticipated the inevitability of a forced exodus of the Copts from Egypt, recalling "the ancient exodus of the sons of Israel from tyranny in Egypt, when they left a great, rich land of plenty, happiness and civilization, for a barren desert. . . . Some say that Israel may welcome the Copts if they are thrown out of Egypt and make their home in Sinai, because Israel will understand what good neighbors the Copts are. Together they might exploit the desert which would become the land of the Copts, its natural owners. . . ." (*Al-Manarat Al-Misriat*, Feb. 19, 1951.)

This somewhat fantastic vision is characteristic of the desperate mood of the Coptic minority.

At the turn of the year 1951–52, when the mounting wave of anti-British feeling degenerated into an indiscriminate intense hatred of everything non-Moslem and non-Arabic, even the physical safety of the Copts was endangered. *The New York Times* of January 6, 1952, reported that riotous Moslem crowds had stormed into a Coptic church at Ismailia and almost completely destroyed it. The church's beadle was murdered.

There has been no anti-Coptic violence under the regime of Gamal Abdul Nasser. But the Coptic minority is leading an isolated, strictly secluded life, acutely aware of the utter shakiness of their present relatively safe existence, warily watching the progressing deterioration of the position held by other Christian groups in the country.

The 200,000 Roman Catholics and the 120,000 Protestants are precariously holding their status quo. Their number has remained unchanged during the past years. Dr. Ibrahim Said, president of the Protestant Council of Egypt, told a newspaper correspondent in the spring of 1959 that no Moslem had become a Christian in the past two decades, though thousands of Moslem children attend Christian primary and secondary schools and an American college for girls, all run by Protestants.[7] Hardly better is the position of the Catholics whose schools in 1959 had a total enrollment of 52,723 pupils, mostly Egyptians and Moslems. In January 1959, the Ministry of Education closed three Catholic schools of the Collège de la Sainte Famille, founded fifty years ago and operated by the Society of Jesus. The Ministry charged that the schools, which since 1956 have been under the protection of Msgr. Oddi, the Papal Internuncio, had a curriculum that "did not truly reflect Arab trends in history and encouraged religious differences." According to Msgr. Oddi, the school authorities received no warning of impending closure; they were summarily replaced by an Egyptian administrator.[8]

In Syria. When Syria achieved independence from the last remnants of the French mandatory regime, her Christian minorities watched the new status with deep apprehension.

As early as 1942, Professor William F. Albright, Head of the Oriental Seminary at Johns Hopkins University, who had had close contact with many Christian Arabs, revealed the intense fear of the Christian population in Syria at the possibility of becoming a minority in a Moslem-ruled state: "The Christians of Syria have no more confidence in their eventual future as a minority in a Moslem State than the Nestorians of Iraq or the Copts of Egypt, both of whom are hated and despised (quite unjustly) by the Moslem."[9] Very soon the Christians began to experience the disadvantages of their minority status. American intelligence sources in the Middle East reported in May 1944 that "there has been an increase in Moslem fanaticism throughout Syria, and several serious anti-Christian outrages have occurred."[10] The situation hardly improved in 1945. In the Jezirah district in northern Syria, where persecuted Christian minorities (Armenian, Chaldeans and Assyrians) from Iraq and Turkey were encouraged in 1924 by the French authorities to settle, about 130 Assyrian families and about 30 Chaldean Catholic families were forcibly removed to Lebanon as refugees by army vehicles. Some 20,000 Christians were said to have fled Syria for Lebanon by November 1945. In 1946, the *Servicio Informasioni della Chiesa Orientale*, Beirut, reported the emigration of thousands of Catholic refugees to Lebanon.[11]

Considerable friction developed in connection with the draft of a new Syrian constitution. Article 3 of the draft text stated that "Islam is the religion of the Syrian State." Christian leaders insisted that this clause would result in their being made subject to Mohammedan civil law in matters of personal status, as Islam is not only a religious creed but also a civil code. A conference at Homs of representatives of the various Christian sects of Syria decided unanimously to ask all Christian deputies in the Syrian National Assembly to resign if Article 3 of the Constitution was adopted by the Assembly. The Syrian Orthodox Patriarch in Damascus, Alexdros Tahar, attacking the idea of an Islamic state religion, said: "Syria belonged to the Christians before it belonged to the Moslems. This time we are not going to embrace Islam in order to be safe in Syria. Either we will leave Syria to the Moslems and go into exile, or else Syria must belong to all Syrians alike, and Islam will not be the official religion of the state as they are trying to make it!"[12]

Faced with this violent opposition, the Assembly dropped the original version of Art. 3. It decided, however, that the religion of Syria's President must be Islamic. In addition, clause number 8 of the preamble of the constitution was worded as follows:

"As the majority of the people professes Islam the State declares its attachment to the Islamic religion and to its high ideals." Art. 36 of the Constitution declared the teaching of the Islamic religion obligatory in Syria's public schools.

There is little charm in being a minority in Syria. Minority groups are regarded as "fifth columns" and serve as scapegoats of every emotional outburst of Arab nationalism. Early in November 1956, "Day of Algeria" was proclaimed throughout Syria as a demonstration of Moslem solidarity with the Algerian rebels. In Aleppo the Moslem mob, with the connivance of the authorities, attacked and plundered local Catholic institutions, both religious and lay. Convents were destroyed, religious schools and the French *Lycée laique* were burned, two persons were killed and nineteen wounded.

In Iran. Iran is an overwhelmingly Shi'a-Mohammedan country. Ninety-eight per cent of the population is Moslem, and 93 per cent of this number are Shi'as; 7 per cent belong to the Sunni sect, which is especially strong among the Kurds."[13]

As early as December 1933, the special correspondent of *The New York Times* in Teheran called attention to the menacing growth of nationalism in Iran and stressed that only "a few practice nationalism from pure patriotism or the love of their country and its past . . . the true patriots may be numbered on the fingers of a hand, and they are not to be found in the chief places of the present government." On the contrary, "a large number practice nationalism from hatred of everything foreign, good or bad. . . . The cult of the 'foreign devil' is particularly noticeable in the police and the army officers."[14] This early trend of nationalistic intolerance grew in strength and intensity during the years to follow. The authors of two competent studies on present-day Iran, L. P. Ellwell-Sutton

(*Modern Iran*, London, 1941), and William S. Haas (*Iran*, New York, 1946) are outspoken in emphasizing this aspect of the young Iran nationalism. "Modern Iranian social and political ideas," says Ellwell-Sutton, "combine in a form of 'nation-worship' . . . which is quite as strong as anything in Europe today. . . . While unorthodoxy of a nationalist character is welcomed, religions which are neither Islamic nor Iranian fare less well. Armenians, Assyrians, and Jews all come in for their share. Minority clubs and societies are generally forbidden (though their religious associations are as yet untouched), and although they do not actually suffer from any disabilities, members of these groups rarely seem to reach high office (pp. 145–146)." An even grimmer picture is given by William S. Haas (p. 172): "Emotions [in Iran] are shifting from the religious to the national sphere. Until the time of Riza Shah, the Parsis, the Armenians and the Jews had been discriminated against and even persecuted because of their religion. Now that legislation had lifted the ban against these groups, by making them members of the nation with equal rights, public feeling and administrative practice use the national criterion to maintain the moral and social discrimination to a certain degree."

The position of the 50,000-strong Armenian minority, concentrated mostly in two large communities, one in Azerbaijan, the other in Julfa near Isfahan, had been historically one of social inferiority. Though they were not directly persecuted, their plight depended upon the arbitrary will of the authorities. It was not before the nineteenth century that as the result of the influence of the foreign powers their position began to improve. Some acquired quite a few important posts in the administration, while the majority was engaged in commercial and financial operations, and so held in Iranian society a place similar to that which the Jews used to hold in Europe.

The new nationalistic trend of the Iranian policy has, however, severely affected the Armenians holding administrative and clerical positions. Religious discrimination of old has been replaced by the barrier of nationality. The Armenians are increasingly banned from government employment, and have difficulties in finding work elsewhere. Modern education is now providing the Government with sufficient cadres of trained Persian intelligentsia, whereas earlier the Armenians had made themselves indispensable for such posts by their superior knowledge and experience. Their positions in agriculture, gardening, trade and business have also been greatly undermined. It is therefore not at all surprising that almost the entire Armenian community of Iran has responded to the invitation of the Government of Soviet Armenia to the Armenian Diaspora to settle in the Armenian Soviet Republic. By the end of 1946, some 30,-000 have already left Iran; in one day, 12,737 Armenians have crossed the Iranian-Soviet border.[15]

A tragic fate befell the Assyrian (Nestorian) minority. In Azerbaijan, where some 15,000 of the about 30,000 Persian Assyrians are concentrated, units of the Iranian military forces have on December 12–17, 1945, massacred scores of Assyrians in the district of Rizaiyeh (Urmia). In December 1946, after the liquidation of the pro-Soviet Azerbaijan regime of Pishevara, twenty-four Assyrian settlements in the same district were wholly or partially looted and burned, and more than 300 Assyrian men from the town of Rizaiyeh alone were murdered. Relating these facts in a memorandum presented to the Secretary General of the United Nations, His Holiness Eshai Shimun, Patriarch of the Nestorian Church, emphatically stated that "the last and only hope for surviving Assyrians in Iran is their removal out of that country; the request is unanimous and irrevocable."[16] When, in November 1947, Maurice Hindus of the New York *Herald Tribune* visited Rizaiyeh, Catholic and Protestant leaders in the forty-three Christian villages of the district told him their people were so frightened they were ready to emigrate and were hoping some Christian nation in Europe or the Americas would offer them asylum.[17] Their fervent hope did not materialize.

NON-CHRISTIAN MINORITIES

Also far from enviable is the plight of non-Christian groups, such as the Kurds and the Berbers, living among the Arabs.

The Kurds, like the Arabs, are Moslems. They constitute, however, a distinct ethnic group, and speak an Indo-European language of the Iranian type. Their territory is divided among Turkey, Iran and Iraq, and in none of them can the Kurds be regarded as integrated into the body politic. Between 1922 and 1945 they staged two major revolts in Turkey, three in Iran and five in Iraq. In Iraq they invariably inflicted crushing defeats on the Iraqi armies, an the Arab domination over this proud and militant race was preserved every time only by the intervention of the British air force, which ruthlessly strafed and destroyed Kurd villages and forced the insurgents into submission. As late as August 1945, Mulla Mustafa, political chief of the Barzani clan, with his 5,000 men, defeated Iraqi infantry and police troops supported by 25 planes. Then the RAF intervened, destroying 55 villages. The revolt was liquidated. The Iraqi Government took revenge in 1948 when martial law was proclaimed. Ten thousand Kurds were thrown into concentration camps, together with thousands of Jews arrested as "Zionists."[18]

The Berbers of Morocco are also Moslems, but they are of a different origin (Hamitic) and have retained their own unwritten language and customs, to the exclusion of Koranic law in matters of personal status. Indigenous inhabitants of North Africa, they were subjugated by Arab invaders in the eighth century c.e. They still constitute over two-thirds of the population of Morocco, however, and are concentrated in the mountainous districts of the Middle, the Great, and the Anti-Atlas, as well as in the plains of the Sousse to the south. Arab elements—and the mixture of the two races known as the Moors —which form only about one-third of the population, prevail in the towns and the fertile plains of the west and north as well as in some of the more arid semidesert plains of eastern Morocco. They have an influence out of proportion to their numbers.

The French administration endeavored to protect the Berbers from artificial and forcible Arabization. The French policy, inaugurated by Marshal Lyautey, tended to provide the Berbers with schools of their own and did not encourage them to learn Arabic. The co-called "Berber Dahir" of May 16, 1930, crystallized this policy by giving legal sanction to the customary laws of the Berber tribes and placing them under French penal code for serious crimes.

Moroccan Arab nationalists have bitterly resented these safeguards of Berber language and institutions and accused the French of "trying to keep the country divided."

The Berbers have no illusions as to their plight in Arab-dominated independent Morocco.

THE OUTLOOK

It is this writer's considered opinion that unless and until a radical change takes place in the entire social and spiritual climate of the Arab world, there is no satisfactory solution to the problem of non-Jewish minorities in the Arab Middle East.

The peculiar mixture of growing Moslem religious fanaticism —as strikingly represented by the Moslem Brotherhood in Egypt and its subsidiaries in other countries—on the one hand, and militant Arab nationalism on the other hand, leaves no visible "living space" for groups which are either not of Islamic faith or not of Arab origin, or both. The position of such groups becomes increasingly untenable. They feel desperately insecure.

In this mood, some Christian groups (the Assyrians, Copts, Armenians, and Syrian Christians) begin to think in terms of mass emigration, of following the Jewish pattern of wholesale departure. But for most of them this is wishful thinking. There is no country to which they could go, no "Israel" of their own which would be willing and eager to receive them. They will have to stay where they are: unhappy, frustrated, often bitter. No less unhappy, frustrated and bitter are the million Moslem Kurds who are increasingly losing hope for the fullfillment of their dreams of unification and statehood.

This state of mind renders all of them extremely susceptible to communist penetration.

To many minority groups, communism appears at times to offer material and political prospects which contrast sharply with the frustrations arising from their present inferior position. Traditional rivalry between the Greek Orthodox Church and the various Christian denominations which are linked with

Rome has made some followers of the Greek Orthodox faith
particularly receptive to renewed Russian support. Since 1945,
the Soviet Union has most skillfully utilized this advantage.
Exploitation of nationalist sentiments has also won many communist sympathizers.

PART ONE

Jews in the Arab Countries

1

Yemen: Ezra's Stepchildren— Operation Magic Carpet

> ". . . they shall mount up with wings as eagles."
>
> Isaiah 40:31

THE END OF GALUT YEMEN

On Sunday, September 24, 1950, the last two planes of "Operation Magic Carpet" landed at Lydda airport, bringing 177 Yemenite Jews from Aden.[1] Two months later, a conference attended by 2,072 Yemenite delegates from 82 settlements in Israel was held at Rehovoth to celebrate the end of *Galut Yemen* (the Yemenite exile), one of the longest-lasting dispersals in Jewish history and the first to be ended by the wholesale repatriation of an almost entire Jewish community to the Jewish homeland.[2]

"On eagle's wings," Operation Magic Carpet brought 48,818 Yemenite Jews to Israel in 430 flights during 1949–50—in contrast to a little more than 18,000 who had succeeded in escaping to the Holy Land in the preceding thirty-eight years.

The dramatic story of *Galut Yemen* and of its end deserves to be reconstructed. It is a part of Jewish history.

THE LAND AND ITS JEWS

The Jews of Yemen. The Imamat (ecclesiastical Moslem state) of Yemen is situated at the southwestern tip of the Arabian peninsula, between south Arabia to the north, the British Aden colony and protectorate to the southeast, and the Red Sea, which separates it from Africa, to the west. The land is mostly hilly and fertile, and the highlands are the only part of the Arabian peninsula with adequate rainfall. Here was the site of the biblical kingdom of Sheba, whose queen visited King

Solomon on one of the world's first good-will missions. Alexander the Great planned to live in Yemen after his conquest
of India. However, the name of *Arabia Felix* given to this country by Roman geographers is merely the result of mistranslation
by Ptolemy of the Arabic *yeman*, which does not signify
"happy" but "land lying to the right."

The data on Yemen's Jewish population have always been
contradictory. At the beginning of the nineteenth century, they
were said to have numbered 30,000, and to have lived principally in the capital city of San'a (10,000), Sada (1,000),
Dhamar (1,000), and the desert of Beda.[3] Since 1905, the
Jewish population has been repeatedly decimated by hunger
and disease. Yomtov Zemach of Beirut, director of a Jewish
school supported by the Alliance Israélite Universelle, who, in
1910, undertook a study trip to Yemen on behalf of the Alliance, reported 12,106 Jews living in about 150 localities; of
this number 2,744 were in San'a.[4] Twelve years later, another
visitor, Ameen Rihani, related that of the 20,000 Jews he found
in Yemen, 6,000 lived in San'a.[5] Wolfgang von Weisl, in 1926,
estimated their number at 35,000 (10,000 in San'a and 5,000
in Sada),[6] Ladislas Farago, who toured the country in 1937, put
the number at 60,000.[7] Professor L. Massignion in his *Annuaire
du Monde Musulman Statistique, Social et Economique*, spoke
of 100,000 Jews,[8] and *The 1949 Britannica Book of the Year*—
of 80,000.[9] However, all estimates upward of 50,000 seem to be
widely exaggerated. Despite early marriages, a high birth rate,
and even occasional polygamy, the natural increase of the Yemen Jewish community has always been very low. Frequent
famines heavily affected the village Jews. Death from starvation
was a common event. "Nothing moves the Jewish traveller so
much," wrote a Jewish explorer, "as the sight of many places
where all of the Jewish inhabitants have been carried off by the
last famine. The average rate of mortality is terrible." "We see
no grandchildren," is the complaint of the people.[10] Public
health in Yemen is notoriously wretched. There are indications
that among the Jews, of every one hundred children born, sixty
die.[11] In San'a, about 80 per cent of the Jews and 90 per cent of
the Arabs were reported affected with trachoma.[12]

At the beginning of our century, Jews were only found in the towns and larger settlements of the highland, where G. Wyman Bury had, in 1915, known entire villages exclusively populated by them. They were seldom found in the towns of the Tihama, and never beyond the Yemen plateau. Eastward, toward the vast inland desert, where raids and counterraids of the nomadic tribes were frequent, the Turkish authorities, having little control, were unable to guarantee the security of Jews.[13] A quarter of a century later, the distribution of the Jewish population in Yemen did not seem to have changed to any considerable extent. Hugh Scott reported in 1942 that Jews are encountered in the Yemen and the western part of the Aden Protectorate, in the cities and many of the villages on the high plateau and at middle altitudes, but not, apparently, near the coast (excepting the large ports).[14]

Physical Characteristics. From the anthropological viewpoint, the Jews of Yemen are very different from other Jews, even from Oriental Jews. They are mostly dolichocephalic (with long heads), smaller in size and of darker skin, and with coal-black hair. Slender and wiry, with fine features and large black eyes, they look as purely Semitic as any desert tribe. Country Jews were described as darker and often more heavily built than the city Jews. The latter were short slender people of light complexion, but with black hair and dark-brown eyes. However, among town Jews of the wealthier families Scott saw "people of a less common type, more slender, with small hands and feet, and very narrow heads projecting at the back; in such persons, the forehead, seen in profile, has a sweeping curve, the face is long and narrow, the nose very long and the lips thin. In stature and dimension of the head and face, the city Jews of San'a greatly resemble the Palestine Jews." A characteristic feature of the men's and boys' appearance were their shaven crowns, little black skull caps, and curling earlocks (*peoth*), similar to those of the orthodox Polish Jews. Women and girls wore a cowl, or hood, rising to a peak at the back of the head and bordered in front with silver embroidery, drawn in under the chin; a long narrow-sleeved blouse, usually of dark color or striped, reaches halfway from the knees to the feet. When out of doors, the women were not enveloped from head to foot like their Arab sisters. But they wrapped themselves in a large flowing shawl, dark blue or black, with a broad-patterned border and round or oval patches in which red predominated. Though not veiled, Yemenite Jewish women used to pull the shawl across the face quickly at the approach of strangers.[15]

Early Settlement. Asked in 1937 about the origin of the Jews in the Yemen, San'a Rabbi Soleiman ibn Mussa answered with a mixture of humility and pride, "How should I know about our origin? We have five thousand years of history, and no man can know so long a story."[16] This is certainly an overstatement. Yemenite Jewry is not five thousand years old. But they were indeed the oldest Jewish community in the Diaspora, and they have remained upon the same piece of land, comparatively unaffected by internal Jewish migrations, longer than any other part of the Jewish Diaspora.

The beginnings of Jewish settlement in Yemen are shrouded in myth. The records of Arab historians and chroniclers abound in legends, of which the most common is the tale about the Israelite malcontents who flouted Moses' order to kill all the Amalekites and were therefore driven to Yemen. Among modern historians, some believe that Jewish colonies in the Yemen may have originated in the commercial and naval enterprises of Solomon and his ally Hiram, King of Tyre, early in the tenth century before the Christian era.[17] A more conservative tradition places the settlement of Jews in Yemen in the sixth century before the Christian era, about forty years before the destruction of the First Temple in Jerusalem, when 75,000 Jews, including priests, Levites, military and civil officials, convinced of the imminent fulfillment of Jeremiah's prophecy of impending national catastrophe, are said to have crossed the Jordan and the lands of Edom and Seir, and settled in Yemen. Another batch of Jewish settlers is supposed to have arrived after the destruction of the First Temple by Nebuchadnezzar. Itzhak Ben-Zvi believes, however, that even the earliest Jewish settlement in Yemen may be definitely traced only to "the days of the Second Commonwealth and the mass migration from Palestine that ensued upon the destruction of the

Temple and Hadrian's persecutions of the Jews." Many Jews came after the abortive rebellion of Bar Kokhba. Others flocked from the Persian dominions. Large Jewish communities had existed in Yemen in pre-Islamic days, as early as the third century after the Christian era.[18]

The Curse of Ezra. Jewish settlers prospered in their new residences. Yemen was then a thriving country, and the Jewish newcomers, energetic, cultured, and ambitious, became an important factor in its development. "At that time," said Rabbi Soleiman ibn Mussa of San'a, "the Yemen was in the hands of prosperous kings and prosperity prevailed in her hills. The Jews, men of considerable wealth and esteem, lived in amity and comfort." And when Ezra the Scribe called upon all the communities to return to Judea and sent word to the Yemenite Jews to join their brethren in rebuilding the Temple and the homeland, "they scorned him and threw stones at him and hired assassins to kill him." Because of this attitude, Ezra cursed the Yemenite Jews, who attributed all their later misfortunes to Ezra's curse, and, in turn, excommunicated him and refrained from calling their children Ezra.

From those days to the present, a matter of at least twenty-six centuries, Yemen has never been without its Jewish community. "The Exile in Yemen" is mentioned in several quite ancient homilies. The country's average Jewish population for the first five centuries of the Christian era was estimated at about 3,000. They seem to have enjoyed prosperity until the sixth century.

Islamic Persecution. Yet since the country adopted Islam, in the seventh century, the Yemenite Jews have suffered almost uninterruptedly. The succeeding twelve or thirteen centuries were a continuous martyrdom. Yemen became an obscure and isolated province of the mighty Moslem Empire. For about four hundred years, little or no information on the life of the Jews has leaked out of the country. Yemen was then ruled by the Imams of the Zeidi sect, which is notorious for its fanaticism and utter intolerance toward all other religions. In the twelfth century, the Jewish plight became so tragic that in 1172 Maimonides, the Great Rambam, wrote his classical *Iggeret Teman*

(*Epistle to the Yemenites*), consoling the Jews of Yemen for the tortures they suffered and exhorting them to remain true to their faith, no matter what the cost.

Despite the remoteness of their abode, the Yemenite Jews never lost contact with the spiritual movements in world Jewry. Their religious life was based entirely upon the Talmud, though the settlement of Yemen by Jews took place long before the Babylonian Talmud was completed. They took a lively part in the creation of that most important Jewish spiritual work of the early Middle Ages, the Haggadic *Midrashim* (homiletic commentaries on the Bible). Cabala was always popular among them, and there were many Cabalistic authors in their ranks. Mori Salim Shabazi (born 1619), who wrote *Hemdath Yamin* (*Charm of Yemen*), was considered their foremost poet. Many Jewish scholars and poets have come from Yemen. Rabbi Solomon Adani, born in San'a, who went to Palestine in his childhood, is known to every student of *Mishnayoth* for his commentary *Mlechet Shlomo*. About two generations after him, Eliya Adani wrote *Piyutim* (religious poems). The Shabazi family gave several poets, and Rabbi Shalom Sharabi was among the greatest Cabalists of Palestine in the eighteenth century.[19]

Turkish Rule. In 1517, Yemen was incorporated into the Ottoman Empire. The Jews greeted the Turkish rule with some hopes for improvement of their status. In the seventeenth century, however, they followed the teachings of Sabbatai Zevi, the false Messiah, with such heartiness that thousands of them left their homes in an attempt to reach the Promised Land. But they were intercepted, and the Chief Rabbi of San'a, More Sulman El Jamal, was tortured to death.

In 1773, the Zeidis succeeded in expelling the Turkish governors. To mark their independence, they decreed the deportation of all Jews from the capital, San'a, to the coastal region, Thema, whose harsh climate made it uninhabitable for any but Nubians. Jewish houses were pillaged and occupied by Arabs. After a while, they were permitted to return to San'a. But their homes were not restored to them and they had to build a separate quarter outside the city boundaries. Occasion-

ally, a few Jews who were particularly useful in the minting
of coins, in financial transactions or foreign trade, had managed
to win the benevolence of the ruling emirs, and their influence
allowed for brief respites from persecution and for relative
prosperity. The Danish-German explorer, Carsten Niebuhr, the
first European to visit Yemen (in 1762), found there a well-to-
do Jewish community. Here is one of the glimpses he gives of
the life in their ghetto:[20]

Completely shut off from the city of San'a is the Jewish village
Qua'al Yahud, where two thousand Jews live in great contempt.
Nevertheless they are the best artisans, potters, goldsmiths, engravers, minters and others. By day they work in their shops in
San'a, but by night they must withdraw to their isolated dwellings. . . . Shortly before my arrival . . . twelve of the fourteen
synagogues of the Jews were torn down, and all their beautiful houses
wrecked. The Jews gave the number of their families at 5000 living at
San'a, Tenalm and Quaulan.

Yemen's independence was, however, short-lived. In 1818,
the Turks reconquered the country and were once again
greeted by the Jews. But repeated Arab revolts against the
Turkish rule made Jewish life miserable. Jacob Sappir, a Jerusalem scholar who made a two-year (1858–59) visit to Yemen,
related:[21]

The Jews who have been living in Yemen for many hundreds,
perhaps even thousands of years, are now in a position of inferiority,
and are oppressed by a people which declares itself holy and pious
but which is very brutal, barbarous and hard-hearted. The natives
consider the Jew unclean, but his blood is for them not unclean.
They lay claim to all his belongings, and if he is unwilling, they
employ force. They, therefore, do not let the Jews live in their
fortified towns so that they should not defile their homes and so
that the property of the Jews should not enjoy the protection of the
city walls. The Jews, therefore, live outside the towns in dark dwellings like prison cells or caves out of fear for murderers and robbers.
Whoever has any money or valuables conceals them in the earth or
in such secret holes as they have in their little houses so that nobody
may see them. . . .
. . . It is particularly bad for the Jew if he is himself accused of a
crime. There is then no mercy. For the least offense, he is sentenced

to outrageous fines, which he is quite unable to pay. In case of non-payment, he is put into chains and cruelly beaten every day. Before the punishment is inflicted, the *Cadi* addresses him in gentle tones and urges him to change his faith and obtain a share of all the glory of this world and of the world beyond. His refusal is again regarded as penal obstinacy. On the other hand, it is not open to the Jew to prosecute a Moslem, as the Moslem by right of law can dispose of the life and the property of the Jew, and it is only to be regarded as an act of magnanimity if the Jews are allowed to live. The Jew is not admissible as a witness, nor has his oath any validity.

In 1872, the Turks succeeded in reoccupying San'a and subjugating the high plateau. Yemen and Asir were transformed into a Turkish *Vilayet* (province), with a governor (*Vali*) directly responsible to Constantinople. This change in the country's status has considerably improved the position of the Yemen Jewish community. In a letter to the Anglo-Jewish Association, dated San'a, 28th of the Second Adar, 5635, (corresponding to April 4, 1875), four "Dayanim of San'a and its dependencies and all the cities of Yemen," after having stated that "in this country we hold an unstable and precarious position, and have during many years been subjected to every manifestation of disregard and intolerance," continued:[22]

Since this country has been subjected to His Imperial Majesty Sultan Abdul Aziz, the hope of better days has dawned upon the Jews, and many of our dispersed and fugitive people have turned back to their homes. Although the hardship of poverty clings to the destitute, it is a satisfaction that the poor may now live in their homes free from the daily terrors of death.

The Turkish rule over Yemen was, however, never stable and undisputed. Local revolts and disturbances were frequent and violent. The Jews suffered greatly under the chaos and lawlessness caused by this permanent internal struggle, and their very existence was repeatedly jeopardized.

In 1910, the Alliance Israélite Universelle sent one of its ablest teachers, Yomtov Zemach of Beirut, to Yemen to study the conditions of the Jewish community. Zemach visited the country several times, observed daily life and submitted a detailed and reliable report.[23]

On March 2, 1910, he wrote in his diary: "San'a. I am here now more than a week. I have made myself acquainted with the life of the Jews in all its phases. . . . They are exceedingly unfortunate. . . . They have forgotten what honor and respect signify. If they are abused, they listen in silence as though they had not understood; if they are attacked by an Arab boy with stones, they flee."

This attitude was largely caused by the almost absolute impossibility for an abused, beaten or robbed Jew to win his case before a judge (*Cadi*), as Jewish evidence was at that time as little recognized as fifty years previous, when Jacob Sappir visited the country. Zemach was, however, unable to make any positive proposals for relieving the depressing situation of Yemenite Jewry. Himself a pedagogue, he merely recommended the establishment of an Alliance school in San'a. Fully realizing that one school could not exercise any substantial influence upon the lot of the Jews dispersed in hundreds of places all over the country, Zemach also was aware of the danger of imparting to a few young Jews of Yemen modern ideas and mode of life and thus converting them into forlorn and frustrated "déclassés," to use his own expression. But, evidently, no other concrete proposal could be made under the circumstances that prevailed in Yemen.

Independent Yemen. The foremost leader of the intermittent struggle against the Turkish regime was Imam Yahia Hamid ed Din, who claimed that the "Covenant of the Prophet," the Moslem religious law, not the Ottoman secular code, should be the law of the land. Yahia won this struggle after two decades of bitter strife. On September 22, 1913, an imperial firman announced that Yemen's civil and criminal law be no longer based on the Turkish judicial code, or *Kanum*, but on the old Islamic code, or *Sheria*.[24]

For the Jews of Yemen this self-effacement of the Turkish regime was a heavy blow. The Turkish Government had done precious little for them. But even under the regime of Abdul Hamid, Turkey could be considered a legally regulated state in comparison with the ruthless despotism of the Yemen tribal rulers and petty Imams. Motives of self-preservation prompted the Jews of Yemen to remain loyal to the Turkish rule during the long-continued feud with the Imam Yahia. "The Jews of Yemen," said the *Osmanischer Lloyd* of Constantinople on July 9, 1912, "have shown a pronounced devotion to the Turkish Government throughout the hostilities between the imams of the country and the government. . . . It now seems that the Jews have been thrown into an evil plight by the agreement concluded with the Imam Yahia, as the latter . . . is apparently inclined to punish them for the loyalty they have shown to the [Turkish] Government." The Imam administration started demanding from the Jews taxes for forty years, i.e., for the whole period of the Turkish rule in Yemen (an amount of about £10,000).[25]

After the First World War, Imam Yahia, in spite of his staunch loyalty to the Turkish cause during the war, was recognized by the victorious Allies as the sovereign ruler of Yemen. The restoration of full independence of the Imamat did not seem to have affected the Yemenite Jews too adversely at first, though they were subjected to much humiliation at the hands of Arab fanatics. But after 1922, the situation again deteriorated. The emigration of a considerable number of Yemeni Jews to Palestine led to representations to the Imam by the Palestine Arab leaders who claimed that these immigrants were "assisting the Zionists to rob them of their country." About the same time, Arab pilgrims from Palestine launched anti-Zionist propaganda in Mecca, which was carried by the Yemen pilgrims back to their homes, with the result that Yemenite anti-Jewish fanaticism became inflamed. Much of the old persecution was revived and intensified.

Jewish Pariahs. The status of the Jews was defined both by Islamic law and the prevailing feudal system.[26] As the only "infidels"—there were scarcely twenty Christians in the country—the Jews were legally considered the property of the Imam or the sheiks. Every Jew over thirteen years of age had to pay a head tax of 12 to 48 silver drachmas, a kind of *Judensteur*, for which he was entitled to the Imam's protection; businessmen had, in addition, to pay 5 per cent of their profits. The ancient hereditary system of clientele continued to exist: every Jew had to choose a protector (gar), usually a member of the noblest caste of the Gabili, to whom he was to pay a special tax.

Jews were not permitted to serve in the army or to carry arms, even though Jewish smiths were practically the only ones who knew the art of arms making. Since Jewish men carried no *jambeya* or weapons, their dress was ungirded and, instead of a belt (the symbol of nobility), they had to wear a rope. A Jew was not allowed to ride a horse or a mule in the street and had to rely on donkeys for his transport. Even beyond town limits he had to dismount when he saw a Moslem pass by. A United States intelligence report (dated May 29, 1946) related that during the visit of the American mission to San'a, a Jewish boy and his mother were put in chains because the child accepted a ride in the jeep. Meeting a Moslem in the street a Jew had to salute him and inquire about his "exalted health." Jews were not permitted to walk on the same side of the street as the Moslems or to touch food to be used by Moslems; not permitted to wear colored clothes (only black or dark-blue smocks that leave the legs bare), or shoes; not permitted to stir from the ghetto at night or to have any lights on the streets of the Jewish quarter. A Jew was prohibited from entering a public bath except to stir the fires of the Arabs' bathhouses—a duty usually imposed on Jews. He could be called from the synagogue on his most holy day and ordered to perform the most degrading task, for which he would not be paid. A particularly degrading practice was the obligation of the Jewish community of San'a to clean the city latrines. Jews were forbidden to build a house more than two stories high. Though allowed to trade in the Arab city, they were forbidden to settle outside the ghetto walls.

A law promulgated in 1922 prescribed that every fatherless child under thirteen years of age—even if his mother was still alive—and every person who has not reached maturity at the time of his parents' death, be taken from the ghetto, converted to Islam, and reared in an Arab environment to become a member of the Moslem society. These waifs were described as "children of the Imam," whose duty was to provide for them until they were able to earn their own livelihood. Even if the relatives of the child undertook to care for him, the child was forcibly taken to a Moslem orphanage. Anxious to avoid this fate, the Yemenite Jews used to marry off their orphans at a very tender age, or smuggle them out of the country. This practice of forcible conversion has created a secret community in Yemen—the marranos of Asia, reported Farago (pp. 272–73): "Some of the Jewish orphans become good Moslems, but most of them are unable to escape the memory of their Jewish tradition and practice both religions. They are afraid to visit the rabbis or to go to the synagogues, but they cherish the Old Testament, and keep the prayer cloth and the phylacteries hidden in unobtrusive places in their homes."

The Jews suffered not only from legal disabilities. Possibly even more painful was the attitude of the native Moslem population, which, related Hans Helfritz in 1935, "regard the Jews as people of lower grade, and despise them utterly."[27] There were apparently significant nuances in the attitude of the Bedouins and that of the townspeople. "The fighting Arab," testified G. Wyman Bury, "has a good-humored contempt for them [the Jews], but respects their skill and industry and would be loath to do them harm. It is the townsfolk who give them a bad time, recognizing the power of their commercial rivalry."[28] Ahmed Rihani also stressed the particularly vicious attitude of the higher classes of Yemen society: "The common people may be rabid in their hatred, but the cultured are subtle and more malevolent."[29] Nevertheless, when Farago asked a "wretched slave" in Mocha to show him the way to the Jewish quarter, the latter jumped to his feet and cried: "I'll tell you the way, but you'll have to go alone. I would not soil my feet in Qu'ul Yahud." As he uttered the word "Yahud," he spat out in disgust and explained: "Whenever the name of Yahuda is mentioned—Allah curse him—I have to spit."[30]

The Economic Position. The economic position of Yemenite Jews has considerably deteriorated in the course of the forty years preceding their exodus.

Of the 12,026 Jews found in Yemen by Yomtov Zemach in 1910, 2,462 were artisans, 582 were peddlers, and 237 were occupied in "various professions"; some practiced agriculture, while the rest were wandering with the Bedouins in the desert. Later, agriculture was barred to the Jews, and life with the Bedouin tribes became too insecure. The Jews concentrated on handicrafts and "became the artisans of the Yemen": blacksmiths, potters, basketweavers, embroiderers, arms manufacturers, goldsmiths and silversmiths. They produced some of the finest workmanship in the world in delicate filigree jewelry, inset with semiprecious stones, colorful and exotic embroidery and basketwork, somewhat similar in color and design to that of the American Indians and the ancient Aztecs. In some of these trades they enjoyed complete monopoly in the country. They were also active in the cloth industry and owned soap factories, iron foundries and carpentry shops.

The business section of the San'a ghetto was composed of narrow streets with long tortuous bazaars and small shop stalls. In 1915, Bury noted that "European prints and calicoes may be bought in these shops, many in oriental designs which you will never see in Europe. Also woolen fabrics and various colors in flannelette are largely sold here and in San'a itself, where the Jews run most of the better shops, but have to clear out before night and go back to their quarter, as no Jew is allowed to live in sacred San'a" (p. 74). In 1922, when Ameen Rihani visited the country, "the best jewelers, big merchants, and those who have an ambition that rises above the two-story equality, have their business in San'a, but their homes are here, among their fellow Jews" (p. 184). Hans Helfritz could not "escape the impression that a certain section of the Jews in San'a have, despite all restrictions and their contemptuous position, amassed considerable wealth" (p. 248). Ameen Rihani, on the contrary, did not find any big fortunes among the Yemen Jews: "The richest merchant is not worth $100,000" (pp. 147–148). In fact, the standard of life of Yemenite Jewry was unbelievably low. Even a rich Yemenite Jew did not eat more than one course at a meal on a weekday; and the Yemenite immigrants in Palestine, employed in domestic service, had to be trained to eat an adequate meal.

Spiritual Life. In the walled ghetto of San'a, or in ghetto-like clusters outside smaller Arab towns, the Yemenite Jews lived a completely isolated life of their own.

The ghetto was the determining feature of the Jewish existence in Yemen. In San'a the *Qu'ul Yahud* had only one gate, well guarded by military and police who closely questioned wayfarers. It formed a mass of buildings penetrated only by a network of narrow lanes, with low houses built of sun-baked brick dressed with mud; all were plain, the windows being simple rectangular or round-headed openings with little or no tracery, and filled with thin alabaster sheets.[31] The cleanliness and loveliness of the Jewish homes—despite utter poverty and overcrowding of the ghetto—was particularly stressed by the few explorers who were allowed to visit Yemen. In the very heart of the San'a ghetto, Ameen Rihani "experienced a very pleasant sensation" (pp. 183–185):

My idea of the ghetto, as it exists on the East Side of Manhattan, or even in the Bronx, was totally but happily upset. I looked for clotheslines, for rags, for overflowing garbage cans, for accumulated filth, for babble and confusion, ragamuffin children, for slatterns with infants at their breasts, for dingy and smelly doorways; but I found instead a labyrinth of incredibly clean lanes, narrowing in places into footpaths, with little doors on either side, far apart, a few people going sluggishly and quietly hither and thither, a woman's face in a window, a flower pot, a sweet-basil plant. No cries, no noise, no confusion, no smells. . . . The little terraces are whitewashed and hedged with flowerpots; in the principal street, a broad thoroughfare leading to the outer gate, the children play; and neither the dense crowd nor the unctuous raggedness of the slums is evident except in its business section.

The German traveler, Hans Helfritz, stressed (p. 248) that "the interior of the houses is scrupulously clean." While noting that the Jewish Quarter was in a state of decay, Farago (p. 266) emphasized that "its spotlessness was a contrast to the smelly dirt of the Arabs' quarters." Hugh Scott also reported that Jewish houses in San'a "showed a high degree of cleanliness" (p. 136).

There was no restriction on establishing places of worship within the Jewish quarter, and Ameen Rihani found in the

San'a ghetto sixteen synagogues (*knis*). None of them was allowed to vie with the mosques, and all synagogues were little one-storied structures, distinguished only by their uniform coat of whitewash.

The Jews were permitted to elect authorities of two different kinds. One was the *Nasi*, generally a wealthy and learned man, who represented his community before the authorities of Imam. The other was the *Mori*, a combination of rabbi, judge, shochet, and teacher. The court of San'a was recognized by all Jews of the country as the supreme court. The chief revenue of the community was supplied by the *gabella* (salt tax) and served for charitable purposes.[32]

Though there were no communal schools in the ghetto, Jewish religious education was on a high level. In daily life their speech was Arabic, but they knew Hebrew and Aramaic, and rare were those who could not make themselves understood in Hebrew. Almost every Jew was well acquainted with the Bible, and biblical quotations were always on their lips. Despite severe restrictions, children always received a Hebrew education. G. Wyman Bury was "much impressed, on passing a Jewish cobbler's shop in a hamlet near Menakha, to see him teaching his children to read Hebrew Scriptures. . . . I understand that this practice is general; it denotes a laudable standard of education and considerable stiffness of mental fibre in a difficult environment" (pp. 30–31).

Rihani noted in the ghetto of San'a "a few schools, where children are taught to speak Hebrew and continue to live in the shadow of the synagogue" (p. 186). They learned the prayers and the Torah, all by word of mouth, so well that they almost had them memorized. One book served each classroom, and the pupils were trained to read it sideways or upside down, at their convenience. In addition to the Scriptures, which they memorized in the Hebrew original in their distinct Yemenite diction and intonation, they also studied both the Aramaic translation (*Targum*) of Onkelos and the Arabic translation of Saadia Gaon (*Taj*). The *Mishna* and the Jewish law were imparted to them by reading Maimonides' *Mishneh Torah* and to some extent through the *Shulkhan Arukh*.

The average Yemenite Jew was imbued with the Torah and its spirit by Hebrew tradition, and they became part of his everyday existence. The least-educated knew large portions of the Bible by heart, and the more oppressed they were, the more ardently did they cling to and cultivate the exalted spiritual vision of their people. They found in it refuge and solace from their abject existence, keeping alive and intense their dream of the Holy Land, fervently longing for the Messiah who would deliver them from exile. It was this dream of Redemption that, more than anything, gave the Jews of Yemen the strength to survive millennia of servitude and persecution.

THE DREAM OF REDEMPTION

Early Trek to Zion. Driven both by their wretched existence and by love for Zion, the Jews of Yemen were among the earliest Zionist immigrants to Palestine. The first group arrived there in the summer of 1881, after a difficult journey of several months, shortly before the coming of the Russian *Biluim.* Upon their arrival, the leaders of the small and struggling Jerusalem community were at a loss as to what to do with them. For many months the Yemenites slept in the open air. Finally, however, they found employment in construction work and, by their industriousness and modest requirements, soon won the community's recognition. The fact that living conditions in Palestine were superior to those in Yemen prompted them to urge relatives and friends to migrate. Thus sizable Yemenite communities gradually arose in Jerusalem and Jaffa. By 1885 they numbered 450.

In 1907, a comparatively large group of three hundred Jews, mostly sturdy and armed villagers from Heidan-Asham in the northeast of Yemen, landed in Jaffa in an exhausted condition, having lost several children and women during their long journey. They found employment as agricultural laborers in Rehovoth and Rishon-le-Zion. Their successful adjustment had its effect upon the Jews in Yemen, whose position had meanwhile grown increasingly difficult after the transfer of authority by the Turks to the local Imam in 1911. Joshua Feldman quotes "a respected head of a Jewish community" who reported severe persecutions and increasing emigration to Palestine despite warning letters. Another letter stated that when some Jews could not find purchasers for their houses, they destroyed them and sold the wood. The Yemenites who arrived in Palestine declared that no letters of any kind could check the emigration, as it was a matter of life and death for them.[33]

The direct call to emigrate to Palestine came to Yemen from the Palestine Office (which was established in Jaffa by the World Zionist Organization in 1908) and the *Hapoel Hatsair*, a non-Marxist socialist party. It was they who, in 1911, dispatched to Yemen Shmuel Eliezer Ben Baruch Yavnieli, a Russian halutz, with instructions to inform the Jews about Zionist revival and to organize their emigration to Palestine.[34] Disguised as an Arab, Yavnieli spent two weeks in Aden and then entered Yemen. Riding a donkey, he visited some forty cities and villages over a four-month period. Wherever he went, crowds of Jews gathered to hear him. Yavnieli told them of the Land of Israel, the new villages under construction and the stirrings of the national liberation movement among the Jewish people. The Yemenites showed great interest and asked many questions concerning the Western (Wailing) Wall and other holy places. Mystically minded, they eagerly asked this "messenger of Zion" whether there were signs of the Messiah's coming. When Yavnieli replied that he was not the Messiah's forerunner but that he could tell them of the coming redemption of the land through labor and devotion, the response was varied. Some decided that it was their duty to leave for Palestine. Others felt that the time of true redemption had not yet arrived and that it should not be "forced." Still others expressed their willingness to go if transportation were provided, as they could not finance the trip themselves. On the whole, Yavnieli noted a "tremendous longing for the Land of Israel." A major hindrance to large-scale emigration was the fact that most of the Yemenites did not have the funds to pay for transportation. Yavnieli, therefore, urged Dr. Arthur Ruppin, head of the Palestine Office, to secure reduced ship fares. Two months later, he was informed that Austrian Lloyd had cut its Yemen-to-Palestine rate by half, to 38 francs per person.

In the late spring of 1911, Yavnieli returned to Aden on a five-month mission. He dispatched a messenger, Mari Yehai Salam, into the interior to spread the news of the reduction in fare and to invite the villagers in the districts nearest to Aden to emigrate to Palestine. Most of these Jews were weavers, silversmiths or potters. Within six weeks, the messenger returned to report that one group from Sala'a was preparing to begin its journey in one month, that another was scheduled to leave in the following month and that additional groups from various villages were to leave in the course of the winter. The migration, as Yavnieli visualized it, was to be a gradual one; thus, each group could be properly cared for on its arrival.

In the month of Elul (August–September) of 1911, the first fifty Yemenite Jews departed for Palestine. Yavnieli felt that "the movement is gaining ground." From various sources it became evident that the resources of the imagination had been tapped and that the movement was acquiring the semblance of a Messianic awakening. In Sala'a, Jews began to sell their belongings at half price. However, according to Yavnieli's report, Imam Yahia, who did not want to lose his revenues from the Jews, forbade Arabs to purchase their houses. This was a heavy blow to the poorer Jews, who had hoped to finance their passage this way. Nevertheless, Yavnieli reported that "they were determined to go anyway." He sent letters to the most isolated communities and, taking a step which he had at first rejected, addressed an open letter to the entire Jewish community. A few months later, he decided to visit the country's eastern and northern regions. While on the road, he heard rumors that large numbers of Yemenite Jews had been arriving in Aden. Returning there, he found that some six hundred Jews had arrived and that most of them had already left for Palestine. Other groups, he learned, were en route to Aden.

A steady emigration to Palestine developed thereafter. In 1912 alone, over 2,000 immigrants disembarked at Jaffa. By 1919, there were 4,234 Yemenites in Palestine, 7.6 per cent of the total Jewish population of 57,000. A small percentage remained in the cities, but most settled as farm laborers in colonies such as Petach Tikva (three hundred families), Rehovoth (eighty families) and Hedera (sixty families).[35]

During the period between the two world wars, Yemenite immigration to Palestine showed a steady increase. While only 184 Yemenites arrived in 1919–23, an average of 37 per year, it rose to 2,500 in the years 1923–31 (277 per year). Between 1932 and 1938 the annual average was 1,005. Nor did the outbreak of World War II halt the Yemenite influx, as 4,703 entered the country between 1939 and 1945. By 1943 there were more than twenty Yemenite settlements in the Holy Land.[36] To summarize, the period of British rule in Palestine (1917–48) saw the arrival of 15,340 Yemenites, or 3.8 per cent of the total Jewish immigration.

Their journeys were perilous. Single men were able to travel without great difficulty. But when entire families were seen along the roads, they were recognized as being en route to Israel and were driven back or jailed. Some adults succeeded in escaping by disguising themselves as Arabs. The children, however, gave themselves away easily when they were tested by being offered nonkosher food.

Aden Way Station. The principal gateway of the Yemenites to the Holy Land was the British Protectorate of Aden which became a Crown Colony after 1937. From there they set out for Palestine in small groups. The number of migrants in each case was determined by the availability of immigration certificates. Some succeeded in leaving Aden relatively quickly. Others, however, had to wait for months and sometimes for years. The British White Paper of May 1939, with its drastic restriction of Jewish immigration into Palestine, converted the escape road of Aden into an almost hopeless bottleneck. The limited number of certificates had to be utilized almost exclusively for the rescue of Jews in the Nazi-dominated European countries. No "illegal" emigration was possible from British-controlled Aden. At the same time, the oppressed Yemenites continued to arrive there. In 1940, only 80 were able to continue for Palestine, and only 57 in 1941. Between November 1943 and October 1945, about 4,300 were able to reach Palestine.[37] Afterwards, immigration was virtually barred, only

55 Yemenites having entered Palestine in 1946; 50 in 1947; and 54 in January through October 1948.[38] The congestion in Aden became increasingly acute. The Aden administration described the situation as follows: "Large numbers of Jews have been induced to leave the Yemen in the hope of securing admission to Palestine. They reach Aden to find no prospect of obtaining Palestine immigration certificates, and, having no sources of livelihood, drag out a miserable existence, sleeping in the streets, in synagogues, or in disused warehouses."[39]

In his July 1946 report to the American Jewish Joint Distribution Committee (J.D.C.) Dr. Gertz Beigel, who had worked among the Yemenite refugees in Aden since the beginning of the year, estimated the number of refugees at 3,000. Over a third of the total were destitute; the others somehow made a living as porters, tinsmiths, cobblers, goldsmiths, peddlers and house servants. However, even those employed were living in misery. Living conditions were appalling. Yemenites huddled in courtyards, back alleys, on stairways; many literally on the streets. There were no sanitary facilities not even water for washing. The refugees were dirty, infested with lice. Many suffered from malaria and skin ailments contracted on the long trip. Scabies, trachoma, malaria, tropical ulcers and stomach troubles were prevalent.[40]

The British authorities permitted the J.D.C. to open at Hashed, a desert spot forty-three miles from the Aden town, a refugee camp named Geula (Redemption); by mid-1947 it had 1,700 inmates. A second camp, with 950 inmates, was organized at the village of Sheikh Othman, not far from Hashed. About 1,200 refugees remained in Aden. Housing conditions at Sheikh Othman, where the inmates lived on rations, were described as poor; an area with facilities for 30 persons housed 300. Conditions were better at Geula Camp where refugee care was rather comprehensive and where a Jewish Agency emissary did considerable educational and cultural work. A great deal of Hebrew could be heard there and the spirit of *halutziyut* was evident.

Describing the mood prevailing among the inmates of the

Hashed camp, Norman Bentwich, former Attorney General for Palestine under the Mandate, stressed that

paradoxically, the Yemenite camp in the desert is a more hopeful place than the Jewish quarter of Aden. It is an amazing community, crowded into a few acres, surrounded by barbed wire and holding their schools and their classes in the huts where they eat and sleep and learn. Compared with their habitations, the camps of the DP's in Germany are splendid mansions. Yet a spirit of hope and of preparation dominates everything. More than half of the inhabitants are young people below seventeen years of age. But the adults as well as the youth and children have the thirst for knowledge of Hebrew and the way of life of the Yishuv. It is quite exhilarating to hear the classes shouting together: "We will come to the Land though we may tarry on the way," reciting the story of the *Bilu*, repeating the doctrines of Rousseau, or chanting the songs of the return as they used, in their synagogues in the Yemen, to chant the verses of the Bible.[41]

The Aden Pogrom. Bloody anti-Jewish riots which exploded in December 1947 in the so-called Crater, the Jewish quarter of the city of Aden, affected the Yemenite refugees only slightly. The Hashed camp, housing by that time 2,400 refugees, was unharmed; the 450 Yemenites who lived in Sheikh Othman were evacuated to the Hashed camp under armed escort. The thousand Yemenites among the 5,200 Crater Jews suffered relatively little, since they had no houses, business or property which could attract the greed of the attacking Arabs. A number of them also sought security in the Hashed camp. In January 1948, a registry showed that only 810 lived in the city of Aden and 3,850 in the camp, which was ill-equipped to care for half that number.[42]

The Aden Government did its utmost to get rid of these unwanted guests and even attempted their wholesale "repatriation" to Yemen. In December 1947, the Jewry Agency representative in Aden reported to the Agency's Immigration Department in Jerusalem that the British District Commissioner had approached Dr. Olga P. Feinberg, a physician in the Hashed camp, and asked her whether she was prepared to pay for the "repatriation" to Yemen of all the 4,000 in the camps, including 300 orphans. He revealed that the Aden authorities had already contacted the Imam Yahia, who agreed to accept them provided that they return within two months. Dr. Feinberg indignantly refused to cooperate, maintaining that the refugees would migrate only to Palestine. After many arguments, she succeeded in deferring the matter.[43] By October 1948, a few months after the establishment of the State of Israel, 7,000 Yemenite refugees had assembled in Hashed camp where the J.D.C. provided for their support. But the British authorities continued to threaten the inmates with deportation. Their transportation to Israel across the Red Sea was impossible because the Egyptian Government had closed the Suez Canal to Israel-bound ships.

THE MAGIC CARPET

First Stage. Under these circumstances, large-scale, unorthodox and speedy action became imperative. The Israel Government made 3,500 visas available. The Jewish Agency began making preparations for their reception and absorption. The J.D.C. undertook to secure their wholesale transportation from Aden by air, thus inaugurating the unprecedented airlift evacuation known as "Operation Magic Carpet," under a contract with the American Alaska Airlines.

Headed by James Wooten, a dynamic and resourceful man for whom there was little in the world that he would consider too tough to deal with, the Alaska Airlines was engaged in rescuing Jewish refugees stranded in China and landing them in Israel. It succeeded in evacuating several hundred Jews from Shanghai, Tientsin and Hong Kong during the worst spell of fighting in the Chinese Civil War. On the Aden-Israel run, the Alaska Airlines was using chartered American planes (C-54 Skymasters and Curtis Commandos). In August 1949, the United States Government, for reasons which need not be discussed here, clamped down on the Alaska Airlines. A new company, the Near East Transport Company (NEAT), headed by James Wooten and Robert MacGuire, took over the airlift. At the peak of the operation (September–October

1949), it had as many as eleven planes from several airlines, both American and British, flying on round-the-clock schedules: those so engaged were the Trans-Caribbean, The Flying Tigers, Seaboard, and Western Airlines, as well as Fairflight Ltd. Some forty ground personnel and some thirty crew members were at that time regularly employed. Among the latter, according to experts, were flyers ranking with the best in the world.[44]

As long as hostilities were in progress between Israel and the Arab countries, the airlift had to be run as a secret operation. On their 1,760-mile nonstop, eight-hour flight, the planes were compelled to follow a route crossing Yemen but skirting Saudi Arabia, Egypt and Transjordan. Edward Trueblood Martin, one of the American pilots flying the Magic Carpet planes, later described their itinerary and its dangers:[45]

We were to fly a narrow corridor south over the Negev Desert to the southernmost tip of Israel, Elath, from there down the middle of the Gulf of Aqaba to the Red Sea, and on down the middle of the Red Sea to Perim Island at its mouth. From that point our course would proceed eastward to Aden along the southern coast of Arabia. It was imperative to stay on course and not fly over forbidden territory. One plane on the airlift had already been damaged by rifle fire while flying off course over Saudi Arabia near Mecca. From Lydda to Elath our course was flanked on the east by Jordan, on the west by the Gaza Strip and Egypt. Once over the Gulf of Aqaba and the Red Sea, we would be flanked on the east by Saudi Arabia and Yemen, on the west by Egypt and Sudan, territories which were all hostile to the operation. Staying within these limits would not be difficult by day, but at night or on instruments the job would be complicated by a scarcity of dependable radio fixes. In over seventeen hundred miles of flight, approximately eight hours flying time, we would have only three: one at Lydda, one at Jidda, the port of Mecca half way down the Red Sea, and one at Aden. It would be necessary, therefore, to depend on the dead reckoned flight plan and the navigator for course correction. And it was important to stay on course not only because of territorial limitations, but also for terrain clearance. Mountain ranges rise up to twelve thousand feet on both sides of the Red Sea, but since we were unpressurized, our cruising altitude would be only eight to ten thousand feet. However, the odds on good weather were in our favor—in the fall there is little precipitation in the Red Sea area—and the radio altimeter would give warning if we flew dangerously close to any terrain higher than our altitude.

. . . The time seemed to pass quickly on the airlift. Things ran pretty much according to schedule. Fly down empty to Aden in eight hours; rest three or four hours, and then in about eight hours return to Lydda with a load of Yemenites; a day or two off between trips. No flying was done over Shabbat, from sundown Friday to sundown Saturday. The Yemenites observed this rigidly and would not fly at that time. This generally resulted in flight crews having to lay over in Aden during Saturday.

They were shot at from the ground by small arms seven times when they were not directly over the Red Sea, and in at least one known instance a pilot had to feather his propeller when the engine was hit by a bullet in the tail section. The pilots fully realized that a forced landing in the event of trouble in flight would have meant disaster. There were only two places, outside the desert wilderness itself, where a forced landing was possible. They were the air strips at Jidda, in Saudi Arabia, and Port Sudan, farther south. The nature of Israel-Arab relations was such that any aircraft landing at Jidda would have been seized, the pilots interned—and there was no saying what would have happened to the passengers. At Port Sudan, which was under joint British-Egyptian control, "reasonable treatment was assured in the event of an emergency." There also was a difficult problem of refueling, which made necessary complicated arrangements. Sometimes fuel was bought in Cyprus, a two-hour return flight from Lydda. But the main fueling base had to be established at the port of Asmara in Eritrea, some 500 miles from Aden. There, on return hops from Israel, the pilots would take on full loads of oil in extra tanks which had been built into them, go down to Aden to pick up the Yemenites, and fly on to Lydda. Or else, the fuel would be siphoned off into storage tanks at Aden and then pumped into Israel-bound planes with a hundred-foot-long garden hose.[46]

The Best Air Travelers. The first group of fifty orphans left
Aden on December 16, 1948. Subsequently, groups of seventy
to one hundred and seventeen refugees were transported almost
daily in trucks to the Aden airport under the eye of Arab police. Their pilots considered them "among the best of air travelers." While waiting on the airfield to board the plane, they
were sitting quietly "under the wing, some of them smoking
water pipes which stood about three feet high off the sand.... If
they were excited about the trip, it certainly was not apparent
from their actions. The women and children also sat around
in small groups, the children quietly disciplined to remain with
their parents and keep out of the way of the ground crews.
Their interest in the aircraft appeared casual and they did not
wander around, touching and fingering the strange marvel of
flight as might have been expected. It seemed as though they
accepted this great metal bird poised on the desert as a part
of the Bible and prophecy in which they were so well versed."
James Wooten was impressed by the fact that "these people
out of an age a thousand years behind our own, had no fear
of flying. They had never seen an airplane or any other machine
before, but they had implicit faith in the words of Isaiah. Our
plane was the eagle whose wings would carry them to the
Promised Land." During the flight, once accustomed to the
steady drone of the engines, most of them dozed off in their
seats, awakening only occasionally for snacks of sandwiches and
fruit offered by the cabin attendant. Others were staring in a
relaxed manner through the windows.[47]

The aircraft loading schedule limited the amount of luggage
they could bring to not more than about fifty pounds each.
Some had to leave behind possessions which were either too
bulky to fit into the belly hatches or cabin, or which exceeded
reasonable weight allowances. Last-minute decisions had to
be made. Particularly painful was the necessity to part with
cherished Torah scrolls and religious books, which many had
carried with them throughout the long, arduous and perilous
journey over the desert. Almost three hundred precious Torah
scrolls and thousands of old Bibles, prayerbooks, Talmud sets,
Midrashim, etc., were accumulated in a Jewish Agency store-

house. They were packed in cases and shipped to Elath in 1950.[48]

At an early stage, the planes had been carrying one hundred and twenty-five to one hundred and forty-five Yemenites per flight, without exceeding the gross weight limit of an aircraft that normally carried no more than about sixty-five passengers in scheduled flight operations in the United States. This was possible because the average weight of an undernourished and emaciated Yemenite male was about eighty pounds. The planes were accordingly refitted. Instead of the regular passenger seats, rows of plywood benches were installed from forward cabin to aft, on both sides of a narrow aisle, to seat eight persons abreast across the cabin. In all, there were twenty rows from fore to aft, providing a total seating capacity of one hundred and sixty persons. Each bench contained one safety belt to cross the laps of four persons. Each mounted a plywood back which would afford some comfort. But even the pilots themselves wondered how long a thin-skeletoned body would be able to sit on a hard, vibrating bench and stand the gaff.[49] Later, the U.S. Civil Aeronautics Authority ruled that a seat belt must be provided for each passenger. Since the NEAT flew under American regulations, it had to abide by this order. Through an ingenious arrangement, it nevertheless succeeded in getting ninety seats into a plane. Infants were carried in the arms of their mothers or tucked into baskets. Rations on the flight were rather meager: hard-boiled eggs and dry cheese sandwiches, and pint bottles for the children. But there were no complaints.[50]

At the end of February 1949, the first phase of the Magic Carpet operation was completed; in two months some 4,500 refugees were flown from Aden to Israel. Almost all of the arrivals were women, children and elderly persons. The Aden authorities retained at first 860 refugees of military age, but early in March they were given permission to leave, and the first group was flown to Israel on March 6. By March 11, a total of 55 flights had been completed, clearing the accumulated backlog of 3,300 Yemenite refugees. The Joint Distribution Committee paid $97 for each passenger flown to Israel, bringing the cost of this phase of the Magic Carpet to $320,000. On British insistence, the Hashed camp was closed.

The Influx Continues. The British authorities in Aden had permitted the J.D.C. to organize the wholesale air evacuation of the refugees on the assumption that this would liquidate the "Yemenite problem" in the crown colony. But they miscalculated. The influx from Yemen continued. Hundreds of other Yemenite Jews were making the six-weeks' trek across the desert.

Faced with the continued flow of refugees, the Governor of Aden, Sir Reginald Champion, formerly District Commissioner of the Galilee under the British Mandatory Administration, took stern measures to stem the influx. Claiming that it was creating an "explosive situation in Aden which might lead to a recurrence of the 1947 anti-Jewish riots," Sir Reginald issued orders to strengthen patrols on the outskirts of the city and instructed the local sultans and sheikhs in the British Aden Protectorate (situated between Yemen and the crown colony of Aden) to strictly guard the area under their jurisdiction. In addition, he warned representatives of the Jewish Agency and the J.D.C. that they were prohibited from extending aid to Yemenite refugees or housing them in the camps.[51] Simultaneously, Sir Reginald requested the Imam to adopt rigorous measures to stop Jews from leaving Yemen.[52] The Imam accordingly decreed that Jews must register themselves and their property, forbade them to leave for Aden and warned that persons caught in an attempt to flee would be sternly punished and their property subject to confiscation.[53]

Yemen Changes. In the meantime, revolutionary developments had been taking place in the traditionally hidebound Yemen. In February 1948, news reached the outside world that Imam Yahia, his chief minister and two of his sons had been murdered by rebels, and that an assembly of ulemas (Moslem priests) and notables at San'a had elected the rebellious chief Sayyid Abdullah Ibn Ahman al-Wazir as the new Imam.

However, the regime proved to be short-lived. Emir Saif al Islam Ahmad, the eldest son of Imam Yahia, who had been designated by his father as his successor, raised an army and established himself as the ruler in March 1948. (In ascending the throne, he changed his name to Ahamad al-Nasir li-Din Allah.) British officials in Aden were unanimous in their opinion that the new Imam was treating his Jewish subjects "with great kindness." They admitted that this benevolence was to them an incomprehensible mystery.[54]

The British Cooperate. In an effort to clarify and normalize the situation, the Immigration Department of the Jewish Agency delegated to Aden Dr. Jacob Vainstein.[55] His mission was to persuade the British administration to agree to the reopening of a reception camp for the Yemenite refugees and to allow them to be flown to Israel from the Aden airport, an R.A.F. base. In addition, he was to secure the permission of the sultans of the British Protectorate areas to allow the transit through their territories, and to obtain the consent of the Yemen Imam to the mass exodus of his Jewish subjects.

Dr. Vainstein arrived in Aden on May 12, 1949. He was welcomed by the British authorities, who by that time were willing to lift the ban on the further influx from Yemen and stated so officially in a letter by the Governor to Selim Banin, head of the Aden Jewish community, only a week before. Dr. Vainstein strengthened this attitude, telling the Governor and his assistants that by helping the Jewish evacuation from Yemen "they would be doing an historic and humanitarian act." The second stage was to obtain the cooperation of the sultans of Audhaly, Sallah ibn Hussein, and Fadhli, Abdallah Hussein, and of Hussein ibn Ahmad Havili, the Sherif of Beihan, through whose territories the refugees had to pass on their way from Yemen. But, recalls Vainstein, "I felt that we would have no difficulties with the sultans, because the British do not want us to have any." In fact, when Major Basil W. Seager, Political Officer for the Protectorate and the real "boss" in the sultanates, arranged a meeting with their rulers, the negotiations "were short and sweet, and they showed much understanding for the cause we had discussed." "Naturally," added Dr. Vainstein, "encouragement on our part was not lacking."[56]

The plan of action presented by Seager, and readily accepted by the Arab chieftains, was based on an estimate that there would be 10,000 Jews trying to leave the Yemen in the course of a year. Once inside the Protectorate border, the migrants had to be directed to three reception centers, whence their dispatch to the camp in Aden could be organized and regulated. One such center was to be at Mokeiras in Audhaly, where the small airfield could be used for dispatching them on the last lap of the journey by plane—a distance of forty-five minutes' flying time to Aden. This had originally been suggested by the Audally Sultan himself, but Seager now proposed that a certain number of the people coming in at this point should be sent on by truck through the adjoining territory of Fadhli—this, in order to bring the Sultan of Fadhli in on the scheme and avoid bad blood between the two rulers. Neither should be able to accuse the other of being a Jew-helper. Another reception center would be set up in the Beihan territory, close to the easternmost regions of the Yemen. Refugees coming from San'a could reach this point in four days by foot, and here too they would be put on planes and flown to Aden in eighty or ninety minutes. Finally, there would be a third assembly point at Dhala, right on the border, almost directly north of Aden; here the Jews would travel by car, passing Lahej, the closest sultanate from Aden. This was to be the shortest route of the three.

Seager, on behalf of the British authorities, undertook to watch over the safety of the Jews moving through the Protectorate. He suggested that those living in the Protectorate itself, some two thousand, should stay last to cover the movement of the others, without attracting too much attention among the Arabs. Jewish Agency emissaries were to be stationed at each of the assembly points to organize and regulate the movement. They would be in touch with Aden by wireless. Strict secrecy was deemed vital to the whole operation, and Dr. Vainstein undertook to have the military censorship in Israel prevent leakages at that end.

The only question that remained unsettled was that of the amount of "head tax" or "transit fees" to be paid for the passage of the refugees through the sultans' territories.[57]

The Imam's "La Man'a Aleikum." The chief task was, however, to obtain the Imam's consent for the departure of his
Jewish subjects. A "high British Security Officer" told Dr.
Vainstein that the prerequisite for the success of the entire
Yemen cum Aden project was "to reach some agreement with
the Imam," who, however, "would certainly not receive a Jew
in audience, and it was doubtful whether he would agree to see
a European. . . . But the Imam's personal representative in Aden
might agree to mediate between us and the Imam regardless of
the price."

It is questionable whether the good offices of this representative were sought and obtained. The suggestion of approach-
ing the Imam on behalf of the American Joint Distribution
Committee was frowned upon by the British: they saw no justification for an intercession by an *American* organization, and
felt that it would be of no avail. Yoseph Zadok, a Yemenite Jew
who had come to Palestine as a boy and, dressed as an Arab,
had, in 1948–49, six times visited Yemen to prepare and organize the exodus, replied by a flat "Never" to a point-blank question whether there were at any time negotiations between outside Jewish bodies and the Imam.[58]

The announcement that, in a momentous reversal of
Yemen's traditional policy, the Imam permitted his Jewish
subjects to leave the country freely, came completely unexpected. Its motivation is still unknown. It is even to this day
not established in which form this authorization was given. It
is usually referred to as Imam's "letter" or "permit"; its wording has, however, never been published. It was rumored that
a group of San'a Jews sent the Imam a petition asking to be
allowed to leave the country, and that it was in a corner of this
paper that he wrote in Arabic, *La Man'a Aleikum* (I shall not
prevent you) and affixed his signature.

The leaders of the San'a Jewish community, interviewed after their arrival in Aden, intimated that the Imam had acted
chiefly out of *hassidut*—a Hebrew word implying anything
from simple human kindliness to piety and saintliness. They
felt that the decision to let the Jews go was prompted as much

by fear of God as by any other reason.* The Imam was said to have stipulated that every departing Jew must sell every bit of his property, and to have told his Arab subjects to buy up these properties. While protecting the Jews in some measure from the price-slashing usual in a forced sale, he wanted them not to leave anything behind which might later form the basis of a Jewish claim on the Yemen. Reports on the actual outcome of this well-intended stipulation are contradictory. Some refugees said that they had "got good money for what they had to sell" because "not a few Arabs believed that the Jews would return one day with the apparently omnipotent armed forces of Israel and take everything back." Shlomo Levy, the son of the chief Rabbi of San'a, related with a chuckle: "The Arab to whom I sold my house told me: 'Look, I am paying you good money, please remember this when you come back, and mark this house, and tell your brethren in Israel not to destroy it with their bombs."

Shlomo Barer who interviewed many other Yemenite refugees, observes that for the very same reason many Arabs were reluctant to touch the property of the departing Jews: "What was the use of buying a house if the Jew would return as a conqueror and take it back from you?" And finally, among those who were not motivated by fantastic speculation about the future, the simple economic laws of offer and demand began to assert themselves: because the Jews had to rid themselves of all possessions before leaving, prospective Arab buyers soon realized that if they waited long enough they would get everything at bargain prices; in fact, many Jews found it extremely difficult to realize their assets and often got pitifully little for their properties.[59]

* Said Major Basil W. Seager in a lecture on Yemen delivered before the Royal Central Asian Society in London: "The State of Israel should be grateful to the Imam Ahmed for putting no obstacles in the way of the Yemeni Jews' mass exodus. I know that Yemeni governors had explicit orders to expedite them on their way. I think I am right in saying that not a single Jew was attacked on his way southwards. Some must have trekked over 600 miles through Arab territory. It is true that they had to pay a lot of money on the way, but the important thing is that they got through, though inevitably many of the sick and elderly fell by the wayside." (B. W. Seager, "The Yemen," in *Royal Central Asian Journal*, July–October, 1955, p. 220.)

A Community on the Move. Economic considerations, however, were the least decisive in determining the scope and tempo of the exodus. When, at the end of May–beginning of June 1949, news of the Imam's *La Man'a Aleikum* had reached the Jewish communities throughout the country, the long pent-up yearning for Redemption exploded with almost elemental force. Very few hesitated. The overwhelming majority went on the move almost immediately. Recalled Zecharia Nissim, from a village situated a fortnight's journey from San'a:[60]

We were instructed by the Rabbi of our village to transfer all we had to the Arabs and whatever they agreed to pay we should accept, for the Miracle of the Redemption was at hand. We did as we were instructed and made ready for the journey. The orders were that no one in the village travel alone, but the whole village together. The money must be divided equally among rich and poor so that all might reach the Land together. Afterward they would return the money given to them as a loan. This we did before we made our way to the city of San'a. The flour and the bread we transported on the camels and the asses together with the oil and the coffee.

In the course of that summer, Jews set out from hundreds of localities scattered all over the country.

They did not proceed from these places all at the same time, nor in the same fashion. From some—cities like San'a, Haulan, Sharab, Sa'da, Ibb, Dhamar—went on the road in fairly compact and continuous groups of forty or fifty or a hundred persons. Of the smaller localities, many were emptied of their Jews at one stroke, overnight. From dozens of villages they proceeded in small detachments, individual families, a man and his wife and his children. . . .

They descended mostly from the densely populated central and southern highlands, but they also came from the far north, whence they had to traverse the mountain line from the Saudi Arabian border and for three hundred miles across the whole length of the Yemen. They came from the humid lowlands and the hot, sandy desert stretches along the Red Sea in the West. . . . They came from places where the existence of Jews had never been suspected. Some made the journey in ten or twelve days. These were the lucky ones. For most of them it took four or six weeks; for some a harrowing three months.[61]

Some of the migrants went on foot, some rode donkeys; very few were able to travel at least part of the way by bus. Leaving aside those from remote districts and taking San'a, roughly in the center of the Yemen, as a convenient starting point, the distance they had to cover on their tortuous trek was a stretch of more than two hundred miles of rough unfriendly territory, along which they were exposed to sharp extremes of temperature; there was no shade from the sun by day and no shelter from cold by night, for most of the time. Thousands fell ill on the way, hundreds died from sickness, hunger and hardship. They were intermittently harried, beaten, robbed by the Arabs whose villages they had to cross, fleeced by local petty sultans and sheikhs, as well as by customs officials. Before departing, each emigrant had to pay a head tax of three Maria Theresa silver dollars (or riyals, approximately one U.S. dollar) for an exit permit.[62]

Once they were over Yemen's state border, the weary wanderers had to make further payments to rulers of the five petty principalities in the British Protectorate, situated along the eighty-mile stretch between Dhala, near the frontier, and the Aden Colony proper. Each chieftain exacted some money: a toll fee per head, varying according to place and time (usually three Maria Theresa dollars per man, woman or child), with an additional tax for each item of their belongings and for their most precious possession, the handwritten Torah scrolls. Zecharia Nissim, who, with his parents, went through the entire journey from his native village to Aden, recalled: "The Arabs were closing the way before us every five kilometers and demanding money. We paid them a little and they asked for more, and we gave them more, for whatever they asked they were given. In one of the places there came Englishmen, who sought to search all our goods as well as our persons, for they thought that we had gold. And they even opened the Sefer Torah and searched, and they pried into every little thing. They took our clothes from our backs, even our shoes, but found nothing. So again we packed and again we traveled."[63] It is estimated that the average amount paid during these peregrinations was from three to six American dollars per person.[64]

Those who were relatively well-to-do paid for those who had no money left.

There was, in itself, nothing exceptional in the head tax the Jews had to pay on crossing from one sultan's territory to another's. Such payments are normal practice in the Aden Protectorate, for Arabs and Jews alike. In some places they were effected, against receipt, in the offices responsible to the British political officer. But very often the Yemenite refugees had to pay more—sometimes double the customary amount taken from Arab travelers.[65]

The Great Influx. The first group of two hundred, the spearhead of the general exodus, appeared unannounced on the border of the Protectorate at Lahej on or about June 9, before Major Seager's orderly evacuation plan had had a chance to be put into operation. For a week, their fate was uncertain, but on June 16 they finally were admitted to the Hashed camp, where nothing as yet was ready for their accommodation. Almost immediately thereafter, the Aden Government received information that within two months an "inflow from anything between five to twenty thousand" Yemenite refugees could be expected. In fact, already by July 1, some two thousand were reported waiting at Dhala, Lodhar and other places in the Protectorate for permission to enter the camp. Another four hundred arrived at Lahej a few days later and told of more on the way.

The elemental mass character of this migration precluded its organization in orderly stages and according to localities. At the outset, those responsible for the evacuation program believed that the number of arrivals would not exceed a few hundred daily and that a reception camp of medium size, and a daily airlift capable of transporting approximately one thousand weekly, would be sufficient. Indeed, the British authorities ruled that the Hashed camp would hold no more than one thousand persons at any one time. But already early in July, the acting political officer of the Aden British Administration, on a tour of the Western Protectorate, was told by Yemenite refugees that they were both unable and unwilling to submit to any measures regulating their arrival in the colony. They would come by any ways and means, in any numbers, and at any time. All plans for an orderly evacuation went overboard.

On July 4, 1949, an additional camp, New Hashed, had been hurriedly declared open. At that time it was little more than a stretch of hot, open desert, with five narrow mud-brick barracks, of which three were set aside as "hospital," "clinic," and "isolation ward." Only two barracks remained available for housing the incoming refugees. Their "absorptive capacity" was forty to fifty people each, but with the arrival of the first few hundred refugees, they had to house many more. There were no beds. The inmates squatted or lay on mats spread on the ground. There was almost no passageway between the bodies. This emergency arrangement proved to be hopelessly inadequate. Countless families had to remain in the open in the blazing sun, with the sands blowing about them. Ten more mud-brick barracks were rapidly being built, but by the time they were ready for occupation, thousands more newcomers were looking for shelter. They had to remain without a roof over their heads in an area which had no rain, no vegetation, and where even thorns and thistles were rare. The refugees were exposed to the scorching sun; mothers attempted to protect their babies by shading them with their bodies. By August 13, the population of New Hashed camp reached the 2,500 mark.[66] By September 1, there were already 7,000; two weeks later, 11,333; and by September 20, over 13,000.[67]

At the early stage, the scope of the airlift evacuation was strikingly inadequate as compared with the intensity of the inflow. Only 159 camp inmates were flown to Israel in the month of May, 108 in June, and 625 in July. In August, evacuation was stepped up, and 2,170 left.[68] But this, too, was of little help. The overcrowding assumed alarming proportions.

Physical Conditions. Arriving after weeks on the road, the refugees were reaching the camp in a state of utter physical exhaustion—dirty, diseased, starved and half-naked. Their power of resistance was gone. There were days with seven or eight deaths each. Many refugees arrived in a state beyond help, and most of the deaths occurred within twenty-four hours of their reaching the camp. One of the camp nurses, Tova Englard, later recalled:[69]

I don't really know how to describe the mass of humanity pouring in. . . . They were hungry and sick, and most of them had terrible sores. Soon there were so many they covered every inch of the ground. You had to pick your way not to step on them. . . . Then came a time when there were nearly fourteen thousand people here, and you can imagine what it meant to wash, feed and clothe them. . . . There would be a day-long queue only for food, and more faintings and pushing and shouting and restlessness. There were still too few tents, only more sun and more sandstorms, and more people to lie about in the open, with little water to go round, no shade, no sanitary facilities; those toilets were not enough; they would urinate and excrete in the sand all about them; there was a smell I would not like to describe, it was felt for a mile round the camp; and they ate and slept in the sand, and women gave birth in the open, on the sand; and others died there.

During the peak of September, when 16,027 new arrivals were registered, 199 died. In October, when the influx dropped to 6,851, there were still 161 deaths.[70]

All during July, there was only one permanent doctor at the camp, occasionally assisted by two local Adenite Indian doctors who used to come on brief visits to the camp and examine 100 to 150 people in an hour. Only July 10, one nurse came down from Tel Aviv, and one more by the end of the month. The two girls "had to attend to everything . . . they worked like hell, from dawn to dusk, fourteen, sixteen, sometimes eighteen hours a day." Somewhat later, two more nurses arrived. In September, an eye specialist arrived, with a wife who was an eye nurse. They were badly needed. Between 70 and 80 per cent of the Yemenites had some eye disease, mostly trachoma, which leads to partial or total blindness. Another widespread disease was ulcers, and great quantities of penicillin were used to counter the ulcer plague. During the month of October, the main problem was malaria. The refugees contracted it on the way, while camping in swampy and infested regions. The number of malaria cases reached several thousands. Later, a team of bacteriologists, delegated from Israel, succeeded in spotting the malaria-infested areas on the refugees' itinerary, and those still on the way were directed to follow other routes. Over a million antimalaria tablets were distributed to those who reached the Aden borders.[71]

Transportation and Food. The camp's administrative and medical staff was doing their very best for the refugees' well-being. Once the weary travelers reached the border of the Aden colony, they were met by Joint Distribution Committee representatives and brought to the camp in trucks belonging to Aden Arabs. There, for sanitary reasons, they were at once stripped of their clothes (which were burned on the spot), washed, vaccinated, sprayed with DDT; they received new clothes. But Yemenite women refused to undress in the open, and during the early stages there was no screen around the washing place, no female attendants. When pressed, they would cower in shame, hiding their faces in the sand. A clinic and a hospital with 300 beds were available. But at first, no refugee would attend these of his own accord. Often it was necessary to seek out those who were ill and bring them to the hospital by force. Those in a critical condition would, as soon as medical care had reduced their temperature, leave the institution in the belief that they were well. The sick would be sneaked out of the hospital by their relatives because of the fear that they would not be permitted to join them on the journey to Israel. Special guards had to be assigned to prevent patients from running away. Force also had to be used to bring ill persons to the clinic. Dr. Yehuda Bar Am, the eye doctor, complained that the Yemenites were reluctant to come for treatment, and once they came and got a silver nitrate treatment they would say that the salve burned their eyes and would not return. It took time before they stopped distrusting the physicians.[72]

Complicated also was the task of feeding the refugees. The Yemenites had their own dietary habits: they drank no milk, refused to eat spaghetti or pudding. Their favorite vegetables and spices were Indian beans and *bishas*, or red pepper onions;

garlic, *pitot*, or flatbreads; and *samne*, or boiled butter. At the
beginning, available food was scarce: a pound of bread a day
per person, fifty grams of meat twice or three times a week,
dates, radish and *samne*. This diet was hardly sufficient for
diseased, undernourished people whose average weight was
eighty pounds. Many were so starved they could not hold their
food and only gradually began to develop appetite and the ability to hold and assimilate the nourishment given them.[73] Later,
the conditions improved. Zecharia Nissim, a Yemenite boy
whose family of six had, after long weeks of travel, finally
reached the Hashed camp, rapturously recalled how his father
had been loaded with provisions for the six members of the
family.[74]

When he appeared in our tent, he could not carry all the rations
he had received. And I can even now remember what they were.
Meat, five kilograms; bread, ten loaves; two kilos of dates, a little
coffee, sugar and tomatoes. I remember when they called to the
young people to come and eat in the common kitchen, I was the first
to go and get food which I had never eaten before in my life. The
women instructors cooked it, nice and clean, and we sat on chairs
and ate from a table.

All this was a complete novelty for the newcomers, and a
most salutary one for their emaciated bodies. It was reported
that those who stayed in camp for four to six weeks would gain
twenty to thirty pounds. But it took time before an adequate
supply and distribution system was organized.[75] The food was
distributed three times daily to heads of families, against rations cards showing the number of children and dependents.
Most of the men carried the precious food cards, which they
were unable to read, in a little white sack dangling over the
breast. They were given a red card for the first ten days, during which they received food only if the whole family lined up
daily to swallow their dose of Paludrine antimalaria pills. On
the eleventh day, after a second typhus injection, the red card
was exchanged for a white one for the rest of their stay in the
camp. Every family head watched his little sack with the cards,
for he believed if he lost them he would not go to the Holy

Land.[76] They were a primitive people in many respects and had to be taught the use of modern conveniences such as toilets. Soon, however, they began to enjoy the shower baths and would take several a day. Many wore shoes for the first time in their lives and were proud of their new belongings. The men had some difficulty in putting on trousers—they had to learn the knack of standing on one leg at a time without falling down.

The Jewish Agency, acting on behalf of the Israeli Government, originally insisted that every refugee be medically examined and if necessary treated at Hashed. But it was established that of a sample batch of two hundred and fifty incoming refugees, only thirty would be found free of diseases and not more than sixty could be treated and dispatched in one day. The sick and their families would have to be detained for adequate treatment at the camp anywhere between five and thirty-five days, thus creating a bottleneck. The Jewish Agency had no choice but to waive the insistence on preliminary medical treatment.[77]

Border Closed and Reopened. It was truly something of a miracle that no epidemics had broken out among the camp population during all those trying weeks. But the British authorities in Aden were not inclined to rely on further miracles. Alarmed by the unrelieved pressure on the camp and fearful of future epidemics, on September 21 they declared the frontier of Aden Protectorate closed to the Yemenite refugees. Several refugee groups totaling some 12,500 people en route to the Protectorate were held up on the Yemen side of the border, mainly in the regions of Shureika (2,300) and al-Rahida (2,500), the latter about ten miles from the frontier. For four weeks they had been wandering, helpless and desperate, camping in the fields and by the roadside, without food, medical help, or milk for the children. It was not before the second half of October that a Jewish Agency emissary was permitted to enter Yemen with fifty sacks of bread, and supplies of flour, oil, dates, salt and baby biscuits, as well as 5,000 rupees for cash distribution among the stranded groups. But, he recalled, the food I took with me was little, far too little for the mass of stranded people suffering terribly from hunger and sickness. They camped in the open. I found men, women and children disintegrating, dying a slow death, minute by minute, lying on the ground with swollen bellies, others with open wounds. No doctors were allowed to go out to them, but a hundred and fifty thousand Paludrine pills were eventually sent, only they could not take the place of food. There was no one to help them, only the savage sun looking down. I get sick when I remember some of the scenes I saw. Worms crawling in the festering wound of a man, eating his flesh. Men in pain pleading with me: "Cut off my leg." I estimate that four or five hundred died in those two places alone in a few weeks. I don't know how many perished in other places.[78]

The Joint Distribution Committee, the Jewish Agency and the Government of Israel made a concerted effort to meet the critical situation. The Hashed camp was hastily enlarged and improved. Two hundred tents, each meant to accommodate twenty persons, were flown from Israel. Barracks and temporary buildings for hospitals, kitchens, children's quarters and staff accommodations were set up. Six doctors and sixteen nurses manned the hospital; experienced camp administrators were rushed to Aden. Additional planes were obtained. Camp personnel, immigration officials and flight crews alike slept little. The congestion was drastically relieved. In September, 68 flights evacuated 8,864 Yemenites, and 11,445 were flown in 89 flights in October. The peak of the crisis was passing. By mid-October, the camp population, for the first time in six or seven weeks, had dropped to some 3,000.[79]

On October 29, the border was reopened. Yet further influx was obviously slackening. Between October 28 and 30 a total of 1,423 refugees passed the gate. However, on the last day of the month there were no convoys, and none on the first day of November. Some 4,000 arrived during the month, but the airlift functioned efficiently, so that 5,478 were flown to Israel during the same period, and 3,055 in December. As a result, from mid-November onward the camp population never rose over 3,000.

The bulk of the Yemenite refugees was transferred to Israel in 1949. In the year 1950, the rate of air evacuation began to decrease.

Rate of Departure in 1950[80]

Month	Number of evacuees
January	1,981
February	2,062
March	1,504
April	1,025
May	989
June	520
July	405
August	437
September	323

Operation Concluded. Operation Magic Carpet came to an end on September 24, 1950, when the last two planes arrived in Lydda with 177 passengers. Among them were twenty-six Yemenite Jews who had traveled from San'a to Aden in the Imam's personal plane, which he put at their disposal as a goodwill gesture on the conclusion of the exodus.

Before the planes left Aden on that Sunday morning, a monument was unveiled at the cemetery of Sheikh Othman, and a smaller one in the graveyard nearer the Hashed camp, dedicated to the memory of the six hundred Yemenite Jews who died there. Scrolls with their names were placed in each monument. The ceremony was attended by representatives of the Government of Aden, or the consular service, the Joint Distribution Committee, the Jewish Agency, and the Near East Transport. Another ceremony had taken place on the same evening at Lydda, attended by the two Chief Rabbis of Israel, representatives of the Government, delegates of Yemenites and the press.[81] A total of 47,140 Yemenites were by that time flown to Israel.

Although the official exodus ended in September 1950, smaller groups continued to arrive at the Hashed camp, where a reduced Jewish Agency staff continued to care for them until there was a party sufficiently large to warrant a flight to Israel. During 1951, 558 arrived in Israel: 89 came in 1952, and 26 in 1953. A slight increase was noticeable in 1954: in February, 250 migrated to Israel via Aden, and in September, 264 more reached Aden after a two-month journey over flooded terrain, and were brought to Israel; the total for the year was 573. In 1955–59 only 13 Yemenites were registered by Israel immigration authorities.[82] *

The entire Magic Carpet operation involved 430 flights, totaling over 1,300,000 miles. Its over-all cost was estimated at the time as $4,500,000, roughly $100 per head. The largest item was the cost of the transport, which, however, due to the mass character of the airlift, did not exceed $70 per adult and $35 per child. Other per capita average expenditure was calculated by the research department of the United Palestine Appeal as follows:[83]

Costs of Operation

	Per capita
Head tax (for passing sultanates between Yemen and Aden)	$ 6.00
Transportation from Yemen to Hashed camp	9.00
Monthly cost of maintenance in camp	15.00
Prorated monthly costs of Jewish Agency personnel in camp	3.00
Basic outfit	9.40
Total per capita	$42.40

The average length of the refugees' stay in the camp ranged from two to three months.

Those Who Remained. It is not known how many Jews remained in Yemen after the great exodus. Early estimates varied between two and three thousand. Subsequent small-scale out-migration reduced this number to one thousand three hundred in 1951 and to some six hundred by 1959.[83a] Those who were unable to join the trek were predominantly skilled artisans whom the Imam had retained for "state reasons." Explained Major Basil W. Seager in a lecture before the Royal Central

* In addition to the above numbers, the Magic Carpet carried to Israel 200 Jews from Djibouti in French Somaliland (two flights) and 200 from Asmara in Eritrea (two flights). As will be seen in the chapter on Aden, 1,770 Adenite Jews were flown to Israel in twenty-eight flights during the period December 1948–March 1950 (Zadok, *op. cit.* p. 232).

Asian Society in London: "When the Imam realized that in course of time all the Jews would be leaving, they were told to teach their trades to the Arabs. I do not say that they taught them very well, but they certainly taught many of them. Strange to relate, the Yemen does not seem to have suffered very much as a result of the exodus."[84] According to Shlomo Levy, in the Hashed camp "there are, apparently, no watchmakers, nor even any cobblers, among the Yemen Arabs, and the King is trying to ensure against the loss of skilled labor. . . . [Levy's] brother is still in the capital of the Yemen, where he is personally responsible to the King for one hundred and fifty Jews (and their families) who will not be allowed to depart before they have taught their crafts to Moslems."[85]

Reporting in the July 1960 issue of the Algerian monthly, *Information*, on his recent visit to Yemen, Attilio Gaudio stressed that the brusque departure of the hard-working Jewish community had "upset the country's internal balance of trade. Because of the absence of a modern native industry capable of replacing the production of highly-skilled Jewish artisans, prices on local markets quickly became prohibitive." The deserted Jewish ghetto of San'a is now a "dead city." "The houses are falling into ruins; the twenty synagogues have been desecrated . . . some of them have been converted into warehouses; private homes have been looted; Jewish stores and subterranean workshops are being nightly invaded by marauders and prostitutes who infiltrate like rats and use them as improvised brothels."

Tenth Anniversary Celebration. In May 1959, thousands of Yemenites from all parts of Israel participated in celebrations held in Jerusalem, Tel Aviv, and Petach Tikva that marked the tenth anniversary of the Magic Carpet Operation. Veteran bearded Yemenites from distant villages, accompanied by their womenfolk with white shawls on their heads, and the new *sabra* generation in open-necked shirts, crammed Jerusalem's 3,500-seat Convention Center auditorium. They cheered President Itzhak Ben-Zvi, who spoke of the redemption of the ancient Yemenite Diaspora. The history-making Magic Carpet Operation was then depicted on the stage in dance and song.[86]

2
Aden: A Community That Was

THE CROWN COLONY OF ADEN

The Jewish Community. Aden consists of the British Crown
Colony of Aden and the Aden Protectorate. The Crown Colony
is 80 square miles in area, with a civilian population of 82,359,
according to the census of October 8, 1946.[1] Occupied by Great
Britain in 1839, Aden was administered by the Government of
India up to April 1, 1937, when it became a Crown Colony.

There are no records in the communal archives of Aden to
show when and whence the Jews first settled in Aden, but it
can safely be assumed that the bulk of the community hailed
from Yemen while a certain percentage were descendants of
Jews who, when traveling from Mediterranean ports to India,
were stranded, or broke their journey at Aden, and became a
part of its community. Tombstones in the two Jewish cemeteries give reliable evidence of the presence of Jews in Aden in
the years 1310 to 1317, but it is thought that some Jews settled
there as early as the fifth century. In 1931, the Jewish population of the Colony was 4,200; it rose to 7,723 in 1946.[2]

Nearly all the Jews of Aden lived in the Crater, a section of
six streets, of which two have names, and the others were
known impersonally as A(1), A(2), A(3) and A(4). Most had
their shops and stores along the main roads that border the
quarter, and sixty-four Jewish small lock-up shops were situated in the bazaar which they shared with Arabs and Indians.
A few wealthy families established their stores in a different
part of the town, in the section commonly known as "Steamer
Point," where the big ships land their passengers.[3]

The community supported several synagogues, which were well attended daily, and two schools. Arabic written in Hebrew characters was their language. The younger generation wrote and spoke Hebrew. Contact with the outside world was maintained by means of Hebrew and English papers.[4]

Most of the Aden Jews were of the poor class and earned their living as small craftsmen, mat weavers, bookbinders, masons, porters, jewelers, goldsmiths, shoemakers and tailors. They were first to introduce tile and fez making in Aden. Many were employed in the cigarette industry, while others worked in the offices of the British administration. Jews have been active in commerce for years. The ostrich-feather trade was entirely in Jewish hands, and before World War I the Jews used to travel and sell their ostrich-feather boas and fans. When the Italian community left Aden during World War II, the Jews took over their trade in piece goods. There were a few rich families of bankers and wholesale traders in the community such as that of the Messas, the "coffee kings" of Aden.[5]

The Background of the Trouble. There is a tendency to present political relations between the Jewish and Arab communities of Aden as having been undisturbed and even cordial till the very outbreak of the pogrom in December 1947, which is alleged to have come completely unexpected. This idyllic pre-pogrom picture is misleading.

There undoubtedly existed a considerable measure of political tension between the ethnic components of the Colony's population. Sir Tom Hickinbotham, who started his career in Aden in 1931 as Personal Assistant to the then Resident, Sir Bernard Reilly, and was in 1951 appointed Governor of Aden, writes in a recent (1958) study:[6]

The colony, to all outward appearances—and they can be very deceptive—always seemed to be one of the most peaceful places on earth where nothing was ever likely to happen, but in fact it only required a minor incident at a wrong time to cause really serious trouble and to do so not within a matter of days, but almost of minutes. The reason, of course, is not far to seek; it is that there are in the Colony three races who have no special love for each other. The Jews are disliked by the Arabs whom they fear, while the Arabs in their turn dislike the Somalis, who are at the best of times a truculent lot. Therefore we are always liable to have trouble between the Arabs and the Jews which might well spread to the Hindu community, or between the Somalis and the Arabs, or between all the three, and in no time. . . .

. . . [The Jews] generally speaking, kept very much to themselves, were self-effacing and their contacts with the Arabs were reasonably good. . . . The Arabs consider that the Jews are their social inferiors and, provided they keep their place, or what the Arabs consider to be their place, there is no trouble at all and the two communities may live side by side in peace for years; but as soon as the Jews tended to forget that they were Jews and began to assert themselves as men, then there was always a likelihood of serious trouble.

Sir Tom's testimony is borne out by a well-documented memorandum on *The Disaster of the Jews of Aden*, prepared on December 12, 1947, by an Adenite Jewish leader:[7]

The Jews of Aden always knew that they were living on sufferance; the local Arab population never harbored anything but hatred towards them. They (the Jews) remembered the "light" pogrom in 1933, when a few people were beaten up and wounded outside the Jewish quarter, when there was some stoning and when a number of rioters entered a Jewish house and did some looting.

Giving evidence before the Commission of Inquiry into the December 1947, disturbances, Col. A. H. Sigrist, since October 1942 Aden's Commissioner of Police, stated:[8]

Since I arrived in Aden there has been a steady growing antagonism between Jews and Arabs. Not strong when I first arrived but shown by many petty assaults and by children throwing stones at each other.

There was distinct worsening in 1947. I think undoubtedly influence of events in Palestine reflected in Aden. We had cases of Arab lorries being driven at Jews walking in the desert. In one case a Jew was killed and an Arab driver was arrested and convicted of causing death by a rash and negligent act.

Nevertheless, neither the Aden administration nor the Jewish community had apparently expected any serious disturbances immediately after the Palestine resolutions of the United Nations of November 29, 1947. Col. Sigrist "did not think

violence would come on the decision to partition Palestine";
he thought "it would come as result of implementation."[9] The
Jews, in turn, relied on the fact that Aden was a British Crown
Colony and hoped that the British administration would protect
them. The author of the memorandum quoted above had "endeavored to arouse the Jews of Aden from a false feeling of security and demanded that they should, with Government help,
establish an armed Jewish Home Guard." But even he "never
seriously believed that such events would occur here."

The Pogrom. The pogrom thus came both unexpectedly and
suddenly.

On December 2, 1947, the Aden Arab leaders proclaimed a
solidarity strike with the Arabs of Palestine. The Jews immediately closed their shops. During the day no disturbances
occurred. But with the fall of darkness, a mob of young Arabs
entered the Jewish Quarter and began throwing stones. The
Jews retaliated by throwing bottles from the roofs of their
houses. The attackers succeeded in setting fire to the girls'
school, *Sukath Shalom,* and burning Jewish cars.

The measures taken by the administration proved to be
completely inadequate. There was no longer a British garri-
son in Aden such as had been maintained during the war, and
the considerable body of Royal Air Force stationed there was
not regarded as available for dealing with civil disturbances.
The military force upon which the Government relied in case
of trouble was a body known as the Aden Protectorate Levies;
it was composed of some 1,800 Arab tribesmen, officered partly
by British officers of the RAF regiment and partly by Arabs.
That force had been constituted to deal with troubles in the
Arab Protectorate of Aden, and was manifestly ill-qualified to
deal with troubles between Arabs and Jews. On the first night
that they were called in, the Levies succeeded in dispersing the
mob, but only after considerable damage had been done to
Jewish property. On the second day, a still larger mob, composed
principally of Yemenite coolies, who constituted the casual
labor of the port and lived in the most primitive conditions, renewed the attack; this time, they broke into the Jewish quarter,

setting fire to shops and houses and murdering their Jewish inhabitants.

It was during that second day that most of the casualties and most of the destruction occurred. The riots spread to the neighboring township of Sheikh Othman, where about 800 Jews, mainly Yemenite refugees, were living, some in houses and some in an encampment. The small local police force was again unable to cope with the demonstration. A squadron of the Aden Protectorate Levies was called in and it was decided that the whole Jewish population should be moved to the large refugee camp of Yemenite Jews at Hashed, a few miles outside the township. The great majority were shepherded by the Levies to that camp, which was not attacked. Some of the Sheikh Othman Jews were unable or unwilling to get away in time: and in the evening, their habitations were invaded, a few were killed, and all the houses and shops were wrecked or burned.

On the second afternoon a party of British Naval Ratings were landed from two destroyers which had been hastily summoned to Aden. They took up positions in the Jewish quarter and were soon able to get the situation in hand.[10]

The balance sheet of the pogrom was disastrous. According to official British sources, 82 Jews were killed and 76 wounded. Of 170 Jewish shops which existed in Aden before the disturbances, 106 were totally looted and 8 were partially looted. In the Crater, 30 houses and both Jewish schools were burned, as well as a number of Jewish-owned motor cars. In Sheikh Othman, 12 houses, 5 shops, 26 huts, 1 synagogue and 1 small school were burned and looted; 61 houses, 10 shops, 40 huts were damaged and looted.[11] The number of Arabs killed during the disturbances were 38; 87 Arabs were wounded and 448 were arrested, 321 of them by the police. Up to December 31, 1947, 226 had been dealt with by the courts. Twelve had been sentenced to two years, 34 to eighteen months, and 128 to one year's imprisonment or less; the latter figures include a few cases of fines and strokes in the case of juveniles. Fifty-two persons were acquitted and 91 persons were awaiting trial. One hundred twenty-seven persons who had been taken into custody by troops at various times and against whom no specific charge could be brought, had been expelled from the Colony.[12]

The British Government appointed a Commissioner, Sir Harry Trusted, formerly Chief Justice of Palestine, to investigate the background of the riots, the conduct of the Aden authorities, the damage to property, and to make recommendations as to the future. The semipublic inquiry started on February 27, 1948, and lasted thirteen days. The Commissioner's report, dated April 7, 1948 (it was published by the Colonial Office as "Colonial No. 233"), absolved the Aden police from any blame, mildly reproached the behavior of the Levies and of the Aden administration, and recommended that a British force be permanently stationed again in Aden.

His Majesty's Government declined any responsibility for the damage to Jewish property caused by the riots, which the Aden Jewish community appraised at 15 million rupees ($4,500,-000). The Colonial Office refuted the very principle of compensation and offered a scheme providing merely for *ex gratia* grants to meet claims in full up to 600 rupees (about $184) and higher claims on a diminishing percentage basis; no grant was to exceed $1,200. Bigger claims had to be met by noninterest-bearing loans under which no person was to receive a total of more than 30,000 rupees ($9,200).

Beyond Recovery. The Aden Jewish community never recovered from the disaster of the December riots, which have irretrievably undermined the very basis of its economic position. In a letter to the World Jewish Congress dated December 28, 1947, the Aden Jewish Emergency Committee stressed that many among the instigators of the riots were "actuated by economical and commercial reasons and wish to destroy all the economic and commercial foundations of the Jewish community in order to replace them. In this, they have succeeded and they will now be able to replace the Jews in this field. Having succeeded in plundering almost all the possessions of the Jews and later introducing the anti-Jewish boycott by intimidation and violence, they have been able to eliminate the Jewish traders and merchants from Aden."

Even more depressing was the feeling of insecurity which prevailed in the community. The Jewish quarter had to be isolated from the rest of Crater and kept continually under guard, and Jews for months did not dare to venture out of it. In January 1949, Rabbi Kopel Rosen, President of the Mizrachi Federation of Great Britain and Ireland, after a visit to Aden, reported that "one felt that the pogrom had taken place not a year ago but a week ago . . . the Jews still live in a state of tension and anxiety . . . so tense is the security position that the Jews still erect barricades at night." All facilities for education and medical treatment had been disrupted, and the school building has not been repaired.[13]

Economic decay, coupled with acute feeling of insecurity, induced Aden Jews to urge for a speedy evacuation to Israel. Joining the Yemenite refugees in the Magic Carpet airlift, 2,200 local Aden Jews registered for emigration.[14] As of April 24, 1949, eighteen flights brought 1,236 Adenites to Israel.[15] During the period from May 15, 1948 (proclamation of the State of Israel), to January 1, 1959, 3,319 Adenite Jews arrived in Israel. Together with the 1,272 who came during the period from 1939 to May 15, 1948, the sum total of Aden Jewish immigrants amounts to 4,591.[16] Jews leaving for Israel were permitted to transfer £1,250 per year in cash or goods, up to a maximum amount of £5,000 over a four-year period.[17]

The Jewish community has shrunk to insignificance. The official Census Report for 1955 gave the number of Jews in the Colony as 831, only 11 per cent of their number eight years ago. In a recent book on Aden, Sir Tom Hickinbotham speaks of "scarcely 700 Jews left in Aden" and flatly says that "the Jewish community has ceased to be a factor in the affairs of the Colony."[18] It became a "community that was." The Government had removed the Jewish member of the Legislature Council, and later also of the Municipal Council. The spiritual and cultural life of the approximately 170 Jewish families almost ceased. There was one Jewish school with 200 pupils, subsidized by the Anglo-Jewish Association; five synagogues were served by two rabbis.[19]

In November 1958, a conflict between the local [Arab] Trade Union Congress and the Aden Government degenerated into violent rioting, mostly by unemployed Yemenis, of whom there were several thousands in the Colony. The authorities acted promptly to put down the disorders and arrested 560 persons, 240 of whom were deported across the border. But during the brief period at their disposal, groups of Yemeni Arabs emerged from hiding in the neighboring lanes and alleyways to attack the Jewish Quarter in the Crater area. The Jewish school and several Jewish houses were set afire. The flames were quickly extinguished, and no Jewish casualties were reported; but the Jewish community, recalling the bitter experience of the 1947 riots, was again alarmed.[20] The prospects of their peaceful existence following these riots are described by an eye-witness: "It would seem that the problem of this Jewish community is not where to turn, but when to turn. They might be wise to remember that 'he who hesitates is lost.' They would not be the first Jewish community that waited too long."[21]

While "passive and wishful procrastination" prevails, this oasis of Judaism "is being overtaken by events more quickly than nature perhaps intended."

THE ADEN PROTECTORATE

The Aden Protectorate is geographically and administratively divided into two areas, the western and the eastern. It is bounded on the east by the western boundary of the Sultanate of Muscat and Oman, on the north and west by the Ruba'al Khali (Empty Quarter) and the Kingdom of Yemen.

Up to the eighteenth century the Aden Protectorate used to be in the hands of the Imam of San'a (present capital of the Yemen). It was administered by the rulers of the tribal districts, who acted as the Imam's "wakils" or governors. With the decline of the Imam's power, the governors declared their independence (1728–1758). After the occupation of Aden by the British in 1839, most of the neighboring chiefs entered into protective treaty relations with the British Government. They managed their own affairs, subject to general supervision by British officials under the control of the Governor of Aden.[22] *Western Aden Protectorate.* Of the nineteen emirates, sheikhdoms and sherifates which compose the Western Protectorate (population 350,000) only seven comprised Jewish communities.

According to figures obtained in April 1949 by Dr. A. Leon Kubowitsky from Major Basil W. Seager, British Agent in the Western Protectorate, the distribution of the 2,600 to 2,750 Jews in the Western Aden Protectorate was as follows:[23]

Area	Number of Jews
Emirate of Amiri	150 to 200
Sultanate of Audhali	1,550 to 1,560
Sultanate of 'Aulaqi	100
Sherifate of Beihan	185 to 195
Sultanate of Fadhli	4
Sheikhdom of Shaib	200
Sultanate of Radfan	12
Sultanate of Yafa'i	400 to 500

The status of these Jewish communities is described by Sir Tom Hickinbotham, who has for more than a quarter of a century held leading positions in the Aden area, as follows (p. 51):[24]

There were then several thousand Jews living in the Protectorate with a greater measure of security than they enjoyed in Central Europe. They were the artisans and the gold- and silversmiths, and their houses were grouped together and generally slightly removed from the Arab quarters of the town. Every small town in the northwestern area had one of these Jewish quarters. They were not interfered with and they could and they did own land and they were useful to the Arabs and lived in peace with them. They were not involved in tribal disputes and it was considered something of a disgrace to kill a Jew.

This carefully retouched picture of the Jewish existence is, of course, a highly idealized one. As can be seen from Hickinbotham's own description of his first visit (in 1932) to Dhala in the Sultanate of Audhali, the Jews were considered and treated as half-slaves.

Somewhat more satisfactory seems to have been, according to Jewish sources, the position of the small Jewish community of Beihan: most of them owned land, some were merchants, gold- and silversmiths, weavers, tailors, shoemakers, etc., and their relationship with their Arab neighbors was cordial.

"When they left some years later," relates Hickinbotham, "drawn almost against their will by a force they could scarcely understand, to Palestine, their need was felt and more than one Ruler tried to persuade them not to go. When they insisted on going, they were not unreasonably treated by the Protectorate Rulers and were allowed to sell their land." An agreement to this effect was reached with Sallah bin Hissein, Ruler of Audhali. A similar attitude was taken by the young Ruler of Beihan, Sherif Hussein bin Ahmad Havili. According to reports of the Jewish Agency delegates, all the Jews of Beihan and Audhali left for Israel in 1949.[25]

The Eastern Aden Protectorate. The Eastern Aden Protectorate is composed of a number of semi-independent sultanates and sheikhdoms with a population of about 300,000. There are scarce data on its Jewish population. The only considerable Jewish community in this area existed in the State of Hadhramaut, which is mentioned in the Bible as *Matzarmavet* and in the Roman and Greek literature, as part of *Arabia Felix.*

Hadhramaut (population 648,521, according to the 1946 census) stretches several hundred miles along the southern coast, meeting the Yemen on the west and Oman on the east, and isolated in the north by desert. It is one of the least-known parts of southern Arabia. Few Western travelers have ever reached it, and none has stayed long.[26] None of them has ever mentioned Jews in the Hadhramaut. This remarkable omission may be due to the fact that many Jews in the country were themselves nomads and that most of the country is still unknown. S. Yavnieli, however, heard of them and visited them in 1922 when he was organizing an immigration of Yemenite Jews to Palestine.

The first direct and reliable information about the Hadhramaut Jewish community became available in 1945, when forty-five-year-old Yechyah (Zecharia) ben 'Awwad ben Ibrahim (Abraham) Habbani, a Jew from the small Hadhramaut town of Habban (situated about 225 miles northeast of

Aden), arrived in Palestine via Aden, accompanied by his wife, three children and a nephew. He related that there were about 700 Jews in the Hadhramaut province of Habban, descendants of early migrants from Palestine.* Some 450 lived in the city of Habban, at the foot of the mountain, and about 250 in the neighboring villages, as arms makers, blacksmiths, and fashioners of household utensils for the whole neighborhood, often visiting settlements situated between two to four days' camel ride.[27]

Their appearance was strikingly different from that of the Yemenite Jews. Wearing their raven-black hair long, in close-grown curls covered by a white headdress, they have a proud upright bearing, are considerably taller than the Yemenites, and, unlike the latter, are tanned brown of complexion rather than dusky. Shlomo Barer, who in 1949 met with a group of twenty-six Habbanis in the Hashed camp, describes them as "men with long-flowing hair . . . more muscular than the others and walking with a manlier gait." Their leader, Mansour Tsadok Jibli, "looked splendid with his crown of black hair parted in the middle, gypsy-like in a way, and yet with a thoughtful and noble air about him, and fine, sculptured features"; Mansour spoke a beautiful Hebrew—"not the functional, everyday language we use in Israel today, but one that may have been spoken two thousand years ago, with many a biblical turn of phrase to it.[28]

Devout in religious observance, all Jews at Habban were literate. They had two synagogues and two elementary schools. Intermarriages were unknown.

Habban Jews were regarded as Sultan's property. Each male was expected to pay to the Sultan a head tax of 30 riyals ($24); those unable to pay this sum, a very large one in Habban, became slaves liable to imposition of any heavy or menial labor.

According to both ben 'Awwad and Mansour, the Habbanian rulers had, on the whole, treated their Jewish subjects

---

* The Habban Jews claim descent from the tribe of Judah and their tradition is that they arrived in Hadhramaut before the destruction of the Second Temple. They possess no written records of history; their history is passed on from generation to generation by word of mouth. The fact that there are among them neither Cohanim nor Leviim is an evidence of their ancient origin.

benevolently. It was only during the last years of the Second
World War that the situation changed. As a result of anti-
Jewish propaganda, Sultan Nasr ibn Abdallah al Wahdi started
persecuting the Jews, imposing exorbitant taxes and heavy fines,
demanding their conversion, and confining them to a ghetto.
When he reached Aden, ben 'Awwad appealed to the British
authorities against the Sultan. The Sultan was incensed by this
intercession and threatened the Jews with deportation.

Upon arrival in Palestine, ben 'Awwad declared that the
Jewish community of Habban had entrusted him with the
mission of exploring every possible channel for bringing them
to Palestine. He swore that he would not rest until he redeemed
his people. In a letter to the Jewish Agency he asked for immediate allocation of 800 immigration certificates. One hundred certificates were allotted; several organizations announced
plans for the settlement of the Habban immigrants in a separate
village.

All these plans have, however, not materialized during the
troubled years 1946–1948. The Habban Jews waited patiently
for their salvation. When, however, in 1949, the news that the
entire Jewish community of the neighboring Yemen was being
transferred to Israel had reached Hadhramaut, their position
became increasingly untenable and their longing for *aliyah*
stronger. In a letter sent to Aden in October 1949, the Habban
Jewish community reported that their Arab neighbors were
convinced that very soon the Israel Government, which "is
caring for all the Jews in exile," would also repatriate the Jews
of Hadhramaut, and they had therefore "already ceased to
trust us. . . . When one of us asks an Arab for a loan, the
answer is: 'We will not advance you money since you are going
to leave the country'." On the other hand, the letter stated,
"the work which is the source of our existence is getting scarcer,
as we have lost the confidence [of the customers]. . . . We
are greatly embarrassed. We have no wings to fly away and no
legs to flee. . . . We are waiting for the help of God, which
is so slow in coming. Each day seems to be like a year, and we
do not know what to do."[29]

In the summer of 1950, after protracted and complicated

negotiations with the Sultan Nasr ibn Abdallah at his palace in Azzam, Joseph Zadok, the Jewish Agency emissary, obtained the release of the entire remaining Jewish community of Habban upon payment of a considerable lump sum (allegedly representing the equivalent of their unpaid tribute to the Sultan) and of extra gifts to the Sultan and the vizier. The fascinating story of this "ransom operation" is soberly told by Zadok himself, in this book *B'Saarot Teyman* (pp. 175–200). Six trucks, packed with 334 men and women, brought them to the Hashed camp in Aden. The first group of 100 was flown to Lydda on August 25, 1950; by the end of September, 221 more arrived. The newcomers were proudly displaying beautiful Torah scrolls written in fine black lettering on thick sheepskin and carefully wrapped in layers of cloth. A number of the party spoke some Hebrew and one young man declared, "It is good to be in Israel."

3

Iraq: "Lost in the Land of Assyr"—
Operation "Ali Baba"

THE PRE-1948 ERA

A Community of Great Antiquity. "My family lived in this country since the days of Nebuchadnezzar, and in Baghdad since this city was founded in 726 C.E. by Caliph Manqur," a young Iraqi Jew proudly told a European Jewish visitor. "My family has seen conquerors come and go, watched plagues and pestilences devastate the inhabitants, lived through massacres and civil war—yet here we are!"[1]

This proud statement might not be fully accurate historically. But no one can doubt that the Jewish community of Iraq is of great antiquity. It is one of the oldest organized communities of Jews in a foreign land. In the Talmudic and Gaonic period, under the Arsacids, Sassanids and Abbasides, Babylonian Jewry grew in power, wealth and culture, overcoming temporary setbacks with constantly renewed vitality. In its golden days, Baghdad's Jewish community was the most influential in the Middle East. Under Persian rule—when Ctesiphon on the Tigris was capital of the Sassanid Empire—the Babylonian Jews spoke their own version of Aramaic, which was close to Hebrew, and which they continued to use long after it had ceased to be the language of the country. They had their own secular administration, complete with courts of law with jurisdiction in all fields. The community was, to a large extent, self-sufficient, as Jews engaged in all occupations, including farming. Baghdad was the seat of the Exilarch, the Prince of Captivity, of whose glories we read in travelers' narratives, and, with the passing of the years, the academies of Sura and Pumbeditha were transferred there. The foremost scholars and personalities of the time—Saadya Gaon, Sherira Gaon, Hai Gaon, David Alroy, Benjamin of Tudela, Saad el-Dawlak, and many others—trod its streets.

However, since the middle of the eleventh century c.e., successive invasions by Mongols and Turks, unsettled conditions in the country and its consequent economic decay, led to progressive isolation of Babylonian Jewry, and the glory of the Babylonian Diaspora began on its downward path.

Unlike most groups of Jews in the Diaspora, Iraqi Jewry was largely homogeneous. There had been no noticeable influx of "foreign" Jews. Such as settled there from outside came mostly from neighboring Persia. Even the wave of Sephardic immigration, which reached almost every corner of the Ottoman Empire, stopped at the gates of the present Iraq territory. Preserving for centuries almost intact their physical type and their cultural tradition, the Iraqi Jews have been in many ways very different from their Jewish brethren in other countries. On the other hand, there has also been no considerable emigration from Iraq, though during the last century or two a number of families left Baghdad and Basra to try their fortune in India and the Far East. They founded prosperous communities in Bombay, Calcutta, Rangoon and Shanghai. In our own days, a number of Jewish merchants and students went to Europe and America.

Under Turkish Rule. During Turkish times, Iraqi Jewry lived the comparatively quiet and stagnant life of people in a remote and neglected Ottoman province. The administration, though generally inefficient and corrupt, did not oppress the Jews as such. In keeping with a Turkish-Moslem tradition of long standing, all religious minorities enjoyed autonomy in communal organization, worship, education, philanthropy and so on, and the Jews were able to make their contribution to the economic and social life of the country. They were known for their industry and skill, and some of them occupied high government positions. They also contributed to the country's commercial development by establishing and maintaining trading contacts between Iraq and other countries. Rabbi David D'Beth Hillel, who visited the Middle East in 1830, described the economic position of the Jews in Iraq as highly satisfactory. They held leading positions in commerce and trade, and some of the 6,000 Jewish families of Baghdad were "extensive merchants and very rich." Many were engaged as weavers, dyers, goldsmiths, silversmiths, and craftsmen in other branches of handicrafts.[1a]

Since the seventies of the last century, Iraqi Jews had been largely profiting by the educational facilities provided by the Alliance Israélite Universelle. The Alliance started its activities in Baghdad in 1865 with one school comprising forty-four pupils. In 1947, there were in the Iraqi capital four schools (two schools for boys and two for girls) with thirty-two hundred pupils. Modern education of Western type, and knowledge of French and English, have contributed a good deal to the improvement of the Jewish position and have given the younger generation a better chance to succeed in business and professions.

During World War I, Turkish governors treated the Jews cruelly, and the latter have eagerly supported the Arab revolt against the Turkish regime and welcomed the establishment of the state of Iraq under the British Mandate.

In Liberated Iraq. After the country's liberation from Turkish rule and throughout the reign of King Feisal I under the British Mandate (1921–1933), the position of the Jewish minority remained favorable. Richard Coke wrote in 1925:[2]

> Though there are many poverty-stricken Jews, and many Jews engaged in very humble occupations—most of the shoeblacks in Baghdad, for instance, are Jewish boys—it is probable that the Jews are much the wealthiest of the various communities. . . . They are large property owners in the towns and practically monopolize the still very active business of petty finance among the large classes of local people who are ignorant or suspicious of European banking methods. They also control an appreciable proportion of the retail trade of the country, especially in the more isolated districts.

Ten years later, another student of Iraq affairs, describing the position of non-Moslem minorities in Iraq, testified that the Christians and the Jews, "who for generations have maintained their own schools, are in the most much better educated than either Arab or Kurd, and they occupy most of the middle-class positions and perform most of the middle-class functions in the towns."[3]

During the first decade of Iraq's statehood, the Jews benefited considerably by the creation of the new administration. Because of their higher standard of education and their knowledge of foreign languages, many of them played a prominent role in government service and trade. They were allowed to expand their school system, and in their schools Hebrew was taught in addition to Arabic, English and French; some of the teachers were from Palestine. Organizations of Jewish youths sprang up, and Zionist activity was not interfered with. The number of Jewish pupils in governmental schools, especially in the upper classes of the secondary schools and among the governmental bursaries sent abroad, increased steadily. There was growing contact with the younger Arab generation, and Jewish sentiment for Arab culture became deeper and more conscious.

The 1947 census counted 118,000 Jews. The great majority was concentrated in Baghdad province (77,542) and in Mosul and Basra (over 10,000 each), but smaller agglomerations were scattered all over the country.[4] Unofficial estimates put the number of Jews in Iraq at 130,000. In Baghdad, the Jews comprised about one-quarter of the capital's population. In contrast to other Middle Eastern cities, there never was a special Jewish quarter in Baghdad. Jews could be found in all parts of the city, though there did exist a noticeable tendency to congregate in certain streets of different quarters.

Jewish communal life was regulated by the "Law of the Jewish Community" (N 77 of 1931).[5] All Iraqi Jews were considered members of their respective communities unless they renounced the Jewish faith. The first three communities to be recognized by the Law were those of Baghdad, Basra ans Mosul; later the community of 'Amara was added. Well organized, Iraqi Jews were a closely knit community, which, subject to Iraq law, enjoyed a certain amount of autonomy in matters of education and charity.

In Independent Iraq. At the beginning of the nineteen thirties, progress toward the formation of an independent Arab state, with looser British control, had gone sufficiently far to allow the army, the schools and the administration to become imbued with an aggressive religious Arab national exclusiveness, deeply inimical to Iraq's minorities. By the side of the Arab population of two and a half million, there were 400,000 Kurds, 130,000 Jews and nearly as many Christians of various denominations. Arab nationalism found a convenient outlet in a policy of persecution of these minorities from the moment it was felt that the latter could no longer count in British protection.

Aware of the necessity to protect the country's minority groups, the Permanent Mandates Commission of the League of Nations insisted, during the discussion of the British proposals to grant Iraq full independence, that the emancipation of the mandated territory "should be made dependent upon . . . certain guarantees satisfactory to the League of Nations. . . . The undertakings of the new state should ensure and guarantee the effective protection of racial, linguistic and religious minorities."[6] The formal declaration of guarantees on matters of international concern communicated to the Council by the Iraq Government on July 13, 1932, provided that nationals belonging to racial, religious or linguistic minorities should be admitted to "public enjoyments, functions and honors" and to the exercise of professions or industries; it was expressly stated that these minority articles should be recognized as part of the fundamental law of Iraq and should constitute international obligations.[7] Yet the very first year of Iraq's full sovereignty was marked by a massacre of the Assyrians, whose tragedy had a strong echo in the Christian world, though in vain. This was followed by expeditions against the Kurds and the persecution of the small "Yezedi" people who for centuries had lived in the mountains of northern Iraq.[8] In this atmosphere, the Jews began to feel increasingly unsafe. A dispatch from Baghdad, published in the London *Daily News* on August 29, 1933, said that Iraq Jews were alarmed over their safety and that "when the Iraq army returned after the weekend [following the raid against the Assyrians], not one Christian or Jew was seen on the streets."

The end of the British Mandate coincided with Hitler's accession to power, and the German minister in Baghdad, Fritz Grobba, succeeded in creating in Iraq an active and influential center of Nazi propaganda. At the same time, the Palestine question became the most convenient instrument of anti-Jewish agitation. After 1929, a systematic and widespread propaganda campaign was launched, led by Arab teachers from Syria and Palestine. It reached its climax when, during the Palestine riots of 1936–1939, some of the followers of the Mufti of Jerusalem and then the Mufti himself, fled from Palestine and took up residence in Baghdad. There, they exerted considerable influence in nationalist and religious circles, spreading horror tales about alleged expropriations, plundering and violence against the Arabs in Palestine. This anti-Jewish and anti-Zionist propaganda provided a convenient opportunity to divert extreme nationalist sentiments from local issues. The Palestine problem was converted into a major issue in Iraq's internal politics.

For years, the Ministry of Education gave preference to Syrian and Palestinian teachers rather than to much better qualified and at that time less chauvinistic Egyptian teachers. Arab history and literature were taught in a spirit of aggressive, declamatory and xenophobic nationalism. Handbooks on Arab history, written mainly by Palestinians, were crammed with vicious, indiscriminate attacks on Jews.

Succeeding Iraq governments have always claimed that the apprehensions of the Iraqi Jews were unfounded. Referring to the Constitution of March 21, 1925, they quoted Article 6, which prescribed that "there shall be no differentiation in the rights of Iraqis before the law, whatever differences may exist in language, race or creed," and Article 18, which stipulated that "Iraq nationals are equal in the enjoyment of civil and political rights and the performance of public duties and obligations. No distinction shall be made between them on account of origin, language, or religion."[9] It is true that there was no anti-Jewish legislation in Iraq. Ostensibly, the Jews were full-fledged citizens. But, admitted A. H. Hourani, a noted Arab scholar, in 1947, although "there is no open and official discrimination against them [the Jews of Iraq] . . . there is however, considerable hostility towards them, because of traditional religious hatred and their economic power."[10] This hostility was not limited to the uneducated masses, but found expression in a consistent policy of anti-Jewish discrimination practiced by succeeding Iraqi governments.

In the early years of Iraq's independence, Jews held many and important positions in the country's administrative machinery. "The first and greatest Minister of Finance, Sassoon Heskail, was a Jew," says Hourani. The Ministry of Finance and the Directorates General of the State Railways, Posts and Telegraphs, Customs and Excise, counted numerous Jewish officials and employees. But in 1935, the Minister of Economics and Communications was authorized to dismiss all employees whom he considered unfit. To conceal the underlying anti-Jewish motive of this measure, the Minister first dismissed both Arabs and Jews; soon afterward, most of the Arab officials were reinstated, while the dismissal of the Jewish officials remained effective.[11] Since then, the position of the Jews in government service has been deteriorating steadily. A United States report from Baghdad, in February 1945, noted that "the trend was undoubtedly toward the employment of fewer Jews in the Government." Jews were also gradually pushed out of state educational institutions. In the early years of independence, Jewish children were admitted to all government schools, but the situation had changed completely since 1933.

Educational Policy. Iraq's educational policy toward the country's minorities followed two fundamentally different, even contradictory, trends. On the one hand, it aimed at the Arabization of minorities, at breaking down their group separatism, and at their complete identification with the state. To achieve this goal, the Government had to admit freely into governmental schools all minority applicants. One the other hand, fanatical Arab nationalism was averse to the treatment of minorities on the basis of real equality, and aimed at their elimination from state educational institutions. Squeezed between these contradictory policies, the Jews experienced the disadvantages of both. From 1933 on, Jewish children in increasing numbers were refused admission to primary and secondary public schools. In 1945, according to the aforementioned United States report, Jewish students in Baghdad, where the Jews constituted 20 to 25 per cent of the population, made up approximately one per cent of the total number of students in government schools. Since then, the situation deteriorated still further, and by 1947, no Jewish children were accepted in the government primary and secondary schools. The entire burden of Jewish education fell on the Jewish community; the Iraq Government's contribution to the Jewish school system was £450.

At the same time, no effort was spared to destroy the Jewish character of this school system. The Department of Public Instruction issued regulations forbidding the teaching of Hebrew and Jewish history in Jewish schools. Only religious instruction was permitted, and this was reduced to a bare minimum. Government school inspectors sometimes objected even to the Bible being read and explained in Hebrew; mechanical learning of some prayers was the most they would tolerate. All teachers from Palestine were dismissed. The appointment of Hebrew and religious teachers from countries other than Palestine was also forbidden. Later, Iraqi authorities demanded that the headmasters of the Jewish schools dismiss all Jewish teachers of history, geography, ethics and Arabic, and replace them with Moslems. The Community Council refused to comply, preferring to close down the schools. The Government then declared that it would be satisfied with the appointment of ten Moslem teachers.

In the government institutions of higher learning, the percentage of Jewish students used to be somewhat higher than in primary and secondary schools, though it was also declining as more Arabs received a primary education. In the school year 1944–1945, the Royal Medical College admitted a total of sixty students, of whom seven were Jews; the Baghdad Law College admitted nine Jews in a new class of three hundred.

The anti-Jewish policy also considerably affected the economic position of the Jews. While they had formerly controlled most of the country's commercial life, their percentage in this field was markedly declining. The Jews of Basra told a United States official, in August 1946, that before 1914 they had conducted almost 95 per cent of the merchant business of the city, but that by 1933, the percentage had dropped to 85 to 90 per cent, and by 1946 it decreased to 65 to 75 per cent.

Official United States reports ascribe this decline to discrimination in taxation and in the granting of foreign currency licenses. One report stated that Jews were treated with exceptional strictness in the matter of income tax assessments; another noted that the Jews of Basra were given foreign exchange licenses, import permits, or passports to travel on business outside the country only after many delays; that taxes were heavier on the Jews and that the courts imposed harder sentences on them. The situation in smaller localities was even worse. "In the provincial towns, with the possible exception of Basra," Jesse Zel Lurie wrote in 1941, "the higher stratum of Jewish society is entirely lacking . . . a large number of Jews live steeped in poverty and ignorance. These live in narrow filthy streets which can compete for dirt with the worst of other Oriental Jewish quarters."[12]

No Future for the Jews. Describing the position of the Jewish minority in Iraq, A. H. Hourani wrote in 1947: "In the past few years, many Iraqi Jews, aware that their future in Iraq is dark, have emigrated to Palestine and America in search of greater security and opportunity."[13] This statement is fully corroborated by evidence from other sources. In 1941, after a visit to Iraq, Jesse Zel Lurie reported: "The feeling of insecurity prevails. The hopes of 'assimilation' are lost. Only a few of the younger generation think of their future in Iraqi terms. Many hope that there may be the possibility of going to America at the end of the war. Many dream of Palestine and make desperate attempts to know something about the Jewish renaissance, whose message was prevented from reaching them for years." The headman of the Jewish village of Sandur, in the Kurd hills, expressed the ardent wish that the fifty Jewish families of this small settlement could "sell their village and emigrate to Palestine."[14] In a communication addressed on January 15, 1946, to

the Anglo-American Committee through the British Foreign
Office, the members of the Committee were begged to "rest
assured that, if a plebiscite is made by you among the Iraqi Jews,
you will find that 100 per cent of them are anxious to emigrate
from Iraq to Palestine, and none of them desire to stay in
Iraq."[15]

The fluctuation of the Jewish immigration from Iraq to
Palestine is shown in the table below:[16]

1919–1923	171
1924–1931	3,290
1932–1938	2,930
1939–1945	1,532
1946–May 15, 1948	65
Total	7,988

The modest extent of the emigration to Palestine (7,988 during twenty-nine years) was largely the result of the Government's policy. Not only immigration, but even visits to Palestine by Jewish merchants were strictly forbidden. Students were
not permitted to attend Palestinian schools; religious leaders
and bona fide pilgrims could not fulfill their vows and visit the
Holy Land. The passports of Jews were stamped "Not valid for
travel to Palestine." In the few cases when a Jew was given
special permission to travel to Palestine, he had to deposit 2,000
to 5,000 dinars ($8,000 to $20,000 at that time) as a guarantee
of his return.

Anti-Zionism. Both public opinion and government of Iraq
have been unfaltering in their enmity toward Zionist aspirations. "Anti-Zionist feeling is strong among the Moslems of
Iraq," wrote Ernest Main in 1935. Jews have been repeatedly
upbraided for their pro-Zionist leanings. At the same time, official spokesmen maintained that Iraq's Jewish citizens were not
at all in sympathy with Zionism; that they looked upon Zionism as another form of fascism, the purpose of which was to exploit the Jewish masses for the benefit of a few Jewish capitalists
and profiteers; and that the Jews and Moslems in Iraq live
peaceably side by side and the Jews are content with their lot.
Testifying in Cairo on March 5, 1946, before the Anglo-Ameri-

can Committee of Inquiry, Dr. Mohammed Fadel Jamali, Director General of the Iraqi Ministry of Foreign Affairs, declared:[17]

They [the Jews] have been living in Iraq for thousands of years. They have been our brethren. We have been living in perfect peace and harmony. They enjoy full political rights; they enjoy all the rights that permit them to practice their religion and communal life as a community. . . . Political Zionism, however, came to poison the atmosphere. The Iraqui Jews, through no fault of their own, feel embarrassed at what the Zionists stand for and at the bitter relationship that exists between us and the Zionist Jews. . . . It is a great burden on the Iraq Government to maintain that peace and harmony which we have enjoyed over a long period in our history.

Dr. Jamali invited the Committee to "come to Baghdad and see our Jewish population there and listen to their point of view." He was apparently sure that Jewish witnesses in Baghdad would never dare to tell the Committee publicly anything that would antagonize the Iraq Government. When the Committee arrived in Baghdad "the Jewish witnesses who testified, publicly declared that all was well. Their lot was not hard, the handicaps to which they were subjected were not serious, there was no danger of another pogrom, and their economic status was generally similar to that of the Arabs."[18]

In fact, terrorist acts against Jews had occurred already prior to World War II. In July 1937, violent anti-Jewish demonstrations took place in Baghdad and tens of thousands marched through the streets. "Most Baghdad Jews realized the seriousness of the situation," cabled *The New York Times* correspondent, "and businessmen closed their establishments and rushed to the safety of their homes, where they bolted doors and lowered shutters. Two Jewish merchants who remained in their shops were killed by a mob that had been told by agitators that the British had given control of a Moslem holy area in Jerusalem to the Jews."[19] Terrorist acts became still more serious in 1938; nitric acid was cast on Jewish passers-by, said a Jewish Agency memorandum to the Anglo-American Committee of Inquiry (p. 409).

Rashid Ali Gailani's anti-British coup in the spring of 1941

brought to power the most violent anti-Jewish elements in the
army and among politicians, filling Baghdad Jewry with fear
and foreboding. The blow struck on the first and second of
June, at the very moment when Gailani fled and the armistice
with the British was concluded. The police, far from preventing the rioters from killing and looting, fired on Jewish homes
and openly took part in the attack. The report of the official
investigation commission appointed by the new Government—
moderate as it tried to be—gives precise account of these bloody
days: 110 Jews were killed, 240 wounded, 86 Jewish enterprises
were looted and 911 Jewish houses destroyed. Unofficial accounts put the number of deaths at 150 and the number of
wounded at more than 700, while the material damage was
estimated at 750,000 dinars, or about three million dollars.[20]

But worse even than these direct cases of violence was the
ever-present feeling of fear and insecurity which permeated
Jewish life in Iraq. A United States consular report on the
status of the Jews of Basra related:

Every Jew talked with had a feeling of insecurity and fear for
his life which predominates over everything else. They expect another purge of Jews in Iraq on a grander scale than during the 1941
troubles but do not know when. . . . It is the unknown future that
continually plagues their imagination, not the present conditions.

During conversations with them, all were very conscious of any
persons near by. They felt every move was being watched and that
somehow it would be found out that the Jewish question was being
discussed. Some of the people approached would say nothing and
others tried to end the meeting as soon as possible. They continually
fear arrests on grounds that they are Zionists or members of some
other 'foreign' organization.

IRAQ GOES TO WAR

Governmental Terror. On May 15, 1948, Iraq, together with
Egypt, Syria, Lebanon and Transjordan, went to war against
the State of Israel. On the same day the Government declared
martial law. Officially, this step was motivated by the need to
secure the rear of the Iraqi army which was sent into Palestine,
and to protect the Jews against possible mob attacks. In prac-

tice, however, it was used as a legal weapon for a wave of governmental terror.

The Jewish community of Iraq, already badly shattered by the inimical government policy of the past fifteen years, had become the object of an unprecedented onslaught obviously aimed at its total destruction and carried on with every means at the disposal of governmental machinery. Information on measures designed to have this effect can be found in the Arab press in Iraq and other Arab countries. Specific excerpts from this source will be quoted in the following survey of events. Most of the data used in this chapter, however, have been obtained from Iraqi Jewish sources which are known to be authentic and accurate. They coincide fully with the scattered data published in the Arab press and in their totality they present an appalling picture of a "cold pogrom" which included searches, arrests, denunciation, torture, mass imprisonment, ruinous fines, deliberate pauperization, and wholesale educational discrimination.

Under the cloak of martial law, the Jews were systematically subjected to relentless persecution. Scores of Jewish homes were searched, often at night, in the most brutal fashion. Walls were sometimes knocked down, cupboards broken to pieces and bedding torn apart. If money or jewelry was found, it was confiscated immediately. The Jews did not dare protest for fear of antagonizing the searchers and being sent to jail. Sometimes the searchers were satisfied with the valuables they found and did not molest their victims further. More often, however, Jews were taken to the police even if nothing incriminating was discovered, and considerable sums of money were demanded for their release. Those who refused or were unable to pay were tortured until they agreed to do so. They were then released; in many cases, however, they were rearrested later and put under similar pressure. Those who did not yield to the threats and beatings were transferred to jail for further investigation. There, they were subjected to an even more cruel procedure of extortion. Several Jews, who were subsequently acquitted by the court, left the prison badly undermined in health; one prominent merchant came out completely blind. Three hundred and ten Jews were arrested by the military authorities in the early days of martial law; 160 were released after questioning during varying periods of detention; 150 were held for further investigation and trial. Simultaneously with the promulgation of martial law, four regional martial courts were established in Baghdad, Basra, Mosul and Diwaniyya. The punishment meted out by these courts have been exceedingly severe. During a single week in September 1948, they delivered thirty-two verdicts; the lightest sentence was one year imprisonment with a fine of £10,000 to be paid to the treasury for the account of the Ministry of National Defense.[21]

Only a fraction of the cases reported in the Arab press contained the two essential components of every judicial or even administrative procedure: the charge against the accused and the penalty imposed. Much more numerous were the cases in which Jews were sentenced with no reason given by the martial court. Arab papers and broadcasts for the period from September 2, 1948, to April 27, 1948, published forty-nine names of Jews who—without indication of charges—were, in their totality, sentenced to prison for 117 years and 8 months (four Jews were, in addition, sentenced to life imprisonment); their fines amounted to 1,012,950 dinars ($4,051,800), and they had to deposit bonds amounting to 12,000 dinars as guarantees of good conduct. (One defendant had his entire property confiscated.) The Arab press also announced the arrest of at least twenty Jews whose cases, as far as can be judged on the basis of available information, never came before the courts; nothing is known about the penalties to which they were subjected. Many Jews had to deposit bonds ranging from 50 to 3,000 dinars as a guarantee for future "good conduct."

On July 14, 1948, two months after the promulgation of martial law, the Iraqi House of Representatives passed an amendment to Article 51 of the Baghdad Criminal Code, making Zionism, together with anarchism, nazism, communism and atheism, a subversive and criminal creed, punishable by death, hard labor for life, or imprisonment up to fifteen years.[22] The amendment was formulated in so vague a form that not only overt Zionist activities but sympathy with the Zionist idea could be considered a crime. The testimony of two Moslem witnesses was sufficient to prove an accusation against any person. This travesty of justice resulted in an avalanche of denunciations. Any two Arabs could blackmail their Jewish neighbors. If they did not obtain satisfaction, they could go to court and prefer charges of "Zionism" or "treacherous behavior" against the state. Sometimes the same witnesses appeared in court several times in one day to give evidence against different Jews, and their testimony was given credence.

When the British Mandate over Palestine ended, the Palestine administration handed over to the Iraqi Post Office a batch of letters from Palestine addressed to Iraqi Jews. These letters had been mailed before May 15, 1948, but had, for unknown reasons, not been forwarded by the Palestine postal service. The Government used these letters to persecute its Jewish citizens. Every addressee and every Jew mentioned in the letters was *eo ipso* considered a "Zionist" and became subject to persecution under martial law. Scores of Jews were arrested, detained for months, often mistreated and tortured, and then brought before the courts. Many were sentenced to imprisonment for terms ranging from three to ten years, subjected to hard labor and to fines which ranged generally from 1,000 to 10,000 dinars. Those who could not pay had their property confiscated and sold at very low prices.

The most spectacular case of Iraq's anti-Jewish judicial terror was the trial and hanging of Shafiq Ades of Basra, the country's richest Jew, whose fortune was estimated at $20 million. He was accused simultaneously of organizing and financing the Communist demonstration and strike and of being "one of the leading founders and builders of the alleged Zionist State"; the prosecution charged that he had for several years been buying all types of arms, irrespective of price, and sending them to the Zionists. The trial before the military court took but three sessions. Twenty-four witnesses for the prosecution fully confirmed all the charges. No witness for the defense was admitted. The sentence was—"hanged until death," and five million dinars to be paid from Ades' estate to the Ministry of the Defense. Ades was hanged on September 23, 1948, in the courtyard of his own house in Basra. The execution was declared a public holiday, and tens of thousands gathered to watch it.*

In October 1948, there were indications that the fury was abating. The number of arrests diminished; some Jewish businesses were encouraged to resume operations; and a few minor Jewish officials were restored to their old civil service posts. In December, however, the persecution was resumed and arrests and arbitrary court judgments were almost as widespread as before. Another wave of repressions was reported in October 1949.

Discrimination. The Supplementary Service Law authorized the Council of Ministers to dismiss summarily any government official. After May 15, 1948, the Government made full use of this provision. Hundreds of Jewish state officials and employees, some of whom had for decades served the country loyally and efficiently, were dismissed, sometimes without any explanation, and sometimes under charges of disloyalty, high treason, misbehavior, lack of efficiency, and the like. *Al-Ahram* of October 19, 1948, reported that all Jewish officials and workers in government offices were cashiered "in order to safeguard State secrets." It was estimated that their number was about 1,500; with their dependents, they represented some 10,000 persons deprived of means of livelihood. Many were arrested and given heavy penalties both in imprisonment and fines. Those who were not molested were put under police supervision and barred from obtaining new jobs. Even Jewish institutions received instructions from the Government not to employ such people, and Jewish schools were definitely forbidden to do so.

In September 1948, a committee of the Ministry of Health decided not to issue new licenses to Jewish doctors and not to renew the licenses of those already practicing in Iraq. This decision was based on alleged "scores of cases in which Iraqi Jews practicing medicine and pharmacy acted against the safety of the Iraqi forces."

Under the Military Service Law, Jews, like other citizens,

---

* Court proceedings and verdict, as well as the ceremony at the hanging have been described in detail in the Arab press (*Al Nair* of September 12; *Al Nida* of September 13 and 14; *Liva-al Istiklal*, September 14, 1948).

were subject to military service, and while no Jewish applicants were accepted by the Military Academy which trained officers, in the army itself, Jewish soldiers had been treated on an equal footing with their non-Jewish fellows. However, after May 1948, Jewish draftees, instead of being trained for military service, were grouped in special work battalions and given hard labor assignments. Sometimes they were sent to cut thorny plants in the desert, or to build mud houses which they were later ordered to destroy and rebuild.

Thousands of Iraqi Jews, born in the country and whose ancestors had lived there for generations, had never bothered to secure citizenship papers, which were normally never demanded in everyday life. Under the new circumstances, such papers had suddenly become a "must" for obtaining jobs or dealing with government institutions. Yet, attempts by Jews to apply for citizenship papers met with systematic obstruction on the part of the officials in charge. A police certificate of good conduct was also needed when a person tried to obtain a salaried job, to enter a high school, or to enter a licensed profession. The police usually refused to issue such certificates to Jewish applicants, who were thus practically excluded from every job and office.

At the beginning of the school year 1948–1949, headmasters of government schools called in the Jewish students and told them that they were not in a position to guarantee their security or even their lives, in the face of the mounting hatred of their Moslem colleagues. The students were advised to transfer to Jewish schools, and many heeded the advice.

Before 1948, the policy of the Ministry of Education, as defined by a United States consular report, was "to give preference to Moslem candidates for admission into schools of higher learning when such preference can be given unostentatiously." This latter face-saving qualification has been abandoned since May, 1948. Jewish students were without exception barred from admission to colleges and high schools. On the other hand, no passports were issued to those who wished to study abroad. Students who attended foreign universities before the ban on traveling abroad became too stringent, were often forced to re-

turn even before graduation since their parents were unable to
send them foreign currency to continue their studies.

Economic Ruin. The Government's policy has badly shattered
the economic position of the Jewish community.

According to a reliable report, Jewish commercial activity in
Iraq was estimated as follows:

Before the Second World War
    a. Imports   95 per cent in Jewish hands
    b. Contracts 90 " " "   "   "
    c. Exports   10 " " "   "   "

During the war
    a. Imports   80 per cent
    b. Contracts 10 " "   (Contracts with British military
                             forces excluded)
    c. Exports   5 " "

After the war
    a. Imports   50 per cent
    b. Contracts   2 " "
    c. Exports   2 " "

After May 15, 1948
    a. Imports   20 per cent
    b. Contracts   0 " "
    c. Exports   2 " "

This catastrophic decline came as a direct result of the government policy aimed at outright elimination of Jewish economic activities. On July 17, 1948, Defense Minister Sadek
al-Bassan Pasha issued an order prohibiting Jewish-owned banks
(the Zelha Bank, the Credit Bank, the Edward Aboody Bank,
the Bank Khardith) from dealing in foreign exchange, sending
money out of the country and conducting credit business.[23]
This drastic curtailment of the normal bank activity, which seriously affected Jewish commercial circles, was organically connected with a series of other discriminatory measures.

Jewish merchants had always played a leading role in the
country's import and export trade. Immediately after the

proclamation of the State of Israel, the Iraqi Government introduced a licensing system for transactions of both kinds; in September, it imposed a wholesale ban on imports and exports. Later, importing was resumed, but import and export permits previously granted to Jewish merchants were canceled[24] and very few licenses have since been granted. It is essential for a merchant dealing in imports and exports to be able to travel outside the country. This has been denied to Jewish businessmen for many years. Article 8 of Iraqi Passport Law N65, published in 1932, empowers the Director of the Passport Division to refuse a passport to any person for reasons of "national security." Even before May 1948, this provision had been applied to Jewish citizens only; after this date, its application became completely prohibitive. As for foreign exchange, none was granted to Iraqi Jews who went abroad either for business, study, or for medical treatment.

In Iraq, income taxes were as a rule paid only by tradesmen and professionals, and most of the taxpayers had always been Jews. But since 1948, they were being taxed beyond any reasonable limit. Moreover, the tax officials have pulled out a forgotten provision in the income tax law that taxes imposed and paid during the past five years are liable to reassessment. The application of this article led to the imposition of fantastic additional sums, the payment of which meant the complete ruin of the taxpayer. In addition, the authorities introduced another ruinous measure known as "provisional seizure." When a Jewish merchant or landlord was accused of any "political crime," all his property, movable and nonmovable, was seized "provisionally." Banks were ordered to freeze his accounts; custom houses were instructed not to allow clearance of the goods sent to him from abroad; and his stores and houses were put under seal. Pending investigation, which usually lasted many months, all his sources of income were blocked. His family remained penniless, and no means were available for organizing his legal defense. Even if he was later released, he could never recover his losses.

The Balance Sheet. On the whole, Iraqi Jewry constituted a fairly prosperous community. S. P. Sassoon, vice president of the

Sephardic Association of Tel Aviv, a person of Iraqi origin, revealed the results of a survey drawn up by himself and others
with an intimate knowledge of the country.[25] According to their
findings, about half of the 30,000 Jewish families of Iraq owned
their own homes, valued at I£30,000,000. Their land was worth
I£5,000,000. Their synagogues, schools and other buildings
were valued at I£2,000,000. Moreover, 9,000 families had property valued at I£750 each; 1,200 owned properties estimated at
I£2,000 each. There were 100 families with possessions estimated at I£150,000 each and 50 families with resources and
properties of I£300,000 each.

A considerable part of this wealth has melted away as a result
of governmental economic discrimination and restrictions.
More was directly appropriated by the Government in the form
of Jewish "voluntary donations," fines, and the wholesale confiscation of the property of Jews found guilty of "assistance to
Zionism." Jews were the largest donors to the officially launched
campaigns for the Palestine Arabs. Early in December 1947, the
Reuter agency reported that following Chief Rabbi Sassoon
Khedouri's appeal, 500,000 dinars were collected among the
Jews for this cause. During one week in September 1948, the
sum total of the fines imposed on Jews amounted to 173,000
dinars.[25a] By the end of October 1948, fines to the amount of
20,000,000 dinars ($80 million) had been levied against Jews.[26]

When, late in 1949, direct mass persecutions of Jews subsided, the economic ruin of the Jewish community became the
dominant line in the policy of Iraq's Government. While insisting that "spectacular stories of persecution circulated abroad
do not appear to be well substantiated in Iraq itself," Albion
Ross of *The New York Times* stressed the economic motives
promoting the urge to emigrate in large numbers, even illegally:

With the Iraqui economy dislocated at present and unemployment rather extensive, the Jews, suspected in general of Zionism,
have a hard time finding employment and have scant chances of
advancement in the present circumstances, unless they are employed
in a Jewish firm. Jewish business men, however, have to a marked
degree cut down their investments and reduced their commercial
activity bcause of uncertainty as to their future status.

EXODUS

Capital Offense. The right of Jews to leave Iraq—either to emigrate or on temporary visits abroad—has always been restricted. After May 1948, emigration to Palestine became a capital offense and scores of Jews were arrested on suspicion of aiding others to emigrate.

In August 1948, it was announced that all Iraqi Jews who went to Palestine and did not return would be considered criminals who had joined the ranks of the enemy and would be tried by military courts *in absentia*.[27] No distinction whatsoever was made between those who had gone to Palestine legally before the commencement of the hostilities between Iraq and Israel and those who left clandestinely after May 1948. Thus all the 1,597 Jews who went to Palestine between 1939 and May 1948 automatically became "criminals." The Minister of the Interior, Tewfiq al-Nale, openly admitted in Parliament that the judgments *in absentia* were also against those Jews who had left the country legally.[28] Since such persons had left through regular channels, the martial courts were able to obtain their names from the emigration officials. They were tried and given death sentences or many years of hard labor plus heavy fines. While the death and jail sentences were of a symbolic rather than actual nature, the fines against those who had left behind some kind of property were quite tangible and supplied the treasury with very substantial amounts of money. Between February 4 and June 8, 1949, the Arab press and radio listed the names of 83 Jews who were tried *in absentia*. Seventeen were condemned to death by hanging, while 66 received prison sentences totaling 449 years. Fines amounting to 79,000 dinars were imposed. The entire property of one defendant was confiscated.[29]

Many Jews have fled and tried to reach Israel through neighboring Iran in a desperate attempt to escape from persecution. The penalty for such attempts to cross the border illegally was five to seven years' imprisonment with hard labor, although the official penal law limits the penalty for such offenses to six months. Despite these severe punishments and the close watch on the Iraq-Iranian frontier, 719 Jews have succeeded in crossing into Iran between May 15, 1948, and August 31, 1949. Here they would be set free upon the payment of a nominal fine for illegal entry. A special Jewish organization established in Teheran took over the care of the newcomers.[30]

Temporarily endangered late in November 1949 by restrictive Iranian measures,[31] this small-scale exodus via Iran continued unabated. It even showed an increase during the following months. Special *shelihim* (emissaries) of the Jewish Agency were active in organizing this clandestine emigration. In January 1950, Albion Ross reported from Khorramshahr on the Iran-Iraqi border that "this crossing point for Iraqi Jews leaving the country is getting a steadily heavier traffic," as the Jews in Baghdad, Basra and the adjoining southern areas "close out their affairs and prepare to leave the country." This sharp increase in illegal crossings was encouraged by the lifting of the severe Iraqi martial law. Henceforth, Jews found near the frontier without adequate explanations for their presence there were fined about 5 dinars ($14). Those caught in the act of illegal crossing were fined about 50 dinars. Ross also reported that one Jew had made five attempts to escape and was fined five times before his successful sixth attempt.[32]

The grim realities of Iraq's economic situation have caused the gradual change in the attitude of the country's ruling circles towards Jewish emigration. Iraq's finances were steadily deteriorating. Royalties from oil, the country's single major source of income, have decreased considerably since the Government imposed an embargo on the petroleum flow to Haifa. The average daily oil production fell from 96,000 barrels in 1947 to 72,000 barrels in 1948. The Baghdad correspondent for the London *Economist* (January 8, 1949) wrote that not only was the Government in arrears in paying its officials and in covering the cost of maintenance of its troops in Palestine, but there was doubt whether it could meet its obligations to foreign contractors. The country's exports dropped from 14 million dinars in 1947 to less than 7 million dinars in 1948, while imports rose from 39 million dinars in 1947 to 50 million in 1948.

Under such circumstances, the prospect of eventually inheriting the property of the Jews following a planned mass evacuation became increasingly tempting. A considerable part of this property has already been taken over by the state in the form of fines, sequestration or outright confiscation. The bulk of it, however, still remained in the hands of its owners and could not be taken away from them without too much unpleasant international publicity.

Gates Thrown Open. On February 13, 1950, Mohammed Saed Maraghai, Prime Minister of Iran, announced that in accordance with his nation's 6,000-year-old tradition of tolerance, the "open door" policy for all religious and political refugees would continue to be maintained.[33] This generous gesture served to increase the number of the illegal crossings. An official Iraqi Government spokesman frankly admitted that clandestine emigration had reached such proportions that there was "practically no possibility of stopping it."[34] Sayid Saleh Jabr, the Iraqi Minister of the Interior, reported to the Parliament that the "Iraqi Jews had resorted to unimaginable devices to get out of the country."[35] The Iraqi Government sadly realized that it would take more authority than it possessed to prevent its own officials from accepting baksheesh.

It is possible that this state of affairs played a considerable role in the sudden decision of Iraq's rulers to reverse their traditional policy and to legalize Jewish emigration. On March 5–7, 1950, both chambers of the Iraqi Parliament passed the following law, which was introduced by the Minister of Interior:[36]

Art. 1. The Council of Ministers is empowered to deprive any Iraqi Jew of Iraqi citizenship, who, of his own free will, chooses to leave Iraq for good, after he shall so signify in writing before an official designated by the Minister of the Interior.

Art. 2. Any Iraqi Jew who leaves Iraq legally or attempts to leave illegally will be deprived of Iraqi citizenship by virtue of a decision of the Council of Ministers.

Art. 3. Any Iraqi Jew who has already left Iraq illegally will be regarded as though he has left for good if he does not return within two months from the effective date of this law; he will be deprived of Iraqi citizenship after the expiration of this period of grace.

Art. 4. The Minister of the Interior will order the deportation from the country of all those who are deprived of Iraqi citizenship under Articles 1 and 2, unless he is convinced, on the basis of sufficient proof, that the temporary stay in Iraq of the person concerned is necessary for legal reasons or for safeguarding his temporary rights.

Art. 5. This law will be in force for one year from the date of its enactment. It may be revoked at any time during this period by a Royal decree, to be published in the *Official Gazette*.

Art. 6. This law will go into effect on the day of its publication in the *Official Gazette*.

Art. 7. The Minister of the Interior shall execute this law.

The bill was introduced with the following explanation:

Consideration was given to the fact that many Iraqi Jews are using all illegal ways in order to leave Iraq for good; indeed, many of them have already left Iraq illegally. Since the presence of such citizens—who are forced to remain in the country and keep their Iraq citizenship—is bound to produce results which will adversely affect security and create social and economic problems it was found that there was no alternative but not to hinder those desiring to leave Iraq for good, and to deprive them of the Iraqi citizenship. It is for this purpose that the present law was enacted.

Reporting Iraq's new decision on March 6, Transjordan's Ramallah Radio stressed that it was "only reached after a stormy debate and much opposition." Senator Mustafa Omari maintained that the bill did not make clear whether Jews would be permitted to withdraw their properties and funds. He demanded that Jewish property be frozen. Ex-Premier Musahim Amin Pashashi urged the Government to consult the member states of the Arab League so that a united policy on Jewish emigration from Arab countries could be formulated: "We should study the question of whether it would not be possible to exchange our Jews for the Arabs of Israel or the Palestine Arab refugees." Pashashi warned that approval of the bill would enable Iraqi Jews to join the Israel army, "while it is the Arab's duty to save Palestine." It was only after the House had been given assurances that the measure was "entirely in the best interests of the country" and would "provide the best method of solving the Jewish problem" that the Government was able to obtain a small majority for the bill.[37]

The well-informed correspondent of the London *Times*

(March 9) explained that this change in policy came in consequence of the large-scale illegal crossings during the past few months, amounting to a huge smuggling operation and that Tawfik as-Swedi's new cabinet decided that it would be best to allow disaffected Jews to leave and to enable the remaining majority to settle down. The correspondent added that the Government "intends to restore to the [remaining] Jews at the earliest opportunity full rights as citizens" of which they had been deprived "for security reasons during the Palestine conflict." This point, he reported, was particularly stressed by Ezra Menahem Daniel, the only Jewish member of the Senate, who urged that the Government accord equal rights to Jews who refuse to emigrate and that the discriminatory restrictions imposed during the period of martial law be abolished.

Mass Registration. Legalization of emigration prompted the Jews to avail themselves of the unexpected opportunity to leave the country. Some two weeks after the promulgation of the law, the Middle East correspondent of the London *Jewish Chronicle* reported that "already feverish preparations for an early departure are in full swing, especially in the great Jewish centers of Baghdad and Basra, where hundreds of families are selling their immovable property, winding up their affairs and packing their bags."[38] However, when shortly before Passover notices appeared in the Iraqi press stating that every Jew desiring to leave the country should register at the Central Synagogue in Baghdad, many thought that this was a trap to round up suspected Zionists, and only 4,000 registered. Later, when it became known that the Government was really permitting emigration, the mass movement began.[39] Very soon six new registration centers were established in synagogues to take care of the rush of applicants. The number of the centers was later increased to eight and to twelve, with the final processing handled at the Central Synagogue. By the end of April, the number of registrants reached 47,000.[40] Jewish officials of the State Railway and other government departments were resigning from their jobs in order to qualify for registration.[41] Of the 50,000 registered until the autumn of 1950, 40,000 were from

Baghdad and the remaining 10,000 from the provinces. Emigration formalities had by that time been completed for over 12,000 applicants, 7,500 in Baghdad, 1,100 in Basra, and 3,500 in other towns.[42] The registration proceeded on a considerable scale but without undue panic. At the end of 1950 about 70,-000 had registered, 8,500 per month.[43] Yet in January 1951, a series of bomb outrages causing several deaths and scores of wounded precipitated a virtual stampede. Between January 14 and March 10, 40,000 registered, over 20,000 per month.[44]

Each applicant was required to sign the following statement:

I declare willingly and voluntarily that I have decided to leave Iraq permanently and that I am aware this statement of mine will have the effect of depriving me of Iraqi nationality and of causing my deportation from Iraq and of preventing me forever afterward from returning.

The names of the registrants were placed on special lists and forwarded to the Council of Ministers for official approval—a procedure normally requiring over two months.[46] The poorer elements of Iraqi Jewry constituted the overwhelming majority of the applicants. The wealthier elements refrained from registering because of difficulties in disposing of their property. Since all applicants were first obligated to renounce their citizenship and were permitted to remain in the country for only two weeks after the grant of the exit visa, the rich Jews feared that should they not succeed in selling their property in time, they would have to leave penniless. The market became flooded with offers by Jews, causing a sharp drop in prices. By the end of March 1950, it was reported that the price of houses had dropped by about 80 per cent. The price of furniture had also sunk abruptly, and the secondhand market was flooded with household goods hurriedly sold at auction. Moreover, violent propaganda was conducted against purchases from the Jews. It stressed that their property would remain in Arab hands should the boycott succeed. Sheikh Mohammed el-Khalesi, a leader of the Moslem hierarchy, issued a *fatwah*—a religious proclamation—forbidding faithful Moslems to buy goods, furniture, or property from

Jews.[47] In consequence, most of the prospective emigrants had to sell their possessions at ridiculously low prices.

Before their departure Jews had to prove to the authorities that they owed no taxes and often had to give up all their cash to satisfy the revenue officers. An emigrant was allowed to take along an Ottoman Bank check for 20 dinars ($56—at the official but nominal rate of exchange) per head for children under ten years of age; 30 dinars ($84) for those between ten and twenty; and 50 dinars ($140) for persons over twenty. They were permitted only 66 pounds of luggage per person or up to 400 pounds per family and had to leave behind all jewelry, including that worn ordinarily.[48]

A major difficulty was transportation. For a time, a thin stream of emigrants continued to trickle into Iran. At the end of April 1950, it was reported from Teheran that some 400 Iraqi Jews had joined the 5,000 earlier illegal entrants. The Jewish Agency opened an office at Teheran and a reception center on the Iraqi-Persian frontier to facilitate the movement of the emigrants.[49]

However, the bulk of the emigrants had to leave directly from Baghdad by air. The plan to ship them by boats from Basra to Elath (via the Indian Ocean and the Red Sea) had to be abandoned because of Iraq's continued refusal to recognize Israel. Nor was overland travel possible because Syria and Lebanon refused to allow the passage of Jews.

The Iraqi Government finally granted permission for air transport to the Near East Air Transport, Inc. (an American chartered company, which had carried out The Magic Carpet operation from Yemen)[50] on the condition that the planes should not fly directly to Israel, but land first in some "neutral country." Nicosia in Cyprus was chosen as such a neutral landing place. Police accompanied the first planes in order to make sure that the arrangements were carried out. The Cyprus authorities granted permission for use of their airfields on the condition that the passengers be immediately flown to Israel. The 400-mile detour increased the cost of transportation by about $15 per passenger. Later, the Iraqi authorities demanded that different planes be employed to fly the Jews from Baghdad to

Cyprus and from Nicosia to Lydda. The Jewish Agency had to
comply with this new and costly demand.[51]

The emigrants were provided—at the cost of one pound and
an additional three shillings tax to "save Palestine"—with special travel documents permitting them to proceed to Cyprus
and carrying a stamped statement forbidding their return to
Iraq.[52]

The Great Airlift. The great airlift transfer from Iraq, which
became known as "Operation Ali-Baba," commenced with the
flight from Baghdad of 175 passengers aboard two giant Skymasters that arrived in Lydda on May 21, 1950. Strict censorship prevented the announcement of their arrival because of
the fear that the Iraqi Government, embarrassed by publicity,
might call off the exodus. But the ban was lifted by Israeli authorities after the disclosure of the operation both by Baghdad
and Cyprus.

On May 27, 1950, a few days after the airlift started, Lawrence Resner recorded in his diary that American pilots of the
Near East Air Transport told him a "hair-raising story" about
the conditions under which departing Jews had to board the
planes:[53]

... [They] are all put through a very nasty type of search. Men and
women are forced to strip together. Iraqi soldiers go through their
garments item by item. Even after a group has boarded a plane the
Iraqis may come aboard and say a mistake has been made and take
one or two passengers back to town. In several instances a whole
planeload of passengers has been taken off and replaced by another.
One of the planes was held up eight hours by this procedure. The
crews themselves, most of them Americans, are put through exhaustive searches. Their papers, their pockets, every little scrap of
paper is thoroughly examined. For each day a plane is idle in Baghdad
the Joint Distribution Committee must pay the airline $1,500.

... Bill Troster, an American pilot in the war and a soldier of fortune,
related how the Iraqi police forced the disrobing of men and women
together under glaring searchlights.... Stanley Bush, another American pilot told me he had to keep the motors of his plane warmed up,
ready for take-off, from 9 A.M. until 5 P.M.; the passengers themselves never had more than a day or a day and a half notice that they
were to go. The Iraqi police apparently thought that too much ad-

vance notice would give those leaving an opportunity to make a more convenient disposition of whatever worldly goods they had. The whole process was elaborately screened and guarded.

On the whole, the air evacuation failed to proceed at a satisfactory rate. Before the beginning of the airlift in May 1950, 4,876 Jews had been brought to Israel, mostly via Iran. The progress of the air evacuation from Baghdad during the months May–December 1950 is shown in the following table.[54]

Month	Number	Month	Number
May	1,133	September	2,875
June	2,739	October	4,449
July	3,999	November	3,773
August	3,948	December	3,841

A total of 26,757 persons were flown during the eight months. But the number of registrants began to exceed that of the departures. Albion Ross who visited Iraq in October 1950 reported that by the end of July some 16,000 persons, including over 8,500 adults, had completed their denationalization processing and were awaiting final cabinet approval; at the end of October, the number increased to approximately 30,000.[55]

Faced with this backlog of denationalized Jews waiting to emigrate, the Government slowed down the rate of the authorization of applications for denationalization. Consequently the number of those with approved denationalization requests awaiting transportation dropped from about 5,000 at the end of July to some 1,000 to 2,000 at the end of October 1950. Some 30,000 were waiting for their applications' approval by the cabinet. Nevertheless, new applications for denationalization and permission to leave the country continued to be filed at the rate of about 250 a day. Together with children entered on their parents' forms the daily average rose to about 400 to 500.[56]

In the meantime, the situation of tens of thousands of now stateless Jews was becoming increasingly critical, as they had been completely cut off from the country's life. Deputy El-Sayed Fayek el-Samerai, vice president of the strongly nationalistic *Istiqlal* (Independence) Party, raised in the House of

Representatives the question whether the six Jewish parliamentary deputies should continue to represent the rapidly dwindling Jewish community. Minister of State Mustafa al-Omari replied that the Government intended to present a bill amending the law governing the emigration of Jews to Israel and to reconsider the reduction in the number of Jewish deputies who would represent the relatively small number of Jews who retained their Iraqi citizenship.[57] Among those waiting to emigrate, many were homeless and had to sleep in the streets, others were living on their meager savings or on aid from relatives and Jewish organizations. Many prospective emigrants were imprisoned on charges that they sought to smuggle gold and jewelry out of the country.[58] Frequent were cases of arrests in the street of Jews carrying parcels or luggage: police accused them of trying to "remove frozen property" and confiscated the seized effects.[59] At a later stage, every departing Jew had to produce a police certificate that he was not exporting anything; such certificates were obtainable only after prolonged police searches and upon payment of heavy bribes.[60] An order was issued to directors of Iraqi firms to pledge in writing that they would have no business dealings with Jews registered for emigration.[61] According to a bulletin published by the Union of Iraqi Jews in Israel, all letters from Israel to Iraqi Jews were opened by Iraqi secret police and the homes of the addressees were searched. Jews in Israel were advised to exercise discretion in writing to their relatives in Iraq and even to stop writing altogether lest they endanger them. The bulletin also reported that customs officials at Baghdad airport were maltreating the Jewish emigrants, taking away from them all khaki clothing, sugar, rice and tea, tearing their clothes and breaking their glassware during inspection. Immigrants arriving in Israel complained that they had been forced to leave their goods in Baghdad airport, and that the baggage delivery was greatly delayed and in some cases never arrived.[62]

... *Intensified*. On January 18, 1951, the Near East Arab Broadcasting Station reported that the Iraqi Government had decided to discontinue the emigration of Jews to Israel on March 1, 1951. Three days later, the Baghdad Radio denied the report, but it soon became known that March 9 was the last day on which application for exit permits would be accepted and that actual emigration would be permitted until May 31 only.[63] The Jewish Agency and the Government of Israel had therefore decided on January 30 (at a meeting of the Government-Agency Coordination Board) to almost triple the number of immigrants from Iraq during the next three months. Thus, 13,500 were to be transferred monthly in order to meet the new timetable set by the Iraqi Government.[64] Unconditional transport priority was given to this biggest human airlift in history, the cost of which was expected to exceed $3 million.[65] The Finance Committee of the Knesset allocated $5 million from the 1951–52 budget for the housing and employment of the newcomers.[66]

However, the new airlift schedule could not be carried out. Only 4,448 arrived in January, 1951, and 6,346 in February.[67] By March 9, 1951, the last day for filing applications, 104,630 persons had registered for emigration. Of these 68,923 were from Baghdad and 35,707 from the provinces. Not more than 25,000 to 26,000 Jews had at that date chosen to remain in Iraq, mostly in Baghdad.[68] All the Jews of Mossul, the second-largest Jewish community in Iraq numbering about 25,000 souls and claiming a 2,000-year history, registered. In Basra, the Jewish Community Council, representing about 20,000 persons, sold some communal properties to cover the cost of passage and closed its three Jewish schools.[69]

It was not before the middle of March 1951, when the situation had become most critical, that the airlift operations began to proceed at an adequate pace. On March 12, planes began to fly directly from Baghdad to Lydda.* On March 14, four Skymasters brought in 478 persons in twenty-four hours, with 550 arriving on March 17. By March 19, arrangements were completed for a shuttle service three times daily with the ulti-

* Of the 106,622 Iraqi Jews flown to Israel during the period May 1950 to June 1951, 61 per cent (65,371) came by the direct Baghdad-Lydda route; 36 per cent (37,791) by the roundabout route Baghdad-Nicosia-Lydda; and the rest arrived via Baghdad-Teheran-Lydda. (The Executive of the Zionist Organization and the Executive of the Jewish Agency. *Reports for the Period April 1951 to December 1955 Submitted to the Twenty-Fourth Zionist Congress in Jerusalem.* Jerusalem, April 1956, p. 87.)

mate daily schedule of 1,000 passengers. Five days later, the airlift brought in 650. Another 100 came by special plane from
Basra where several hundred Jews were stranded by the Government's prohibition of travel to Baghdad. A total of 15,018 was
flown to Israel during the month of March. However, this impressive record was surpassed in April with 21,651 passengers.
The total for May was 18,094.[70]

The exit deadline of May 31 was extended till June 30, 1951,
because of the large number of registrants for emigration, with
the result that 14,889 were flown during that month.[71] Jewish
Agency spokesmen expressed the hope for another extension in
view of the unforeseen slow-downs resulting from shortage of
aircraft at the Israel end and from the stoppages in Baghdad following alleged discoveries of arms.[72] The airlift continued, with
5,757 transported in July. The total for the first eight months
of 1951 was 86,788, and the grand total from the beginning of
the "Operation Ali-Baba" on May 19, 1950, until December 31,
1951, was 113,545 passengers flown[73]—three times the number
of Jews who had returned from Babylon with Ezra and Nehe-
miah, nearly 2,500 years ago.

On August 5, a Jewish Agency spokesman declared that "Operation Ali-Baba" was concluded.[74] The Near East Airlines at
that time was already carrying Jews to Israel from Iran, where,
in addition to many Iranian Jews, over 7,500 Iraqi refugees were
awaiting their turn.[75] In fact, 1,298 Iraqi Jews arrived in Israel
in August, via Iran, in addition to those who came directly from
Iraq, 415 in September and 245 in October–December. Thus
88,161 were repatriated in 1951 from Iraq, constituting 50.7
per cent of the entire year's immigration, as compared with 18.7
per cent in 1950. According to official statistics, 121,512 Iraqi
Jews came to Israel since the establishment of the state. Small-
scale immigration from Iraq, mostly via Iran and Turkey, continued throughout the following years: 868 arrived in 1952; 375
in 1953; 232 in 1954; 166 in 1955; 76 in 1956; 119 in 1957;
and 77 in 1958.[76]. These latecomers were mostly wealthy Iraqi
Jews who had delayed their departure in order to be able to sell
their businesses and to liquidate other assets. During the pe-

riod May 15, 1948, to January 1, 1959, a total of 123,425 Iraqi Jews have settled in Israel.[77]

The Fate of Jewish Assets. Early in 1948, forebodings of inescapable economic doom induced many wealthy Jews to look for means of transferring their liquid assets abroad, through Kuwait, Iran and other countries. Neutral economic observers at foreign embassies and legations in Baghdad reported to their governments that it had been relatively easy to transfer funds from Iraq to neighboring countries with little risk involved until fairly recently. The Government did not have adequate machinery of control while channels for free transfer of funds were well established. Dr. Saleh Haydar, Deputy Director of the Iraqi National Bank, told the Arab News Agency in June 1951 that the Jews had sent to Israel or elsewhere abroad approximately $30 million during the preceding two years alone and that in fact the movement of funds had begun even earlier.[78]

This estimate appears to have been highly exaggerated. The bulk of the Jewish wealth consisted of immovable property, houses, land, factories, goods in stock, furniture and fittings. The capital of the small local dealers was used for current trade operations and could not be transferred abroad. The emigrants were allowed to take with them only small sums of money in cash. Their movable and immovable property remained theirs legally to be disposed of at some later time. However, on March 10, 1951, the Parliament passed (at a closed session, to which the six Jewish deputies had no access) "The Fifth Law for the Supervision and Management of Assets of Jews Who Have Lost Their Nationality,"[79] ordering the freezing of bank accounts and property of Jews who have applied for immigration to Israel and have thus forfeited their Iraqi citizenship. Immediately afterward "The Third Decree of 1951" was issued by the Minister of the Interior, stipulating the purpose and establishing the machinery for the implementation of the Law.[80] In order to prevent premature leakage of information which might have given Jews the chance of withdrawing their deposits, the Government and Parliament deliberations were held in strictest secrecy and the Baghdad telephone service was suspended for several hours before the issuance of the decree. All

Iraqi banks were closed for two days following its promulgation.[81]

By passing this law on March 10, the day after the deadline
for registration for emigration, the Government deliberately
tricked its Jewish subjects who had registered in good faith, be-
lieving that they would retain their right of property. Moshe
Sharett, Israel's Foreign Minister, rightly recalled before the
Knesset on March 19 that the laws on emigration provided only
for the loss of Iraqi citizenship but carried no other conditions,
and it had been on this basis that the Jews had registered: "Only
after they had done so, was their property robbed from them
without prior notice."[82] The premeditated character of this
measure was frankly acknowledged by Al Ahd, organ of the
Prime Minister Nuri Said's Constitutional Unity Party. In the
article, "A Blessed Move," the paper particularly praised the
timing of the Fifth Law after the registration's deadline, arguing
that "if the law had been enacted earlier, most of the Jews, particularly the rich, would have hesitated to relinquish their
[Iraqi] nationality, and subsequently a great number of them
would have stayed in the country."[83]

On March 22, 1951, less than a fortnight after the enactment
of the Fifth Law, Parliament at a secret session, again without
the participation of the Jewish deputies, enacted a new law
dealing with Jews who had left the country otherwise than on
the basis of Law No. 1 (1950). It provided for freezing of assets
of all Jews who had left Iraq with a passport on or after the first
of January 1948. The provisions of Law No. 5 (1951) were to
be applied to such property. Every Jew affected by this law
was to return to Iraq within two months from the day of posting
a relevant public notice by the Iraqi diplomatic or consular
services abroad. (Such notices appeared thereafter in practically
all countries.) Those returning to Iraq within the prescribed
period would have their property restored after deduction of
all expenses assessed thereon by the public administrator. Those
failing to return were to be considered as having forfeited their
Iraqi nationality and their property was liable to sequestration.[84]
It was estimated that about 3,000 Iraqi Jewish citizens in Great
Britain, the United States, France, Iran, India and other coun-

tries have been affected by the new legislation. Most of them were rather rich and their aggregate assets amounted to vast sums of money.[85]

The property of the denationalized Jews was vested in a special office named *Amanu Ama* (General Secretariat), headed by the *Amin Am* (General Secretary), with functions similar to those of the Custodian of Alien Property. He was authorized to freeze, administer and liquidate all the assets of the denationalized persons; to appoint special custodians for the administration of estates and assets; to pay for the support of all the dependents of the owners of the property if they had no other income or means of sustenance; to give the necessary funds to any person who had forfeited his citizenship to support himself until his departure. The *Amin Am* was also empowered to sell the frozen assets in order to pay the debts that were due to the Tax Office and to other official institutions as well as to private persons whose loans were recognized by a court of law, and to cover the expenses involved in the administration and the supervision of the properties. The *Amin Am* prohibited the sale or transfer of Jewish nonmovable property. The land registration office was closed in order to prevent land transactions.[86]

Arab sources indicated that the funds frozen by the Fifth Law amounted to about six million dinars ($16,800,000). The value of frozen property was estimated to be over twelve million dinars ($33 million).[87] An item in *The New York Times* of September 23, 1951, estimated the value of the blocked accounts alone (not including other movable and nonmovable property) as amounting to from $84 million to $120 million. All establishments owned by Jews who registered for emigration were at once put under seal by the police. "Tens of thousands of Jews were converted overnight into paupers," stated a report from Baghdad in the *Davar* of March 20, 1951.

On March 19, 1951, Foreign Minister Sharett declared before the Knesset that

by freezing the property of tens of thousands of Jewish immigrants to Israel—stateless today but citizens of Israel from the moment they arrive—the Government of Iraq has invited a reckoning between itself and the State of Israel. There already existed an account between

us and the Arabs for compensation due to the Arabs who left the
territory of Israel and abandoned their property there as a result of
the war of aggression by the Arab world against our state. The act
now perpetrated by the Kingdom of Iraq with regard to the property
of Jews who neither violated Iraqi law nor in any way threatened that
country's position nor undermined its security, compels us to link
the two accounts.

The Israel Government, therefore, has decided to inform the appropriate United Nations institutions—and I hereby make this
public—that the value of Jewish property frozen in Iraq will be taken
into account with regard to the compensation we have undertaken
to pay Arabs who abandoned property in Israel.[88]

An official note outlining the Israel Government's attitude
to the freezing of Jewish assets was submitted to the U.N.
Palestine Conciliation Committee, which forwarded it to the
Iraqi and other Arab governments.[89] The Amman paper *Falastin* asserted on March 21, 1951, that the Iraqi Government was
legally right and that the property of the Iraqi Jews could not
be subject to bargaining between Israel and Iraq.

There the issue rested for some sixteen months. In July 1952,
the U.N. Palestine Conciliation Committee approached the
Israel Government on the long dormant question of releasing
the blocked bank accounts (estimated at I£5,000,000) of Arab
refugees who left Palestine in 1948. In reply Abba Eban, the
Chief Delegate of the state of Israel to the United Nations,
called attention to the blocked accounts of Israeli residents who
had fled from Iraq and other Arab countries. Israel, he stated,
considered it reasonable that equal concern should be shown
for Jewish refugees from Arab countries. However, he stressed
that Israel, prompted by the desire to assist the Palestine refugees and their resettlement, was willing to discuss measures for
the gradual release of accounts of the Arab refugees, subject to
"the over-all foreign exchange position of the country," and
offered on behalf of his government to release I£500,000 of the
Arab blocked accounts. According to a spokesman of the Israel
Foreign Office, "this offer was not linked with any request for
the defreezing of any Jewish money in Iraq, but it was hoped
that action (by the Conciliation Commission) would be taken

to this end.[90] Later, the amount of Arab frozen accounts to be released was increased to I£1,000,000. Again no mention was made of linking this payment with the defreezing of Jewish assets in Iraq.[91] But the Israel Government has not given up its claim for the Jewish assets in Iraq. In October 1952, Israel residents with property in Arab and Arab-held territory were invited to register their claims at the Foreign Claims Registry Office. These were to include real estate, movable property, business enterprises, patents and similar rights, securities and other properties, bank balances, supplies and other services by trade agreement and other claims.[92] As late as November 17, 1958, Ambassador Abba Eban, reiterating Israel's readiness to pay compensation for the property left behind by the Arab refugees, stressed: "In fixing the level of compensation owed by Israel, it would be necessary to take into account the claims of Israel citizens who have the right to compensation for their property left behind in Arab lands."[93]

The Plight of the Remnant. The transfer of Iraqi Jewry to Israel was the largest of the series of airborne repatriation operations since Israel's statehood. As was the case with Yemenite Jewry, this was a "total" repatriation, virtually the liquidation of the Iraqi Jewish community. In 1955, the Chief Rabbi of Baghdad estimated the total number of the Jews in the country at 5,000 persons. Other sources speak of 4,000, 5,000 and even 8,000, concentrated predominantly in Baghdad. The number of Jews in provincial areas is small: Basra had a community of 300, while 80 Jews lived in Diwaniya, about 100 miles south of the capital.[94] Latest information puts the total Jewish population of Iraq at "some 600 families." They are almost exclusively wealthy importers and exporters who stayed on because they were reluctant to abandon their lucrative business.[95]

Under the Nuri Pasha regime, their plight was most unhappy. A communiqué published on March 26, 1951, by the Iraqi Director General of Propaganda assured that the Jews who retained their Iraqi citizenship would be granted "all rights and the just treatment guaranteed by the Iraqi Constitution to all Iraqi citizens."[96] This promise proved to be of little value. The order providing for the freezing of Jewish bank accounts was for three weeks applied also to the deposits of those who had not registered for emigration. Later such Jews were given special (yellow) passports certifying that the citizenship of the "Jew" so and so has not been withdrawn.[97] Under a penalty of up to two years imprisonment or a fine of $7,200, they were ordered to sign declarations swearing that they were not in possession of goods or articles which had formerly belonged to intending emigrants.[98] Jews were forbidden to ride bicycles.[99] They were refused import licenses, restricted in the right of travel abroad. Jewish religious courts and the Jewish courts of appeal, which were in existence in Baghdad for over a century, were abolished in December 1951.[100] Some tenuous vestiges of the ancient and once famous Baghdad Kehilah and of its institutions still exist. There is a five-member administrative committee appointed by the Ministry of Justice. The Chief Rabbi Sassoon Khadouri has managed to keep all the twenty-six synagogues intact, though only one is in use. Of more than fifty schools once run by the Kehilah only one (the "Shamash School" consisting of a kindergarten, a secondary and a high school with some 500 pupils) was still functioning in 1958. But here, too, the main language is Arabic, with French and English as secondary languages; the only Jewish subject is religious instruction and there is an acute shortage of Jewish teachers. Of the six Jewish members of Parliament who represented the Jewish minority not a single one is left: The Government's argument is that there are practically no Jews left to be represented.[101]

An unexpected and seemingly far-reaching turn for the better occurred after the July 1958 bloody revolution. Though the new regime is as strongly hostile toward Israel as were its predecessors, Premier Kassem said in one of his pronouncements that Jews must be treated like all other citizens of Iraq. In 1959, the Minister of Education attended as guest of honor the prize distribution of the "Shamash School." For the first time, too, ten Jewish boys and girls have been admitted to the University of Baghdad. The Government has also canceled the legislation abolishing the Iraqi citizenship of Jews who emigrated from the country, and rescinded compulsory custodianship over their "abandoned property." According to Arab press reports, the Government considered the denationalization of such emigrants "contrary to the Iraq constitution" under which citizenship "is the inalienable right of all Iraqis." There is no restriction of emigration.[102] The few hundred Jewish families that are still "lost in the Land of Assyr," are so of their own volition.* Their "Babylonian captivity" is self-imposed.

* According to latest information, 450 Iraqi Jews who had left the country returned after the publication of the new decree (*Jewish Chronicle*, April 1, 1960).

4

Libya: Total Transfer to Israel

An Autochthonous Community. Libya extends along the Mediterranean Sea from Egypt on the east to Tunisia and Algeria on the west; on the north it is bounded by Algeria, French West Africa and the Sudan. Its area includes the former Italian colonies known as Tripolitania (capital, Tripoli) in the western part and Cyrenaica (capital, Benghazi) in the eastern part of the territory.

The Jews of Libya are an indigenous community, with their roots deep in the centuries and the millennia of North African history. There have been Jews in the town of Tripoli from the earliest times, perhaps even from the period of Phoenician colonization. It is certain that in the fourth century the town boasted rabbis well versed in Hebrew, as related by St. Augustine (*Epistolae*, 71, 3–5). Cyrenaica attracted Jewish traders and settlers long before the destruction of the First Temple (586 B.C.E.). Shortly before the destruction of Jerusalem, Jews and Jewish proselytes formed a large part of Libya's population. Successive waves of Jewish immigrants, in particular the influx of Jews from Spain and from the Balearic Islands in 1391 and 1492, have contributed a noticeable admixture of European blood. The Jews of Libya are thus of dual origin, some of them coming from Europe and others descending from an autochthonous race. But, as is indicated by their type, their names, their manners, customs, and traditions, the first nucleus was formed of Jews native to the country. Their customs, laws and traditions are, however, distinct from those of the native Arabs. Even where they had been partly Europeanized, mostly in the larger towns such as Benghazi and Tripoli, they have maintained their Jewish associations, hardly taking any part in the civic, social, cultural, or professional life of the majority population.

Formerly one of the Barbary states, Tripoli became independent in 1714 and was conquered by Turkey in 1835. Under Turkish rule, new and better prospects opened for Tripolitania's Jews. In the major centers they were able to devote themselves to skilled trades, such as goldsmiths and silversmiths, and lived in relative security; yet, in the interior, they were always exposed to the fanaticism and jealousy of the local Arab population and had to endure many privations. In 1885, there were in Tripoli 7,500 Jews with eighteen synagogues, eleven yeshivoth and two schools of the Alliance Israélite Universelle. By 1909 their number increased to 14,000, of whom hardly one-tenth lived under decent conditions. Of the 2,000 Jewish families in the Tripoli Hara (ghetto), 400 lived on public charity, while more than a thousand earned just enough to keep alive.[1]

Italian Rule. During the Turko-Italian war of 1911–1912, Italy proclaimed the annexation of Tripoli which was recognized by the Great Powers in the Treaty of Ouchy (October 18, 1912). The attitude of the Italian conquerors toward Libyan Jews in the years that followed was, on the whole, a fair one. It was, however, marred by frequent cases of violence and discrimination on the part of Italian colonists.

Under Italian domination the Libyan Jewish population was divided into three groups which were treated differently from the point of view of the Italian law.

a. *Italian citizens,* i.e., citizens of the Kingdom of Italy residing in Libya; their number was very limited.

b. *Italian-Libyan citizens,* i.e., Libyan natives of Jewish faith. Under the Royal Decree Law, December 3, 1934, No. 2012 and the Law of April 11, 1935, No. 675, concerning the organization of the Colony of Libya, they were granted equality of rights with the other citizens of the colony. These rights included respect of creed and of local traditions; in governmental schools, Jews were not to be taught views or subjects that conflicted with their religion (Royal Decree Law, December 3,

1934, Art. 39–42). Like the Arabs, they were exempt from military duty.

c. *Foreign Jews* who were neither Italian nor Italian-Libyan citizens; they enjoyed the same position as all other foreigners and were protected by their respective consulates.

The administration of the Libyan Jewish community was in the hands of a "Jewish Commission" appointed by the Italian administration. The main source of community income was taxation, levied by a special community committee, which imposed taxes in accordance with the income of individual community members. In the year preceding World War II, some 3,000 out of Tripoli's 23,000 Jews were paying £6 or more in community taxes.[2]

Elementary education was provided by Hebrew schools (Talmud Torahs) devoted almost entirely to the study of Hebrew and religion, and by public schools which were under the direct control of the Italian administration. In the scholastic year 1939–1940, 2,074 pupils (1,272 boys and 802 girls) attended Jewish elementary public schools in Tripolitania, and 436 (286 boys and 150 girls) in Cyrenaica. In addition, Jewish public kindergartens in Tripolitania had 256 pupils (68 boys and 188 girls), and 77 students (58 boys and 19 girls) attended a Jewish secondary school. Talmud Torahs (not in receipt of government grants) had an enrollment of 1,235 students in Tripolitania and of 511 in Cyrenaica.[3] Both public schools and Talmud Torahs were badly organized and poorly run. Progressive Jewish leaders have in vain stressed the need for a single and unified school system, under a coordinated direction and with a broader curriculum and range of subjects, including Hebrew as a separate subject. Before the enactment of the racial laws by the Italian Government, the Jews had access to the secondary schools and colleges. These were barred to them after 1938. Since the outbreak of war, all schools have been closed, and a survey taken in 1946, three years after liberation from the Fascist regime, showed that out of a total of about 6,000 Jewish boys and girls between the ages of twelve and eighteen, about 4,500 were not attending school, and had not received any general education for the preceding six years.[4]

Numbers and Economy. From 25,103 in 1931, the Jewish population increased to 30,046 in 1939. The largest communities were those of Tripoli (18,980), Benghazi (3,300), Amrus (1500), Misurata (1,222), Homs (930).

The 7,000 Jews living in the interior of the country have adapted their pattern of life to that of the local Arab population. They dressed like the Arabs, except on Sabbath. A peculiar group formed the 345-strong troglodyte, cave-dwelling Jewish community in the "Tigrina Concession" high in the hills. Their dwellings were grottos built in round craters 35 yards deep and 25 yards across. They could be reached only by a rough descending passage through the rock, protected by stout-beamed bolted doors which could be moved only by those who were familiar with them. The homes were cool in summer and warm in winter. Although these Jewish cave dwellers seemed to be completely assimilated with the Arabs in dress, custom, and language, they attended synagogue daily for morning and evening prayers, and observed the Sabbath strictly.[5]

The economic resources of Libya are limited. With the shifting of the communication centers toward the Atlantic coast, the development of such ports as Casablanca and Pointe Noire, and the creation of railways and roads in West Africa and Congo, Libya has lost its former important position in world trade.

Commerce and trade being the prevalent occupation of Libyan Jews, the decline of the country's commercial traffic strongly affected their welfare. Only a minority were able to derive a satisfactory income from their commercial activities; about two-thirds of the community were composed of people who barely managed to subsist or who were utterly poverty-stricken and lived on charity. Some endeavored to earn their living as petty artisans (mainly in the production of jewelry, trinkets, etc.) or as unskilled laborers; neither of these occupations secured an adequate income. As in all cities of North Africa, the Jews of Tripoli had their own quarter, called *Hara* or *Hora*—a Berber word of Greek origin, meaning "segregated place"—a labyrinth of narrow and tortuous streets, a survival of the Moslem Middle Ages which has remained unchanged either by Turkish or by modern European architectural influences. These crowded areas became hotbeds of disease; trachoma, tuberculosis, venereal diseases, malnutrition and rickets were rampant; prostitution and high infant mortality were common phenomena.

Mussolini—"Protector of Islam." On the whole, the Libyan Arabs did not begrudge the Jews their modest commercial standing. It could in no way interfere with the interests of the Arab population, which is almost exclusively engaged in agriculture and cattle-breeding. Arab-Jewish relations have therefore been peaceful as long as they have not been interfered with by outside influences. The Fascist Italian administration has in this respect played a sinister role.

Mussolini's government cherished the dream of a new Roman Empire centered around the Mediterranean which was to become the Italian *mare nostrum*. Moslem countries were attributed a major part in this ambitious scheme, and Mussolini declared himself "Protector of Islam." Libya, the only Arabic-speaking province in Italian possession, was chosen as the center of Italian imperialistic designs and a springboard for Fascist propaganda in the Moslem world. It was singled out to become an example of a Moslem province under Italian rule. After the Senussi rebellion had been ruthlessly quelled by 1932, the Italian administration made it a point of Fascist honor and efficacy to build up the desolate province as a model colony. Thousands of desert acres were converted into blooming fields. These were, of course, allotted mostly to Italian colonists, but the natives, too, were given some aid in rebuilding and bettering their settlements.[6]

Striving to win popularity among the Libyan Arab population, the Italian administration displayed marked hostility toward the Jewish community and its traditions. Even before anti-Semitism had become the official policy of the Fascist regime, it used to be common practice for the Italian authorities to ingratiate themselves with the Arabs by anti-Jewish pronouncements and discrimination. The Fascist organ of Libya, the *L'Avvenire di Tripoli*, frequently published anti-Semitic material and conducted a systematic campaign of incitement against the Jews. In 1938 and 1939, a series of royal decrees and laws placed Italian Jewry in a kind of moral and economic ghetto. The Royal Decree N 1728, of November 18, 1938, extended to Libya all the metropolitan racial laws and regulations. In addition, Italian authorities of Libya published a number of local decrees which often went farther than the original racial legislation. In December, 1942, all these anti-Jewish decrees, metropolitan and Libyan alike, were combined, added to, and issued as an integral code, to become effective in January 1949. This code excluded the Jews from military service, but made them liable to labor duty in wartime. Jews were forbidden to own or manage firms engaged in work for national defense or employing more than twenty persons, to possess land valued at more than 300,000 lire, or buildings and lots of gross value of 500,000 lire. They were barred from owning or managing import, export, credit or insurance businesses; shipping, transport or forwarding agencies; and theaters or theatrical agencies. Jewish doctors and lawyers could practice their professions among Jews only. Jewish children were barred from Italian and Arab schools. No Italian or Arab servant could be employed in Jewish families.[7]

The effect of the anti-Jewish measures on native Libyan Jews seems to have been slight during the first few years following their successive enactment. Local authorities were often lenient in their application, and corruption, which was rife in the Fascist regime, always left an open door for bribery. The most affected were Jews of foreign origin whose citizenship, if granted later than 1919, had been revoked; they had, therefore, lost the right of residence. Some of them were expelled from Libya, and others interned in concentration camps.

The bulk of native Libyan Jewry began to feel the full impact of the governmental anti-Jewish policy after Italy's entrance into war. The vicissitudes of war had an almost immediate effect on the fate of the Libyan Jewish communities. The defeat of the Italian army on the Egyptian frontier was a severe blow to the Fascist prestige in Libya. In an attempt to divert public attention from the unfortunate military campaign, a number of Libyan Jews were arrested in December, 1940, on charges of

pro-British activities. Again, in April, 1941, after the reoccupa-
tion of Bardia by Axis forces, Italian authorities arrested many
Benghazi Jews on similar charges. All members of the Tripoli
Jewish Community Board were also arrested. The recapture of
Benghazi by the British forces on December 24, 1941, was
followed by an order of the Axis commander in Tripoli forbidding Jews to leave their homes between 4 P.M. and 6 A.M.[8]

In May 1942, the Italian authorities, acting on the instruction of the German military commander, ordered the deportation of 2,800 Jews of Cyrenaica to Giado, a military outpost in
the mountains; 218 of them died from undernourishment before they were freed by the British Eighth Army. Later on, 1,400
Jews of Tripoli were conscripted for work on the railway and
road, and 200 Jews of Sirta were sent in chains to Misurata
where they were, together with 800 local Jews, to be mobilized
for forced labor.[9]

On the evening before Tripoli fell, Axis troops raided the
ancient ghetto quarter and summarily executed a number of
leading Jewish personages; according to various reports, 162 to
700 Jews were massacred. Thirty Jewish leaders had been
deported to Italy as early as December 1942, to be held as
hostages "to prevent Tripoli Jews from taking revenge on the
Italians after the British occupation."

Under British Administration. By the end of January 1943, Ger-
men and Italian forces were driven out of all of Libya. A British
Military Administration of Tripolitania came formally in existence on December 15, 1942. Subsequently it was extended
over the entire territory of Libya.

The Allied armies were hailed by the Jews as liberators. Their
enthusiasm was all the greater as the victorious British forces
comprised a considerable number of Palestinian Jewish units.
The first action of the British military authorities was to tear
down the barbed wire fence surrounding the Jewish quarter, to
free 1,400 Jews employed in forced labor, and to rescind the anti-
Jewish laws. They assumed responsibility for the maintenance
of the 3,000 Jews in the concentration camp at Giado and organized their repatriation to Cyrenaica. Owing to an outbreak
of typhus and a necessity for quarantine, the repatriation

proceeded slowly, but by October 1943, the first 1,200 deportees had already been brought home. Many of the released Jews joined the Fighting French Army.[10]

Jewish communal activities were quickly revived. The British Military Government appointed a twelve-member Council of the Jewish Community of Tripoli. All the Jewish communities of the province affiliated themselves with the *Communita Israelitica del Tripolitania*, so that it became the official organ of the whole of Tripolitanian Jewry, and was, as such, recognized by the British military authorities. Similarly, the Council of the Jewish Community of Benghazi was recognized as spokesman for Cyrenaica Jewry. The Tripoli Community Council has established special committees for education, welfare, synagogues and the like.[11]

In the field of education, the Community Councils had the hard task of providing for the needs of some 3,000 children who for three years had not received any education. Jewish military units stationed with the British forces helped to repair the damaged synagogue and organized schools for Jewish children.[12] In Cyrenaica, the Palestinian Jewish soldiers serving with the British Army opened Hebrew schools for liberated Jewish children.

The economic position of the Jewish population began to improve. While the number of contributors taxed directly for the Tripoli Community budget did not exceed 1,267 in the year 1942, it rose to 1,873 in 1944. The amount of taxation, which was 749,328 lire in 1943 (when the lira had quite a different value), was raised to 3,166,950 lire in 1944.[13]

The 1945 Pogrom. After some twenty months of calm and safety, the laborious recovery of the Libyan Jewish community was shaken by bloody anti-Jewish riots in Tripolitania. On November 2 and 3, 1945, anti-Jewish violence broke out in neighboring Egypt. During general strikes called by Arab nationalistic organizations on the twenty-eighth anniversary of the Balfour Declaration, Jewish shops and homes were attacked by the Arab mobs in Cairo, Alexandria, Port Said, and El Mansura. Radio and press reports of this onslaught had reached Tripolitania within two days. They were followed by anti-

Jewish riots in Tripoli which started on November 4 and continued the next day. On November 6 and 7, when violence was checked in the city, leaving behind 35 dead and hundreds of ruined and looted shops and homes, disturbances spread to the suburbs and outlying towns: Zanzur (34 killed), Zawiya (13 killed), Cussabat (3 killed), and Zilten.[14]

There is a striking difference between the outbreaks in Egypt and Libya which so closely followed each other. Whereas in Egypt the rioters were chiefly bent on looting and were predominantly members of the underworld always eager for easy gain, the pogroms in Tripolitania were directed in the main against the lives of Jewish men, women and children and were evidently motivated more by nationalistic and religious fanaticism than by loot. The murderous and viciously cruel character of the Tripolitanian pogroms was stressed by Clifton Daniel, who, on November 7, cabled to The New York Times from Tripoli: "Many of the attacks were premeditated and coldly murderous in intent." Later, the same correspondent added terrifying details:[15] "Babies were beaten to death with iron bars. Old men were hacked to pieces where they fell. Expectant mothers were disemboweled. Whole families were burned alive in their houses. Two brothers lost twenty-seven relatives in one attack. . . . When the riots were raging, the thirst for blood seemed to have supplanted the desire for loot and revenge."

Accordingly, the results of the riots were greatly different in Egypt and Libya: in Egypt, 10 Jews were killed and 350 injured; in Tripolitania, according to a survey by the Tripoli Jewish Community, 130 were murdered and 450 seriously wounded. Several Jewish women and girls were raped before the eyes of their families. Many were compelled to embrace Islam in order to save their lives. At least 2,000 were driven from their homes. Another noticeable difference was that while in Egypt a good many non-Jewish stores and houses were looted and destroyed, in Libya the destruction and murder were directed solely against the Jews. According to British Army figures, only two Italians were hurt so seriously as to require hospital treatment. In Souk-el-Turk, in the Old City of Tripoli, shops on which owners had chalked "Italiano," "Greco" or "Arabic" were spared, while all Jewish shops were smashed open and looted.[16]

Heavy losses have been sustained by Jewish property. Nothing was spared by the attackers. Whatever they did not want or could not carry away, owing to bulk or weight, was damaged, destroyed or set on fire. Massive safes were demolished; pieces of furniture destroyed or burned; glasses and mirrors, even the smallest, were smashed to pieces. The main sufferers were the small merchants, shopmen, and artisans. Nearly all were reduced literally to penury.[17] The Jewish community, as a body, also sustained heavy damage. In the nine synagogues attacked in Tripoli and in the minor communities, the furnishings, household goods and furniture were destroyed by fire or damaged; 35 Torah scrolls and 2,084 holy books were desecrated, and 89,086 kilograms of silver (sacred ornaments) were plundered. As of December 31, 1945, 1,435 restitution claims had been filed by Jews for damages, totaling 268,231,752 M.A.L. (Military Authority Lire), or 558,816 English pounds (the official rate of exchange being £1 = M.A.L. 480). The value of Jewish property damaged or lost in Tripoli amounted to M.A.L. 239,168,-088.[18]

Jewish spokesmen insisted that full reparation must be paid by British occupying authorities who were responsible for maintaining order in Libya and whose passivity and inefficiency were largely to blame for the loss of life and property. Four hundred and fifty Jewish property owners retained a London lawyer to press legal claims for restitution. But the British military authorities, while having spent, up to May 1946, about $64,000 to provide food, clothing, household equipment, and temporary shelter for the victims of the pogrom, categorically disclaimed responsibility for the loss of property.[19] They allotted the sum of $46,000 as small interest-free loans for the rehabilitation of riot victims. But the terms of the loans—supplying of a guarantor and undertaking to repay within four years—were beyond the means of most would-be beneficiaries. In fact, only twelve loans were granted (while 240 applications were submitted by the Jewish Community Council); after considerable haggling and delay the administration declared that the matter must be considered closed.[20]

Punitive action on the part of the British authorities was both inadequate and inefficient.

A total of 550 Arabs were arrested during the riots (other arrests followed in consequence of the police searches or of denunciation by Jews).[21] According to a survey by the Jewish community of Tripoli, until the end of 1945, only 295 persons were put on trial and only 208 found guilty. The majority of those found guilty received prison sentences up to eight years; one Arab was sentenced to fifteen years, and one to ten years.[22] Thirty cases which had been still pending on November 26 were expected to end in capital sentences.[23] But as late as May 1946, Jewish circles in Tripoli pointed out that by that time only two Arabs were executed for murder. In the beginning, local Arab leaders were rather dumfounded by the beastly killings and mass looting and were afraid that this savage outbreak of fanaticism and lawlessness might endanger their hopes for independence. The British-controlled Arabic newspaper in Tripoli, *Tarabulus el-Gharb* said in a leading article (November 9) that rioters and plunderers have done immense harm to the cause of the Libyan people "by the attacks on a minority which had lived with us for centuries in perfect peace." The paper warned that Libya was "on the threshold of a new destiny, and any action would bear on the future of its people." The Mufti of Tripoli, Mohammed Bulasad El Alem, denounced the riots as "a most disgraceful and lamentable episode." He stressed that the Jewish and Arab communities "have such mutual interests that one cannot live without the other."

Very soon, however, the Arab chieftains realized that their fears were exaggerated. No "irreparable damage" was done to their aspirations for independence by the killing of 130 Jews and the looting of Jewish property, and they have by no means lost the British support for their demand for Libya's self-government. This has completely changed their original attitude. They began to blame the Jews for the worsening Arab-Jewish relations. One week after the riots had been checked, Mustafa Bey Misran, member of the Arab Advisory Council to the British

Military Administration, said in an interview that during the past year or two the Arabs "have become annoyed by the increase in Zionist activity"; the Jews formed Zionist clubs, he said, and Jewish Boy Scouts went through streets singing Zionist hymns; Zionist flags appeared and signs applauding Zionism and its leaders were on Tripoli's walls. The Tripolitanian Jews, insisted Mustafa Misran Bey, must renounce "militant Zionism" if they expect race relations to return to the basis on which they were conducted for thirteen centuries before the riots.[24]

In keeping with this attitude, Tripolitanian Arab leaders two weeks later were reported to have refused to guarantee that order would be maintained unless the following demands were met: removal of the Palestinian company attached to the British troops; disbandment of the Jewish Boy Scouts Association; cessation of all Zionist activities; dismissal of the Jewish members of the city's mixed police.[25]

Uncertainty and Fears. Libya's status has remained uncertain for almost five years. The largest Arab party of Tripolitania— the United National Front—advocated the independence of unified Libya (including Cyrenaica, Tripolitania, and Fezzan). The Jews, officially represented on the executive of the party, made this demand their own. In the spring of 1946, when discussions as to the future of the country were taking place, a combined Arab-Jewish delegation called upon the head of the British Military Administration. Zachino Habib, the leader of the Jewish delegates, declared that 30,000 Jews fully supported the cause of Libyan independence and all the members of the delegation recited in chorus the following words: "In spite of the sad events, we are still holding fast together through our firm brotherhood and confidence in one another." A few days later, Zionist youth groups announced their affiliation with the United National Front.[26]

Dr. Raffaele Cantoni, President of the Union of Italian Jewish Communities, on the basis of information from confidential sources, claimed that both statements were made "under the severest moral pressure, under threats, allurements and blackmail, and under the increasing fear of a repetition on an

even larger scale of the 1945 pogrom." The Tripoli Jews knew
what they, as a minority, could expect from an Arab regime, but
they also knew that any disagreement on their part with the
Arab nationalist claims would provoke Arab ire and violence.
F. E. Stafford, British member of the Commission dispatched
by the Big Four to investigate the wishes of the people in the
former Italian colonies, described the atmosphere in Tripolitania as follows: "Only an insignificant minority suggested their
[Italian] return. Undoubtedly the violence of public opinion
acted as a deterrent to open admission of pro-Italian feelings.
. . . The Jews, possibly with some private misgiving, officially
aligned themselves with popular demand."[27]

The protracted uncertain status of the area, and the continued
international deadlock on the Libyan question constituted a
permanent source of uneasiness and friction. The increasingly
acute feeling of insecurity, often bordering on panic, has since
1945 been a constant reality among the Libyan Jewish community. "Libya's Jews are today living in an atmosphere of
terror," reported an authoritative Italian-Jewish source in April
1948: "Any rumor, any threat uttered by even a small Arab boy,
sends the Jews in panic-stricken terror to the ghetto which they
had abandoned during the Italian administration, but where
they feel safer now, because the old Jewish quarter is easier to
defend from the Arab attack."[28]

The 1948 Pogrom. These fears proved to be too well founded.
On June 12, 1948, anti-Jewish riots again broke out in Tripoli's
Old City and continued unabated on June 13.[29] Largely at the
incitement of 400 Tunisian Arab volunteers en route for the
Palestine war front, an Arab mob tried to penetrate the Hara,
but the Jews, knowing from the bitter experience of the 1945
riots that they could not rely on the protection of the British
authorities, organized a defense of their own and repelled the
Arab attacks. The Arabs then concentrated on the new city,
where Jewish houses and shops were scattered, isolated, and
without protection. A number of houses were set afire. "The
most abominable cruelties have been perpetuated," reported
a correspondent of the Alliance Israélite Universelle. "Old persons and children have been literally cut to pieces; their corpses

were but a pulp of flesh and bones."[30] Authorities ordered a curfew at 7 P.M. Troops and police patrolled all main streets. According to an Associated Press cable, 4 Arab rioters were killed by the police and 29 injured. The number of Jewish fatal casualties amounted to 12; 21 Jews were injured. Two hundred eighty-seven Jewish houses were destroyed, and more than 300 Jewish family heads have lost their means of livelihood.[31]

As in 1945, the British administration quickly disclaimed any responsibility, financial or otherwise, for losses incurred by the Jews. It was left to the impoverished Jewish Community to carry out relief work. No public inquiry was held by the Administration concerning the causes of the disorders.

The June 1948, outrages broke out anew and intensified the fears of Tripolitanian Jewry. J. B. Segal, who, early in 1949, visited Tripolitania on behalf of the Anglo-Jewish Association, the Central British Fund, and the Board of Deputies of British Jews, described the "feeling of insecurity" as the most striking feature of the plight of Tripolitanian Jewry: "The Jews of Tripoli and the interior are in the grip of a veritable fear psychosis. The two violent and bloody attacks have left them full of dread, awaiting almost hourly an onslaught that may never come. The young teacher is afraid to venture by night outside the Jewish quarter. The Jewish pedlars are frightened to visit the Arab encampments since one of their number was killed by Arabs over a year ago. Even the children are nervous and scared. It is not surprising that in the interior some Jews and Jewesses have found security in Islam."[32]

Coupled with the fear of further violence was the feeling of utter hopelessness of the Jewish economic situation. General depression, severe droughts in the years 1947 and 1948, and the loss of trade due to the change of Libya's position, coming as they did on top of two pogroms, reduced the Jewish population to a pitiable state. Even more ominous was the inevitability of the further "inexorable decline" of the Jewish community, as Jon Kimche put it in his penetrating survey of Tripolitania:[33]

The Arabs here and elsewhere want to conduct their own commerce, their own banking, their own export and import; they want to bring business to the Arab artisan and the Arab shopkeeper. Who can say that the Arab should not "Buy Arab" any more than the British should not "Buy British" or "Fly British"? But inevitably the "Arabization" in these mixed communities inexorably takes place at the expense of the Jew.

Inevitably therefore the economic position of the Jews is deteriorating as the drive for economic and political independence of the Arabs grows in emphasis. Competition and the battle for survival becomes sharper and tension inevitably follows. . . . The Jews find that their future has become economically precarious and offers little by way of settled prospects—particularly for the younger generation.

Thousands of this oldest among the Jewish communities now find—after all these settled centuries—that in fact they must either perish economically or emigrate—somewhere.

"Clamor for Transportation." The first pogrom of November 1945 had already generated a powerful, irrepressible longing for emigration. Hundreds of Jews were reported fleeing Tripoli daily, hoping to make their way across the Tunisian border and relying on the promises of Arabs to smuggle them over the frontier. Many refugees vanished before ever reaching Tunisia. In a single village, Kamutov, near the Tunisian border, fourteen corpses were found early in December 1945, including three women and five children. They were identified as Jews from Tripoli who had been promised by Arab smugglers that they would be led across the frontier, and then had been "disposed of." On the other hand, Tripoli Arabs, taking advantage of Jewish panic, were buying up Jewish possessions cheaply.[34] George Santillano reported from Tripoli that Jews in evacuee camps, who lost their homes and possessions during the outbreaks, "clamor for transportation to Palestine, Europe or anywhere so long as it is out of this country."[35]

This popular "clamor for transportation" did not subside in the months and years to come. In May 1946, Zachino Habib head of the Tripoli Jewish community, stated that "because of economic distress and a feeling of insecurity, the Jewish community had asked that a large number of its members be admitted to Palestine or the United States. . . . Tripolitanian Jews would prefer Palestine because they are a Mediterranean people."[36] The June 1948 outbreak considerably intensified the emigration trend. "The slogan of every Jew without exception is now 'to go away,' irrespective of destination," reported an Alliance Israélite Universelle correspondent. "This is the only goal of every Jew here. They expect in advance to suffer hunger, to abandon their property and their friends, their native country —in order not to become a victim, not to be suddenly slaughtered or burned alive."[37]

In August 1948, a group of some thirty-five Jewish refugees who fled from Tripoli in fear of Arab terror arrived in Rome; they had been granted visas by the Italian Consul in Tripoli. "Individual refugees continue to arrive—some with visas and some without," a Rome dispatch went on.[38] In December 1948, the Jewish Agency's *Digest of Press and Events* (December 31, 1948) reported that about one hundred Libyan Jews had arrived at Syracuse, Sicily; they declared that they had fled from Tripoli to escape persecution by Arabs and the local administration. In January 1949, a *J.T.A.* message from Rome stated that "the number of Jews arriving in Italy from Tripolitania is increasing almost daily." The International Refugee Organization refused to extend its aid to these refugees, considering them to be "Italian citizens who entered Italy legally from former Italian colonies"; hence, their maintenance was secured by the American Joint Distribution Committee.[39] Italy was, however, but a stopover on the way to Israel. About 2,500 Jews left Libya clandestinely via Tunisia and Italy from July 1948 to January 1949.[40] In the months January to May 1949, about 1,500 arrived in Israel via Italy. For the entire year 1949, the number of such immigrants amounted to 2,107.[41]

Direct Crossing to Haifa. For a considerable period of time, direct emigration to Israel was practically banned by the British authorities. But in March 1949 it was announced that while in the past emigration to Palestine was possible only by way of Italian ports, it would henceforth be permitted by direct crossing to Haifa.[42] On April 5, the S.S. *Caserta* picked up at Tripoli the first 400 Tripolitanian Jews sailing for Israel.[43]

The Immigration Department of the Jewish Agency has established an office in Tripoli. In cooperation with an Immi-

gration Commission composed of representatives of all public
Jewish bodies, a register was drawn up of all candidates for immigration. Medical services were organized in collaboration
with the Joint Distribution Committee and the O.S.E. (Jewish Health Society) which looked to health conditions and
the treatment of sick would-be immigrants. The office had become, in fact, the recognized representative of Israel in Libya.
It was on its responsibility that all travel documents were issued
to prospective immigrants.[44]

The opening of the gates for unrestricted immigration to Israel has precipitated an almost elemental, enthusiastic urge for
immediate aliyah.

A correspondent of the New York *Jewish Journal* (March 8,
1949) described the situation after the British authorities finally
permitted emigration as follows:

> Seven thousand of the 26,000 Jews living in Tripoli have obtained
> permission from the British military authorities to leave the country
> in order to go to Israel.
>
> A short time ago the Jews were notified that they would have to
> wait until the arrival of an Israeli representative, who would issue
> entry visas for the state of Israel. But the local Jews find waiting too
> much for them and have begun to leave the country without Israeli
> visas. For weeks now, one has witnessed in the narrow streets of
> the Jewish quarter scenes of Jews selling their few belongings, both
> their household goods and the merchandise of their shops. One
> also sees whole families, which often comprise three and four genera-
> tions, making their way to the harbor of Tripoli.
>
> The urge to emigrate to Israel is not limited to the poor. Even
> the well-to-do are straining to leave. A number of Jews have resigned
> their government posts and are preparing to go to Israel.

A. Kirschenbaum, head of the Jewish Agency Immigration
Department in Italy, who witnessed the departure of the first
transport sailing directly to Israel on the S.S. *Caserta*, reported
that a spontaneous holiday was observed at this occasion in the
Jewish quarter of the Old City of Tripoli: shops were closed,
synagogues were crowded, and there was singing, shouting, and
great rejoicing among the Tripolitanian Jews. When Dr.
Maurice L. Perlzweig of the World Jewish Congress visited

Tripolitania in September 1949, he heard everywhere "the steady rhythmic cry of a single word, '*Ali*[*y*]*ah*,' '*Aliah*,' '*Aliah*.' The word '*Aliyah*' was written up on every wall in Hebrew and Latin characters. It represents the main activity of Jewish communities, it embodies a whole philosophy and represents what now amounts to a religion."[45]

Emptying Cyrenaica. The Jews of Cyrenaica, the first province of Libya to become independent in internal affairs under the Emir Sayid Idriss el-Senussi, were the most anxious to emigrate to Israel and began streaming to Tripoli in the hope of obtaining passage on Israel-bound vessels. In the summer of 1949, about 1,300 of Benghazi's 3,000 Jews arrived in Tripoli and the influx continued at the rate of 100 to 150 a week. By March 8, 1950, 3,726 Cyrenaica Jews had already left for Israel.[46] By August 1950, of the 6,000 Cyrenaica Jews only some 300 remained.[47] The rest had in the meantime either reached Israel or still awaited their turn in Tripoli.

The highly unsafe position of the over 7,000 Jews in fourteen smaller Jewish communities in the interior of Tripolitania made imperative their almost wholesale evacuation to Tripoli.

The 1,300-year-old Jewish community of Garian-Tigrina, the oldest in Tripolitania, (numbering 464 in January 1949) ceased to exist when the last group of Jews arrived in Tripoli in August of the same year on their way to Israel. The two synagogues, one of which is 830 years old, have been closed down, and the last of the Torah scrolls held by the community have been brought to Tripoli. The Jewish Community of Jeffren (some 650 years old; 391 Jews in 1949), has also ceased to exist. The two synagogues have been closed, and the four remaining Torah scrolls have been brought to Tripoli. Not a single Jew remained in Zlitten (604 Jews in January 1949).[48] Of the evacuated provincial Tripolitanian Jews, 3,714 had left for Israel by March 8, 1950, together with 9,372 from the city of Tripoli.[49] This mass departure has brought about the liquidation of many Jewish religious institutions. By August 1950, twelve Tripolitanian synagogues, most of them in the interior, had been closed and handed over to the Libyan authorities who use them as schools.[50]

The bulk of the emigrants left during the year 1949, when 15,130 Libyan Jews arrived in Israel. During the first two months of 1950, 3,809 arrived. Beginning with March 1950, the emigration trend somehow subsided. Slightly improved relations between Arabs and Jews, coupled with better economic conditions brought about by a bumper harvest, induced some Jewish groups to delay their departure. While the desire to emigrate was still strong among the poorer elements of the community, merchants, shopkeepers and other well-to-do community members were inclined to wait till conditions in Israel improved. Simultaneously, the Jewish Agency, faced with great financial difficulties and with the necessity of maintaining at any cost the high rate of immigration of endangered Jewish communities in Rumania and Iraq, had considerably curtailed the immigration quotas from Libya. During the seven-month period March–September 1950, arrivals from Libya were sharply declining. The monthly average was 543 (as against 1,904 in the previous two months); in September, only 9 arrived in Israel.[51]

Now or Never. Lawrence Resner relates that, by that time, of about 18,000 Jews still remaining in Libya, a few thousand with independent means planned to stay, or, if they would leave, go to Europe or some other country. But "about fifteen thousand wanted desperately to get out." Their plight was both pathetic and hopeless. At a hastily summoned meeting in Paris, Reuben Hassan, the Libyan director of the Joint Distribution Committee, observed soberly, "We have four thousand people who are considered healthy and can go to Israel today. However, if they have to remain in Tripoli for many months, I am convinced that when the day for their departure arrives they will not be able to pass a physical examination because of undernourishment." He also warned of other, more critical factors. With the large-scale departure of Jews from Tripoli, the British Military Administration started to move homeless Arab families into the Jewish Hara. What had been an exclusively Jewish walled section was now vulnerable to any sudden Arab uprising. In the fall of 1950, the British permitted a number of Palestinian Arabs to enter Libya. These were Arabs who felt that the

Jews in Israel had driven them from their ancestral homes, and one did not have to be an alarmist to sense the dangerous possibilities in this situation.[52] Meeting this emergency, the Jewish Agency resumed the evacuation program, though on a reduced scale. During the last three months of 1950, 1,220 Jews arrived from Libya, bringing the total for the year to 8,818.

Emigration was considerably handicapped by difficulties of transferring property. G. L. Glutton, British representative to the United Nations Political Committee, declared on October 10, 1949, that each emigrant family was permitted to take out £250 (sterling) in belongings and to transfer up to £250 (sterling) of liquid assets through normal channels of transfer. The rest had to be placed in blocked accounts. The emigrants were not permitted to take along any currency.[53] The wealthier elements of Libya's Jewry, eager to migrate to Israel, were naturally strongly affected by these regulations.

The Immigration Office of the Jewish Agency in Tripoli has set up a special department for the registration of Jewish capital in Libya, and a trust company, which, in order to avert a haphazard disposal of nonmovable property, was issuing advances, thus enabling property owners to avoid selling it at rock-bottom prices.[54]

Those Who Left and Those Who Stayed On. Emigration continued in 1951, which saw the departure of 6,534. In 1952 it slowed down to 1,146, and only 641 arrived in Israel in the years 1953–1958. Together with the 873 pre-May 15, 1948, immigrants, the grand total amounts to 35,142.[55]

Not more than 4,300 Jews remained in Libya:* about 4,000 in the city of Tripoli and some 300 in Benghazi. The Libyan constitution guarantees full equality to all of the country's citizens, regardless of creed or race. The following material, received in 1954 from a visitor to a neighboring country, shows the extent to which these constitutional safeguards have been circumvented since Libya, in March 1953, joined the Arab League:[56]

---

* Professor Louis Dupree mistakenly puts the prewar number of Jews in Libya as 33,000 and the number of those "ferried" to Israel at 26,000 (instead of 35,000), coming to the wrong conclusion that 7,000 Jews remained in the country. (Louis Dupree. "The Non-Arab Ethnic Groups of Libya" in *The Middle East Journal*, Winter 1958.)

Libyan Jews cannot vote or be elected to public office. No Jews
are employed by the government. There is only one Jew occupying
any public post at all—an interpreter at a court. Jews are not admitted
to the army or police forces. The last four Jewish police officers were
dismissed recently simply because they were Jews.

Jews going abroad receive a laissez-passer valid for only six months,
instead of the usual five-year passport. Failure to return to Libya
before expiration of this period may entail the loss of citizenship
and the right of residence in Libya. A Moslem Libyan is readmitted
even if he has no valid passport at all. It is worth mentioning that the
color of the laissez-passer is yellow-orange, a color painfully reminiscent of the medieval 'Jewish badge.'

Libyan Jews who leave the country are not permitted to take their
belongings.

Correspondence with Israel is strictly forbidden, although almost
all Libyan Jews have relatives there.

Moslems who used to be friendly to Jews, now avoid all contact
with them and make no attempt to hide their contempt. The Jewish
population feels that its position is most precarious, that none of its
legitimate rights can now be considered secure.

The authorities tolerated the existence of organized Jewish
communities in Tripoli and Benghazi, but deprived them of
the right of taxation which they had enjoyed before 1948. The
Tripoli community had no rabbi, but maintained a day school,
a Talmud Torah and synagogues.

By a decree effective as of December 31, 1958, the provincial
government of Tripolitania dissolved the Jewish Community
Council, appointing a special commissioner to administer the
community and replace the Council. The commissioner was
instructed "to take over all papers, books, correspondence, files
and other things concerned with its affairs."[57] There is no evidence that property or status of individual Jews have been affected by the decree. A reliable non-Jewish observer who visited
Tripoli in April 1959 reported that the economic positions of
the Jews was described to him "as prosperous by some sources,
as excellent by others." Anti-Jewish attitude "rarely finds its
outlet in open acts of harsh treatment, but rather, as told by all
sources, in covert and subtle forms of obstructionism in all
spheres of public life. . . . Thus, for example, in public bid-

ding for supplies for the Government or for public works, a Jewish bid is rarely taken into consideration, although it might be the lowest and most advantageous one." As to the appraisal of the general Jewish situation, the observer established that Jewish leadership was split into two groups. One of them had close business and personal ties with influential Arab circles and believed that those connections would protect them should the Jewish situation deteriorate. The other group, much larger in number and apparently less successful, both economically and socially, had no hesitation in stating that they "lived a 'day-to-day' existence, in constant anxiety about the future."[58]

5

Syria: Disappearing Jewish Community

The Background. The principal cities of Syria had Jewish populations even in biblical times. At the time of the destruction of the Second Temple, the Jewish community of Damascus numbered about ten thousand. For some time into the Middle Ages, Damascus and Aleppo had more Jews than all of Palestine. They were the home of many Jewish scholars and poets and served as places of refuge during evil days.

The position of Jewish and Christian minorities after the Arab conquest of Syria is on the whole accurately described by a competent Arab author as follows: "Christians and Jews . . . were regarded as in a sense standing outside the community; they were not allowed to carry weapons, to bear witness against Moslems in courts of law, or to marry Moslem women; and they were subject to special measures of taxation. But they were permitted to retain their beliefs and their property, to worship as they pleased, and to manage the internal affairs of their communities according to their own laws and customs. . . . Moslems would no more have thought of compelling Christians and Jews to conform to Moslem law in matters of personal life and relationship, than they would of abandoning their rigid religious code. Law was personal." The ruling Moslem-Arab majority and the subjugated but tolerated Jewish and Christian minorities coexisted, the latter being allowed "a certain status on the side of the Islamic community."[1] Each group formed a community of its own, or, as it was called in Arabic, a "millah," and in Turkish a "millet," within the state and coterminous with it. Under Ottoman domination the Jews of Syria lived un-molested for several centuries.

The middle of the nineteenth century brought a significant change. At that time, the Turkish central government's in-fluence became considerably weaker. The influence of Christian missionaries and of foreign consuls, who encouraged Arab na-tionalism while taking the local Christians under their protec-tion, left the Jews as the only unprotected ethnic and religious minority. The notorious "Damascus Affair" of 1840, when a ritual-murder libel was leveled against the Jewish community, brought in its wake anti-Jewish riots.

Under the French Mandate. In 1920, at San Remo, the Allied Powers assigned the mandate over Syria (including Lebanon) to France; on July 24, 1922, this decision was officially sanc-tioned by the League of Nations.[2] Under the French adminis-tration Syria and Lebanon had separate budgets and also a "common interests" budget covering customs, posts, tele-graphs, etc.[3]

In Syria the French have met constant difficulties of ad-ministration, economic troubles, armed uprisings. The coun-try's population, though predominantly Moslem, is a con-glomeration of at least twenty ethnic and religious groups, with the Arabic language as the strongest unifying link. The Mos-lems are split into Sunnites, Shi'ites, Allowais, Druses and Ish-maelites; and the Christians go even further in sectarianism: Maronites, Greek Orthodox, Greek Catholics, Jacobites, and Protestants are but a fraction of the long list. Sunni Moslem Arabs constitute, however, an overwhelming majority. Of the 1955 estimated population of 3,806,973 about 2,400,000 be-longed to this dominant ethno-religious entity.[4] An increas-ingly intransigent Arab nationalist movement firmly opposed French control and demanded full independence of the coun-try. The French mandatory administration alternately made concessions to the nationalists and tried to rule by "strong hand" methods. Throughout all these vicissitudes, the French mandatory administration has consistently protected full per-sonal and communal rights of Syrian Jewry. But growing anti-

French and antiforeign feeling had found an easy outlet in hatred of the weak and isolated Jewish minority.

Arab outbreaks against the French Mandate authorities have always affected the Jewish population. During the anti-French riots of 1936, Damascus Jews suffered attacks in streets and cafés. The anti-Jewish sentiment was not appeased by the patriotic gesture of the Jewish community of Aleppo which cabled the French Government in support of the position of the Arab delegation then in Paris,[5] and by the fact that, according to an American historian of the "nationalist crusade in Syria," "the majority of Syrian Jews opposed the French Mandate and supported the nationalist demands.[6] Syrian Jews were accused of being Zionist and unpatriotic.

During the three years of the Arab riots in Palestine (1936–1939), Damascus was the headquarters of the anti-Jewish and anti-British propaganda and activities. The outlawed Palestine Arab Higher Committee was recruiting volunteers and buying arms in Damascus to be smuggled into the Holy Land. Anti-Jewish propaganda was intensified since December 1937 by the visit in Damascus of Baldur von Schirach, head of the Nazi youth organization of Germany. Accompanied by fifteen Nazi agents, von Schirach conferred with leading Nazi representatives in the Near and Middle East. It was decided to increase propaganda in existing German schools in this area, to create others, and to establish closer contact with Arab youth groups. The armed extremist Arab National Youth Organization announced a boycott of Arab merchants who were buying "Zionist goods from Palestine." The boycott campaign gained momentum in April 1938, in connection with the inquiry by the British Palestine Partition Commission (Woodhead Commission). Anti-Jewish demonstrations and a protest strike in Damascus induced the Syrian Parliament, on May, 1, unanimously to adopt a resolution against the proposed partition of Palestine and to send a protest to local representatives of foreign powers. On October 10, 1938, the "Arab Defense Committee" in Damascus addressed a warning to Dr. Chaim Weizmann, President of the Jewish Agency for Palestine: "Your attitude will lead you and

Jews of the East to the worst of calamities that has been written in history up to the present."

The emergence of the Vichy regime in France (June 1940) considerably affected the position of Syrian Jewry. Highly placed Jewish government and state officials were dismissed from their posts, and economic restrictions were imposed. However, even during the Vichy period, the French authorities defended the Jews and did not permit the Arab extremists to attack them. In July 1941, British and Free (Fighting) French forces occupied the country, Jewish equality was restored. Yet German propaganda continued to incite the Arab population against the Jews. On February 18, 1942, Axis radio stations spread the lie that Roosevelt and Churchill intended to incorporate Syria into a postwar Jewish state as reward to the Jews for their support of the Allies. Even the French, engaged in bitter competition with the British for Arab sympathies, in the spring of 1945, began taking an anti-Jewish line. United States intelligence sources reported that the Press and Propaganda Section of the French Delegation in Aleppo had launched a propaganda campaign representing France as the champion of the Arab world in the struggle against "Zionist imperialism backed by Britain and the United States."[7]

The Economy. Paralleling the growth of anti-Jewish feelings went the disintegration of the economic position of Syrian Jewry.

In "normal" times, many Syrian Jews earned their livelihood by peddling in Arab villages. Some became importers, bankers, and state officials appointed by the French mandatory administration. During the last prewar decades, individual Jews who received their higher education in France, after having been trained in the schools of the Alliance Israélite Universelle, took their place in the professions. Many were artisans, skilled and unskilled; in the decade of 1925–1935, the copper industry attracted Jewish artisans. Incomplete data on the occupational distribution of Jews in Damascus in the interwar period shows that about 40 per cent of the Jews were peddlers; 20 per cent workers (of whom substantial numbers were engravers on metal and marble); 15 per cent merchants; 10 per cent artisans and

craftsmen; and 15 per cent were living on charity.[8] Indigenous
competition was increasingly felt. The Christian population,
taking advantage of modern education received in missionary
schools, began a successful drive to push the Jews out of their
economic positions in commerce and trade. Later on, Moslem
Arabs who had learned Western methods started to enter into
competition. The Jews were losing one economic position after
another.

In 1946, it was estimated that not more than 5 per cent of the
Damascus Jews were wealthy; 15 per cent belonged to the
middle class; the remainder were peddlers or small merchants.
Practically all the Jews who lived above subsistence level belonged to the merchant class. There were only six Jewish physicians, no lawyers, no industrialists, no engineers or architects.[9]
According to a report published in March 1946, in the newspaper *Hechayal*, half of the Jewish population in Damascus was living in such poverty that they would have starved but for the
financial help sent by Damascus Jewish immigrants in the
United States, Mexico and the Argentine, amounting to 2,000
Syrian pounds yearly, along with personal gifts from relatives
abroad.[10]

Thousands of Syrian Jews have found their way to other
countries. In the early stages, they emigrated to America (by
1943 about 10,000 Syrian Jews were living in the United States),
Brazil, Shanghai, Bombay, and Cairo. Later, Palestine became
the principal goal. It is estimated that between the two World
Wars some 27,000 Jews had left for Latin America, Palestine
and Lebanon. This migration drastically reduced the number
of Jews in Syria. In the first decade of the twentieth century
there were aproximately 50,000 Jews in this area.[11] The latest
census—that of 1943—gave the number of Jews in Syria as
29,770, with about 17,000 in Aleppo and 11,000 in Damascus.[12]
Early in 1947, not more than 13,000 Jews remained,* and the
Syrian Government was reported to have launched "an investigation into the disappearance of some 17,000 Syrian Jews since

* According to official Israeli data, 4,811 Syrian and Lebanese Jews arrived in
Israel in the years 1942–1946, and 585 in 1947–May 15, 1948. (Israel, Central
Bureau of Statistics, *Registration of Population*. Part B. Special Series W53.
Jerusalem 1956, pp. 20–23)

the last government census."[13] In February 1949, the Middle
East correspondent of the London *Jewish Chronicle* reported
that 80 per cent of the Damascus Jewish community had left
the Syrian capital during the past four years.[14]

The communal organization of Syrian Jewry was never truly
democratic. The boards, or committees, of the single communities were mostly "appointed" by cliques of wealthy Jews from
among the rich families. The Government recognized these
committees as spokesmen of the Jewish population and as
administrators of the local Jewish institutions for mutual aid,
charity, medical assistance, etc. The communal budgets were
covered by direct taxes paid by the wealthier families and indirect taxes paid by all community members; a considerable
portion of the budget was provided by contributions from
Syrian Jewish emigrants in North and South America.[15]

Since the convocation of the first Syrian Parliament in December 1936, there has been one Jewish representative in the
Chamber of Deputies (Syria dispenses with a Senate).[16] Yet
the electoral law of 1949 did not provide for Jewish representation in the Syrian Constituent Assembly.

Education. Jewish education in Syria (and Lebanon) has largely
been provided by the network of the Alliance Israélite Universelle, which in 1947 comprised ten schools with 2,485 pupils.
The language of instruction was French—as in all Alliance
schools in the Oriental countries—but Arabic was not neglected,
and many Alliance students won distinction in the Arabic language and its literature. In spite of the deficiency of purely
Jewish subjects in their curricula, these schools were of para-
mount importance in the development of local Jewish life; a
great number of their former students occupied leading positions in communal affairs.[17]

Following Syria's liberation from the last remnants of the
French mandatory regime, the Syrian Ministry of Public Instruction on October 15, 1945, summarily closed all Catholic
schools with French as language of instruction.[18] This measure,
anti-French in its motives, also affected the Alliance schools,
which remained closed till February 18, 1947, when they were
permitted to reopen under the name "Ecoles Nationales de

l'Alliance Israélite Universelle," with a contingent of some 275 boys and girls. Their curricula had, however, to undergo far-reaching changes. Ten hours weekly had to be allocated to the study of Arabic, with particular stress on the study of Arab history and subjects fostering the development of Arab national sentiment; native school directors were to be appointed.[19]

The Jewish communal and religious schools have not been affected by the new ordinances of the Ministry of Public Instruction, but they, too, had to undergo changes in their educational program. The Talmud Torahs came under the close supervision of the Ministry; without interfering with their religious character, the Ministry insisted that its educational program be complied with, i.e., that Arabic be taught and that history, geography and the natural sciences be taught in Arabic. The Jewish religious schools were also permitted to teach English as a foreign language instead of French. The use of Palestinian textbooks was strictly forbidden, though for their Hebrew studies Jewish schools had no other. The teaching of the Hebrew language remained restricted, and teachers suspected of "Zionist sympathies" were summarily dismissed.[20]

After World War II. Antagonism toward and persecution of the Jewish minority rose sharply after World War II, with the Arab-Jewish conflict over Palestine being used as a welcome irritant.

Demonstrations by Damascus Arab students against Jewish immigration to Palestine (March 20, 1945), were followed in May by anti-Jewish riots; the police had to prevent the rioters from breaking into the Jewish quarter of Damascus. In June, Jacques Franco, Assistant Headmaster of the Alliance school in Damascus, was murdered in broad daylight. In October, a meeting of Islamic religious leaders in Damascus, presided over by the Mufti of that city, warned the Allied governments that a Holy War against the Jews would be declared in all countries of Islam if Jewish immigration into Palestine were to continue. In the same month, Sheikh Mustafa Al-Siba'i, leader of the Young Moslems' Association, ascended the pulpit of the Umayyad mosque in Damascus after the Friday prayers and delivered a sharp anti-Jewish speech: "If the Palestine problem is not solved in favor of the Arabs," he declared, "the Arabs will know how to deal with the Jews living in their countries." On November 18, 1945, on the Moslem holiday of Qurban Bayram, a Syrian mob, headed by students, broke into the Great Synagogue of Aleppo, smashed the memorial candles burning before the Holy Shrine, beat up two old Jews reading in the synagogue, and burned prayerbooks in the street.[21]

At the same time, Jews were practically made prisoners within the frontiers of Syria. Syrian Jews requesting permission to travel abroad were invariably denied passports. Only an insignificant number of well-to-do Jews, with influential friends in government departments, were able to obtain permission to leave, after depositing cash guarantees of 200 to 300 Syrian pounds. Those in possession of a passport and a British visa to enter Palestine were denied an exit permit. In many cases, Syrian Jews who wished to travel to neighboring Lebanon were deprived of their passports because of the suspicion they might continue to Palestine. Prevented from emigrating legally, Syrian Jews took recourse to clandestine emigration. In June 1945, Damascus Sûreté (Security) sources quoted "a leader of the Jewish community in Damascus" as saying that about 1,200 Jews, mostly of the younger generation, had lately left the Syrian capital for Palestine. The same sources reported that "a regular transport service exists for Jews leaving Damascus," and that Rahmo Nahmad, former Jewish deputy from Aleppo, had been playing a leading part in the illegal emigration of Aleppo Jews to Palestine, arranging their travel facilities and illicit entries into the country, mostly via Mardjayun, Metulla and Bint Jubayl.

The Syrian Government took drastic steps to curb this migration. Syrian frontier guards were instructed to open fire on any Jew attempting to cross the border illegally. Those caught trying to cross the Syrian border into Palestine were liable to a heavy fine and imprisonment. Many were arrested on the charge of helping "illegal emigrants" to enter Palestine.[22] Some Arab policemen, detectives and informers took advantage of this governmental practice and began blackmailing rich Jews, threatening to denounce them to the police as being involved in illegal emigration. Relatives of Jews who had gone to Palestine years ago were often severely interrogated by the Syrian police and pressed to reveal the present whereabouts of their kin.[23] Syria also eagerly joined the boycott of Jewish industry and commerce proclaimed by the Arab League in December 1945.

Early in 1946, the situation became so strained that leaders of the Damascus Jewish community decided to take urgent steps to protect their civil rights. A meeting called on February 25 by the Religious Court Council was attended by a large number of community notables and youths. According to a report in the Beirut Jewish paper *El Alam El Israeli* (The Jewish World) of March 8, the meeting decided to send a delegation to the President of the Syrian Republic and to submit a memorandum concerning "the discrimination against the community in all matters concerning Jews without heed to their citizenship." The next day, the delegation was received by President Shukry Bey Quwatly, to whom they presented a memorandum stressing that they had been Syrians for thousands of years, had loyally worked for the country, and were taking an active part in the national movement: "We have sacrificed much for the independence which Syrians are enjoying today. We did so out of national feelings, the same as other loyal citizens. We like to hope that we shall live in freedom and independence like all other citizens, especially in the present epoch of democracy whose slogan is fraternity, freedom and equality." It pained them to state, the memorandum continued, that "we are treated as though we were strangers in the country, and are deprived of rights granted to others." Previous appeals to the authorities for justice and equality were of no avail: "We received replies full of sympathy and hope, but nothing was done to improve conditions." The memorandum asked for the President's protection and urged him to do away with the idea that they were strangers in Syria, "so that nationality and not religion shall determine our status." Verbally, the delegation informed the President of the arbitrary attitude toward Jewish tradesmen by the Visas and Security Departments and other government agencies. Complaint was also lodged against the harsh sentences imposed on three Jews for having smuggled their wives or children into Palestine. One of the delegates said: "The Jews of America and Britain do not emigrate to other countries because they are living in safety and security in their homelands, and their governments do not oppress their Jews." The President, concluded the *El Alam El Israel* report, promised to instruct the various government departments not to "degrade and insult the Jews and to treat them as other inhabitants. The parting was cordial."

The presidential assurance has, however, eased very little the plight of the Syrian Jewish community. The Paris radio reported in July 1946 that several Jews had been arrested in Damascus following a police raid on the Jewish quarter and would be tried for maintaining "illegal contacts with Zionists."[24] In September, the Syrian Government confiscated Arab-administered Jewish-owned lands in the Hauran district.[25] But the heaviest blow came in March 1947, when Jamal el-Husseini, vice-chairman of the Palestine Arab Higher Executive, visited Damascus. He asked the Syrian Government for more drastic measures to curb illegal entry of Syrian Jews into Palestine and the sale of land to Jews by Arab landowners living in Syria and Lebanon who had titles to almost 400,000 acres in Palestine. After Jamal left, Syrian Premier Jamil Mardam Bey informed the leaders of the Syrian Jewish community that unless they publicly denounced Zionism and surrendered all Jewish refugees attempting to reach Palestine via the overland route from Europe, death sentences would be imposed both on captured refugees and those assisting their flight; legislation to this effect was drafted, and was to be considered when Parliament reconvened. Shocked and frightened, the Jewish community sent a delegation to Premier Mardam, asking him to nullify the proposed measure. The Prime Minister agreed, but told the delegates that the Jews must comply with three conditions: surrender all persons aiding the movement of refugees; cooperate with security forces in capturing refugees; and issue a public statement denouncing Zionism and calling on all Jews in the Arab states to support the struggle against Zionism. The delegation promised to abide by these conditions. Apparently mollified by Jewish acquiescence, the Syrian Government amended the original anti-emigration draft law. The bill introduced in the Syrian Parliament provided for life imprisonment instead of the death penalty for Jews caught fleeing to Palestine.[26]

This kind of governmental intimidation of the leaders of Syrian Jewry was undoubtedly accountable for the amazing behavior of Jewish representatives before the Anglo-American Committee of Inquiry on Palestine, which had to investigate, among other questions, the position of the Jewish minorities in the Arab states.

A subcommittee of this Committee, headed by the Committee's chairman, Judge Joseph Hutcheson, visited Damascus in March 1946, and heard evidence of representatives of Syrian political and religious groups and organizations. The Jews were allotted twenty minutes. But, reported Bartley C. Crum, himself a Committee member, the spokesman of the Jewish delegation "used forty-five seconds of his allotted time. He raced through a one-sentence written statement in which he said that the Jews of Syria were happy and not discriminated against; that their situation was excellent under the present Syrian government; and that they had absolutely nothing whatsoever to do with Zionism." Judge Hutcheson, surprised at the brevity of this presentation, asked: "You have nothing else to add?" The Jewish spokesman shook his head. "Very well," said the Judge, nodding his head, and with the dismissal, the three members of the delegation hurried to their seats in the rear of the room amid murmurs of sly amusement from the Moslem audience which said, as clearly as words, "They knew what was best for them."[27]

On December 1, 1947, anti-Jewish riots broke out in the Jewish section of Aleppo. One hundred and fifty Jewish homes, fifty shops and offices, ten synagogues, five Jewish schools, one orphanage, and one youth club were destroyed; one hundred and sixty holy scrolls and one of the oldest and most priceless manuscripts of the Old Testament which was housed in the ancient Bashita Synagogue were burned.[28] The Syrian firemen who were called upon to fight the fires refused to intervene. Policemen and gendarmes actively helped the attackers.[29]

"Rabbis, public servants and leaders" of the Aleppo community sent to American Jews an urgent appeal for aid, which could have been taken from Lamentations:[30]

> May God have pity and put an end to His people's troubles. . . . Our hearts are standing still at this misfortune, and we are writing listlessly. . . . Hundreds of poor houses were set afire and then destroyed to the very foundations. Hundreds of people are now sitting on the ash heaps without a garment to cover their bodies and without a roof over their heads.

The President of the Syrian Republic received a delegation of Aleppo Jewish leaders, expressed his "regret at the incidents," and gave assurances that "steps had ben taken to prevent a recurrence of the rioting." Notwithstanding these assurances, nearly 2,000 Aleppo Jews left the city and sought refuge in the Lebanon, although the Syrian authorities tried to stop this exodus.[31]

The Scapegoat. The United Nations resolution of November 29, 1947, providing for the creation of a Jewish state in part of western Palestine, and the following outbreak of open Arab-Jewish warfare were the signal for a new and particularly vicious wave of anti-Jewish propaganda and violence.

In a letter to the Jewish organizations in America, dated December 21, 1947, which was smuggled out of Damascus, the anonymous author who signed himself "Yoav Ben Tzroya,"* gives an eloquent picture of the Jewish situation in Syria at that time:

> The war against Zionism has turned into a war against the entire Jewish people, and of course, against the Jewish citizens. . . . Anti-Jewish propaganda is rampant in the press, over the radio and in special pamphlets. Poisonous articles, full of degradation and employing the lowest form of expression, are read over the radio and in the mosques. The masses follow faithfully, since the sheikhs promise them a considerable part of paradise.

* "I am writing anonymously," explained the author, "as I cannot give you my name for fear of vengeance on the part of the *Reshaim* (evildoers). However, I promise, with the help of God, to keep you informed about the happenings in our midst, whenever I can, and when daylight returns to us, you will know my name."

Following the classic, well-established pattern of Jew-baiting, the Syrian press used every occasion to make Jews the scapegoat for all troubles befalling the country. Complained Ben Tzroya: "Cholera broke out in Syria—the Jews are blamed. Accusations of the Middle Ages have been revived: the Jews poisoned the water. . . . Counterfeit money was found—the Zionists are the ones to blame. In short, the Jews are blamed for everything."

Aleppo Jews who, relying on the assurances of the Syrian President, had remained in the city, paid dearly for their confidence. On April 28, 1948, several rabbis of Aleppo addressed the following pathetic letter to the Mogen David Congregation in Brooklyn:[32]

This is the third day we are in hiding. The Arab mobs are raging and threatening our lives. Pray for us. Act in our behalf before your Government. Our lives are in total danger. Send a large sum of money to be used for graft expense. . . . Hurry up, help us! The water is engulfing us.

The Jews of Damascus fared not much better. At the end of February 1948, a bomb was thrown in front of the Alliance Israélite Universelle school in the center of the Jewish quarter, causing considerable damage. Disheartened and terrorized, leaders of the Jewish communities of Damascus and Aleppo felt compelled to cable to the Syrian President protesting against Zionism and the partition of Palestine and declaring their willingness to "stand side by side with the Arabs in defense of Palestine." The Jews were also intimidated into contributing funds for the Arab war effort in Palestine. In March 1948, it was estimated that the Jews of Aleppo and Damascus had paid 40,000 Syrian pounds under pressure of threats.[33] In the previously quoted letter from Damascus the anonymous author wrote: "The Jews are being discriminated against in all walks of life; but their money is 'kosher.' They are forced to give money—and immediately—'to free Palestine from Zionism.' The Board of the community itself had to collect the funds and hand them over to the Arab committee heading the Arab recruits. Is there pain more severe, is there a 'galuth' (exile) more bitter than to give money for the purchase of arms to kill our brethren in Palestine?"

Pauperization. Simultaneously, almost all avenues of economic activity were successively closed to Syrian Jews.

As early as April 1947, the New York *Herald Tribune* correspondent quoted Damascus Jewish leaders charging the Syrian Government with "making their livelihood impossible by denying them jobs in the government, withholding import and export licenses, and making virtually impossible the admission of Jewish youths into secondary schools."[34] Even more outspoken were Syrian Jewish leaders at a closed meeting organized on December 30, 1947, at the New York headquarters of the World Jewish Congress. One of them (whose name had to be withheld for understandable reasons) said: "The present anti-Jewish propaganda in Syria is being conducted under the cover of religion and nationalism. In reality, the Arabs want Jewish property and Jewish lives. Some years ago, when Turkey applied the infamous Varlïk laws (see Chapter 8), an Arab leader from Aleppo told me that what the Turks did, the Arabs wanted to do in Syria—and even more: 'When it will come to Syria,' he said, 'we will take everything.' "

Following a violent anti-Jewish press campaign, the Syrian Government inaugurated a policy of systematic dismissal of the few Jews still employed in governmental services. On January 12, 1948, the Beirut *Al Massaa* reported that the telephone company had dismissed all fifty Jewish employees, "so as to guarantee the security of secret telephone conversations." On December 23, 1947, *Al Nida* announced that only one Jew, Rafoul Batchi, remained in the Syrian Home Office: "He will be transferred very soon," predicted the paper. In the fall of 1948, the London *Times* reported that the Security Departments of Syria and Lebanon ruled that marriages between Lebanese or Syrian citizens and Jews be forbidden and that government officials married to Jews be dismissed.[35]

In February 1948, the World Jewish Congress submitted to the United Nations Economic and Social Council except from letters received from Syria, which contained revealing facts on governmental economic policy toward the Jews.

Following the dismissals of Jews in governmental employ, a special committee requested all businessmen and manufacturers also to discharge their Jewish workers, who are 'Zionist traitors and enemies of the Arab nation.' The peddlers were warned not to go to the villages, as no responsibility would be assumed for their safety. . . .

Manufacturers of textiles, hosiery and rayon, who employed Jewish girls, were warned against this practice and asked to discharge all of them immediately. In spite of the fact that their enterprises are at a standstill as a result of this, they were compelled to send away the girls and advertise in the press for new help, as may be seen from the enclosed clipping.

All clerks working for businessmen are to resign. It seems that a Jew worked at the famous Nair transportation offices, and he, too, was discharged as a result of the boycott. I am enclosing a clipping in which the Nair offices declare that their enterprise is free from Jewish employees.

All this in in addition to discharges effected by Government and businessmen's boycott, as well as fear on the part of Jewish farmers to proceed to their work.

The economic life of the Jews is almost completely paralyzed. Every day brings a new affliction. . . . The number of unemployed Jews grows from day to day, and on the other hand there is a decree, 'No Jews shall be allowed to leave or proceed from one city to another!'

Early in 1949, all banks in Syria were instructed to freeze Jewish accounts, to hand over a list of Jewish assets and the names of Jewish depositors to the authorities, and to refuse requests to transfer Jewish funds to foreign countries. No effort was spared to enforce the return of Jewish refugees. In December 1947, the Government notified all Syrian citizens residing in Palestine to return to Syria immediately under the penalty of having their Syrian citizenship rescinded.[36] This "repatriation" order was later extended to the thousands of Syrian Jews who fled to Lebanon following the United Nations partition resolution, and in October 1948, the Syrian and Lebanese police authorities issued a joint statement ordering all Jews who fled from Arab countries to neighboring states during the past year to return to their previous places of residence.[37] In May 1947, the Syrian Government promulgated a law providing for a three-year prison sentence for anyone smuggling a Jew into Palestine from Syria,[38] and in January 1948, an order was issued prohibiting Jews from leaving Syria—not only for Palestine, but for any other country as well—and even from changing their residences within the Syrian territory; they practically became prisoners within a limited pale of settlement.[39] In December, the Jews were forbidden to liquidate their private property in Syria in order to prevent them from transferring money outside the country.[40]

Coup and Countercoup. On March 30, 1949, a bloodless army led by Brigadier Husni Zayim eliminated the Syrian Government of President Shukri Quwatly and Premier Khalid el-Azem, and put the country under military dictatorship.

Although fiercely nationalistic, the new regime inaugurated a somewhat milder policy toward the remnants of Syrian Jewry. On May 3, a high government official stated that Husni Zayim considered all citizens, regardless of creed, to be of "complete equality in rights and liabilities," and that restrictions preventing Syrian Jews from traveling freely, from operating business and from transferring properties had been lifted. The new President's good intentions had, however, to overcome violent anti-Jewish feelings firmly implanted in the Syrian population by years of vicious anti-Jewish propaganda.

On August 5, 1949, a bomb was thrown into the entrance of a synagogue in Damascus just as preparations were being made for the Sabbath Eve service. The building was damaged. Twelve Jews were killed and twenty-six injured. President Zayim sent a representative to visit the wounded. On his orders to apprehend those responsible "without fail," the police arrested numerous suspects. On August 9, a seventeen-year-old Syrian veteran of the Palestine war confessed that he and two friends had thrown hand grenades into the synagogue.[41] President Zayim was quoted as saying that the three criminals were now in prison "and will be judged and condemned to death if the evidence so indicates." He ordered the authorities to prevent further anti-Jewish terrorism at all costs. Yet, a few days later, on August 14, a second military coup led by Col. Sami Hinnavi succeeded in overthrowing the Husni Zayim regime. Zayim was executed before a firing squad and Hinnavi installed himself as chief of Syria's armed forces, with Hashim al-Atasi, a former president of the Republic, as Prime Minister.

The new Government took the position that the fate of Syrian Jews is tied up with the fate of the Arab refugees from Israel; as soon as the refugee problem was settled satisfactorily, it was stated, full rights would be restored to the Jews of Syria.[42] The Jewish community was treated with extreme severity and was largely confined to a ghetto. Although liable to stern penalties if caught, they were ready to take any risk to escape by secret channels from their unhappy surroundings.

Clandestine Emigration. Some succeeded in doing so, but several transports of "illegal" emigrants were intercepted. In September 1949, thirty Syrian Jews were sentenced to terms of imprisonment ranging from one to three months for attempting to cross into Israel illegally.[43] A Jewish Telegraphic Agency dispatch, datelined Tel Aviv, November 10, 1949, reported that twenty-two Jews from Aleppo had been arrested for attempting to cross the Lebanese border into Israel. Another group of thirty-nine, including three women and four children, were rounded up by the Syrian police.[44] On December 29, the Beirut police announced that they had arrested two hundred Syrian Jews and seized nine motorboats after discovering a "big Levantine-Jewish band smuggling Syrian and Lebanese Jews into Israel."[45]

In May 1950, Beirut sources indicated that the Syrian Government was allegedly prepared to follow the example of Iraq and allow Jews to emigrate on condition that they renounce their Syrian citizenship. The first party of ten legal emigrants was reported to have reached Beirut en route to Israel. It was asserted that a general law permitting wholesale emigration was "imminent."[46] Intermediaries suggested that on payment of 100,000 Lebanese pounds (approximately $50,000) such a measure could be easily secured. Responsible Jewish bodies in Jerusalem, however, refused to enter into transactions of this kind. In the meantime, illegal emigration continued. Arab smugglers sometimes took cruel advantage of the Jews who confided in them. In November 1950, thirty Syrian Jews were smuggled out of Syria by a band of Arab seamen who promised to bring them to Israel. Halfway between Beirut and Haifa, the Arabs turned on their passengers, stripped them of their valuables, murdered them and threw their bodies overboard. Twenty bodies were washed ashore and buried in Haifa.[47]

Today, the miserable remnants of the once flourishing Jewish community of Syria feel doomed and are ready to brave any danger in order to reach Israel. In the autumn of 1959, eight Syrian Jews were arrested and tried on charges of attempting "to reach Israel via Lebanon in order to join the Israeli army." The prosecutor demanded the death penalty. Five of the accused were found guilty and sentenced to prison terms of six to twelve years; the other three were released for lack of evidence.[48]

Since May 1948, a total of 5,525 Syrian and Lebanese Jews arrived in Israel:

Year	Number of Immigrants
1948–1949	2,132
1950	931
1951	634
1952	230
1953	197
1954	251
1955	175
1956	207
1957	209
1958	664

Together with the 9,118 who arrived before May 1948, they make a grand total of 14,643, with emigrants from Syria constituting a large majority of this total.[49] Refugees from Syria also constitute the majority of the 11,000-strong Jewish community in Lebanon.

The Balance Sheet. There is a striking discrepancy between the official Syrian data on the Jewish population of the country and the firmly established unofficial data supplied by Jewish sources.

Statistical Abstract of Syria, 1955, published by the Ministry
of National Economy, gives the number of Jews as 32,000. The
same figure is uncritically repeated by N. A. Ziadeh in his otherwise excellent study, *Syria and Lebanon* (pp. 25–26). A Christian Lebanese author, Emile Bustani, is more moderate and
claims in his recent book, *Doubts and Dynamite: The Middle
East Today* (London 1958), that "even today there are 20,000
Jews in Syria" (p. 31). The actual size of the Jewish minority
in Syria was, however, estimated in 1957 at 5,300[50] and in the
autumn of 1959 as low as 2,800.[51] Damascus and Aleppo have
organized Jewish communities, with one synagogue and one
rabbi each. The Alliance school network has been disbanded.
But the Orthodox *Otzar Hatorah,* whose center is in New York,
is permitted to maintain two elementary schools in Aleppo
(with 426 pupils) and one in Damascus (340 pupils).[52] The
communal institutions in both cities receive a large portion of
their budget from abroad. About one-third of the impoverished
Damascus Jewish community is dependent on relief from a
fund for the poor and on medical treatment from a communal
Jewish clinic.

On February 1, 1958, Syria merged with Egypt in the United
Arab Republic. Thus far, the numerically shrunken, impoverished, and cowed Jewish minority seems not to have been
in any way affected by this new development: they are neither
worse nor better off than before.

However, the young Arab generation is being educated in
the spirit of violent hatred against everything Jewish. The reading primer, *Qira'ati* (My Reading), published by the Syrian
Ministry of Education and in use in the first grade of elementary
schools in the school year 1959, contains the following item:[53]
"The Jews are wicked criminals, who invaded Palestine and
drove out the people of Palestine. We Arab children will always
remember Palestine and will drive out from it these wicked
criminals."

6

Lebanon: Between the Crescent and the Cross

Minority Among Minorities. Lebanon is the country of minorities. Its present population, estimated by the United Nations sources at 1,450,000, is a mixture of at least a dozen ethnic and religious groups: the largest group are the Maronites, then come Sunnites, Shi'ites, Greek Orthodox, Greek Catholics, Jews, Armenian Orthodox, Armenian Catholics, and Protestants. It is also the only country in Asia with a slight (53 per cent) Christian population majority. The Lebanese constitution of May 23, 1926, guarantees all citizens equality before the law (Art. 7), freedom of conscience and faith (Art. 9), and freedom of religious education (Art. 10).

The Jewish minority in Lebanon has always been a very small one. Returns published by the French Government in 1923 counted 3,303 Jews in Greater Lebanon.[1] The census of 1932 registered 3,588 Jews in the Lebanese Republic, of whom 3,060 resided in the administrative district of Beirut.[2] Organized religious communities existed in Beirut and Saida (Sidon). There was no central body representing all Lebanese Jews, but the Community Council of Beirut was recognized by the Jews of Saida and the interior, as well as by the Lebanese authorities, as the sole representation of Lebanese Jewry. Beirut counted several cultural and philanthropic organizations and a Jewish weekly in Arabic, *El Alam El Israeli* (The Jewish World). Education was provided mostly by the Alliance Israélite Universelle; the Beirut Alliance school had 673 pupils in 1935. Approximately 90 per cent of Lebanese Jews were engaged in commerce, some 5 per cent in liberal professions, and the remaining 5 per cent belonged to various professions.[3]

On the whole, the tiny Jewish minority in Lebanon had for a considerable time enjoyed a peaceful and uneventful life.[4] Their relationship with the majority population, though restrained, was definitely not hostile. The Government's attitude was far more liberal than in any other Arab country. The Jews were full-fledged citizens, with the right to vote and to participate in the country's political and cultural life. However, they played an insignificant role in Lebanon's political and administrative machinery. The modern political structure of Lebanon is based on the principle, established in the Constitution of 1926, of proportional representation of the numerous religious communities in the Chamber of Deputies, in the distribution of ministerial portfolios, and in administrative functions.[5] The Jewish share in this "equilibre of communities" has always been infinitesimal. In an open letter, addressed on April 22, 1937, to Khaireddin Ahdab, then Prime Minister of the Lebanese Republic, Jacques Lezmi, one of the leaders of the Jewish Community of Beirut, complained: "If our community does not noisily demand its rights, it does not mean that it is resigned. . . . Our minority group is represented in the administration by three employees only."

In other respects, however, Lebanon, a "country of minorities" par excellence, did protect its Jewish minority as well. The Lebanese Constitution contains a unique clause:

Within the territories of Sovereign Lebanon every denominational group which consists of twelve members or more may be regarded as a constituency and may be either directly or indirectly represented in the Parliament, which is to recognize and impose national recognition and observance of any such holiday as the respective constituency may demand on grounds of its religion.

This unusual clause has been faithfully observed. Continuing the Ottoman tradition, Government offices were closed on Fridays because of the Moslems, on Saturdays because of the Jews, and on Sundays because of the Christians; this in addition to observance of all the religious holidays of all the religious groups in the country.

End of the Idyll. During the late forties, the relatively idyllic Jewish existence in Lebanon was violently upset by repercussion of the Palestine events.

On October 15, 1937, the Jerusalem Mufti Haj Amin al Husseini, disguised as a beggar, fled from Jerusalem and settled down in a villa at Juniah, a small coastal town about ten miles northeast of Beirut.[6] There, he resumed his anti-Jewish activities and carried them on for some two years undisturbed. His propaganda did not fail to produce results. In May 1938, the Beirut police had to fire on a large demonstration, against British policy in Palestine and the plan of partition.[7] In July, strong police guards had to be posted in the Jewish quarter in Beirut as a precaution against an anticipated attack. In south Lebanon, Arab terrorists were putting to the torch fields belonging, or suspected of belonging, to Jews. On August 7, Palestine terrorists bombed a Beirut synagogue. On July 24, 1939, bomb outrages were again perpetrated at Beirut.

The outbreak of World War II has, for a limited time, improved rather than adversely affected the Jewish position in the country. The Lebanese population, both Moslem and Christian, showed considerable resentment against anti-Jewish measures imposed by the Vichy regime in 1940. The Mufti of Beirut and the Maronite Patriarch of Lebanon submitted a memorandum of protest to the French authorities against the discharge of Jewish government and state officials. Following the entrance of Free (Fighting) French and British forces into Lebanon in July 1941, all anti-Jewish restrictions had been abolished. Alfred Naccache, then President of the Republic of Lebanon, upon his visit to the synagogue of Beirut in December 1941, pledged that the Jews would be given a full share in the responsibilities of government.[8] Several scores of Palestinian Jews who had been interned by the Vichy administration were released.

Joining the Arab League. In 1943, with the proclamation of independence, and later, in 1945, with the withdrawal of the French mandatory power, Lebanon became a sovereign state, free to shape its own destiny. But the newly elected President of the Republic, Sheikh Bichara al-Khoury, and its successive governments, instead of keeping the country truly independent, have forced predominantly Christian Lebanon, the only Middle East country which has no Islamic stamp, into the Arab League, composed of Islamic states under theocratic governments. Because of this unnatural alignment, the Khoury regime had to follow a domestic and foreign policy of submission to extremist Moslem elements in Lebanon. With certain strata of nationalistic Christian leaders following the pro-Arab League policy, the Christian groups feel increasingly uneasy and apprehensive. In a series of articles published in the oldest and most influential Lebanese newspaper in the United States, the daily *Al Hoda* (Guidance), Father Joseph E. Awad, rector of the St. Joseph's Maronite Church in Waterville, Maine, and one of the foremost leaders of the Lebanese emigration in the United States, after having visited Lebanon in the spring of 1948, wrote:[9] "The Christian majority live in perpetual fright, fearful for their lives, their property and their economic position." If such was the status of the Christian majority, the position of the tiny Jewish minority was incomparably more precarious.

When, in November 1944, news of the assassination by two Palestine Jewish youths of Lord Moyne, pro-Arab British resident minister in the Middle East, reached Lebanon, Moslem leaders in Beirut launched a violent campaign directed not only against Palestine Jewry, but also against the local Jewish population. American Intelligence sources reported that on November 10 a Moslem gathering addressed a letter to the then Lebanese Premier Riadh Solh condemning "Jewish acts of terrorism"; two days later, a delegation told the Premier and the Mufti of Lebanon that they had decided to boycott "all Jewish activity within the country." Riadh Solh pleaded with them "not to lose their heads or direct their activity against Lebanese Jews, as they were not responsible for the Palestinian events." In September 1945, the same sources related that "a group of fanatical Moslems was making plans for mobbing Jews in Lebanon and Syria."

These plans materialized two months later when anti-Jewish riots broke out in the Lebanese town of Tripoli; fourteen persons were killed.[10] The terrified Council of the Beirut Jewish community hastily called upon the Minister of the Interior to express their loyalty to Lebanon and to disclaim any connection with Zionism; in return for this self-denial, the Minister promised that the demonstrations on the anniversary of the Balfour Declaration would pass off quietly.[11] Anti-Jewish terror was resumed in May 1946: two persons were injured in Beirut as Arab terrorists threw bombs into the Jewish stores in the center of the city.[12] In October of the same year, a Moslem demonstration marched to the Lebanese Parliament with cries of "Down with Zionism."[13] Together with Syria, Lebanon joined in the boycott of "Zionist goods" proclaimed by the Arab League in December 1945. By an act of the Lebanese legislature, anyone caught dealing in "Zionist goods" was subject to fines totaling twice the value of the goods. Persistent offenders were liable to a maximum of fifteen years imprisonment.

Simultaneously, the Lebanese Government spared no effort to thwart Jewish immigration into Palestine. The Jewish youth organizations Maccabi and Bnei Zion in Beirut were, in the fall of 1945, accused of smuggling Jews into Palestine and engaging in Zionist activities; the Maccabi sport club was forced to sever connections with its head office in London.[14] In October 1946, the Lebanese chiefs of state had met their Syrian opposite numbers in the Syrian village of Zabadani, near Damascus, and decided upon common measures against "unauthorized Jewish immigration into Palestine" across the Syrian and Lebanon frontiers. In the same month, Lebanese authorities refused to grant transit visas to 105 Jewish refugees from Bulgaria, so that a vessel had to be chartered to bring them directly from a Turkish port to Haifa.[15]

On the whole, however, the Jews of Lebanon have, till the end of 1947, enjoyed greater liberty than their brethren in Syria. They have been tolerated, and although the atmosphere in the country was violently anti-Zionist, it seldom became anti-Jewish. Being largely a Christian Arab land, Lebanon showed more tolerance for its Jewish community than other Arab countries. On government instructions, the Lebanese press usually endeavored to differentiate between "Zionists" and Jews. Sometimes the same paper published a pro-Jewish article on the first

page and a virulently anti-Jewish one on the second page. The
Government tolerated the normal functioning of the schools of
the Alliance Israélite Universelle and did not forbid the study
of Hebrew.[16]

Influx from Syria. During the post-World War II period, the
number of Jews in Lebanon has considerably increased, mainly
through influx of refugees from neighboring Syria where existence became unbearable. According to a Chicago *Tribune* dispatch, about 25 per cent of the Aleppo Jewish community migrated to Lebanon after the December 1947 pogrom.[17] After the
outbreak of the Arab-Israeli war of 1948, the influx from Syria
grew considerably. A recent report estimated that some 14,000
Syrian Jews had crossed the border and found asylum in Lebanon. The report stressed that

tribute should be paid to Lebanon as the only country in the Middle
East willing to open its doors to these Jewish refugees. Its govern-
ment was well aware of the fact that by granting asylum to the Syrian
Jews it would be straining the already unfriendly relations between
Lebanon and Syria. But this consideration was fortunately not
decisive.[18]

Jewish educational needs and institutions increased accordingly. The Beirut Alliance school, which had 673 pupils in
1935, augmented its contingent to 923 in 1946 and to 968 in
1947. According to a report submitted in June 1947 by the Jewish Community Council, there were in Beirut 431 pupils (223
girls and 208 boys) in the elementary classes of the Alliance
school, 251 in the kindergarten, and 84 boys and girls attended
the class "*de brevet*"; besides, 202 pupils attended the "Community People's School" managed by the Alliance. In 1948, the
total number of pupils in the Beirut Alliance schools rose to
1,043. This increase was mostly due to the influx of refugees
from Syria. "Beginning with mid-December, 1947," reported
M. Elmaleh, Director of the school, in March 1948, "no day
passes without one or two enrollments. Since February 1948,
to our regret we had to suspend new admissions to the school."

The language of instruction was French; eleven hours weekly
were devoted to the study of Arabic. The Alliance report admitted that the study of Hebrew in the school was unsatisfac-

tory and ascribed this to the lack of competent teachers; several foreign Hebrew teachers had to depart, and the Lebanese Sûreté Générale refused to replace them by others.[19] Another educational institution was the "Selim Tarrab" school, organized by the Beirut Jewish Community and attended by some 250 children of poorer families, who not only were educated but also clothed and fed at the expense of the community. In the Selim Tarrab school, Hebrew was taught thoroughly: in the primary classes, thirteen hours weekly out of a total of thirty-eight were devoted to the study of Hebrew, and in the kindergarten thirty-two hours out of thirty-eight. There was also an Alliance school in Saida (65 pupils) with Hebrew as the language of instruction. Approximately 200 Jewish students attended non-Jewish schools and universities.[20]

In War with Israel. The position of Lebanese Jewry had deteriorated sharply at the end of 1947 when open Arab-Jewish hostilities started in Palestine. The Lebanese Government's anti-Jewish course reached its climax in May 1948, when Lebanon sent her tiny army against the newly proclaimed state of Israel.

In a statement before the UN Security Council, Lebanese representative, Dr. Charles Malik, on June 2, 1948, assured the Council that nothing would happen to the Jews in the Arab countries as long as they "remain loyal to their own motherlands" and maintain no relations "with the Zionists of Palestine." The Lebanese police, reported Dr. Malik, halted, "by use of force, an anti-Jewish demonstration and dispersed the demonstrators, causing some casualties among them."[21]

Notwithstanding these official assurances, the Jewish community of Lebanon suffered greatly from a deliberate anti-Jewish governmental policy.

In keeping with the practice of all anti-Jewish regimes, the Lebanese Government made foreign Jews residing on Lebanese territory the first victims of its repressive measures. The influx of Syrian Jewish refugees provoked violent opposition in nationalistic Arab circles. The paper *Al Yom* published an article insisting that the Lebanese Republic must not show itself more lenient toward the Jews than Syria by accepting Jewish refugees from Syria. "Our country," warned the paper, "will finally create the impression that it is more friendly toward the Jews than toward its own sister countries."[22] The governments of Lebanon and Syria were reported to have agreed on the establishment of control posts at their common frontier in order to check on the movement of Jews and to prevent them from moving from one country to another without a special permit from the police[23]; it was decided to prepare a comprehensive list of all alien Jews residing in both countries and to return to Syria all alien Jews who had previously resided in Damascus and then migrated to Lebanon; Syria in turn undertook to expel these returnees from her territory within the shortest possible time.[24] Stern measures were also taken against Palestine Jews dwelling in Lebanon. The Beirut correspondent of the Jaffa Arabic daily, *Falastin*, reported that the Lebanese authorities issued a warning to all Palestine Jews to leave Lebanese territory not later than January 1, 1948.[25]

Foreign Jewish residents were the first to suffer from the intense hostility generated by the Lebanese-Israeli war. But "native" Lebanese Jews fared not much better. All Jewish institutions were gradually closed down "on grounds of Zionist tendencies." The Maccabi group was declared illegal, the Maccabi House with all its property confiscated, and Dr. Abraham Hellmann, the organization's President, was jailed for three weeks. Rabbi Dr. Kurdagi was summoned to the Beirut police headquarters and advised that for each service conducted in his synagogue he was to obtain a special police license at a cost of five Lebanese pounds, and that persons attending or conducting unlicensed services would be arrested. A special "defense tax" was imposed on every Jewish person with earning capacity. Several minor Jewish officials in the Ministry of Commerce were discharged.

Organized Blackmail. One of the most widespread and disturbing forms of anti-Jewish pressure was extortion of money "for the Arab refugees from Palestine," which had become a highly organized and dangerous racket.

Father Joseph E. Awad, who spent several months in Lebanon, described the working of this racket as follows:[26]

In Beirut there are four committees, each one singing a different tune and all collecting monies for Palestine. They use every means in their power to coerce the people and make them contribute to their funds. Their activities consist of visiting the shops and houses and the bureaus of the Government, asking them to help the refugees of Palestine. One committee comes today, the other tomorrow, the third and fourth later on. The shopkeeper, the family man, the poor civil servant have to contribute to all of them. If they have contributed to the first and second committees, as is usual, when the third and fourth committees arrive and these poor people state that they have no more money to contribute, they are insulted, threatened, and called traitors to the Arab cause.

The Jews suffered greatly from this organized blackmail. The Beirut paper *Al Hayat* ominously wrote on January 12, 1948:

In our issue of the day before yesterday we reported that the collector of funds for Palestine had visited Jewish businessmen and that she has met with some opposition from Mr. Rahmine Derviche. We do not know whether this opposition was at the bottom of the throwing of the incendiary bomb yesterday into the apartment of the brother of Mr. Derviche, Mr. Saleh Derviche.

The same *Al Hayat* revealed that a "meeting of Jewish personages" called for the purpose of inducing Jews to donate money for the Arab struggle "has had the desired effect on the Jewish businessmen; they offered considerable gifts for the collection"; a Jewish delegation visited the Lebanese Premier and assured him of "their desire to fight Zionism and to prove this desire by deeds"; 82,000 Lebanese lire were collected for that purpose among Jewish businessmen. *Al Hayat* published the names of contributors and amounts contributed by each; another list contained the names of Jews who had not yet contributed to the Arab fund. "Let us thank God for having created rich Jews at Beirut so that they can pay for the Arabs of Palestine," commented the paper. But even the most generous Jewish contributions evidently did not guarantee the security of the Jewish community. Another Beirut paper, *Al Beyrag* (January 12, 1948), acknowledged that "in spite of the fact that the rich Jews have liberally contributed for the Arab cause in Palestine, several disagreeable incidents have happened which have caused the Jews to close their stores."

Not content with extorting money through intimidation, Arab nationalist leaders also applied more "direct" means of terrorizing the Jews.

On January 8, 1948, a Beirut Jewish merchant was stabbed to death by three unidentified assailants; the next day, a bomb exploded in the Alliance Israélite school in the Rue Georges Picot. No casualties were reported, but windows were smashed and part of a wall was ripped out. Arab sources asserted that the school was "the headquarters of Zionists in Lebanon." The Beirut paper *Telegraphe* reported that in the morning of the day following this outrage "a number of Jewish storekeepers hesitated to open their stores" and did so later "protected by the vigilance of the police"; police squads patrolled the Jewish quarter "to prevent all anti-Jewish incidents."[27] A majority of the Jewish butchers were afraid to go to the slaughterhouse to obtain their meat and asked for police protection against attacks.[28] Reviewing acts of anti-Jewish violence, another Lebanese paper, *Al Amal*, editorially said on January 12, 1948, that "the troublemakers have a right to act as they do, for how can you expect them not to attack the Jews when the Lebanese non-Jews can hear the cries of their unhappy brothers in Palestine?"

On May 24, 1948, a fanatical Shi'ite mob attacked the Jews at the Lebanese village of Teybl; the police fired at the attackers, killing four of them. Two months later, "unidentified persons" threw a hand grenade into the Jewish quarter of Beirut; three Jews were wounded by flying glass splinters.[29] After the alleged discovery of a munition depot in the garden of a Beirut synagogue, the Grand Rabbi and the Jewish Community Council of the Lebanese capital had to issue a statement denouncing "Zionist propaganda" and proclaiming their loyalty to the Government. The Grand Rabbi also condemned "the violence perpetrated in the name of Zionism in Palestine." The Government, in return, pledged itself to take the necessary measures to protect the Jewish quarter of Beirut.[30]

Christian Leaders Defend Jews. Christian Lebanese repeatedly voiced their disapproval of the Government's anti-Jewish policy.

Leaders of the Beirut Jewish Community, in November 1947, reported to the World Jewish Congress that Beirut Jewry owed much to the protection of their Christian neighbors and of organizations such as the "Falange Lebanese," which was first created in 1936 and had by that time counted 30,000 to 40,000 members (among them some 100 Jews); squads of the "Falange" often patrolled the Jewish quarter in case of anticipated attack. In April 1948, the clandestine "Falange" radio station, operating secretly somewhere on Lebanese territory, repeatedly advocated close cooperation between Christian Lebanon and a Jewish state in Palestine.[31]

Some French-language Lebanese papers warned the Government that the continued anti-Jewish propaganda and outbreaks might lead to results harmful to the Lebanese cause. Enumerating the threats uttered against the Jews and the acts of violence already committed, *L'Orient* (January 13, 1948) questioned whether the police will be able to continue to provide adequate protection for the Jewish quarter; the article insisted that the anti-Jewish violence in the Arab countries "might have international repercussions and serve as food for Zionist propaganda." In an editorial "Our Jewish Fellow-Citizens," *Le Jour* (January 13, 1948) likewise stated that "our Jewish fellow citizens are living in great insecurity" and demanded: "We must reassure them immediately. They must be shown by actions that they are protected by the law in the same way as the members of other communities."

The pro-Jewish attitude of the Christian population considerably affected Lebanon's military potential in the Arab war against Israel. The *Weekly Intelligence Report N 45*, issued by the headquarters of the British Forces in the Middle East, significantly stated:

The Lebanese contribution to the Palestine "war effort" will, it appears, be confined to the provision of materials rather than men. Owing to the pro-Jewish attitude of the Lebanese Christians, who form a considerable proportion of the population, no training will take place in the country, but the best of those who wish to volunteer will be selected and sent to the Syrian centres.

The Christian opposition bitterly criticized the dispatch of the Lebanese army to Palestine to fight the Jews, while "thousands of Palestinian (Arab) youth, strong and healthy, who have fled the war, throng the bazaars and streets of Beirut and the villages of Lebanon . . . promenade and enjoy themselves . . . happy in the safety of Lebanon, far from danger."[32] Lebanese Christians apprehensively reminded each other that when Syrian troops rode through Beirut to fight in Palestine, they chanted a song, the burden of which was: "Saturday today, Sunday tomorrow." To every Christian listener the intent and meaning of this song was clear: "When we finish with Jews we'll get rid of the Christians."[33]

Abatement. After the cessation of hostilities between Lebanon and Israel, the Lebanese authorities gradually moderated their anti-Jewish policy. Senior Jewish officials who had been suspended during the Palestine war were reinstated in their old positions, while in some cases Jews were appointed to higher posts.[34] Most of the thirty to forty Jews who were detained in the camp at Baalbek were set free. Many who at one time had fled Beirut for the rural districts where the Maronite population was more sympathetic toward them, returned and resumed their businesses. Lebanese Jews were again permitted to travel inside the country and to other Arab countries without special permits. It was also announced that "foreign but not Israeli Jews" would be permitted to enter the Lebanon, provided their records are clean. Many Jewish citizens were given facilities to visit Europe for business and other reasons.[35]

A certain abatement took place also in regard to Jewish emigration to Israel. At the meeting of the Israel-Lebanese Mixed Armistice Commission on May 7, 1949, it was agreed that a limited number of Jewish families residing in Lebanon would be allowed to enter Israel.[36] Seven months later it was announced that thirty Jewish families were permitted to leave for Israel and the first group of fifty-five Lebanese Jews crossed the Israel-Lebanese frontier at the Rosh ha-Nikra custom post on February 22, 1950.[37] Simultaneously, foreign Jews residing in the country were allowed to cross into Israel taking with them all their property and valuables. Jews who fled to the Lebanon from Iraq, Syria, and Iran after the outbreak of hostilities in Palestine, were thus enabled to enter Israel under the supervision of the mixed Lebanese-Israel Armistice Commission, whereas hitherto they were compelled to pay large sums of money to Lebanese bands engaged in smuggling people across the border. The first party, consisting of 170 Syrian Jews, left Beirut early in March. Israel, in turn, agreed to accept Christian Arab refugees from Palestine living in Lebanon; about 150 were to be admitted each week.[38]

Notwithstanding this "softening" of governmental emigration policy, the Beirut radio on July 10, 1950, announced that twenty-five Lebanese Jews had been captured while attempting to flee Lebanon for Israel in several rowboats, and two weeks later Radio Baghdad related that Lebanese police authorities had arrested a party of twenty-five Iraqi and Syrian Jews who tried to cross the Lebanese border into Israel.[39] An Arab News Agency report alleged that a Jew named Samuel Abadi, who was arrested by the Lebanese police, "admitted that he assisted many Jews to escape to Israel from Syria and Lebanon.[40]

In the early winter of 1952, a correspondent of the London *Jewish Chronicle* who had visited Lebanon, reported that the Jewish minority "lives a more normal existence than in other Arab countries." There was at that time "no group which is actively propagating anti-Jewish measures." Like all other minorities, the Jews who paid taxes were allowed to vote for a joint representative in the Lebanese Parliament, but "it was explained that they are not directly represented in Parliament because they do not have enough votes.[41]

In the Wake of the Sinai Operation. The crisis caused by Israel's Sinai operation and the Anglo-French attack on Egypt in 1956 affected Lebanon's external and internal policies to a lesser degree than that of other Arab states.

Though a member of the Arab League, Lebanon refused to follow Syria's example in breaking off diplomatic relations with French and Britain after their attack on Egypt. A considerable section of Lebanese public opinion, both within the country and abroad, boldly opposed Nasser's attempts to draw Lebanon into his own military grouping. Particularly vocal were Christian groups. Sheikh Pierre Gemayel, the leader of Al-Kataeb, the National Youth Organization, publicly declared: "We didn't fight the French Mandate in order to accept the Arab one." The paper *Lisan-al-Adl* denounced "flirtation with pan-Arabism, inside and outside the Arab League" and accused "the aggressive Egypto-Syrian group" of striving "to do away with Lebanon as a state, as a Christian nation, as a 'bridgehead of the West,' to use Nasser's words."

Predominantly Western in spirit, apprehensive of the mounting wave of Arab-Moslem fanaticism which is threatening to engulf the last Christian stronghold in the Middle East, wary of her "twin sister," Syria, afraid of being completely isolated, looking for truly kindred alliances, Lebanon was unable to follow a consistent policy because she is a country divided against herself, half her population being Moslem and pan-Arab in their allegiance.

This internal rift exploded in the summer of 1958, degenerating into a civil war between pro-Nasser Moslem groups, instigated and armed by the United Arab Republic, and predominantly Christian adherents of the pro-Western Government of President Camille Chamoun. In July, the United States landed forces in Beirut "to assist the Government of Lebanon in the preservation of Lebanon's territorial integrity and independence." The acute phase of the conflict ended with the establishment of the compromise regime of President Fu'ad Chebab, and a rather vague joint declaration of all Arab League members pledging "respect for the independence and sovereignty of these states."

The Jewish minority, though alarmed and apprehensive, seemed not to have been directly affected by the disturbances and the fighting. They practiced the difficult and delicate art of remaining inconspicuous, avoided arousing the wrath of both Moslems and Christians, stressing their aloofness from both world Jewry and Israel.

In 1958, about 11,000 Jews were living in the Lebanon. Their position is described as bearable and, compared with conditions in other Arab countries, quite satisfactory. Economically, they share in the general prosperity of the country, which is largely based on the extensive and profitable tourist traffic. Most tourist and catering enterprises, including ski trails in the mountains, are run by Jews, especially those of the "old-timers" who constitute Lebanon's Jewish "upper class."[42] The "lower class" comprises mostly newcomers from Syria, who belong to the lower income brackets. They live in poorer circumstances than the "native" Lebanese Jews, and a number of their girls (despite a good Jewish education they receive in the Alliance schools) marry Moslems for lack of suitable Jewish grooms. Attempts by the Syrian Government to obtain the expulsion of these refugees were steadfastly resisted by the Lebanon authorities. The only concession they made was the promise not to grant them (as to Syrians in general) Lebanese citizenship.[43]

Politically, no far-reaching anti-Jewish measures have lately been taken. The Government claims that in Lebanon there is no anti-Jewish prejudice whatever, and the Jews themselves admit that they suffer only from the "conventional forms of anti-Semitism." Nevertheless, no further building licenses are being granted to Jews. Many schools have expelled Jewish children, although elementary education in Lebanon is compulsory. One missionary school, where education is free of charge, did admit sixty Jewish boys on condition that, within the school premises, they wear uniform white shirts with blue stripes as a sign that they are Jews. Their parents, who are poor and cannot afford private tuition, agreed to this discriminatory condition. Curiously enough, the Beirut Jewish school of domestic science, owned by Dr. Elias Abarbanell, has been left alone and the two hundred Jewish girls there continue their training undisturbed. Of the three universities in Beirut only the American University (with 1,935 students in 1955) has so far refused to follow the "advice" of the Government to expel its eighty Jewish undergraduates. The French-sponsored Academy of Science, having expelled its Jewish students, still employs four Jewish lecturers. Of the 101 private, 8 state and 7 foreign hospitals in Lebanon, only the American-owned Cedars of Lebanon Clinic admits Jews at any time.[44]

The Alliance Israélite Universelle in 1959 maintained six schools with a total enrollment of 1,443 pupils. The largest is in

Beirut, with 446 boys and 642 girls; after the Sinai conflict, a
number of Jewish refugee children from Cairo were admitted to
the school. One elementary school with 100 pupils is maintained by *Ozar Hatorah*. A small Alliance school at Saida (Sidon) has about 50 students. A Talmud Torah in Beirut, with
over 250 students and a dozen teachers, is supervised by the
Community Council, but is supported largely by contributions
from abroad.[45]

No Readjustment. The impact of dramatic political development having abated, the Jewish community of Lebanon hoped
to be able to reintegrate themselves into the mainstream of
the country. In the summer of 1959, however, they came under
heavy attack in Parliament when the government of Premier
Rashid Karame brought before the chamber a bill allowing
persons who had emigrated from Lebanon and non-Lebanese
Arabs to own land in Lebanon. Deputy Kamel el Asaad argued
that the measure would enable Jews of Lebanese descent to buy
large tracts of land in Lebanon for Israel, and that Israel "had
plans to dominate Arab countries economically as a forerunner
to military domination." Added Deputy Takieddin Sohl: "I
don't believe Lebanese Jews owe their allegiance to Lebanon.
. . . It is to Israel that their allegiance goes." Defense of the
Jewish community came from Deputy Joseph Chader, who
told the Parliament that no Jew, in Lebanon or Syria, had been
convicted of spying for Israel; Jews in Lebanon "are more loyal
to this country than many other citizens." *The New York
Times* Beirut correspondent reported that "periodic press attacks, occasional incidents such as the Parliamentary proceedings, and the general stringency of Lebanese economic life have
induced many Jewish families to transfer their business interests
abroad and to emigrate. . . . Businessmen and bankers extend
their interests abroad when an opportunity arises. Later they
emigrate, but still in many cases maintain business connections
in Lebanon."[46] Particularly eager to leave are Jews of Syrian
origin.

The pattern of Lebanese Jewish emigration differs considerably from that of other Arab countries. It is not oriented exclusively, or even predominantly, toward Israel. Many went to

Italy, France and England, where they have relatives or business connections. In November 1958, it was reported that in recent weeks more than 500 Jews had left Lebanon for Mexico, Brazil, Argentina, and other Latin American countries; a further 500 had registered with the U.S. Immigration Department to enter the United States.[47]

The emigration trend became even more accentuated in 1959, when the Beirut daily, *Kŭl Shey*, quoting Lebanese security sources, related that half of the remaining Jews had left the country "in a panic." The paper noted with satisfaction that the Jewish section of the capital city had been half emptied, and added: "We will not regret it if another half of Lebanese Jews will leave the country. . . . It is better that they leave on their own at the earliest opportunity than wait until we shall ask them to leave, when we might get in trouble with the United Nations."[48] Despite this apparent assent to Jewish emigration, a Jewish lawyer, Albert Levi, a Lebanese Maronite and a Moslem merchant were, according to another Beirut paper, *Al Hayat*, arrested for organizing a "spy ring" engaged in smuggling Jews and money through Turkey and Cyprus to Israel.[49]

7

Egypt: Abandoning the Ruins

Two Thousand Years of History. Jews have lived in Egypt almost continuously for more than two millennia. Some were established there prior to the Babylon captivity; others, seeking refuge, were later allowed to settle in the Delta towns. In Upper Egypt, Jewish mercenaries founded a colony on the Island of Elephantine. A papyrus in the Cairo Museum of Egyptian Antiquities records—in Aramaic—the sale of a plot of land negotiated between two Jews, "To last for all time."

The most important Jewish group to settle in Egypt, after the first Exodus, arrived there following the conquest of Judea by Alexander the Great (322 B.C.E.). Ptolemy I (323–283) encouraged the Jews to settle in Alexandria. According to legend, it was upon the wish of Ptolemy VI that the Pentateuch was translated into Greek (the Septuagint). When Julius Caesar arrived in Egypt in 48 B.C.E., he assured the Jews of their ancient political rights and privileges, among others that of being governed by their ethnarch. But their growing prosperity aroused hostility: the first anti-Jewish riot, accompanied by looting and murder, in the year 38 C.E., occurred under Caligula, who deprived the Jews of their privileges. In the year 66 C.E. new riots took the lives of thousands of Jews in Alexandria. Four years later, Jerusalem having fallen into the hands of Titus, Jewish prisoners were sent by the thousands to Egypt to be used for public works. In 415 C.E., Cyril, Bishop of Alexandria, instigated a riot after which a large number of the more than 100,-000 Jews were compelled to emigrate. Better days returned with the rule of the Caliphs of Baghdad (638).

In 1517, the Ottoman Sultan, Selim I, conquered Egypt. The following three centuries were eventful but rarely directly affecting the life of the Jewish community. It was not before the Greek revolution in Morea (1821–1824) that Egypt experienced a new wave of Jewish immigration. Under Mehmet Ali, who for a time united Palestine and Syria with Egypt (1833), Jews lived undisturbed and prospered. Edward William Lane, whose classic study *Manners and Customs of Modern Egyptians* was first published in 1836, estimated the Jewish community of Egypt at about 5,000.

The opening of the Suez Canal in 1860 inaugurated an era of numerical growth and material prosperity, which lasted until the close of World War II. In 1910, the noted historian and leader of the Alliance Israélite Universelle, Narcisse Leven, wrote in the second volume of *Fifty Years of History:*[1]

The situation of the Jews in Egypt is now [1910] excellent. They have contributed substantially to the prosperity of the country. They have founded numerous establishments of commerce, industry and credit, and these have been of great benefit to Egypt.

The census of 1937 recorded a Jewish population of 62,953. *Foreigners and Jews.* Egypt was the first Moslem country to experience the full impact of Western penetration, both in economic expansion and cultural influence. Ethnic and religious minorities (Greeks, Armenians, Christian Syrians, Jews) were strongly attracted by these advantages. Successive waves of immigrants were streaming from Turkey, Iraq, Lebanon, Iran, Syria, North Africa. Their legal status was most favorably determined by the system of "Capitulations" and "Mixed Tribunals," which provided that no foreign resident is subject to the jurisdiction of Moslem courts. Few of the newcomers were therefore eager to acquire Egyption citizenship. In 1937, there were in the country over 150,000 foreign subjects—chiefly Italians, British, French, Greeks and Persians. Among the Jews, whose number was prior to Israel's War of Liberation (1948) estimated at 75,000, some 30,000 were foreign nationals, about 5,000 had Egyptian citizenship, and 40,000 were stateless persons. The last named were for the most part descendants of families who had lived in Egypt for generations. They did not enjoy either the privileges of foreign citizens or the rights of Egyptian nationals. Those among them who tried to become naturalized met with insuperable obstacles. Art. 22 of the Nationality Law of February 27, 1929, which provided that a "resident is to be considered Egyptian until his nationality has been formally proved," did not apply to Jews. Until the turn of the century there was no office in Egypt which recorded births. When, under increasing xenophobia, Egypt passed a naturalization law stipulating that to become an Egyptian one had to prove that one's grandfather had been born in Egypt or that his family had lived in the country continuously from 1849, most of the Jews of *Haret-el-Yahud* (the Jewish quarter of the large cities) could produce no such documents.

The overwhelming majority of the Jewish community was not integrated into the country's fabric, not only legally, but also culturally and spiritually. Most of the French-educated middle-class Jews could neither read nor write Arabic. The school curriculum was strictly "European." Classes were conducted in French, and English was a required subject. The younger generation avidly grabbed every new French book and were well posted on every French government crisis. But they were disinterested in Egypt's cultural, social and political problems. Better education, geared to the needs of an expanding business community and its employment opportunities, enhanced the position which the Jews, together with other Europeans, had for decades been occupying in the country's economy.

It was due to the combined effort of the foreign builders of modern Egypt—British, French, Italians, Greeks, Jews—that Egypt has become the most advanced Middle Eastern country. The most beautiful portion of Alexandria was built by a British Jew, Joseph Smuha, and was called in his honor the Smuha City. The National Bank of Egypt and the Agricultural Bank, the Egyptian railroads, the large sugar factories, the transport enterprises, were all created by Jews. Most firms, from the director down to the typists and the errand boys, were manned by Jews. In comparison with the average Middle Eastern norms, the Jewish community enjoyed a good standard of living. Except for a small number, not in excess of 4,000, who were aided by communal institutions, extreme poverty was unknown. Nor did the attitude of the authorities and of the public seem strongly inimical.

Early Violence and Discrimination. The first indication of violent animosity was the demonstration organized by Egyptian nationalist organizations on November 2, 1945, the twenty-eighth anniversary of the Balfour Declaration. The demonstration turned into an unbridled outbreak of plundering and looting not only of stores but of synagogues and churches. All non-Moslem Egyptians and Europeans became the targets of mob attack. The Ashkenazi synagogue in Cairo was burned, as were a home for the aged, a soup kitchen for children, a shelter for indigent transients, a Jewish hospital, the quarters of an art society, and numerous other Jewish public buildings.[2] This mob outbreak was, however, considered of little symptomatic significance, and as late as March 1946, the Jewish Agency for Palestine confidently asserted, in a memorandum on the position of the Jewish communities in the Oriental countries submitted to the Anglo-American Committee of Inquiry, that "the general position of the Jews in Egypt is beyond comparison better than in any (Arab and Moslem) country so far surveyed."[3]

The next few years, however, witnessed an abrupt and dramatic decline. Growing general hatred of foreigners among all classes of Egyptian population found a most convenient outlet in Jew-baiting. The Government was not averse to making use of public excitement for political purposes. On July 29, 1947, it enacted the so-called Company Law, Loi No. 638 de 1947, providing that within three months after its official publication (which took place on August 4), all Egyptian Societés Anonymes and all Egyptian branches or offices of foreign societies must maintain among their salaried employees a staff at least 75 per cent Egyptian, receiving not less than 80 per cent of the total salaries; among their laborers at least 90 per cent, receiving at least 80 per cent of the total wages; and on their boards of directors, at least 40 per cent.[4]

Prior to Egypt's entry into the Palestine campaign, this measure was part of a general drive against foreigners and minorities. Coupled with the expiration of the Mixed Tribunals on October 15, 1949, which left foreigners without any guarantee against the arbitrariness of local courts, it transformed the nationalism and xenophobia which had for years saturated the Egyptian press into solid economic and legal substance. The full force of the impact of the Company Law upon Egypt's Jews can be appraised only when taking into account the fact that not more than some 5,000 Jewish residents were able to qualify as "Egyptians" within the terms of the Company Law. This led to mass dismissals and joblessness.

Ten months later, after the outbreak of the Palestinian War, the economic life of Egyptian Jews, already shaken, was dealt a new crushing blow. Proclamation N 26, issued on May 30, 1948, subjected to sequestration the property not only of any person who was interned in Egypt and of any person residing outside of Egypt whose activities were deemed "prejudicial to the safety and security of the State," but also of any person merely placed under surveillance (Art. I). Since there was no legal barrier to placing anyone "under surveillance," Proclamation N 28 could be, and was, applied indiscriminately. All business organizations, either under the control of any such person or in which any such person had a substantial interest, were within the stated scope of the proclamation. Upon taking over any property, the Director General named to manage it was entitled (Art. 2) to do "all acts appropriate to normal exploitation," including cancellation of debts owed to the owner of the property.[5]

A notice appended to the Proclamation explained that the Government had finally concluded "with regret" that "a certain number of persons and establishments who possess goods in Egypt have committed acts against the safety and security of the state," and that it therefore had to take "necessary measures to prevent these persons from pursuing their activities prejudicial to the safety of Egypt and of the Arab countries in general." Orders were issued placing the property of 68 persons and firms under sequestration. Nothing was mentioned about the purported grounds for the action, but 67 of the 68 sequestrations were in fact either Jewish or establishments under Jewish ownership or control. In addition, a blanket order placed under sequestration all property in Egypt belonging to individuals or establishments residing in Palestine or even temporarily sojourning there.[6] During the month of October, 14 more Jewish enterprises were sequestrated,[7] 12 in November,[8] and 10 in December.[9] January 1949 saw the sequestration of 8 Jewish concerns,[10] February of 3 more.[11] Branching out from commerce and trade to professional activities, Law No. 142 of September 22, 1948, made Egyptian nationality a prerequisite for practicing medicine,[12] and a general regulation of the Stock Exchange of August 28 allowed only "Egyptians" to become brokers.[13]

The cumulative effect of these measures within a few months wrecked the entire structure of the Jewish economic life in Egypt. It destroyed the position not only of the 111 enterprises directly affected by the sequestration, but also of a much larger number of those who had by that time still been spared. Their owners felt acutely insecure, knowing that being Jewish was per se sufficient reason for being under suspicion and liable to application of Proclamation No. 26. On the other hand, anyone entering into a contract or agreement with them was on notice not only that the transaction could be retroactively nullified if their goods were sequestered, but that his own resources connected with it might be involved. This apprehension actually paralyzed any commercial activity.

When Egypt Attacked Israel. When, in May 1948, Egypt joined in the invasion of Israel, Jews became an easy prey to administrative abuse and mob terror.

On May 14, 1948, King Farouk issued a royal decree imposing martial law throughout the country and invested Prime Minister Mahmoud Fahmi El Nokrachi with extraordinary powers. Mass arrests followed. On the night of May 14, 600 persons were rounded up and interned; within a short time the number of internees reached 1,300. Some 1,000 of them— Jews and non-Jews, Arabs, Egyptians and Europeans alike— were people known for their opposition to the Government, as well as for their Communist association. The remaining 300 were Jews selected for their past association with Zionist organizations or activities which up to that time were completely legal.[14]

Administrative repression was followed by mob terror. On June 20, 1948, twelve houses were blown up in the Harat al Karayim, part of the Musk quarter inhabited by Jews of the Karaite sect. Twenty Jews were killed and 41 wounded. The office of the Public Prosecutor declared the occurrence an "unpremeditated homicide by unknown persons."[15] After the Israeli air force attack upon Cairo on July 15, Arab mobs twice marched upon the Jewish quarter, attacking Jews in the streets and in public conveyances, breaking into Jewish homes and plundering them. On July 19, high explosives caused extensive damage to the Jewish-owned Cicurel Department Stores, damaging also 500 shops in the neighborhood, killing 3 persons and injuring 17. Another explosion in a Jewish store took place on July 28 (with 4 persons injured), and still another on August 1 (with 28 injured).[16] According to an account in the Basler National Zeitung (August 10, 1948) more than 150 Jews were murdered or seriously wounded during mob attacks on July 18 to 25. The New York Times reported on August 5 that 3 rabbis were murdered by the mob in slaughterhouses.

The wide coverage of the riots in the foreign press and strong intervention by foreign governments in behalf of their nationals caused a brief end in anti-Jewish outbreaks. On August 3, the semi-official Al Ahram editorially condemned terrorism. But the lull was short-lived. On September 22, several Jewish houses in Cairo were demolished by a heavy explosion: 19 Jews were killed and 62 injured; Jewish homes and shops were looted. This time, the police intervened and a state of emergency was proclaimed in the Jewish quarter.[17]

Jewish leaders were doing their best to mollify official and popular anti-Jewish ire by demonstrating their loyalty to Egypt and their hostility to Zionism. Jewish members of Parliament had solemnly reasserted their Egyptian patriotism. Chief Rabbi Hayim Nahum Effendi had declared that Egyptian Jews must defend their country against the Zionists, and urged them to contribute for the relief of Arab refugees from Israel.[18] Ac-

cording to *The New York Times* of June 6, 1948, the Jews of
Egypt had been donating large sums for the War Chest; the
Egyptian press reported that the Jews of Alexandria had contributed $80,000 and those of Cairo $160,000 to the Egyptian
Soldiers' Fund. The *Bourse Egyptienne* of July 2 confirmed a
gift of 41,000 Egyptian pounds, while the *Journal d'Egypte* of
June 26 reported a donation of £1,000 by the small Jewish community of Port Said. On the other hand, Egyptian spokesmen
endeavored to absolve themselves from accusation of conducting an anti-Jewish crusade. *Tour d'Horizon* (Paris), an Arab
publication in the French language, asserted in its issue of
August 15, 1948, that the Egyptian Government had not taken
any measures against the Jews. M. Bishr Fares, member of the
Egyptian Institute and of the French Archaeological Institute
in Cairo, claimed in *Paroles Françaises* (September 3, 1948),
that the agitation had been due solely to anti-Zionism, which
was steadily gaining adherents among the Arab population,
while anti-Jewish bias was nonexistent.

Sealing off the Exit. Characteristically enough, one of the first
measures taken under the martial law was to ensure that the
Jews be prevented from leaving for Israel and remain hostages
in Egypt. Before the establishment of the State of Israel, Egyptian Jews contributed little to immigration into Palestine: only
1,845 were listed prior to May 15, 1948. Governmental measures, however, strove to seal off every possibility of exit. Proclamation N 23 of May 25, 1948, stipulated that no one, "even
the holder of a passport," could leave Egypt without a special
exit visa obtainable from the Ministry of Interior.[19] For several
weeks after this proclamation went into effect, no Jews at all
were permitted to leave Egypt, while at the same time permission was being obtained with relatively little difficulty by non-
Jews in like circumstances. The ban was applied to Jews regardless of their nationality and in spite of the protests of
various foreign consular offices in Egypt on behalf of their
respective nationals. These protests were probably instrumental
in causing a slight relaxation in the enforcement of restriction in
July and August. But Proclamation N 52 of September 26, by
transferring jurisdiction over infractions of the laws on illegal

entry and departure to courts-martial, again set an ominous tone in this field.[20]

Companion pieces to the Proclamation N 23 were quick to follow. On May 28, Proclamation N 28 narrowly limited the amount of money, securities, and jewelry which could be taken out of Egypt without special authorization, and directed that in no case could authorization be given for an aggregate amount exceeding 4,000 Egyptian pounds (£11,200). Moreover, it provided that everyone carrying out jewelry must post a bond guaranteeing the return of the particular articles to Egypt within a year. Proclamation No. 25 of May 30 placed comprehensive controls upon transfers of funds to the neighboring Sudan, whether through banking transactions or otherwise. Both proclamations stipulated that any property or funds transferred in contravention of their terms would be administratively confiscated, and both established prison terms and fines for violations.[21] These measures created in the entire Jewish community an acute sense of imprisonment. Even illegal exit was impossible, since the Egyptian frontiers are either at the sea or at the boundaries of countries in which a Jewish refugee could expect no shelter.

. . . *and Lifting the Ban.* Early in August 1949, the Egyptian Government suddenly reversed its policy. Exit visas, introduced in 1948, were abolished and all restrictions lifted.

Immediately, a hasty exodus started. The Cairo correspondent of the London *News Chronicle* cabled on August 15 that approximately 300 persons, "most of them Jews," have been leaving Egypt daily. In November 1949, it was reported that over 20,000 Egyptian Jews had left the country since the cessation of hostilities in Palestine. Officially, they were bound for Italy or France. The Egyptian press used to refer to Jews leaving the country as "tourists going to Europe for a short period." However, in January 1950, *Al-Ahram* admitted: "It may now be revealed that the Jews leaving Egypt are known to be proceeding to Israel from France or Italy, which is only their first destination." In the last months of 1948 and in 1949, a total of 7,268 Egyptian Jews have found their way to Israel.[22]

In the second half of 1949, the general situation abated considerably. In August, fifty prominent Jews arrested in May, 1948 were released, their sequestered properties were returned, and they were permitted to emigrate.[23] Sequestration of seven Jewish-owned large industrial and commercial concerns had been revoked. Improvement continued in 1950, when the more moderate Wafd Party came to power. Several anti-Jewish decrees were rescinded, many detainees freed, and a number of sequestrated properties returned to their Jewish owners. The mood of the Jews changed to greater optimism, the Jewish community resumed normal operation of their schools, hospitals, etc. By 1951, the tension had eased further; those who remained regained faith in their future. Jewish bankers and businessmen pursued their vocations; Jewish lawyers made their appearance in the courts; Jewish professionals followed their careers; Jewish books were on display, etc.

Nevertheless, emigration continued strong in 1950, when Israel alone admitted 7,154 Egyptian Jews. It slowed down in 1951, when 2,086 arrived.[24]

Naguib and Nasser. In July 1952, a military junta, headed by Maj. Gen. Mohammed Naguib, overthrew the regime of King Faud and forced him into exile; the infant Ahmed Fuad was proclaimed King. In June 1953, the monarchy was officially abolished and the Republic of Egypt proclaimed, with General Naguib as President and Premier for a transition period of three years; Colonel Gamal Abdul Nasser was appointed Deputy Premier and Minister of the Interior.

President Naguib displayed marked friendliness toward Egyptian Jewry. He visited several Jewish institutions, including Cairo's main synagogue on the first day of the Jewish New Year (September 10, 1953), extending greetings to the Jewish community; he embraced the seventy-year-old Chief Rabbi Hayim Nahum Effendi and made a number of friendly public pronouncements.[25] Jewish schools in Cairo, which had been burned during the 1948 riots, were rebuilt. There were rumors that several hundred stateless Jews would be naturalized. At the same time, however, a number of foreign Jews were expelled, and a special police contingent to deal with Jews was established. In November 1953, thirteen Jews were arrested on charges of conducting "Zionist and communist propaganda"; a military court sentenced eight of them to prison terms of three to seven years. In February 1954, sixteen Jews were arrested in Alexandria on the same charges.[26] During this period emigration continued, though on a modest scale: 1,251 Egyptian Jews arrived in Israel in 1952, and 1,041 in 1953.[27]

In February 1954, Naguib was overthrown by his second-in-command, Gamal Abdul Nasser. Under the new regime, the Jewish position considerably deteriorated. In July, three young Jews were arrested on trumped-up charges of having set fire to the United States Library, the Alexandria Post Office, and a number of cinemas. Unlike Naguib, Nasser and his senior officials displayed the utmost reserve in relation to Jews; he even refused to see the Chief Rabbi in connection with the arrests. By October 1954, arrests of Jews had assumed such a massive character that the World Jewish Congress urgently appealed to the Cairo Government to halt the wave of repression. Recalling that reports reaching the Congress indicate that in recent weeks more than 150 Jews had been arrested and charged with Zionism as a crime and with other crimes, ranging from attempted arson to Communism, the statement continued:[28]

Earlier hopes that Egypt would not permit its hostility towards Israel to influence its treatment of its own Jews have been shattered. . . . The mass arrests have created panic among the local Jewish population. . . . The World Jewish Congress is reluctant to believe that these violations of human rights and decency represent a settled policy on the part of the Egyptian Government. The Congress makes a most earnest appeal to the Egyptian Government, before it is too late, to take measures to halt a process which not only threatens the survival of Egyptian Jewry, but is bound to damage the reputation of Egypt among the civilized nations.

The appeal remained unheeded. In December, twelve Jews were brought before Egypt's Supreme Military Court, accused of being operatives of a Zionist espionage apparatus. In fact, they were Zionists who were meeting secretly in contravention of the ban on Zionist activities.[29] As the Washington, D.C. *Post and Times Herald* pointed out on December 22, 1954, the trial started immediately after the execution of the leaders of the anti-government Moslem Brotherhood as an attempt to divert public attention from these by playing the anti-Israeli card. The two alleged leaders of the group were sentenced to death and, despite a storm of international indignation and protest, executed; two defendants were sentenced to lifelong imprisonment at hard labor and two were acquitted; others received sentences from seven to fifteen years. Two other trials involved in one case 7 Jews and in a second 77; they ended in milder sentences. Apparently in order to justify these repressions, the Egyptian Embassy in Washington began distributing, in February 1955, a pamphlet titled *The Story of the Zionist Espionage in Egypt*, whose main theme was that "Zionism and Communism are two distinctive forces with one political objective—world domination. Both powers cooperate secretly and in public without friction since the power in the end will eventually go to Zionism," In 1956, the semi-official fortnightly *Al Goumhouria* launched a violent attack against Jews in general and those in the United States and Great Britain in particular, predicting that, following the Nazi pattern, world Jewry will sooner or later be exterminated. In June of the same year, the notorious ex-Mufti of Jerusalem was permitted to launch his anti-Jewish propaganda on the Cairo radio. The "Voice of the Arabs" told its audience that "the Jewish religion wants to enslave the entire world, to spread terror and corruption, in order to secure Jewish world domination."[30]

Jewish communal and cultural institutions have been increasingly interfered with. Rabbinical tribunals, with an Appellate Court, which were competent for litigations among Jews and in certain cases of personal status (divorce, alimony) were abolished by the law of September 21, 1955. Since October 1956, existing Jewish community councils have lost their representative status with the Egyptian authorities and have ceased to function as intermediaries between the Jewish population and government officials in matters concerning work permits, registration of documents, or vital statistics. The Government recognized the eighty-two-year-old and virtually blind Grand Rabbi of Egypt, Hayim Nahum, as the only spokesman of Egyptian Jewry. The Jewish communities of Cairo, Alexandria and

Tonta, which had for years been maintaining schools where Hebrew was taught along with secular subjects, have since the middle of 1956 been ordered to accept Moslem pupils as well. Their distinctive character was thus practically obliterated (the Cairo Jewish school had to admit 236 Moslem students).[31]

Emigration. Emigration during this period had its ups and downs. In 1954, 1,069 Egyptian Jews arrived in Israel. Without completely prohibiting emigration, the Egyptian authorities have established a complicated and annoying system of delays and checks in granting exit permits. Such permits were to be approved by the so-called Arab Department, which, in fact, was concerned mostly with Jewish affairs. The department kept a dossier of every Jew in the country and if the applicant was known to have any connection with Zionism his application for an exit visa was denied. The Division of Jewish Affairs in the Secret Police Department (for a time there had existed the "Zionist Police") was re-established. It was believed to have a first-class staff with many Nazi German technicians who had specialized in Jewish affairs. The division set up, in 1955, a system of control to follow closely the activities of the members of the Jewish community—without, as a rule, interfering with their daily life. In Cairo and Alexandria, every head of a Jewish family had his own file where all his activities were registered; all letters sent and received by him were photographed, and the photostats put in the file.[32] As a result of this administrative practice, immigration to Israel dropped to 677 in 1955 and to 880 in 1956. The grand total for the period May 15, 1948 to January 1, 1957, was 21,482.[33] Many more remained in the European countries to which they had obtained visas. It can be assumed that by October 1956 not less than 25,000 Jews have left Egypt.

In the Wake of the Sinai Campaign. On October 29, 1956, units of the Israeli army entered the Sinai Peninsula. Three days later, British and French aircraft bombed Cairo, Alexandria and Port Said. Within seventy-two hours of this thrust, the Egyptian Government promulgated a series of decrees which established a state of siege, imposed strict censorship, provided a juridical basis for seizure of hostages, mass arrests, denaturalization of entire groups of Egyptian citizens, as well as for the subsequent sequestration and confiscation of property of a large section of the Jewish population. When the United Nations imposed the withdrawal of Israeli and Franco-British forces, repression began.

An Associated Press dispatch from Port Said on November 26, 1956, reported that "Jews began leaving Port Said today, leaving behind hostages seized from each family by the Egyptians the night before the British and French landings." The practice of seizing hostages extended beyond the immediate emergency of the British and French landings. On December 15, the *Washington Star* reported: "Jewish families had been visited by Egyptian secret police in the early morning hours just before British and French troops landed here last month and one member of each family was taken hostage."

Making ample use of the Emergency Law of 1954, which authorized the Military Government of Egypt to "order the arrest and apprehension of suspects and those who prejudice public order and security," Egyptian authorities rounded up and interned large numbers of Jews. On November 24, 1956, Osgood Caruthers, *The New York Times* correspondent in Cairo, reported that arrest orders "according to authoritative estimates, affect thousands of Jews in Cairo who are of foreign nationality, many of them British and French subjects, or who are in the status of stateless persons. It was not known how many others might be affected throughout the rest of the country."

The Egyptian Foreign Minister, Mahmoud Fawsi, admitted that "a few Jews" were taken into custody "because they were dangerous to the security of the state." Five days later, these "few Jews" became, by the admission of Lieut. Col. Zakariah Mohiedine, Minister of the Interior, "288 Jews" who were being detained "for reasons of security."[34] Conditions in the improvised detention centers were described as appalling.

On November 1, 1956, Military Proclamation No. 4 conferred on the Director General for the administration of the property of persons interned and put under surveillance, unlimited powers to sequester personal possessions, business and industrial enterprises, and to dispose of or to liquidate them with the consent of the Minister of Finance.[35] Within a week, a series of implementing decrees was issued. Decree No. 170, published on November 8, 1956, listed 440 persons whose properties were to be sequestered and who were made liable to arrest and expulsion.[36] Decree No. 171, published on November 11, mentioned 25 additional persons, including the president of the Jewish community in Cairo. Decrees No. 174 to 196, published in the period November 11–13, 1956, named for sequestration 13 of the principal mercantile or commercial enterprises owned by Jews. Virtually every Jewish-owned enterprise of any significance had been taken over, and the lists included the names of Egyptian citizens, Egyptian-born stateless persons, as well as persons of various nationalities. By far the greater part of the possessions of Egyptian Jewry has been taken over. Many thousands have lost their means of livelihood, or have been suspended without compensation from their posts, or prevented by various measures from exercising their professions. By March 1957, assets of 500 Jewish-owned firms were sequestrated and their bank accounts frozen; 800 more Jewish-owned enterprises were placed on an economic blacklist and their assets frozen.[37]

"Clearing out the Jews." There can hardly be any doubt that, following the pattern of Nazi Germany, the Egyptian Government was determined to make Egypt judenrein—cleared of Jews. A Jewish escapee told an International News Service correspondent in Paris that the "fairly high official" who came to arrest him said: "We've got a list of 6,000 Jews we're going to imprison or expel. And that's only a first list of 6,000. Soon there'll be no more Jews in Egypt. You'll all have to go."[38] Major Hadid, a blue-uniformed police official in charge of the internment camp at the Sebil School in Cairo, was "often proclaiming that Egypt had no place for Jews."[39]

"Cleaning out the Jews" took various forms.

In a series of articles published in December 1956 in the Scripps-Howard chain of newspapers, Fred Stark described his departure from Cairo "on a plane cargoed with unhappiness." Among the passengers, a few were Christians, most were Jews, all were native born, forced out—stripped of all possessions—because they held British and French passports; they were "enemy aliens" . . . [there were] three couples and their children who read and write only Arabic. . . . Officially, none are expelled solely for religious reasons, but because of nationality, British or French. It is true that British and French Christians have also been expelled, but if an "enemy alien" is also a Jew his deportation chances soar.

The government has yet to oust all French and British, Jew or Gentile. But many, seeing countless problems ahead, worried by endless police checkups, liquidate and go. Airline and shipping offices are crowded through the day with refugees seeking transport. Seats and berths are priceless.

"At this time," reported Stark, "there is no 'anti-Jewish terror' in the manner of a Hitler-style pogrom. . . . The government has condemned anti-Jewish threats and violence; such publicity cannot serve Col. Nasser in his battle for world opinion. . . . The pressure—subtle and unofficial—is a 'shadowy persecution.' "[40]

As a result of such "subtle pressure," a total of 14,102 Jews had left Egypt between November 22, 1956, and March 6, 1957. By September 1957, the number increased to 21,000.[41]

An official United Nations report, published in February 1960, established that more than 36,000 Jews were forced to leave Egypt since the end of 1956.

A statement issued in January 1957 by a conference of the world's major Jewish organizations, specially called to deal with the plight of the Jews in Egypt, said:[42]

Large numbers of Jews of all nationalities have either been served with orders of expulsion, or were subjected to ruthless intimidation to compel them to apply for permission to depart. Hundreds who have reached lands of refuge have testified that they were taken in shackles from prison and concentration camps to board ships. In order to ensure that this deliberate creation of a new refugee problem should not evoke protests from international public opinion, documents proving expulsion were taken away from expellees before departure. Furthermore, they were compelled to sign statements certifying that they left voluntarily. The victims of this barbaric process were deprived of their possessions.

Spoliation. When leaving the country, Egyptian nationals were deprived of their passports; their laissez-passer carried the stamp: "Not valid for return to Egypt." A variety of government regulations prevented a Jew or a foreigner from transferring capital abroad. No one was allowed to take along more than $84 in cash and $390 worth of jewelry. Theoretically, up to $14,000 could be transferred abroad, but the checks were issued on blocked Egyptian accounts in the United States, Great Britain and France. No limit was set regarding the value of personal belongings, such as clothes, shoes, etc. This generosity was obviously motivated by the desire to induce the would-be emigrant to spend all his money in Egypt by buying Egyptian-made clothes, shoes, and furniture, which could be bought at more reasonable prices and which, if it were possible to purchase such goods in Europe or elsewhere, would be of far better quality. The only alternative for a Jew was to put himself in the power of Egyptian black-marketeers, thereby often losing over 50 per cent of the value of his assets in the transaction, which usually involved excessive commission fees. Moreover, even with the small amounts realized from the sale of his goods, he was liable to arrest on the charge of smuggling capital.[43]

At first, departing Jews were permitted to take with them only two suitcases; later this restriction had been mitigated somewhat, but they had to leave behind their nonmovable property, house furnishings, valuables, to be padlocked by a public custodian for "future disposition." "Naturally," reported Fred Stark, "deportees don't expect to hear again from the custodian. They make every effort at salvage. I was approached on a Cairo street and offered a vast amount of currency and jewelry for my word that I would have a bank pay the deportee a trifling amount of dollars in Paris. I rejected the deal, but there is profitable traffic with these unfortunates; many participating are in government service. When police have the power to deal with 'enemy aliens' they are seldom gentle, often corrupt."

Frequently, property left behind was being auctioned off. The paper *Al-Kadem* reported on August 10, 1957, that in Cairo, 22 Jewish houses, 8 factories, and other buildings, which were allegedly left by their Jewish owners in a dilapidated state, would be auctioned off. Similar auctions were announced for Alexandria and Ismailia.

By the end of 1958, the Jewish position was described by the *Jewish Chronicle* correspondents as "increasingly difficult"[44]:

> Foreign firms are reluctant to employ Jews for fear of antagonizing the authorities. . . . The Egyptians have desequestrated two large shops belonging to Jews, 'Benzion' and 'Chemla,' but these shops are still under Egyptian management and their former Jewish directors are still in France. Each of the shops once employed over 300 Jews. They now have no Jewish personnel . . . Jewish-owned business firms which are still functioning in Egypt are being blacklisted by the authorities, and export and import licenses are being withheld from them. Realizing that they are faced with ruin, Jews are desperately trying to dispose of their businesses to Egyptians and to transfer the money received to Europe.

Vistas of Emigration. Israel was by far the main, though not the only, haven of refuge. In 1957, a total of 13,003 Egyptian Jews arrived. But in 1958 the figure dropped to 523. Overseas countries started attracting Egyptian emigrants. Between January 1957 and October 1959, 2,804 Egyptian Jews settled in Brazil. About 2,500 have been admitted to the United States under the 1957 law permitting entry of 5,000 aliens who had fled their countries "because of persecution." But about 2,000 more who had applied for emigration to the United States were, in the autumn of 1959, still stranded in France and Italy. They could not be fitted into existing United States immigration quotas, and their only hope was that unused quotas from other countries might become available.[45]

The Jewish Agency directed the emigration to Israel, and the United Hias Service took care of the emigration to Latin America, the United States, Canada, Australia, and other immigration areas, directly from Egypt, as well as from France, Italy, Greece and Great Britain. No Jewish organization, of course, could function in Egypt itself. It was the excellent cooperation between the United Hias Service and the International Red Cross that made it possible to accomplish this task.

Of great help also was the attitude of the French Government, which did all in its power to help not only the Jews of Egypt who were French citizens, but also other Jewish refugees who asked French assistance.

Some 45,000 Jews have left, or were forced to leave, Egypt during the period May 15, 1948 to January 1, 1959. Of this total, 34,787 went to Israel. About one-half (17,761) of the latter number did so under the reign of King Farouk (1948–1952). The other half (17,026) arrived when Egypt was ruled by Naguib (July 1952 to February 1954) and Nasser (since 1954). So powerful apparently was the urge to get rid of the Jews and to get hold of their properties and assets that Nasser acquiesced in a considerable increase of Israel's manpower. Thus he violated the basic Arab League principle that further immigration into Israel be prevented. In Syria, which in February 1958 joined Egypt in the United Arab Republic, any attempt to leave for Israel is still considered and treated as treason.

A Vanishing Community. The Jews of Egypt are now a fast dwindling community. Early in 1959, a correspondent who recently returned from Cairo reported that they were enjoying one of the "quieter periods of decline." Outwardly, their existence could be considered as untroubled:[46]

Public sentiment does not much hinder Jews in their daily routine of business and family life. Social life is likewise relatively free. I saw Jews in the 'best places,' and they are once again free to go wherever they can afford to do so. Religious institutions thrive as best they can. Virtually all of the Jews still in Egypt are relatively well off financially. The poorest having gone, there are very few who still need to accept money from the community's relief agency. An abnormally small proportion of these who remain are below 40 years of age. It is a community of older people who are pessimistic about their future in Egypt but consider themselves too old to make a change now.

The numerical decline is spectacular. From 75,000 in 1948, not more than 13,000 to 14,000 remained at the end of 1958. Of these, some 7,000 held Egyptian citizenship, the others being in the main Italian, Greek and Spanish nationals. One year later, their number was already estimated at 4,000 to 5,000.[47] A report submitted to the 1960 annual meeting of the Cairo Jewish Community Council gave a distressing picture of the community's decline. Of the 3,000 eligible members in 1949, only 400 remained, and of that number only 30 to 40 attended the meeting. The deficit for the year 1958 amounted to £15,000 Egyptian (£52,000), and, said the presiding officer, "cannot be overcome nor sensibly reduced"—the only likely reduction being in the size of the community. Though the community had 70 properties, only a few buildings were bringing in some income. The big problem was to try to maintain community services with a steadily declining income. Receipts by the Rabbinate for administrative services were less than one-third of income received the previous year; gatherings at the various temples were down by the same amount, and the school deficit had increased by about $10,000 to $30,000. Of the twelve old synagogues in the Jewish quarter of Musk, only one was functioning, and the Jewish quarter became almost entirely inhabited by Moslems and Copts. Only 150 Jewish children were attending the Jewish school of Abbassia (instead of 7,500 in 1948) and about 100 attended the "Goutte de Lait" school in Cairo (instead of 1,000). The Heliopolis Jewish school, which in 1948 had 1,500 pupils, has been closed because of lack of support. Of the 500 students in the community schools, only some 300 were Jews—the others were Moslems imposed by the government regulations.[48]

The Plight of the Deportees. Extremely precarious also is the financial position of the thousands of Egyptian Jews who departed leaving their properties behind.

In August 1958, a French-Egyptian agreement was concluded in Zurich providing for "desequestration" of, or reimbursement for, properties and businesses of the approximately 8,000 French citizens expelled from Egypt; a similar agreement was signed in February 1959 with Great Britain. As of September 1959, 2,800 such applications had been received by the General Administration of Sequestrated Property and about

700 French and between 250 and 300 British "desequestra-
tions," large and small, have been disposed of.[49] Yet no satisfaction was given to Jewish claimants of British and French
nationality. A total of 2,078 Jewish "evacuees" from Egypt
have found refuge in England: about 1,100 of them were British
subjects and 978 were stateless persons. Among them, the
Smouha family, the David and Nessim Ades families, and
the Hettena families are reported to have amassed a fortune
estimated at $84 million. But Jews applying for visas to Egypt
to settle claims arising from their sequestrated property were
being refused, without any reason given. Jewish organizations in London have obtained a secret Egyptian document in-
structing UAR consuls to issue visas only to applicants able to
submit a baptismal certificate.[50] Hardly better is the position of
French Jews. "So far," reported the London *Jewish Chronicle*
on October 31, 1958, "no French Jew expelled by the Nasser
Government since 1956 has obtained an entry visa to Egypt to
regain control of his sequestrated properties or business." One
year later, speaking before the Council of Frenchmen in Foreign Countries, René Seydoux, Vice-President of the *Conseil
Superieur*, said that more than 95 per cent of the claimants
would not be able to come to Egypt and arrange their affairs
because the majority are of Jewish faith.[51]

Particularly difficult is the position of about 12,000 to 15,-
000 stateless Jewish refugees, as well as those holding Egyptian
nationality. Their properties left in Egypt are estimated to be
worth up to $28 million. They have, however, no government
to present their case, and no attempt has so far been made to
open negotiations on their behalf, though the American Joint
Distribution Committee, together with the World Jewish Congress, the Alliance Israélite Universelle, and the American Jewish Committee, started in 1957 to register the claims of these
Jews all over the world. Most of them, as mentioned before, are
now settled in Israel, but a large number have emigrated to
Brazil and other Latin American countries, and some to Britain.
The Cairo Government announced that it will treat the claims
of the stateless and Egyptian Jews residing in the United King-

dom in the same way as it deals with the claims of British nationals. No such promise was given to those residing in France or elsewhere. The World Conference of Jewish Organizations held in New York in January 1959 deliberated on the steps necessary to protect their interests.[52]

PART TWO

Jews in Non-Arab Moslem Countries

8

Turkey: Jewry on the Move

Status and Numbers. Jews lived within the present boundaries of Turkey many centuries before the Turks conquered the country. After the expulsion of Jews from Spain in 1492, Turkey admitted more than one hundred thousand Jewish expellees and received them with extreme friendliness. Ottoman Sultans, Selim and Suleiman, early in the sixteenth century, invited Jews to Constantinople. There was also a small influx of Ashkenazic Jews, especially after the revolution and pogroms of 1905, from Russia.[1]

Christian and Jewish minorities in the Ottoman Empire lived under the remarkable regime of the *millet*. Each religious community was organized autonomously, like a state within the state, in most cases under a religious head, and had power, under the general authority of the Sultan, to manage its own affairs. The Moslems were headed by the Grand Mufti of Constantinople. Next in importance was the "Millet-i-Rum," the community of Orthodox Christians under the Ecumenical Patriarch, again at Constantinople. There was an Armenian millet under the Gregorian Patriarch, a Catholic millet under the Pope's delegate, and a Jewish millet under the Grand Rabbi. The minorities had their own schools where the teaching of Turkish was not obligatory, retained their own language, customs, and were free to preserve and cultivate their identity.[2]

The Ottoman Empire, which included Mesopotamia (Iraq), Syria, Palestine, and Libya, had a large Jewish population. Estimates vary greatly as to the number of Jews in Old Turkey at the beginning of the twentieth century. Arthur Ruppin assessed

it at 375,000, of whom 210,000 were living in Asiatic Turkey
(1.1 per cent of the total population); 150,000 (2.7 per cent
of the total) in European Turkey; and 12,000 in Tripoli.[3] The
Alliance Israélite Universelle estimated the total number of
Jews in Turkey at 463,688; of these 188,896 were in Europe
(65,000 in Constantinople, 17,000 in Adrianople).[4] Ernest
Jäckh, a German authority on Turkish affairs, quoting statistics
available in 1908, counted 300,000 Jews.[5]

Successive territorial losses which culminated in the Lausanne Peace Treaty of July 24, 1923, have reduced Turkish territory to a mere fraction of the former Turkish state (294,416
square miles instead of 710,224 square miles as late as 1916).
The new Turkish Republic had a considerably smaller Jewish
population. This decrease was due not only to the curtailment
of territory, but also to an intensive Jewish emigration after the
First World War. The first postwar Turkish census of 1927
registered 81,872 Jews—55,592 in Europe (4.7 per cent of the
total population) and 26,280 in Asia (0.2 per cent of the total population).[6] The census of 1935 showed a further decline; the number of Jews in the whole of Turkey dropped to 78,-
730.[7]

In 1948, 82,622 Jews lived in the Turkish Republic.[8] More
than two-thirds was concentrated in Istanbul (55,000); 15,-
000 resided in Izmir (Smyrna), and 2,750 in Edirne (Adrianople); Brussa or as it is now called, Bursa, had a Jewish population of 1,000; Canakkale, 1,200; Ankara, the capital of new
Turkey, only 500; and there were groups of 100 to 2,000 Jews
at various towns and townlets in the provinces.[9]

Replacing the defunct Treaty of Sèvres (August 10, 1920),
the Treaty of Lausanne, signed on July 24, 1923, contained articles 37–45 providing for the protection of ethnic and religious
minority groups. Yet, while acknowledging that these articles
constituted "obligations of international concern" placed under the guarantee of the League of Nations, the Turkish Government urged non-Moslem minorities to forego their rights
under the Treaty in order not to be excluded from the protection of the new Turkish civil code.[10] Yielding to this pressure,
the Temporal and Spiritual Council of the Jewish Rabbinate

in Turkey notified the Turkish Government in October 1925, "in the name of the Jewish community," that "they renounced their internationally guaranteed minority rights in view of the coming introduction of a Western civil code."[11] Similar statements followed in the name of the Armenian and Greek minority groups.[12] After the enactment of the new civil code on February 17, 1926, the Turkish Minister of Justice informed the aforementioned communities that in return for their renunciation of minority rights, the new code would be applied to all citizens of the Turkish Republic without distinction of race, nationality or religion.[13]

This renunciation of collective minority rights had undoubtedly no legal validity. Turkey's minorities were not a party to the Treaty and had, therefore, not the legal power to cancel any of its provisions. The League of Nations regarded the renunciation by the minorities of their rights as null and void. It never prevented either the minorities themselves or others from drawing its attention to any violation of the rights of Jewish, Armenian, or Greek communities in Turkey, and was dealing with a number of petitions emanating from minorities in Turkey without objection on the part of the Turkish Government.[14]

Turkish legislation was almost indifferent to the status of minorities. The unique provision of the Constitution of 1924 which was of some significance was Article 80, securing freedom of instruction under the control of the state. On the whole, the status of the minorities was based on old statutes, such as the *Kbatt* of 1839 and the *Firman* of 1858, which had permitted non-Moslems to maintain temples, hospitals, welfare organizations, and cemeteries, and allowed religious communities to establish schools in their own language.[15] Actually, however, the young Republic never looked with favor on autonomous minority organizations. As a result of the territorial changes following the first World War, present-day Turkey emerged as a smaller but ethnically homogeneous state entity which cast off the age-old traditions associated with its former territory and spiritual life. The radical secularization of the country was unavoidably reflected in the Government's treatment of the minority creeds. In view of the close historic ties between the religious and cultural factors within the minority groups, this governmental attitude was bound to affect the entire spiritual life of the minorities.

Education and Culture. Destruction of cultural autonomy, which all the minority groups had enjoyed under the old regime, started as early as 1923, when all teachers in Jewish schools were ordered to teach in the Turkish language; no exception was made even for the schools maintained by the Alliance Israélite Universelle. All Jewish schools had to be closed on Friday, the official Moslem day of rest. In 1926, the Turkish language was declared to be the sole medium of instruction. In December 1937, the Ministry of Education appointed government commissioners for all Jewish and other minority schools, with unlimited powers both in regard to curriculum and general financial administrations.[16] Under these circumstances, very few distinctive Jewish features remained in the Jewish educational system in Turkey. In addition, fewer and fewer Jewish children were being covered. In 1929, out of 8,000 of school age, only about 6,000 were receiving any instruction; of them 3,500 attended Jewish schools and 2,500 various Christian missionary schools.[17] In 1947, there were seven Jewish schools in Istanbul and Izmir, with 4,500 pupils between them; of this number the Alliance maintained four schools with 2,083 pupils. Many Jewish parents were compelled to send their children to foreign or governmental schools where they were brought up in complete ignorance of everything Jewish. The college for higher Jewish studies in Istanbul, which was supported by the B'nai B'rith until 1928 when a government decree barred all such supports from abroad, could do little to remedy this state of affairs (351 pupils in 1948). Jewish students preferred to attend French, English and American schools after completing their secondary courses either in Jewish or public schools. In August 1950, the college closed down its two senior classes because of lack of students.[18]

The inadequacy of the Jewish school system is particularly striking when compared with the school systems of other non-Moslem minorities which were subject to the same unfriendly administrative attitude as were the Jews. In 1939, the situation was as follows:[19]

	Colleges	Elementary Schools
The 125,046-member Greek community had	8	52
The 55,229-member Armenian community had	3	31
The 78,730-member Jewish community had	1	8

Under these circumstances, it was only natural that the process of Turkization gained momentum.

Of 81,872 Jews in Turkey in 1927, 68,900 or 84.1 per cent gave Ladino (Spanish-Hebrew dialect) or Yiddish as their mother tongue. Eight years later, in 1935, of 78,730 Jews, only 42,607 or 54.1 per cent gave these languages as their mother tongues.[20] It became increasingly difficult to speak a language other than Turkish in public. In 1937, the Istanbul papers launched a campaign against public use of all languages except Turkish. The drive was particularly aimed against Ladino, but Greek and Armenian were also targets of the campaign. Yielding to this pressure, the Jews of Izmir, at public assemblies held in all synagogues of the city, decided thereafter to speak only Turkish in public. An "Association of Turkish Culture" was founded by young educated Jews for the purpose of spreading Turkish customs and language among the Jewish population. An appeal to use the Turkish language instead of Ladino was read in all synagogues of the country on Rosh Hashanah of 1938: Jews were urged to consider Turkish as their native tongue, as "we constitute an integral part of the noble [Turkish] nation and there should be nothing to distinguish us from our brethren." Many Jewish families changed their names for Turkish-sounding surnames. In 1950, for the first time in the history of Turkish Jewry, a weekly *Turkiyenin Sesi*, devoted to Jewish news and printed in Turkish, began to appear in Istan-

bul. Previously, Jewish periodicals used to be published in Ladino, which was steadily declining.[21]

In 1948, the ban on religious instruction in state and communal schools, in force since the Republic was founded in 1923,
was lifted. The Jews received this new governmental policy
with mixed feelings. They were apprehensive of the possible
psychological and political implications of the revival of the
Mohammedan religious influence in public affairs. On the other
hand, however, they felt heartened by the chance to reintro-
duce instruction in Jewish religion and history and in the
Hebrew language. Under the twenty-five-year-old former system, no specifically Jewish subjects could be included in the
school curricula, and only limited instruction on Jewish religion
and tradition could be given at certain synagogues. The new
regulation, published in July 1949, announced that minority
educational institutions which, since 1937, had been under the
supervision of Moslem superintendents appointed by the Department of Public Education, would henceforth have complete autonomy of administration.[22]

Communal Organization. Communal affairs of the two largest
communities, Istanbul and Izmir, are vested in two distinct
bodies: the twenty-member Religious Council dealing with religious matters and the sixty-member Lay Council dealing with
administrative, financial and similar affairs. Smaller communities have only an administrative council, with religious matters
under the supervision of the Istanbul Chief Rabbi. But even
in Istanbul, the Religious Council had for several years been
reduced to three members out of the statutory twenty, because
of the death or departure of a number of its members and the
impossibility of finding well-qualified candidates for these posts
in the country. Similarly, fifteen of the sixty seats of the Lay
Council had been vacant for fifteen years. The post of the Chief
Rabbi was not occupied since 1932, and the shortage of religious
leaders, especially in the smaller communities and in the suburbs of Izmir, Istanbul and Ankara, was such that during the
High Holidays of 1949 no rabbi could be found to officiate at
the services in the synagogues, since those who had emigrated
could not be replaced.[23]

Communal organization of Turkish Jewry was deeply affected by governmental policy of separation of church and state, which deprived the Chief Rabbinate of Turkey of its position as Jewish representative and the Jewish religious and cultural organizations of their official status. The Religious and Lay Councils were closely watched by government bureaus, which prevented their democratization and development. Speaking in the Turkish Parliament on April 13, 1948, the sole Jewish M.P., Solomon Adato, complained that under the existing set-up, the Jews, as well as other minority groups, suffered considerable hardships from the centralized government authority which controlled all synagogues, the Jewish hospital, and other communal institutions. Adato introduced a bill providing for reorganization of the existing system of jurisdiction over the Jewish community in Turkey; local committees elected by the Jews would be responsible for the administration of all communal matters.[24] The Parliament passed the Adato bill in June 1949, thus removing important obstacles in the path of the development of the Jewish communities.[25] In January 1950, the Chief Rabbinate announced the appointment of eighteen members (approved by the Turkish authorities) to the General Assembly of the Istanbul Jewish Community, thus bringing up to its statutory strength this eighty-member body composed of sixty lay and twenty religious members[26]

Equality and Discrimination. There was no lack of attempts to stir up anti-Jewish agitation in Turkey, but they were consistently frustrated by strong action on the part of the Government.

After the death of Kemal Pasha in November 1938, there was some apprehension that reactionary elements might attempt to create a Jewish problem in Turkey after the German model. The new President, Ismet Inönü, solemnly declared, however, that "a Jewish problem had never existed in the Turkish Republic: the Jews are equal with all other citizens; the spirit of justice and tolerance—which is characteristic of the Turkish nation—as well as its ideas of morality and humanity, make it impossible for Turkey to harbor anti-Semitism." This credo was repeated eight years later, in March 1947, by Turkish

Premier Racep Peker, who, addressing students of Istanbul University, declared that "anti-Semitism is the shame of the twentieth century. The Turkish people will have nothing to do with it." Turkish nationalism, the Premier explained, is "based on tradition and love of family and country; it repudiates any religious or racial prejudice. The Christians in Turkey possess the same rights as their Moslem brethren. The same applies to the Jews.[27]

Notwithstanding these solemn declarations, the Turkish Republic, which was conceived by Kemal Ataturk as a modern secular state, where all citizens would enjoy equal rights regardless of race and creed, was hardly living up to this lofty concept. The Jews, like other minorities, have no share in political life. They are not admitted into the People's Party, which was till the end of 1945 the sole recognized party in Turkey. There is hardly a Jew in the civil service or in the numerous economic institutions established by the state (banks, industrial enterprises, etc.). When the Government acquired the electric corporation of Istanbul from its Belgian owners, it removed all the Jewish employees with the exception of one or two indispensable experts. Jews were excluded from the Turkish Chamber of Commerce and dismissed from the transportation and communication agencies. In the army, discrimination against members of minority groups became an invariable rule. "Although Christian and Jewish citizens must perform the same term of service as others, they are assigned to menial tasks; even young men of the greatest ability failed to pass the examinations for advancement into the officers' training school, if they were not of the Faith," says Donald E. Webster. Conscripted Jews had to serve in labor battalions without arms.[28]

Throughout the first years of World War II, Turkish foreign policy was vacillating and ambiguous. Having concluded a treaty of alliance with Great Britain and France (October 19, 1939), the Turkish Government refused to participate in the war on the side of the Western democracies; and after the German conquest of Yugoslavia and Greece, it concluded a friendship pact with Nazi Germany on June 18, 1941.

The internal policies of the Government followed the vicis-

situdes of its foreign policy. In 1940 and during the first half
of 1941, anti-Jewish propaganda and incitement were energetically suppressed, while in the summer of 1941, much greater
tolerance toward Nazi activities was shown.

Under Nazi influence, Turkish authorities in May 1942 dismissed seventeen Jewish employees of the Ankara main office
of the official Anatolian Telegraphic Agency and six employees
of this agency's Istanbul branch, accusing them of "distributing
news furthering a policy incompatible with Turkey's neutrality." Reporting this move, the *Essener Nationalzeitung* triumphantly announced that "shortly even in the ministries all
Jews will be dismissed," and that already now, many ministries
have decreed that "Jews only exceptionally may be appointed by
the state." Turkish public opinion began to become increasingly "Jew-conscious," and the Nazi *Voelkischer Beobachter*
of June 11, 1943, noted with satisfaction that "everyone who
reads the Turkish press systematically can notice lately that
discussion of the Jewish question increases in scope and liveli-
ness."

Turkey's Role in the Rescue of Nazi Victims. Notwithstanding the increasing anti-Jewish trend of its policy, Turkey played
a considerable and commendable role in the rescue of European Jewry from Nazi extermination and in the maintenance of
at least a limited stream of Jewish immigration into Palestine.

When Italy entered the war on the side of Germany in June
1940, both Trieste and the Greek ports were closed to Jewish
refugees from the European countries. The only remaining
avenue of escape to Palestine was overland, via the Balkans and
Turkey. After long negotiations, the Turkish Government, early
in 1941, agreed to facilitate the transit of Jewish refugees to
Palestine. An official order was published on February 12, 1941,
empowering Turkish consulates to grant transit visas to Jews of
foreign nationality suffering persecution in their countries of
origin. Applicants for such Turkish transit visas had to produce entry visas to the country in which they wished to settle,
as well as transit visas through the territory they intended to
cross after leaving Turkey; they also had to be in possession of
travel tickets to a point beyond the Turkish frontier.

All refugees who had received immigration certificates in their own countries were thus able to pass through Turkey and to reach Palestine. Up to June 1941, 4,401 refugees had made use of this opportunity, mainly from Rumania (1,668), Lithuania (1,121), Hungary (518), Yugoslavia (404), Bulgaria (250), etc. In 1942, a total of 1,090 reached Palestine via Turkey. Early in 1943, the first group of the "Youth Aliyah" from Rumania and Hungary arrived in Palestine via Istanbul. In the spring of 1943, when the Sofia Government suddenly prohibited the exit or transit of Jewish refugees through Bulgarian territory, the Turkish consuls in Bucharest, Budapest and Sofia were instructed to grant individual visas at a rate of nine per week (for families) in each country. Until the end of 1943, 1,-128 such refugees passed through Turkey. The total for 1940–1945 was 18,783.

The summary of immigration through Turkey, says the Report of the Executive of the Jewish Agency for Palestine, submitted to the 22nd Zionist Congress at Basle in December 1946, presents us with a very small figure when compared with the magnitude of the disaster that had befallen the Jews of the Diaspora. Special importance is, however, attached to this immigration, since it was a source of hope and encouragement to the oppressed masses in the Diaspora, to whom Palestine was the only goal and a ray of light in the darkness of their lives. . . . The Turkish Government showed great humanity in allowing the transit of immigrants through its territory at a time when all other routes were closed to Jewish refugees, and made an important contribution to the rescue of thousands of Jews from extermination and their immigration to Palestine.[29]

Varlık Scourge. The bulk of Turkish Jewry is engaged in commerce. During the Ottoman Empire, Jewish business and industrial undertakings were among the most important of their kind, and Jewish merchants played a leading part in Turkey's trade relations with foreign countries. Other professions followed by Turkish Jews were medicine, engineering and law; many Jews were employed also as sailors, boatmen, porters, and fishermen.

In the modern Turkish Republic, the economic position of the Jewish population deteriorated considerably. Kemal Pasha was determined to transform Turkey into an industrial country. He saw the only way to implement this ambitious scheme in state socialism, in developing and running public utilities and most of the key industries by the state out of public funds and along nationalist lines. Barbara Ward formulated the dilemma that faced Ataturk as follows: "The only capitalists were foreign capitalists. The only merchants were foreigners, or local Greeks, Armenians and Jews. There was no private Turkish capital. There could thus be no private Turkish capitalist economy. Either the state built industry, or left it to the foreigners—a solution excluded by the political revolution—or there was no industry."[30] The state-ruled economy deliberately favored the young ethnic-Turkish bourgeoisie at the expense of the traditional minority businessmen. Turkish competition in business was constantly increasing, Donald E. Webster, a keen student of Turkey's realities, wrote in 1939:[31]

During the centuries while the business of the Turks was politics and the business of the Jews was business, there was no conflict. Now that the Turks are becoming commercially conscious and ambitious, a degree of tension has developed, a minority problem in the sociological sense—for while the Jews are not a tenth of the population in the principal commercial centres, their number exceeds 10 per cent of the business population. In the summer of 1934, the strain reached a point at which a hundred Jews fled from Edirne [Adrianople] to Istanbul.

In the sphere of private business no less than in state-controlled enterprise, the minorities began to encounter ever increasing difficulties. The semi-official trade associations (*Birliks*), which issue import and export licenses and control prices, discriminated, though not overtly, against all non-Moslems. Contracts for public works were given mainly to Moslem firms.

This antiminorities economic policy reached its peak in 1942. On November 11, 1942, the Turkish Grand National Assembly passed a "Law Concerning the Tax on Wealth" (*Varlĭk Vergisi*) imposing on all residents of Turkey, citizens and non-citizens alike, a heavy capital levy on wealth and excess profits.[32] The minimum assessment was set at 500 Turkish pounds ($275), a sum staggeringly beyond the capacity of most peo-

ple to pay.[33] The sum total of the levy imposed amounted to
456 million Turkish pounds, an exorbitant amount if we take
into consideration the fact that in the fiscal year 1942–1943 actual state receipts amounted to 394.33 million Turkish pounds,
and that total currency in circulation did not exceed 732 million Turkish pounds on June 30, 1943.[34] Of the 456 million
Turkish pounds which had to be raised by the way of Varlik,
the 260,000 members of the minority groups (of whom only
some one-third were breadwinners) were assessed 280 million
pounds (61.4 per cent), while the 17 million Moslem Turks
were assessed 176 million pounds.[35]

Speaking before the Congress of the governmental People's
Party, the Turkish Prime Minister, Shukru Saracoglu, charac-
terized as "low slander" allegations to the effect that the Government imposed the Varlik "in order to destroy the minorities."
The real intentions of the Turkish Government were, however,
disclosed in correspondence from Ankara published on January
18, 1943, in the well-informed German newspaper *Der Neue
Tag* in Prague. The correspondent flatly stated that the levy
imposed by the Varlik law "does not represent a purely financial
measure, but in addition is of political importance. . . . A
glance at the list of assessments on the property tax shows that
the minorities have been much more affected than the Turkish
national elements within the Turkish economic body. Whereas
the Turkish taxpayer, although affected rather heavily, is still
taxed according to his ability to pay, the taxation committees
assessing Jewish, Armenian and Greek property took a much
stronger and firmer hold of it and imposed upon such property
a tax beyond the capacity of payment of the individual involved,
which means total economic liquidation."

The anti-Jewish character of the Varlik has been particularly
stressed in the following revealing report: "The fact that particular rigor is being exercised not only against the Armenian and
Greek business classes, but also against the Jewish population
in all cities, especially in Istanbul, shows that the Turkish Government has considered in its measures the Jewish problem and
the question of the Jewish influence upon national economy and
trade, without saying so expressly. It is a tendency which cannot

be misunderstood."[36] This tendency found its expression also in the application of the *Varlĭk*. John Gunther reported that Jewish stenographers who had never owned 100 Turkish pounds in their lives were assessed 5,000 pounds; in Istanbul, twenty Turkish shipping firms had to pay 465,000 Turkish pounds, while the single Jewish shipping firm was assessed 1,000,000 pounds.[37]

The impact of this obviously antiminorities, and in particular anti-Jewish, measure on the Jewish economic position was rightly predicted by *Der Neue Tag:*"As matters develop it will be seen that in wide trade groups, especially in the import trade, which is almost without exception in the hands of the Jewish and Armenian population, important shiftings will take place in the course of the property tax collection in favor of the Turkish national elements. . . . All these measures were doubtlessly aimed at discrimination and at the elimination of undesirable elements in Turkish economic life, in addition to financial aims."

Articles 12 and 13 of the Law of November 11, 1942, contained special provisions for penalty for noncompliance with the tax decisions by the taxation boards. These provisions included confiscation of merchandise, of movable property and real estate, and forced labor.[38] At the beginning, 86,000 people were sentenced to forced labor in the mines and on the roads in East Anatolia, reported John Gunther, "and for many elderly Greeks and Jews it was the direct equivalent of a death sentence."[39] Later the number was, according to the *New International Yearbook* (p. 681), reduced to 30,000, "almost all of them members of the minorities." The Ankara correspondent of the *Neues Wiener Tageblatt* (July 2, 1943) meaningfully stressed "the high percentage of Jews among the deportees to East Anatolia," and the *Donau Zeitung* (January 26, 1943) said that "a number of individuals, mostly Jews, who wanted to evade the tax by flight, were arrested while trying to pass the border."

The discriminatory tendency and practice of the *Varlĭk* law and the forced-labor penalty aroused a vigorous protest from the Greek Government and brought indirect but insistent protestations from the British and U.S. governments. At the end of January 1943, the Turkish authorities announced that those taxpayers who paid at least 20 per cent in cash and procured a credit with a Turkish bank for the balance of the amount, would be spared deportation to forced labor camps.[40] By August 1943, about 300 million Turkish pounds had already been collected.[41] On December 2, 1943, just before President Inönü left Ankara for his meeting with President Roosevelt and Prime Minister Churchill at Cairo, a decree was issued ordering the release from forced labor camps those who had paid part of the amount assessed against them. The U.S. Ambassador, Laurence Steinhardt, was officially informed that the prisoners were to be freed.[42] In March 1944, the Varlĭk law itself was abrogated and all the inmates of the labor camp were released. But none of the confiscated property was returned. The suggestion that it should be returned, in part or in full, in the form of Turkish treasury bonds, redeemable over a reasonably long period of time at a low interest rate, was not followed up.

Turkish Jewry never recovered from the crippling effects of the Varlĭk. Many Jewish businesses passed into the hands of Moslems or the state. A particularly distressing situation developed in Istanbul, which had to pay the lion's share of the 300 million Turkish pounds collected through the Varlĭk levy. In 1944 and 1945, the Turkish Jews were unable to support their communal institutions and free-loan agency, and funds from American Jewry helped to maintain them. Some 7,000 of the 50,000 Istanbul Jews were dependent on Jewish community relief, to which a considerable part was contributed by the American Joint Distribution Committee.[43] Of the nearly 16,000 Jewish families living in the country, only about 6,000 were estimated to be in a satisfactory economic position.[44]

New Regime. At the end of 1945, in the wake of democracy's military triumph, democratic trends began slowly to gather momentum in Turkey's internal policy. Successive Ankara cabinets since 1945 have permitted the creation of an opposition Democratic Party, have accorded increasing freedom in elections and have tolerated wider and stronger parliamentary criticism. Certain police powers have been abolished and censorship has been relaxed.

The new tendency also found its expression in some improvement of the position of Turkey's minorities. Anti-Jewish propaganda in the state-controlled press abated considerably. For the first time in the history of the Turkish Republic, two young Jews were admitted to the military academy (*Harbiye*), while several Jewish clerks were engaged by the state banks.

In May 1950, in the wake of the first truly free election campaign ever permitted by the Government, the opposition Democratic Party scored a decisive victory. The Jews, most of whom supported the party in the elections, felt certain that the new regime would fully implement the principle of equality for all citizens and also would give them the opportunity of developing Jewish communal life. The Minister of the Interior, R. Nasuhoglu, emphasizing the complete equality of all citizens, instructed all mayors and governors by circular letter to "promote mutual respect and confidence" among the various sectors of the population.[45] The new Government adopted a more favorable attitude toward the religious life of the country, rejecting the anti-religious bias of the strictly secular Kemalist nationalism.

These symptoms of relaxation in the regime's attitude toward the minorities have, however, not eliminated the apprehensions of non-Turkish ethnic groups. In a study, *The United States and Turkey and Iran* (Cambridge, 1951), Lewis V. Thomas and Richard M. Frey flatly state (p. 113) that "even in the best seasons under the Republic, the minorities were still the object of continuing discrimination, and they are so in fact today." The Cairo *Egyptian Gazette* wrote on January 4, 1946: "Reports by Greeks, Armenians and Jews all agree in one respect. These minorities prefer emigration to economic ruin or social humiliation as outcasts." In fact, out of the 57,599 Armenians in Turkey, some 30,000 have registered for repatriation to Soviet Armenia, notwithstanding administrative pressure on the part of the Turkish authorities. Among the Jews, this feeling found its expression in a growing tendency toward emigration.

. . . *and Emigration.* Under "normal circumstances" Turkish Jewry was a modest but steady contributor to the immigration movement into Palestine. During the period of British rule

(1919–1947), 1.8 per cent of all immigrants came from Turkey.[46] During the war years the demand for immigration permits
to Palestine grew steadily. The number of immigrants from
Turkey, legal and illegal alike, was 14 in 1939, and 4,697 in
1940–1945. However, from 1945 onward, when all attention had
to be given to the resettlement of the remnants of Jewry who
had escaped annihilation in the liberated countries of Europe,
immigration certificates could no longer be allocated to Turkey.
In 1945, only 227 Turkish Jews arrived in Palestine; in January–
September, 1946, a mere 35. The year 1947 was an "empty"
year. A total of 4,747 was absorbed by Palestine during the
period January 1939 to September 1946.[47]

The establishment of the State of Israel in May 1948 inaugurated a new era in the Jewish emigration from Turkey. In
the beginning the Turkish Government unequivocally sided
with the Arab states and discouraged its Jewish citizens from
leaving for Palestine. Only 500 exit visas have been issued during
the five-month period, May–October. This early anti-emigration
policy was reversed on October 17, 1948. The political section
of the Istanbul police was instructed to put no obstacles in the
way of Turkish Jews wanting to go to Israel. During the following three days, October 17–20, close to 2,000 Jews received authorization to leave for Israel. Prospective emigrants in line in
front of the Istanbul police building cheerfully told *The New
York Times* correspondent that they were receiving "all kinds of
speedy facilities from the Turkish officials."[48] This precipitated
a mass emigration movement among the Jewish population.
Over 6,000 Jews applied for passports, and it was expected that
10,000 of the 80,000 Jews living in Turkey would move to Israel.[49] In the course of the first two weeks following October 17,
approximately 2,500 Jews were reported to have sailed for Israel. Of these, 700 were members of the Izmir community, the
largest Jewish community outside of Istanbul. "Very few young
Jews now remain in Istanbul," the correspondent of the London
Jewish Chronicle reported in December 1948. The effect of
this mass emigration was felt particularly in smaller Jewish communities with a membership between 500 and 1,000.[50] According to Lewis V. Thomas and Richard N. Frey, "Those who have

gone represented no overwhelming loss in the Turkish point of view. By and large they were the very poorest urban class from Istanbul and from Izmir."

On November 1, 1948, the Turkish policy on Jewish emigration again underwent a sharp reversal. The political section of the Istanbul police was instructed to grant no further exit visas for Israel and to consider void all passports previously issued to Jews of Turkish nationality wanting to emigrate to Israel. Exit visas which were being issued were marked "valid for all countries but Palestine."[51] It was generally understood that the new turn of Turkey's policy originated with the pressure put on the Turkish Government by representatives of the Arab League.* The Minister of the Interior announced that Jewish emigration was illegal and that those who left for Israel would not be permitted to return. The Turkish press maintained that, under the law, Turkish citizens may not leave for countries "where the present situation is confused." The Ankara radio, reporting that over 500 young Turkish Jews queued up to apply for visas to go to Israel, quoted a "legal opinion" to the effect that the Jewish population was being misled by propaganda and that those who were "running after ambitious and greedy interests would soon regret their decision." Wild accusations were launched in the papers against several leaders of Turkish Jewry who allegedly were responsible for the growth of the emigration movement. It was asserted for instance that Dayan Raphael Saban, President of the *Beth Din* (Jewish religious court) "received secret instructions from Italian Communists and Zionists requesting that Turkish Jews should emigrate."[52]

This new course of the Turkish policy caused consternation among the thousands of Turkish Jews preparing to emigrate. Officially, only Jews of military age were forbidden to leave the country, but those of other ages were also practically debarred by various difficulties placed in their way. The result was that "6,000 Turkish Jews are almost literally sitting on their suitcases, ready packed, waiting to take a ship for Israel," reported

* Lewis V. Thomas and Richard N. Frey believe that, while doing so and thus "giving the Arabs technical satisfaction," the Turkish Government was "confident that this would not deter the Israeli authorities from admitting [Jewish] immigrants." (*The United States and Turkey and Iran*, p. 132.)

the Istanbul correspondent of the Johannesburg *Jewish Herald* in December 1948. "The money and property which they had hoped to take with them has been placed under a ban so that they are now left without means. In most cases the waiting emigrants are women and children, the fathers or young sons had left soon after the establishment of the State of Israel."

Obstacles. Because of the ban on direct emigration to Israel, many Jews were compelled to proceed to ports in Italy and France to await transportation. During the month of November, more than 800 Jews left for ports in France and Italy, hoping to proceed from there to Israel. During the same month, more than 1,000 Turkish Jews arrived in Haifa, most of whom left before Turkey banned emigration to Israel, while others traveled via Italy and France. Those who were obliged to choose the detour were notified by the Turkish authorities that they would lose their Turkish nationality automatically if they proceeded to Israel. "But," reported *The New York Times* correspondent, "that apparently had been no deterrent." During the first week of December, about 600 Jews left Turkey. A total of 7,000 emigrated to Israel in 1948.[53]

Widening its anti-emigration stand, the Turkish Government indicated in December 1948 that no Turkish Jew would be permitted to leave the country for any point in Europe if he intended eventually to go to Israel. In certain localities, local authorities had refused to issue exit permits even for Western Europe, and in Adrianople 100 Jewish applicants had sent a strong protest to the Minister of the Interior against the denial of permits to them. New governmental regulations published early in January 1949 had imposed further restrictions on would-be emigrants: Before leaving the country, prospective emigrants had first to obtain visas from the French or Italian consulates. Since neither of these consulates would issue such visas, the emigration movement had come to a standstill. Some 4,000 Jews who were scheduled to leave on the eve of the promulgation of the new regulations were stranded. The situation of some 1,500 Jews from the interior who came to Istanbul to await transport to overseas countries became increasingly precarious. The majority of them had no homes in which to stay and no jobs. Those who were completely destitute had to be assisted by the Istanbul Jewish Community.[54] Seven Turkish Jews, attempting to sail for Israel in spite of governmental restrictions, were arrested by coast guardsmen when their small Haifa-bound vessel was searched in the Dardanelles. They admitted that they intended emigrating "illegally" because the authorities refused to issue exit permits for Israel. A Spanish Jew, Abram Mayer, who had lived in Istanbul for many years, was arrested on his return from Israel under the accusation of "encouraging Turkish Jews to emigrate to Israel."[55]

In surprising contradiction to this anti-emigration practice, Nejmeddin Sadak, Foreign Minister of Turkey, declared in mid-February 1949 that there was no ban on the emigration of Jews from his country to Israel: "Jews, in common with all other Turkish citizens, are free to leave Turkey whenever they wish, and no difficulties are put in the way of their obtaining exit permits"; they are subject to the same laws governing foreign exchange (as regards taking their property or money out of the country) as are other Turkish citizens.[56]

This new turn of governmental emigration policy has precipitated an unprecedented emigration movement. During the month of March a record number of 5,700 Jewish emigrants left Turkey for Israel; 1,500 of them embarked at Izmir, while the remainder sailed from Istanbul. During the month of April, some 3,500 Turkish Jews emigrated to Israel; 2,600 embarked in Istanbul and the remainder in Izmir. A total of 32,985 Turkish Jews landed in Israel from May 15, 1948 to December 31, 1950.[57]

Character and Motivation. While Jewish exodus from other countries had been organized by the Jewish Agency and largely subsidized by the American Joint Distribution Committee, the emigration of Turkish Jews to Israel was in the main a spontaneous and self-supporting movement. Emigrants from Turkey have been leaving the country on independently chartered boats, big and small, often without any consideration of their seaworthiness and the reliability of their owners and captains.

The most characteristic feature of this mass movement is that it was not motivated by direct persecution or discrimination. Turkish Jews enjoy full legal equality and there is no militant government-sponsored anti-Semitism. In response to queries in the press and elsewhere, Henry Soriano, president of the Jewish Community of Istanbul, averred that economic conditions were chiefly responsible for the great migration. Turkish Jewry never completely recovered from the crippling effects of the *Varlïk*, and thousands were leaving the country in the hope of finding better conditions in Israel. Many were emigrating with a view to joining their relatives there. Some—particularly among the intelligentsia—did so because they had discovered that they "don't belong." Geoffry Lewis reports an animated discussion with a young Jewish engineer who had been educated in France:[58]

"I am going because, although I have lived here most of my life, and my family has been here for nearly five hundred years, I don't feel at home here. It's not that we're illtreated, it's just that I can't talk to a Turk on equal terms: it's his country, not mine, and he won't let me forget it." The suggestion that he, too, was a Turk was greeted first with incomprehension and then with amusement. "I've met Jews in France who regarded themselves as 'Frenchmen of the Jewish faith.' Such a thing isn't possible here. If you are a Jew, how can you be a Turk?"

Again, many—particularly among the youth—were actuated by an almost Messianic longing for full and normal national existence, by an ardent wish to contribute to the building of the State of Israel.

The 1948–1949 migration from Turkey was a spontaneous movement without planning or guidance. There was no grading and selection as to the suitability of the immigrants to the conditions in Israel. As a result, small groups, totaling 1,312, returned to Istanbul in 1949 (412) and 1950 (900).[59] They were mostly old, middle-class family men who were unable, and sometimes unwilling, to adapt themselves to difficult conditions of resettlement in Israel. A number of Turkish newspapers have, in connection with this, launched a campaign to prove that life in Israel is "intolerable" because of the economic difficulties which the country is passing through, and claimed that Turkish Jews who settled in Israel were living under "miserable conditions."

Partly because of this return movement and partly because of some stabilization of domestic conditions, immigration to Israel slackened. In 1951, a total of 1,228 immigrants, a monthly average of some 100, left Turkey; 271 departed to Israel in 1952, and 534 in 1953–1955. Up to the end of 1956, the grand total of immigration to Israel reached 37,538 (some 3,000 left for other countries). A total of 4,811 re-emigrated during the eleven-year period 1948–1959.[60]

In September 1955, the Greek-Turkish dispute over Cyprus provoked violent anti-Greek demonstrations in the major Turkish cities. The riots soon turned into pogroms on Greek and Jewish property in Izmir and Ankara. Jewish losses were estimated at half a billion Turkish lire, or $70 million. In the town of Canakkale in the Dardanelles an inscription appeared on a tree in the main street, warning the Jews to leave Turkey because "the Turks do not want them any more," and threatening them with a massacre if they did not heed the warning. There were persistent rumors that this was not an isolated incident.[61] The Istanbul correspondent of the *Jewish Chronicle* reported that, in the wake of this event, "a growing number of Jews have this week applied to the Israeli Consulate here about the prospects of settling in the Jewish State."[62]

The Impact of Emigration. As a result of emigration to Israel, Turkey's Jewish population decreased from 76,975 in 1945, to 49,196 in 1950 and to about 40,000 in 1958, i.e., by almost 50 per cent. Particularly affected were the Jewish communities in Asiatic Turkey. Of a total of 18,462 Jews in this part of the Turkish Republic, only 6,756 remained in 1950. The Jewish community of Izmir, which counted 15,000 in 1948, was reduced to 4,500 in 1950. Of Edirna's 2,750, 1,300 remained.[63] The community of Bursa lost 500 of its 1,000 Jews; the community of Tshurlu was reduced from 1,200 to 80; that of Intab from 420 to 240. The Kurdistan Jewish communities of Diarbekir (390 Jews) and Marash (600), the most ancient in Turkey, have practically ceased to exist, with 54 and 36 members left, respectively, as the result of wholesale emigration to Israel.

European Turkey was considerably less affected by the emigration: of the 64,200 Jews who lived there in 1948, 42,440 remained in 1950.[64] Of Istanbul's 55,000 Jews, some 35,000 remained in 1950 and only 32,946 in 1958.[65]

The emigration of nearly one-half of Turkey's Jewry has strongly influenced its economic and social structure. The overwhelming majority of the emigrants came from the poorest strata of the population—the unemployed, minor clerks in private business, peddlers, porters, etc. Their departure resulted in the raising of the economic level of the present-day Jewish population of the country. Noticeable also is a growth of the intellectual class. There are now among Turkish Jews eminent writers and poets, historians, professors, doctors, engineers and jurists.[66] On the other hand, cultural assimilation is making spectacular progress. While the 1945 census showed that 51,019 of the 76,965 Turkish Jews had declared Ladino as their mother tongue, only 29,000 did so in the 1955 census.[67] Of the three Jewish periodicals published in Istanbul, two used Ladino (the third appeared in French), but they were no longer printed in the Rashi characters such as the Sephardim have always used, but in Latin letters, adapted in the same way as modern Turkish. The Istanbul community maintains four elementary schools and one secondary school. However, only 2,000 Jewish children receive their education in the Jewish schools.[68]

9

Iran: Community in Transition

Twenty-Five Centuries of Recorded History. The Jews have
been a permanent element in the history of Iran (Persia) since
the time of their captivity. The Jews of Persian Azerbaijan still
speak Aramaic and believe that they had come there before the
destruction of the Second Temple, and that they stem from the
ten lost tribes of Israel.

In 641, Persia was conquered by the Arabs, and Islam became
the dominant faith instead of the Zoroastrian religion of old.
The Arab domination continued for about 400 years, till 1037,
when the Seldjuk Turks became the masters of the country. In
1258, when the Turks were driven out by the Mongol Il-Khan
rulers, Islam lost its dominant position and became just one
religion among others. In the thirteenth and fourteenth centuries, the non-Moslems, Jews and Christians alike, enjoyed the
greatest political and religious freedom ever experienced in this
country before or after. The Jews became prominent in public
and cultural life. In 1502, all the alternating foreign rulers were
substituted by a native Persian dynasty, the Safavids (1502–
1736) who have made Shi'ism the state religion.

Under all these varying regimes, Jewish life in Persia continued uninterruptedly for no less than twenty-five centuries.
"Unclean." Under Shi'ite domination, the position of Iranian
Jewry has been that of an inferior and often persecuted religious
minority. The attitude of the dominant Shi'ite Mohammedanism toward all "nonbelievers" (Christians, Jews, etc.) is based
on the concept that they were ritually unclean (*padges*), and
must therefore be distinguished by differences in costume,

architecture of houses, and in many other more cruel and humiliating ways.[1] T. Goldzicher, one of the most authoritative
students of Islam, testified that throughout the nineteenth century the charge of ritual uncleanliness continued to dominate
the attitude toward the Jews and other "infidels."[2] J. Perkins,
who toured Persia about the middle of the nineteenth century,
wrote in 1851 in the *Journal of the American Oriental Society*
that "the hostility cherished by Mohammedans toward the Jews
is inconceivably more bitter than their hatred for Christians."[3]
Ten years later, M. Peterman confirmed that "Jews live in Persia
under dire oppression; they are the most despised of all peoples
and are subjected to constant maltreatment."[4] Elgin Groseclose, author of a recent study on Iran (1947) similarly stresses
that "the Jews have in general suffered greater disabilities than
the Christians."[5]

The intolerant policy inaugurated by the Safavids was strin-
gently continued by the Kadjar dynasty (1795–1925). In his
two-volume study, *Persia and the Persian Question*, published
in 1892, G. N. Curzon described the Jewish situation in Iran
as follows: "Usually compelled to live apart in a ghetto, or
separate quarter of the towns, they [the Jews] have from time
immemorial suffered from disabilities of occupation, dress and
habits which have marked them as social pariahs from their fellow creatures. . . . In Isfahan they are not permitted to wear
a *kolak*, or Persian headdress, to have shops in the bazaar, to
build the walls of their houses as high as a Moslem neighbors, or
to ride in the streets. . . ."[6] "In the old days," reports Groseclose, "a Jew could not go in the streets in wet weather lest he
contaminate one of the faithful."[7] As late as 1894, the Jews of
Persia had to wear a patch on their clothes to signify their
origin.[8]

Due to the persecution of their Moslem neighbors, many
once flourishing Jewish communities entirely disappeared.
Maragh, for example, ceased to be the seat of a Jewish community around 1800, when the Jews were driven out on account
of a blood libel. For similar reasons, Tabris, where over fifty
Jewish families are supposed to have lived, became *judenrein*
toward the end of the eighteenth century.[9]

Marranos and Converts. In some localities persecution took the form of forced conversions. Rabbi David D'Beth Hillel wrote that in Shira "a number of Jews turned Mohammedan owing to great oppression from the Mohammedans."[10] M. Peterman related that because of constant maltreatment "thousands of them [Jews] have renounced their faith . . . the entire Jewish population of Lar and Meshed have become converted to Islam."[11]

The case of Meshed is particularly striking. The tolerant Sunni ruler Nadir Shah (1736–1747) transferred a number of Jews from Kaswin to this Shi'ite holy city, which harbors the tomb of one of the greatest Persian leaders and saints, Imam Rizah. The existence of this small Jewish community among a fanatical Moslem population never was an easy one. But in 1839 their very lives were threatened by the incensed mob, and in order to escape certain death they embraced Islam. Their descendants live in Meshed under the name of *Jadid al-Islam* (New to Islam) and form the most interesting Jewish community of Iran.[12]

The forcibly converted Jews of Meshed are, however, not the only loss Iranian Jewry suffered from the Islam. A fair proportion of the Moslem population of the town of Shiraz is also believed to be of Jewish origin. The American missionary, Henry A. Stern, who visited Shiraz in 1849, asserted that all the silk merchants of that town's bazaar were Jews forcibly converted to Islam, who had become thoroughly Moslemized and had lost any connection with Judaism. In several other Iranian towns, where no Jews are left today, the peculiar dress of the local population still strongly indicates their Jewish origin.

Substantial inroads into the ranks of the Iranian Jewish community were also made by Christian missionaries and by the powerful Bahai movement.

Conversions to Protestantism started some seventy years ago. English and American missionaries took advantage of the plight of the impoverished and persecuted Jewish communities in Teheran, Isfahan and Hamadan to induce about five hundred Jews to embrace Protestantism. Some of the converts did so in

exchange for a specific sum of money or the promise of a job
in a foreign company; others were induced by the prospect of
protection and help on the part of the British or American Le-
gation. The missionaries tried to make it easier for the Jews to
abandon their creed by presenting Protestantism as a "development of Judaism." Their task was considerably facilitated by
the almost complete lack of organization and spiritual leadership within the Jewish communities. Change of faith did not
usually prejudice private relations with one's family, and converts fully preserved their connections with their former coreligionists.

With the establishment of the Alliance schools and the subsequent increase of Jewish consciousness, the conversions to
Christianity practically stopped. The historian of the Protestant mission in the Near East sadly acknowledges that "among
Jews the fond hopes of the early days have not been fulfilled.
. . . The close connection of the Jews with the Jewish world
outside Persia and the munificent donations of the French Alliance Israélite make the Jews less accessible to missionary influences."[13] According to local Jewish evidence, almost all the
converts returned to Judaism. The few who did not, became
the most militant members of the small Christian community
in Iran.[14]

Conversion to Bahaism proved to be of more serious and last-
ing nature. The liberal, humanizing tendency of the Bahai sect,
an offspring of Babism, and its spiritual dynamism attracted a
considerable number of Jewish souls who were deeply disatis-
fied by the lack of religious guidance in many Jewish communities. Bahai missionaries successfully argued that Bahaism was
but "pure Judaism, which had been distorted by the rabbinical
reforms." They stood for peaceful relations among the various
faiths, abolished the principle of the uncleanliness of "nonbelievers" and freed them from their old stigma. It is this aspect
of Bahaism which mainly accounts for the great influence exercised by the movement upon the Jews. Besides, there also
were considerable advantages of a practical nature that contributed to the success of the Bahai propaganda. The first (non-
Jewish) converts to Bahaism were rich and influential people

who were ready to help poor Jewish proselytes, and generously. The fact that the Bahai were officially registered as Moslems also was a strong inducement to join the sect. Abdul Bahai, an outstanding Bahai leader, claimed that "the day is not far off when there will be not a Jew in Persia who has not become a Bahai."[15] According to Curson, this claim is highly exaggerated: the British scholar estimates that not more than 150 Jews in Teheran, 100 in Hamadan, 50 in Kashan, and 75 per cent of the Jewish population in Gulpayyan (variously estimated at 120 to 900) had formally joined the movement (Wilson counted only 59 Jewish Bahais in Hamadan).[16] Jewish sources, however, offer considerably higher figures of converts to Bahaism. The Teheran Committee of the World Jewish Congress reported that about 5,000 Jews, mostly in Hamadan, embraced the Bahai creed. Many have in the meantime returned to Judaism, but some 2,000 to 3,000 remained faithful to their new creed and are known as fervent adherents of this sect, which is spread over forty countries in the East and in more than five hundred communities in Iran alone. Unlike converts to Christianity or Mohammedanism, the Bahai converts do not take part in Jewish activities and keep aloof from their former coreligionists.[17]

Numbers. Estimates of the number of Jews in Iran vary greatly. The Alliance Israélite sources spoke of 40,000 Jews in 1873 and of 49,500 in 1882.[18] In 1904, Greenfield put their number as low as 32,000,[19] while E. Sikes in a study published in 1911 spoke of 136,000 Persian Jews.[20] As late as 1942, Walter J. Fischel, an authority on Oriental Jewry, stated in the *Universal Jewish Encyclopedia* that there were not more than 50,000 Jews in Iran.[21] The same figure was accepted by the Institute on Overseas Studies of the Committee of Jewish Federations and Welfare Funds in 1948.[22] The *Palestine Year Book* for 5708 (September 1946–September 1947) more than doubled this figure, estimating the number of Jews in Iran at 115,000 in 1939 and at 120,000 in 1945.[23] More detailed data worked out over a period of four years by the Jewish community of Teheran for purposes of social and relief work, and published in the spring of 1950 by S. Landshut in a survey of the Jewish communities in the Moslem countries of the Middle East, put the number of Jews in Iran at between 88,000 and 100,000.[24]

Legal Equality. In 1906, Persia became a constitutional monarchy. The Jews obtained an equal legal status with the Moslems, and access to all professions. But a turn for the better in the history of Iranian Jewry began earlier, with the establishment of modern schools by the Alliance Israélite Universelle. The first Alliance school was founded in Teheran in 1898, and was followed by others at Hamadan (1900), Isfahan (1901), Shiraz and Senhe (1903), Kermanshah (1904), etc. These schools have contributed greatly to the cultural development of Persian Jewry, imparting a knowledge of European languages, and raising the general educational standard of the younger generation. But the constructive role played by the Alliance schools by far exceeded purely educational standards. A report submitted on February 18, 1947, to the World Jewish Congress by its Teheran Committee rightly stressed that, since the very inception of the Alliance schools, their directors were in every town "to some extent Jewish consuls protecting their coreligionists," The director and the teachers of every Alliance school were highly respected by the local Jewish population, with whom they were in daily contact and who sought their advice and help on every occasion.

Since the Alliance was on good terms with the French, British and Russian legations and consulates, its representatives were in a position to render valuable practical services to the Iranian Jews. Jewish merchants recommended by the Alliance have established far-reaching business relations with European firms, and a number of Jewish business and transport enterprises have been thus created or developed in Iran. Young men with a diploma from Alliance schools have found employment in Jewish trade firms whose Moslem employees have gradually been replaced by Jews. Upon the recommendation of the Alliance, a number of young Jews who have learned French—and some who have learned English—better than the Moslems, have, prior to the upsurge of the Nazi influence in 1936, obtained positions with the government. A correspondent of the New York *Day-Jewish Journal*, who visited Iran in 1951, testified that "were it

not for the Alliance Israélite Universelle, the last three generations of Jews in Persia would have been completely covered with
the spiritually blinding and crippling dust that has shrouded the
vast masses. . . . If the mass of ghetto Jews in Persia use a knife
and fork, know the benefits of soap, can read and speak a bit of
Hebrew, a good deal more French and their own native tongue
—it is due to the Alliance."[25]

The Reza Shah Regime. The advent, in 1925, of Reza Shah
Pahlavi, who proclaimed the supremacy of "Iranism" without
consideration of race and religion and broke the absolute power
of the fanatical Shi'ite clergy, was hailed as the beginning of a
new and bright era for the Jews of Iran. However, the eulogists
of the Reza Shah regime (1925–1941) overlooked its most outstanding feature—the dominant nationalistic spirit, which was
not more favorable to the Jews and other minorities than the
old Islamic fanaticism. Describing the status of the Jewish community, William S. Haas wrote in his competent study, *Iran:*[26]

Legal equality has not freed them [the Jews] from social ostracism,
which, in fact, remains unchanged. They . . . are considered foreigners; administrative posts are barred to them, and despite their recognized qualification as teachers, they have great difficulty in finding employment in governmental schools. In some ways they may
be said to be even worse off than before. For, as long as the discrimination was based on religion alone, conversion to Islam opened the
way to social equality and to the opportunity of public career, and,
indeed, a considerable number availed themselves of this. Now that
nationality is the criterion, conversion to Islam does not carry the
same guarantee of success as it did before. In adopting the nationality principle with regard to minorities the Persians are falling
in line with one of the less praiseworthy achievements of Western
political ideology.

During the first decade of the Reza Shah regime, the Jews
still had access to some government jobs and had occupied important positions in the customs administration, in the public
health service, and as teachers in the educational institutions—
though they never were able to obtain any dominating positions
even in these fields.[27] But after 1936, with the growth of the
Nazi influence, a definite policy of anti-Jewish discrimination

started to prevail in the administrative machinery of the state. Jewish officials were discharged one after another. An actual *numerus clausus* was introduced in the higher schools and in the officer corps.

Nazi Influence. German influence in Iran was constantly increasing. "To all intents and purposes Reza Shah handed Persia over to Hitler," testified Arthur C. Millspaugh, who was Administrator General of Iran's finances from 1922 to 1927, and again in 1943–1945. "After Hitler's rise to power, some if not all the German experts became Nazi representatives in disguise. . . . When the Second World War broke out, they were supplemented by political and military agents, secret or otherwise, and when, in June 1941, the Nazis invaded Russia, their activity in Persia intensified."[28] Their agents played a leading role in Iran, distributing Hitlerian propaganda in Persian, and in general spreading Western anti-Semitism in the country. Dr. Schultz, German Consul-General in Teheran, published a viciously anti-Semitic weekly, *Nabard* (Battle). After the collapse of the pro-German rebellion in Iraq in April 1941, Haj Amin-al Husseini, the former Mufti of Jerusalem, found refuge in the Japanese Embassy in Teheran and from there continued his anti-Jewish propaganda. Fearing a possible repetition of the bloody pogroms which the Mufti provoked in Baghdad, many Iranian Jews fled to Istanbul.

In August 1941, the Allies put an end to the Nazi domination in Iran. British and Soviet troops occupied the country. The pro-German Reza Shah was forced to abdicate and was succeeded by Mohammed Reza Pahlavi. Ahmad Qavam Sultaneh formed a pro-Allied cabinet. A Jewish Telegraphic Agency dispatch from London, dated August 25, 1941, reported that "a radical change in the life of the Jews in Iran is expected in Jewish circles here as a result of the entry of British and Russian troops into Iran." On September 10, the same agency reported that "the first group of 23 Jews from the city of Isfahan who fled when Nazi influences began to be dominant in Iran, returned yesterday following the Russo-British occupation of the country."

These expectations did not materialize. As far as the Jewish position is concerned, no "radical change" took place in the years to come. The German agents were driven out, and a noticeable effort was made to eliminate the influence of such Persians who had been in the pay of Hitler Germany. But Jewish employees who were discharged from nearly all governmental institutions during the period 1936–1941 were not reinstated. Except for a few Jewish officials in the postal and customs departments, scarcely any Jews remained in the Iranian administration. A Reuters report from Teheran illustrated the striking discrepancy between the legal equality of Iranian Jewry and its actual position by stating that, though Jewish rights are unrestricted by law, "Jews are rarely accepted in practice as government officials, and concessions, always a prosperous business in Iran, are granted only in exceptional cases. Few Jews are admitted to the high schools, and promotion of Jews in the army is reduced to a minimum."[29]

Nor did the new pro-Allied regime succeed in eliminating religious intolerance and hostility toward the minorities. Maurice Hindus, who toured Iran in November 1947, found that in the preceding two and one-half years fanatical Moslem leaders had been feverishly seeking to swing Iran back to the religious intolerances of the pre-Reza Shah days and to incite hostility toward "the unclean" and "the infidels," that is, Christians and Jews. This campaign, Hindus admitted, was frowned upon by educated Iranians, cabinet ministers and the Shah himself; "but it has scored no small triumph with the uneducated masses who constitute at least 90 per cent of the population."[30]

Poor, Stagnant Economy. In the first half of the nineteenth century, the economic position of Persian Jewry was on the whole favorable. It started deteriorating toward the end of the century. In 1892, G. N. Curzon wrote: "The majority of Jews in Persia are engaged in trade, in jewelry, in wine and opium manufacture, as musicians, dancers, scavengers, pedlars, and in other professions to which is attached no great respect. They rarely attain to a leading mercantile position."[31] In 1931, striving to protect the country's economy against the Soviet economic policy, the Teheran Government monopolized foreign trade, increasingly taking direct charge of sales and purchases, production and transportation of goods. Stated a "Report," published in 1945 by a government economic committee: "Today by far the greatest part of imports and exports of this country is being handled directly by the government, or controlled and supervised by it."[32] For the Jewish merchants who had ventured into commerce on a higher level, this governmentalization of foreign trade was tantamount to their complete elimination.

Most of the Iranian Jews are city dwellers. The overwhelming majority live in the five urban centers: Teheran, Isfahan, Shiraz, Hamadan, Kermanshah. Among the approximately 18,000 Jews of Azerbaijan a majority were engaged in farming; most of them were field hands, in actual bondage of the landowners; some were wealthy landowners. The rest were petty traders; many among them were itinerants peddling their wares in the villages. They usually obtained these wares from Moslem or Jewish retailers on credit, at exorbitant rates of interest, and as their profit scarcely sufficed to pay off the debt, they were always at the mercy of their creditors. In turn, the peddler was obliged to extend credit to his peasant customers, and the collection of debts in the villages presented a difficult, often dangerous task. There are no Jews in Iran's poor industry and a Jewish working class is unknown. A good many Jews are artisans (weavers, carpenters, shoemakers, coppersmiths), unskilled and poorly trained. Jewish officials in government institutions have virtually disappeared. Jews are excluded from legal professions. There are practically no Jewish engineers, and approximately seventy Jewish medical doctors, dentists and midwives.

Indicative of the Jewish economic position in Iran's urban centers is the situation of the Jews in Teheran and Isfahan.

While other Jewish communities are on the whole homogeneous, the Jewish community of Teheran is a mixture of people from various regions of the country, as well as from abroad. One can find there Jews from Baghdad, Russian Jewish refugees, Jews from Bokhara, French Jews (who came since the foundation of the schools of the Alliance Israélite Universelle) and German Jews (refugees from Hitlerism). Each of these native and foreign groups has preserved its special features and lives in almost complete isolation. Economic and cultural differences are far-reaching. Some 150 families belong to the influential and wealthy Baghdad Jewish community; a further 80 families of Russian origin have succeeded in establishing for themselves a fairly satisfactory economic position. There are some Jewish-owned large stores in the better parts of Teheran. Since the Royal Court, the government institutions, and the foreign embassies are all in Teheran, smaller groups of Jews have created for themselves a relatively higher economic standard. But the overwhelming majority live in utter poverty. Their main occupation is in petty trade, dealing in carpets, textiles, antiques, and luxuries. They rank from the peddler, who goes from house to house, from town to town, up to the shopkeeper operating stalls in the bazaar. Jews are also engaged in all kinds of handicraft: they are coppersmiths, shoemakers, joiners, tailors, weavers, and manufacturers of hosiery. Almost all of them live in the *Mahal al-Juhad*, the ghetto, and form a pathetic unity of misery, illness and superstition. Their lodgings are narrow, dark, overcrowded and lacking sunlight and air. Carpets take the place of chairs and tables; fingers and hands are used rather than knives and forks. In 1945, of the 25,000 Teheran Jews, at least 12,000 had to be supported by the community.[33] The first national census of Iran, conducted in 1956, found 35,101 Jews in the capital city.

As late as 1958, Mr. Habib Elghanayan, representative of the Iran Jewish community, told the Annual County Directors Conference of the American Joint Distribution Committee:[34]

In Teheran, a small number of people could leave the ghetto and go into trade and central lucrative employment; however, part of the Jews in Teheran and 90 per cent of the Jews in the provinces still live in ghettos, and they are the great majority of our community and can hardly earn a living for themselves and their families. They lack necessary facilities, they lack education, they lack technical instruction, they lack necessary economic help in order to leave the ghetto.

Similar are conditions in Isfahan, in the south of the country. The city harbors the oldest Jewish community in Iran, and its original name was *Jahudijja*, "Jews' town"; it was also called "Little Jerusalem." Now, the overwhelming majority of the 4,500 Jews who remained in Isfahan live in narrow, dirty streets and in small and low mud huts. A recent survey of 960 Jewish families found 700 so poor that they are barely able to meet the most primitive necessities; 50 families were occupationally classified as "scavengers."[35] Another report established that one in four are either beggars or unemployed. The most common Jewish occupation is that of itinerant peddler, whose stooped figure is seen wandering among the remotest mountain villages, usually at great personal risk. The younger generation sees no prospects of shifting to new and higher economic or social positions. "In practice," soberly stated a former student of the Ecole Normale Israélite of the Alliance Israélite Universelle, "our students, on finishing school, are as a rule unable to get government jobs; therefore, despite their superior education, they are forced to take up the professions of their parents, and become peddlers, shopkeepers, etc."[36]

Other provincial Jewish communities are reported to be in the process of disintegration. In Shiraz and Yezd, where the Jews used to work at home on hand spinning wheels, mechanical spinning mills established by the Government, deprived them of their means of livelihood.[37] Mrs. Eleanor Roosevelt, who visited the Shiraz Jewish Community in the spring of 1959, saw there a "picture of poverty":[38]

The average poor family may consist of a mother and father and many children—six or eight is not unusual—and they live in one room, with no sanitation. There are not even doors or windows in the room—holes are cut in the walls to be used for coming in and going out and for letting in a little light. . . . The occupation of most of the Jewish men is that of a peddler. . . . The man who is making as much as $1 a day is considered quite rich.

A very pronounced emigration movement to the capital (Teheran) has been taking shape for several years, and particularly since the end of the war. The once 6,000-strong Jewish community of Hamadan "has lost its value," Elie Silvert, Director of the town's Alliance school, reported in 1947: "Its former activity has disappeared; the rich people have emigrated. . . . Unemployment is widespread and the misery is great."[39] By 1959, only 3,000 Jews remained in Hamadan. Similar is the situation of Kermanshah's 3,500 Jews: "Kermanshah has lost its importance. This provincial town is deserted; there is a rush toward the capital, the great city. Here, everything is gloomy, weary. The commercial highway Kermanshah-Hamadan-Teheran has been substituted by the trans-Iranian line Persian Gulf-Caspian Sea. Here is a town which again becomes a village."[40]

Education. The education of the Iranian Jewish community is largely dominated by the Alliance Israélite Universelle. The first three decades of the Alliance work are vividly described by one of its old-timers, Albert Confino, in *L'Alliance Israélite Universelle en Perse* (Paris 1950). Its first concern was to create a network of modern schools which would enable the Jews to acquire the essentials of modern European civilization. "The task was not easy," testifies André Cuenca, the Director of the Alliance network in the country. "Even among the Iranian Jews there were those who opposed such innovations as modern schools. This opposition was especially strong with regard to girls' schools. The necessity for girls to be educated was inconceivable. Perseverance overcame all obstacles, however, and practically everywhere schools were opened not only for boys, but for girls as well." (In 1957, girls' attendance constituted 46.4 per cent in the Alliance schools.) Since at the early stage of the Alliance effort there were virtually no educational facilities for the Moslem majority of the country's population, several non-Jews were admitted to its schools, which trained many of Iran's cultural and political leaders (as late as 1947, there were 314 non-Jewish pupils in the Alliance educational institutions, 180 of them in Hamadan and 60 in Teheran).[41]

The development of the Alliance school network during the last decade is shown in the following table:

Year	Number of Schools	Number of Pupils
1948	20	6,360
1949	22	7,760
1950	23	7,985
1951	23	8,259
1952	22	7,577
1953	23	7,599
1954	23	7,994
1955	23	8,052
1956	23	8,052
1957	23	7,848
1958	34	7,955
1959	34	6,357

The decrease of the school complement during 1952–1954 was caused by the emigration to Israel of 27,933 Jews from 1950 to 1953. It is, however, significant that while the Jewish population of the country lost during this period about one-third of its number, the number of Alliance pupils decreased only by some 6 per cent: the place of those departed was taken by children who had thus far not been taken care of because of scarcity of school facilities. By 1955, the school attendance had again reached the 8,000 mark, but renewed emigration in 1957 and 1958 (6,940 emigrants) reduced it by 1,600.

The Alliance network comprises kindergartens and elementary and secondary schools in Teheran, Hamadan, Isfahan, Kermanshah, Yezd, Seneh, and several smaller localities. In addition to teachers who received their diplomas from the Ecole Normal Israélite Orientale of Paris, established by Alliance some ninety years ago, the primary schools alone employ some three hundred teachers of Iranian origin and training. Teheran's two secondary schools, which prepare young people for baccalaureate degrees, have recently introduced English into their curriculum, so that their students now learn four languages: Persian, Hebrew, French and English. Their high standard is recognized and appreciated by the Iranian Ministry of Education.[42] A recent study on Iran (1957), edited by Herbert H. Vreeland, praises the secondary school at Hamadan, whose "graduates are said to be the most brilliant in Iran."[43]

In addition to its purely educational effort, the Alliance, in cooperation with the American Joint Distribution Committee, took on the task of clothing and feeding the children. In 1958, 1,554 children in day care centers and 6,521 older school children were receiving clothes, including underwear, shoes, etc. Free lunches were served to 6,000 school children in Teheran and 4,500 more in six other cities.

Since 1946, the educational work of the Alliance was substantially supplemented by the network of national-religious schools maintained by the *Ozar Hatorah* organization: 29 schools with 5,296 pupils in 16 localities. Since the teaching of Hebrew, Jewish history and religion was admittedly inadequate in the Alliance schools, the *Ozar Hatorah*, in cooperation with the Joint Distribution Committee, took over the task of religious instruction in thirteen Alliance institutions with 5,-789 pupils, supplying them with 50 Hebrew teachers.[44] Twenty-two vocational schools of the ORT, with a teaching staff of 67 and a budget of $197,000, had 1,296 pupils in 1957 (see p. 247). About 4,560 Jewish children study in general schools of the Iranian Ministry of Education, and about 1,500 in Christian missionary schools. Nevertheless, as late as 1957, Eugene Weil, Secretary General of the Alliance Israélite Universelle, revealed that in Teheran alone there were 3,000 Jewish children who could not be admitted to any school because of lack of school facilities.[45]

Up to 1926, Iranian authorities did not interfere with the curriculum and management of the Alliance schools. The language of instruction was French, while Persian and Hebrew were also taught. Since 1926, every school had to follow the curriculum laid down by the Iran Department of Public Instruction, and the Persian language was introduced as the obligatory medium of education, with French as the first foreign language, and Hebrew included into the "religious education" program: 70 per cent of the basic curriculum is being taught in Persian, 15–20 per cent (in accordance with the grades) is devoted to the study of French, the remaining 10–15 per cent is allocated to religious education. In the *Ozar Hatorah* schools, the foreign language taught is English, and with the increasing influence of the English language in the country, responsible Iranian Jewish circles are now advocating its introduction, instead of French, into the Alliance schools. This demand is, however, determinedly resisted by the leadership of the Alliance, bent on preserving French cultural positions.[46]

Joint and ORT. A major role in the life of the Iranian Jewish Community plays the American Joint Distribution Committee (known as "Joint"), which entered the Iranian scene in 1947. As formulated by Maurice Lipian, its director for Iran, the organization strives "to help the Iranian Jews attain a state of physical, intellectual and spiritual readiness to be able to move forward with the times and to find their place constructively in the advancing currents of progress." This broad aim is being implemented in two main directions: "First, actual services, programs and subventioning of programs to improve the conditions of the people, and second, community organization and development of local community spirit and know-how towards the goal that the local Jewish community will ultimately be able to maintain and carry on its own programs and services independently."[47]

To that first category belongs a widespread network of medical institutions and services (hospitals, nursing, curative and preventive health service, maternity care, home sanitation, a dental program, care and treatment of some 10,500 school children); subvention to 26 educational institutions of the Alliance, 17 of *Ozar Hatorah* and 2 ORT schools, as well as to day care centers and summer camps; university students' aid—and many, many more.[48] Not less important is Joint's insistence on the development of self-help among the Jewish community. As a recent observer put it, the Joint had from the very beginning "laid down the first rule: Help will be given only if the people are willing to help themselves. . . . If one comes to JDC for something, he is immediately asked, 'What will you do to help?' . . . The response is slow, but the situation is improving."[49] In a report to the World Jewish Congress, dated February 25, 1958, the Congress representative in Teheran summed up the situation by stating that the Joint "forms actually the backbone of all Jewish organizations in Iran."[50]

An extremely valuable contribution to the rehabilitation of Iranian Jewry constitutes the work of ORT—Organization for Rehabilitation through Training—which started its activities in 1950. By 1957, ORT maintained 23 trade schools and training workshops in Teheran, Isfahan and Shiraz, where three-quarters of Iran's Jews are concentrated, with 45 teachers and 1,190 students, who, in addition to vocational instruction, are given six hours' tuition per week (teachers are supplied by *Ozar Hatorah*). Needy pupils receive meals and clothing, often even pocket money; many of these "extras" are provided through the Joint. To provide employment for its graduates, ORT schools are helping their students in establishing themselves in their respective trades; future electricians, tailors, and carpenters engage in the manufacture of products for outside customers and are getting paid for their labor. When they graduate, tools, equipment, advice and guidance are made available to them in private or cooperative workshops, which numbered 38 in 1957. *ORT Yearbook* for 1957 stresses that

far more than a vocational education program in Iran, ORT is a conveyor belt for modern culture, knowledge and a progressive outlook. Pupils brought to ORT in their adolescent years are introduced to a world their parents never knew existed. They learn personal hygiene, the value of time, habits of work . . . go through a process of awakening that is almost being reborn in one's own lifetime. . . . There seems to have been an increased interest in emigration to Israel recently. The ORT schools have been preparing many for life in Israel.[51]

Communal Life. In no sense can the Jews of Iran be said to be a well-organized body. The existing Community Councils are recognized by the Iranian authorities as representative of the local Jewish population, but, reported Dr. I. Kleinbaum in May 1946, they are not formed along democratic lines and are dominated by plutocratic cliques: there is no over-all Jewish representation, nor is there any contact between single Community Councils. Organized public life is still in its initial stages. In the larger cities regular communal institutions exist, such as *Hebra*, or consistories, youth centers, ladies' committees and clubs. Their membership consists chiefly of Alliance alumni. But national and political consciousness is very poor even among those who are active in public life. The Teheran Committee of the World Jewish Congress said in a detailed and outspoken report: "The small number of people who are interested in public affairs unite and quarrel with each other. No social or political program differentiate one group from the other. Besides, these groups exist among the well-to-do classes only, while the majority live in greatest poverty and misery, and are ready to follow every group for a penny."[52]

There is no organized country-wide rabbinical body in Iran. The rabbis in single communities usually possess no great Jewish knowledge or spiritual authority. There is also no organized central Rabbinical Tribunal (Beth Din). In each community, the local Chief Rabbi, assisted by two others of his choice, deals with legal disputes in matters concerning marriage, divorce, inheritance, etc. An Iranian law promulgated in 1935 transferred all these matters to the authority of the respective religious tribunals of the minority groups. The rabbis are as a rule appointed by the Government in conformity with written suggestions of the local community councils (Hebra), supported by a sufficient number of observant Jews.[53]

A laudable attempt to establish a truly representative body of Iranian Jewry was made by a responsible group of Jewish leaders, with the encouragement and help of the American Joint Distribution Committee, in November 1957, when the First All-Iranian Jewish Medical-Social Congress (this innocuous name was chosen to stress its nonpolitical character) convened in Teheran. The Congress opened by Prince Gholam Reza Pahlavi, brother of the Shah, is reported to have been "highly successful, received considerable recognition, and generated much enthusiasm." It "culminated in the establishment of the Jewish Central Committee, a consummation we had long considered, devoutedly to be wished," said one year later the Joint representative in Iran.[54] But he sadly admitted that

the local leadership has unfortunately not shown much capacity for sustaining this enthusiasm, and thus far the Central Committee has existed largely on paper. A really strong dynamic Central Committee would hold much possibility for the strengthening and structuring of Jewish community life in Iran, but clearly a great deal of effort must still be invested in this endeavor. It is expected that this may be a long, slow process, since fundamentally it involves changing the attitudes and habits of hundreds of years, of generations. The same holds true for almost all other levels of Jewish community organization in Iran.

In 1946, there were two Jewish weeklies in Teheran, both published in Persian: *Haolam Hayehudi* and *Israel*. The first was edited by a group of Jewish "bourgeois" intelligentsia and supplied with material by the Palestine Office. The second was edited by Dr. R. Cohen, one of the Iranian delegates at the Twenty-Second Zionist Congress, and combined Zionism with extreme leftism, close to the pro-Communist *Tudeh* (Masses) party; it was forced to close publication when the Arab states invaded Israel. Somewhat earlier, the same group that backed *Israel* had initiated the monthly *Rahmia Yahud* (The Jewish Hope), a Jewish scientific revue; its chief editor was one of the collaborators of the big Communist daily *Mardom* in Teheran. At the present time, the Jewish press is represented by a single bimonthly in Persian, *Alame Yahoud* (The Jewish World), edited by Moussa Kermanian, representative of the World Jewish Congress.

As a rule, Iranian Jews kept aloof from the general political life of the country. However, certain groups among the young intelligentsia strongly sympathized with the Communist-sponsored *Tudeh* party. Other Jewish elements joined the Democratic party of Ahmad Qavam Sultaneh. In Azerbaijan, Jews have been accused by reactionary Moslem elements of having pro-Soviet leanings, of being Soviet agents during the Soviet occupation, and of doing business with the Soviet authorities.

Communist influence continued to be strongly felt for years thereafter, in particular during the two years of Mossadegh's regime. At the Third Plenary Assembly of the World Jewish Congress in Geneva (August 4–11, 1953), Moussa Kermanian, delegate from Iran, deplored "the clandestine activities of the Jewish Communist Party." The *Tudeh* party, he reported, was accepting Jewish members more readily than other political movements. The majority among Jewish Communists, especially among the leadership, were intellectuals and students: "Their cradle is in the schools, in particular those of the Alliance Israélite, which accepts teachers commonly reputed as known [Communist] militants. . . . They are working under the name of "L'Association Culturelle et Sociale Juive" and their organ is the weekly *Nissam*. All Jewish world organizations working in Iran (the Joint, the Jewish Agency, the ORT, etc.) are the target of all kinds of attacks and are being branded as spies."[55]

On August 19, a few days after Mr. Kermanian had delivered his report, a *coup d'état* by general Fazlollah Zahedi put an end to the leftist regime of Mohammed Mossadegh. All Communist organizations were outlawed and Communist publications banned. Jewish communal and cultural life was resumed and the damage caused by Communist propaganda slowly repaired.[56]

Under the totalitarian and pro-German rule of Reza Shah Pahlavi, all other than purely religious communal activities were prohibited. After the establishment of the pro-Allied regime in September 1941, Jewish organizations from abroad were permitted to work in Iran. The ban on Zionism was lifted, and the foundations were laid for the reorganization of Zionist work, which had been inaugurated in 1912, with Hamadan as the main center. Two delegates from Iran attended the Twenty-Second Zionist Congress in Basle, in December 1946.[57] In spite of its extended aloofness and utter poverty, Iranian Jewry very quickly learned the noble art of helping in the upbuilding of Palestine, and a Reuters correspondent related in September 1949 that "the small minority of wealthy merchants among them is making an important contribution to the aid of the Palestinian Jews."[58]

By the end of 1941, Iran became an important transit center for Polish Jews who found refuge in—or had been deported to—Soviet Russia in 1939–1941 at the time German troops entered Poland, and were now coming to Iran together with the Polish evacuation groups. Among the approximately 75,000 Polish soldiers and members of their families, numbering 37,750, who had reached Iran in 1942, some 7,000 were Jews.[59]

Emigration. The Arab-Jewish conflict in Palestine was utilized to stir up anti-Jewish feelings in the country. On November 4, 1947, a few weeks before the United Nations decision to partition Palestine, Maurice Hindus reported from Teheran to the New York *Herald-Tribune* that the bazaar area of the Iranian capital had been plastered with posters calling on the faithful to come to the support of the Arabs fighting the partitioning of Palestine. The posters contained an eleven-point program of action which included volunteer enlistments in the Arab armies and a boycott of Jewish merchants in Teheran and throughout the country. The appeal ended with a warning that in the event of hostilities between Arabs and Jews, the public could not be held responsible for the death of Jews in Iran. In January 1948, violent anti-Jewish demonstrations took place in Teheran, with fanatical Moslem demonstrators shouting "death to the Jews." Seyd Abolghassem Kashani, a Moslem leader who was imprisoned for Nazi sympathies during the war, addressing a mass meeting, called for a *Jihad* (holy war) against "Jewish atrocities" in Palestine. The Iranian paper *Mard Embrooz* even charged that branches of the Haganah were active in Iran.

The Iranian Government, it is true, refused to be directly involved into the Palestine conflict, despite repeated appeals by the Mullahs and several members of Parliament to send an expeditionary force "to drive out the Zionist immigrants from the holy soil" of Palestine The well-informed Bombay *Chronicle* (September 8, 1948) formulated the official government position as follows: "Iran will give her Arab cousins the wherewithal, in supplies and money, according to her own meagre means, to wage their war, but the Arab world has, probably, realized by now that there will be no Persian *Mohajid* [one taking part in the *Jihad*] to fight in its ranks the Jewish invaders."

In March 1950, a violent wave of anti-Jewish outbursts, staged by local fanatical Sunni Moslem religious leaders, broke out in Iranian Kurdistan. Twelve Jews were murdered at Bakan, Tikab, Saggar and en route to Teheran. Several Jewish girls had been raped. The Teheran Government ordered local authorities to do all possible to protect the Jewish population of the area, but

the terrorized Jews put little faith in the efficacy of these orders. "They decided to leave Kurdistan and to go to Israel,"
reported the Joint Director for Iran, Stanley Abramovitch:[60]

Communities whose history goes back over 2,000 years uprooted
themselves, sold their property at ridiculous prices, took their ancient *Sifrei Torah* and their few belongings and proceeded to Teheran. Here they sought refuge in the Jewish cemetery, the only
Jewish public property in Iran. Not one of them knew how they
would get to Israel, but they heard that others had gone and they
too trusted in God.

In spite of the primitive conditions, there were thousands of
Iranian Jews who were also seeking admittance into the Kurdish
camp. About 1,000 people besieged the gates of the camp for over
a month. Finally, they entered the section filled with graves. A
thousand Iranian Jews live among these graves.

Almost 10,000 Jews have streamed into Teheran from all over
Persia. Not all of them reached Teheran. Some fell on the road. And
not all have sold their property. Many Moslems would not buy it,
knowing that the Jews could not take their houses with them.

By October 1950, an estimated 6,000 Kurdish Jews had come
down to Teheran, with 6,000 to 8,000 possibly still remaining in
Kurdistan.[61]

Iranian Jews started settling in Palestine some seventy years
ago. First immigrants came from Shiraz, to be joined later by
those from Teheran, Yezd, Bushir, Isfahan, Kashan, etc. Some
were rabbis and well-to-do merchants, but the bulk consisted
of poor people, without general education or professional skill.
They settled in Tiberias and Safed, in Haifa and Jaffa, but
mostly in Jerusalem, where, together with immigrants from
Bokhara, they formed a colony of Persian-speaking Jews.[62]

In the pre-World War II period, movement of Iranian Jews
to Palestine was numerically insignificant. In 1936–1938, only
207 Jews arrived from Iran. Immigration was intensified after
the establishment of the State of Israel. In May 1949, the first
plane with 55 immigrants aboard arrived in Lydda from Teheran; in June, a second group of 50 was flown to Israel. During
the period from May 15, 1948, to December 31, 1949, 2,925
Iranian Jews arrived, mostly by air; 11,935 in 1950; and 10,048

in 1951. The 1952 immigration amounted to 4,856, and that of 1953 to 1,096. It declined to 505 and 128 in 1954 and 1955 respectively, but increased again to 652 in 1956, to 1,255 in 1957, and to 5,685 in 1958. Since the establishment of the state, some 39,000 Iranian Jews—nearly one-half of the country's Jewish community—left for Israel. Contrary to prevalent notion, the re-emigration trend was insignificant. A total of 1,510 immigrants from Iran have chosen to return to their country of emigration during the eleven-year period 1948–1958. The return movement was strongest in the years 1951 (132 re-emigrants); 1952 (300); 1953 (462); and 1954 (298). Prior to and after these four years, the number of re-emigrants never exceeded one hundred.[63]

Attitude of the Government. The official position of Iran—the second Moslem country to extend, on March 15, 1950, *de facto* recognition to Israel (Turkey was the first)—was that the Government had no desire to see the departure of its Jewish citizens, but that those who wished to leave were at liberty to do so. The Government only wanted the migration to be gradual and orderly, so as not to overly disturb the country's economy by precipitous liquidation of Jewish holdings.

The Government of Iran also, in 1949, rejected a request by the Iraqi Government for the extradition of several Baghdad Jews who fled to Iran to escape persecution. During his visit in Teheran in the autumn of 1954, the Iraqi Minister of the Interior urged the Iran authorities to curb the activities of the Jewish Agency and of other Jewish educational organizations, and the communiqué published before his departure stated that the Iranian Government had assured the Arab countries that it will check "such activities." It was noted that, on the occasion of the United Nations Day, the Shah had for the first time mentioned in his speech the plight of the Arab refugees from Palestine and voiced his opinion that Israel ought to admit them.[64] But this deviation from benevolent neutrality toward Israel was short-lived. By the end of 1955, observers of the Iranian scene reported that "the attitude of the authorities had considerably improved recently"; indicative of the change was the moderate speech of the Iranian Foreign Minister at the meeting of the Baghdad Pact members.[65] The situation became strained during the 1956 Sinai campaign. Officials of the Jewish Agency, the Joint, and the ORT were told bluntly that if Israel did not get out of Sinai, the Jewish organizations would have to get out of Iran. Jews were not permitted to meet in groups of more than five.[66] But this tension gradually abated, and in 1958 several influential Teheran newspapers, especially the dailies *Firman* and *Musawar*, were demanding the renewal of full diplomatic and economic relations with Israel, interrupted in 1952 under strong Arab pressure.[67]

There are no official statistics on the present Jewish population of Iran, and estimates vary greatly. Though some 39,000 have, in 1948–1958, left for Israel, a 1957 survey published by Human Relations Area Files still puts the number of Jews in that country at 75,000,[68] while the 1959 survey of *Jewish Communities in the World*, issued by the Institute of Jewish Affairs of the World Jewish Congress, speaks of 75,000–85,000.[69] More conservative is the figure of "some 40,000" in *The Middle East, A Political and Economic Survey*, published in 1958 under the editorship of Sir Reader Bullard.[70]

10

Afghanistan: Joining the "Magic Carpet"

Origin. Reliable data on the history of the Afghan Jewish community are meager. It began to reach Europe only toward the middle of the nineteenth century, when the advent of British rule in India led to better communication between India and Afghanistan. Casual travelers left written records of their visits. From their reports it appears that the present Jewish community of Afghanistan is of recent origin. Joseph Wolff, clergyman and a missionary, a German-born Jew who became a convert to the Church of England, and who visited Afghanistan in 1832, reported that there were fifty Jewish families in Kabul that had been "brought here by Ahmed Shah from Meshed, Persia, sixty years ago; but as they were no longer to sell brandy, most of them left Kabul. The Jews went back to Meshed."[1] Abraham Emanuelson, who after World War I traveled extensively among the "remnants of the Jews," related that the present generation of Jews in Afghanistan were descendants of the Marranos who had escaped from Meshed and had come here to live openly as Jews; "the Jewish inhabitants in the country now date their residence back only ninety years."[2] Itzhak Ben Zvi describes the Jewry of Afghanistan as "an integral part of Persian Jewry: its speech is a Persian vernacular."[3] Erich Brauer also stressed "closest relations with Persian Jewry."[4]

Another component of Afghan Jewry were emigrants from Russian Bokhara. A Jewish traveler who visited the country about 1850 reported that Kabul "is very large and well populated. . . . Of my brethren in the faith I found there but few, and these had wandered from Bokhara."[5] A Bokharan Jew, Ga-

briel Barukhoff, who arrived in Israel in 1947, related that there
were at that time about 200 Jewish families of Russian Bokhara
origin in Afghanistan, of which about sixty families were living
in Kabul.⁶

Numbers. Statistical data on the population of Afghanistan,
where there has never been a census, are few and contradictory.
Estimates range from 7 to 15 million. Similar discrepancies exist
with regard to the size of the Jewish community. In 1928, the
Encyclopedia Judaica (Vol. I, p. 927) spoke of 18,000, while
the *Universal Jewish Encyclopedia* (Vol. I, p. 106) stated that
the number of Jews in Afghanistan "dwindled to a few hundred
by 1939." Walter Fischel, an authority on Oriental Jewry, put
the number at 4,000 in 1937,⁷ and Erich Brauer, who, in 1942,
devoted an extensive study to the Jews in Afghanistan, insists
that "despite the larger estimates given by some writers, the
Jews number no more than 3,300." In reply to a request by the
U. S. State Department for information about the status of the
Afghanistan Jewish population, Ambassador Ely Elliot Palmer
cabled on August 21, 1946, that "local and refugee Jews in the
country total about 3,000."⁸ This estimate largely coincides
with the figure 3,500 supplied by the representatives of the Afghan Jewish community in reply to a questionnaire of the
Jewish Agency (October 20, 1949).

In 1927, there were in Afghanistan some 60 Jewish communities. By 1949, the Jewish population was virtually limited
to three towns: the 2,211 Jews in Herat and about 200 in Balkh
lived in voluntary ghettos (*Mahal Yahudi*), while in Kabul,
where the 400 Jews rent their homes from the Moslems, there
is no Jewish quarter.

Organization and Culture. The few existing Jewish communities in Afghanistan are organized on the patriarchal system. For
instance, Herat's 2,200 Jews are divided into twenty families.
The heads of these families elect for a term of one or two years
the community leader (*kalantar*) who represents the Jews vis-
à-vis the authorities, receives a salary from both sources, and is
responsible for the collection of the head tax, which every Jewish male from fifteen to sixty must pay and which, even at the
highest rate, never amounts to more than a dollar and a half a

Immigrants from North Africa crowd a boat to Israel.

ERRATA

In the illustrations that appear as a group after page 256 the caption appearing on the eighth page of the section that reads "A group of blind Yemenites . . ." should read "Moroccan Jewish family entering their new house."

The captions on the last page of the section should read "A group of blind Yemenites in an Israeli *Ma'abara*," and "Moroccan Jews on the way to Israel," respectively.

Magic Carpet plane in flight. On it are over 130 Yemenite passengers.

Yemenite Jews, barefoot, on a 200-mile trek across the desert from the Yemen interior to Aden.

Passengers waiting to embark in Aden.

Yemenite Jews in Israel learning how to plow.

Hadhramaut woman.

Jew from Hadhramaut.

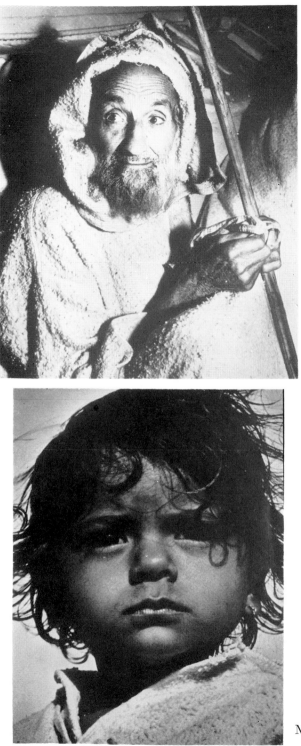

Moroccan Jew.

Moroccan immigrant girl.

A group of blind Yemenites in an Israeli
Ma'abara.

Yemenite worker.

Iraqi youths on flight to Israel.

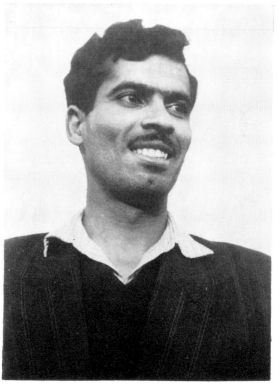

Iraqi immigrant. *Zionist Archives and Library of the Palestine Foundation Fund.*

Youth from Syria.

Jew from Iran.

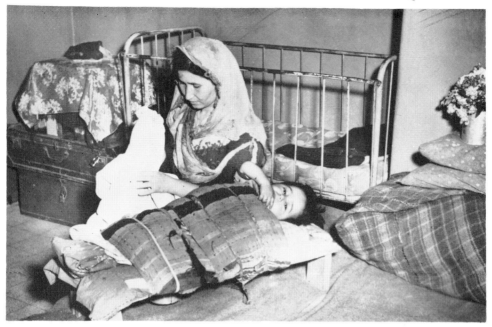

Mother and child from Iraq.

Oldster from Iraq. *Zionist Archives and Library of the Palestine Foundation Fund.*

A family of Marrano Jews from Meshed (Iran) in their new home in Israel.

A group of Marrano children from Meshed.

Egyptian Jew in Israel.

Husband and wife from Libya.

Moroccan immigrants in the customhouse at Haifa.

North African Jews in a **Ma'abara**.

Laborer from Kurdistan.

Bokhara woman.

Girl from Tripoli.

Moroccan Jews on the way to Israel.

Moroccan Jewish family entering their new house.

year. The internal affairs of the community, in which the Jews enjoy full autonomy, are administered by the *hevra*, which, in Herat, is composed of the heads of the ten most important families. Criminal cases as well as civil and religious matters come within its jurisdiction. Whenever possible, offenses committed within the community are dealt with by the *hevra* instead of being turned over to the authorities. Cases in which Jews are committed for trial to the courts of the state are very rare. Those who refuse to accept a judgment are formally excommunicated. Cases involving divorce, levirate marriage, etc., are referred to a special court (*Bet Din*), composed of learned men (*mulla*).[9]

In a book on Afghanistan published in 1937, a French author asserted that the Jews had no synagogues because the Sunnite Islamic law would not tolerate a house of worship of another religion.[10] Actually Herat had eight synagogues, and Balkh also had a few; in Kabul services were held in one of the rooms of the caravanserai.

Polygamy is permitted, but, as in the case of the other oriental Jewish groups, plural marriages are relatively rare. The most common reason for such a marriage is the lack of male issue. Families are usually numerous. The wife bears a child almost every year, but more than half of the children are said to die in infancy.

The spiritual life of Afghan Jewry is poor. Talmudic and rabbinic writings are unknown to them, but they strictly observe the Sabbath, festivals, circumcision, and ritual slaughtering. At the age of three or four the boys begin to attend the school (*midrash*), which every synagogue maintains. The teacher (*mulla* or *khalifa*), himself a product of the local schools, imparts a very limited education to his pupils. The boys are taught to read and translate the Bible and to say the prayers; later on they begin to read Mishna and receive instruction in writing and in the elements of arithmetic. The boys attend the *midrash* until their fifteenth or sixteenth year, by which time they have learned enough to read the weekly portion of the Torah. The girls grow up without any schooling whatever.[11]

Economic Decline. For some time, the Jews held important

economic positions in Afghanistan. But they have successively lost most of them.

Such wealthy Afghan Jews who had owned large herds of cattle and great warehouses in Russia lost them in the 1917 Revolution. In other branches of economic activities, Jews found themselves in competition with rivals for whom they were no match. They have, for example, been ousted by the hundreds from money-changing and the trade in drugs, which were traditional vocations among the Jews in the Orient. By buying their drugs cooperatively, the Hindus, who had followed this vocation for generations, eliminated their Jewish competitors.

But the most decisive role in ruining the Jewish position in the country's economy was played by the governmental policy of monopolizing Afghanistan's foreign trade. No merchandise was to be exported or imported without a government license. An export license was granted only after depositing the value of the goods as security for the return of the money to Afghanistan. On the initiative of the Minister of Finance, Hashim Khan, the Government founded joint stock companies, whose shareholders received the exclusive right to engage in particular trades. The object of this measure was to eliminate all middlemen and ensure that all profits made should accrue to the Government or the shareholders. High governmental officials were largely represented among the beneficiaries of these companies. Of the Jewish traders, only about a hundred were allowed to register as partners or shareholders. Jewish merchants have thus practically been deprived of the possibility of carrying on independent trade. Some Jews were, however, employed during the first years as experts in buying and selling, and there were, as late as 1942, still some Jews on the staffs of these associations.

After the assassination of Mohammed Nadir Shah in November 1933, Jews were expelled from the towns of Mazar-i-Sharif, Tash Kurgan, Maimane, Shiburgan, Mazar, etc. Most of the expellees were robbed of their possessions. Even in the two towns, Kabul and Herat, compulsorily assigned to them, the Jews were forbidden to work without special permission or to engage in any foreign or domestic trade; in the shops they were allowed to open, merchandise could be sold to the local inhabitants only; some entered into partnerships with Moslems and did business under the firm name of their Moslem partner, who secured for himself the lion's share.[12]

Professional Structure. The economic structure of the Afghan Jews is in many respects similar to that of the Jews in Iran. There are almost no agriculturists among them. In countries under Islamic law, authorities very seldom encourage a non-Moslem minority to engage in agriculture, for only the head tax (*jizyah*), and not the tithe (*ushr*) or land tax, may be levied on unbelievers. On the other hand, it is not easy for a small and unprotected community to engage in agriculture where public security is so uncertain. The few Jewish farmers and vincyard owners of Herat and Balkh are an exception. The number of artisans among the Jews is also insignificant. Indicative, in this respect, is the situation in Herat where the Jewish community of 2,200 counted only ten Jewish builders, six tailors, five cobblers and three carpenters.

For the most part, Afghan Jews have always been traders. Before the governmentalization of foreign trade, they held an important position in this field, enjoying the advantage of their foreign connections. Some had settled in London and Leipzig, as well as in the chief cities of Russia and India, and their purchases of wool and of hides were extensive. They exported carpets to England, Russia and India, and imported textiles for the most part. Among the Jewish merchants who limited their activities to the territory of Afghanistan, many have taken recourse to a peculiar type of existence in their endeavor to reach out beyond Herat to areas in which no Jewish communities existed. Leaving their families behind to spare them the risk of traveling, the men proceeded by difficult caravan routes to distant points of the country. Such merchant colonies existed, for example, in Maimane (with 100 Jewish males), Qaleanu and Marqua. The men lived there for several years without visiting their homes, and used to earn a satisfactory livelihood for themselves and their families. The relatively small number of Jewish peddlers carried their goods to nearby villages on the backs of donkeys. They were badly handicapped by the lack of

security on the highways and the necessity to join caravans.[13]
Legal Status. The legal position of Afghan Jews has always been
one of medieval inferiority. They must pay the head tax (*jizyah*)
imposed on all infidels, and the payment of this tax is accompanied by humiliating ceremonies. They may not buy food
in the market. No Jew is employed as a government official or
in the police force. While every Jew of twenty years of age is
enrolled in the army, Jewish soldiers are not permitted to don
the army uniform; nor are they trained in the handling of weapons. They are confined to the cleaning of the stables and to
the lowest form of servant's work for the Moslem soldiers. To
his small army pay, a Jewish soldier must usually add an equal
sum of money to bribe his superiors so that they will not vex
and torture him too much.

Violent anti-Jewish propaganda is not only tolerated by the
Government, but appears actually to be originated and con-
trived from above. The only paper published in Afghanistan is
the government newspaper, and it repeatedly contains anti-Jewish material. In recent years, periodic arrests of Jews without any
specific charges, and apparently affecting Jews only, have been
reported to Jewish organizations abroad. Due to intervention of
the World Jewish Congress, some of the imprisoned have been
subsequently released. But there was no indication that such
periodic arrests of Jews have ceased or that all of those inno-
cently imprisoned have been released.

In the summer of 1946, when Afghanistan made an application for membership in the United Nations, the World Jewish Congress drew the attention of the Great Powers to the
desperate plight of the Jewish community in Afghanistan and
sought to bring about their intervention with the Afghanistan
Government in behalf of the Afghan Jews. Following an interview of an emissary of the Congress with the Chief of the Division of Middle Eastern Affairs of the State Department, Mr.
Ely Elliot Palmer, U.S. Ambassador to Afghanistan, was requested by the State Department to secure information as to
the actual conditions of the Jews in that country. On August 31,
1946, a cable was received from the Ambassador stating that

the Afghanistan Government is not predisposed to admit that the question of Afghanistan Jewry is pertinent to [Afghanistan's] United Nations membership application. The Government has authorized the Undersecretary of the Foreign Office to assure the U.S. Ambassador, on a personal basis, that there is no persecution of Jews in Afghanistan and to inform him that the actual status of the Jews in that country is as follows: Local and refugee Jews in the country total about 3,000. There are no Jews in the army, in Parliament, or in government positions. Jews are permitted to practice their religion freely and to assemble to worship, which they do "noisily." They are allowed to trade freely and have, in fact, a trading organization.[14]

Ambassador Palmer's cable revealed that he had made inquiries only of the Afghanistan Government, without communicating with any members of the Jewish community to secure firsthand evidence. Naturally, the Government presented a largely idyllic picture, even though it had to admit anti-Jewish discrimination in the army, Parliament, and governmental machinery.

The actual conditions under which Afghanistan's Jews live have been authentically described in a letter addressed by seventy rabbis and other representatives of the Afghan Jewish community to the "Great and Noble Government of Israel." Written in a typical Oriental style, the letter says:

We want again to tell you about our great worries and our terrible plight. Our *galut* is much harder than the *galut* in Egypt and Babylon. Apart from the special tax on occupations we have also to pay a levy for our rights, but they [the authorities] take our money and do not accord to us any rights. The doors to trade are closed to us, and so are the gates of the country. There is no way in or out. We have no longer the strength to cope with the difficulties of earning our livelihoods. We have already sold our movable property and are left with nothing. A Jew is barred from work in offices, cooperatives, and many other places, and there are no factories to work in. We meet interference and hostility from the government, and the population treat us badly. We are living in a wild country and consider ourselves to be in great danger.

Emigration. Erich Brauer, a noted student of Oriental Jewry, said in 1942: "How the future of the Afghan Jews will shape itself under the present rule of brute force cannot be foretold

in view of the swiftness with which situations change today.
In the writer's opinion, this group is too weak numerically and
spiritually to withstand any severe pressure. It is not unlikely
that the two thousand Afghan Jews who have settled in Palestine will be the sole survivors of a once flourishing Jewry."[15] The
Committee of the Afghanistan Jewish Community in Palestine, in a letter to the World Jewish Congress (dated June 25,
1947) also came to the conclusion that "their [the Afghan
Jews] only salvation is the Aliyah to Eretz Israel."

Until May 1948, aliyah from Afghanistan was small. During
the eight year period 1924–1931, 154 Afghan Jews have come to
Palestine; 721 arrived during the period 1932–1938. The war
years (1939–1945) saw the immigration of 79 only. Between
1946 and the proclamation of the State of Israel on May 15,
1948, 63 arrived.[16] During the great famine in 1944, about 1,-
000 Jews sold what was left of their possessions and left for India in the hope of reaching Palestine. In April 1946, 100 Afghan
Jewish families were reported in sore plight in Bombay, where
they lived in the synagogue courtyard, sleeping on the floor,
with little food.[17] Their situation did not improve in the course
of the two years to come, and Dr. Henry Shoskes, overseas field
director of the Hias, reported in July 1948 that while in Bombay he saw a group of approximately 600 Jewish refugees from
Afghanistan "in deplorable condition."[18]

Since these Jewish Afghan refugees entered India without
residence permits, they were under constant threat of being
deported. The efforts to obtain for them British certificates for
Palestine were for a long time in vain. In despair, several refugees committed suicide. In the spring of 1947, a deportation decree was issued by the Government of India, ordering 280 Afghan Jews to leave the country immediately. The World Jewish
Congress requested the Indian Government to postpone their
deportation. It also approached the India League of America to
intercede with the Government of India. Sirdar J. J. Singh,
President of the India League of America, in turn approached
Pandit Jawaharlal Nehru, Prime Minister of India, requesting
him to give favorable consideration to the matter. Thereupon,
he received a communication from the New Delhi Government

that they had extended the stay in India of this group of Jewish refugees up to December 31, 1947.[19]

Joining the Magic Carpet. In the course of the following fifteen and a half months (up to August 31, 1949) immigration increased considerably: 405 Afghan Jews were brought to Israel.[20] But this rate of immigration was also far from satisfying the needs of Afghan Jewry. In the above quoted letter to the Israeli Government, representatives of the Afghan Jewish com- community wrote:

Since the rise of Jacob's star and the birth of the Jewish State, the animosity toward us has greatly increased. Pray take measures to avert the impending catastrophe before it is too late. Our desire is to emigrate to Israel. . . . We are in extreme danger. If our captivity lasts a few more months we may all perish. . . .

We are separated from many of our close relatives who are already is Israel. There is no mail service between Afghanistan and Israel and we cannot hear from them. We beg you to reunite us with our parents and children.

Jewish bodies in charge of repatriation of Jews to Israel have done their best to respond to the emigration urge of Afghan Jewry. Evacuation from Afghanistan became part of the Joint Distribution Committee's Operation Magic Carpet. In the spring of 1949, it was announced that more than 500 Afghan Jews were to be transported to Israel by plane within the next two weeks, and that planes from Afghanistan would leave once or twice a day, flying by way of Bombay. The first group of 180 Afghan Jews landed in Israel during the week beginning March 20.

Emigration from Afghanistan, however, encountered considerable difficulties. Afghanistan is a Moslem country and since it had become (on November 19, 1946) a member state of the United Nations, its delegation had consistently voted with the Arab bloc on all questions affecting Jewish rights and interests in Palestine. In accordance with this policy, the Afghanistan Government took a rigidly negative attitude toward emigration of its Jewish subjects to Israel. News given out in October 1949 that Afghanistan "had authorized unrestricted Jewish emigration to Israel" proved to be erroneous. In fact, only a group of about 100 Russian and Bokharan Jews, who had been living in the country since 1917 under conditions of difficulty and distress and had not been able to acquire Afghan citizenship, were permitted to leave. The Indian Government granted transit visas, yet, in order to transfer them by plane from Kabul to India, permission of the Pakistan Government was needed.[21] This permission never came. Unreservedly supporting the Arab position on Palestine, the Pakistan Government refused to grant transit visas to Afghan Jews wishing to migrate to Israel. Limited immigration to Israel nevertheless continued in a roundabout way, mainly via Iran (94 Afghan Jews arrived during the first eight months of 1950).[22] Jewish organizations persisted in their efforts to obtain from the Afghanistan Government permission for an orderly Jewish emigration. In February 1950, the World Jewish Congress requested the Afghanistan Ambassador to the United States, Punre Sardar Mohammad Naim, to transmit to his government a plea that it "abolish its prohibition against Jewish emigration" and let Jews who leave for Israel "take their meager possessions with them." The Ambassador undertook to convey the request to his government in a sympathetic spirit.[23] In October 1950, the Afghanistan Government decided to permit a "slow, orderly" emigration of its Jewish citizens.[24] Since 1948, 3,880 Jews had left Afghanistan for Iran, from where the great majority proceeded for Israel. Not more than some 100 Jewish families are still living in Afghanistan.[25]

PART THREE

Jews in the Moghreb

Introduction

The Arabs called entire French Africa Moghreb, "the land of the setting sun," running as it does to the westernmost edge of the Moslem world. Long before the French came into the picture, this great natural area of 1,060,000 square miles was split into three distinct entities. In the thirteenth century c.e. three Arab kingdoms were founded on the ruins of the Almohad empire, roughly corresponding to modern Morocco, Algeria and Tunisia: that of the Merinids in the west, that of the Abd-el-Wadites in the center, and that of the Hafsites in the east. This division survived six centuries of incessant struggle among dynasties, chronic unrest, insurrections and raids. It was upheld when the three countries successively came under French domination, and has become, if anything, more accentuated now, since Morocco and Tunisia have obtained independence and Algeria is well on the way to establishing her own "personality."

The population of the Moghreb, which has from the most ancient times been a meeting ground for races of different origin, is predominantly Moslem, with the indigenous Berbers and Arab invaders as its main ethnic components. The considerable European minority is a motley one: Frenchmen, Spaniards, Maltese, Greeks, Italians—mostly of relatively recent origin, but occupying positions of wealth and power. The Jews, on the contrary, have lived in the Moghreb for more than two millennia. They first made their appearance after the destruction of the First Temple, when some exiles from Judea sought refuge in North Africa. Another large-scale wave of Jewish refugees came after the destruction of the Second Temple. Flourishing colonies of Jewish merchants and artisans, clustering mainly within the militarily secure coastal areas, emerged in Roman Africa in the third century c.e. These early settlers, identified as *tochavim*, maintained close contact with Palestine and later Babylonia. Rome's domination spelled relative peace and prosperity, though during the fourth century the rise of Christianity caused considerable friction between the Jews and Roman Christians. The fifth century Vandal invasion, which laid waste most of the Moghreb, forced some Jews to flee to the interior. Vandal rule was followed in 535 by Byzantine hegemony. Despite violent anti-Jewish trends, general pacification contributed to the stabilization of the Jewish position. Many Jews, driven from Spain in the seventh century, sought refuge in North Africa. These exiles and their descendants are called *migrashim* and form the Sephardic component of Moghreb Jewry.

At the turn of the eighth century, Arab conquerors rode into the Moghreb, and the long reign of Islam was imposed on the entire area. As elsewhere, throughout Islamic domination, Jews were placed in the position of *dhimmi*, the protected minority (see Introduction). After the rise of the Almohades in the twelfth century, they were segregated in ghettos and forced to wear special dress designed to mark them for contempt. The Jewish plight in Catholic Spain, however, was such that refugees from Spanish massacres (1391) and expulsion (1492) streamed into the Moghreb in great numbers. Their influx revivified the existing Jewish communities, which became a center of Sephardic life and produced some notable scholars. The Spanish newcomers differed in their customs and ways of life from the native Moghreb Jews, but in the course of time the two groups amalgamated.

From the sixteenth century on, under Turkish rule, conditions were generally tolerable. The growth of the independent authority of the Deys of Algeria, always rapacious and cruel, and of the fanatical Rashid dynasty in Morocco (from 1670) greatly affected the Jewish position.

Tolerated but despised, the Jews were made to live in their ghettos, know as *mellahs* in Morocco and as *haras* in Algeria and Tunisia—either a walled quarter within a town, or a small adjunct to rural Arab or Berber settlements. They performed functions which the Moslems were too proud or too lazy to do. The Jew became the scavenger, cobbler, tailor, peddler, serving special needs of the Moslem population, exchanging their goods and services (clothing, jewelry, imported goods, moneylending) for the agricultural staples and craft skills of the Arabs and Berbers. This ethnic "division of labor" established a pattern which reduced economic competition and provided for the Jews a niche in the area's economy. Contacts with the Moslem majority were limited to the strictly "business" field. In the towns, the *mellahs* and *haras*, surrounded by thick walls, adjoined the fortified *medina*, which exacted heavy taxes for "protection," but from which incensed Moslem mobs all too often broke through their heavy gates to plunder and to kill. Outside the ghettos, a Jew had to wear distinctive black garments, was not permitted to walk through the *medina* with his shoes on, to ride a horse, to raise his hand in self-defense. But within the *mellah* or *hara* he was free to live his own life, enjoying internal autonomy in both religious and lay affairs. Among themselves, the Jews spoke their own Arabic dialect, and spoke Arabic and Berber with non-Jews.

The appearance of France in Algeria (1830), Tunisia (1881), and Morocco (1912) spelled revolutionary changes for the Moghreb and its Jewish communities. The French "were received by the Jews with an enthusiasm unequaled anywhere in the Diaspora," testified André Chouraqui, head of the Department of Education of Alliance Israélite Universelle, in his report on North African Jewry at the Jerusalem Ideological Conference.

Those who had suffered under tyrannical rule, who in the eyes of the Moslem masses were 'Jew dogs,' saw the light, new vistas they never dared dream of. . . . The transformation of the Jews of the Moslem Middle Ages to modern men was often accomplished with unexpected speed. In many families in North Africa it is possible to see gathered around one table the grandfather who speaks only Arabic with some Hebrew words required for prayer, wearing the old traditional coat, with a turban on his head, a complete stranger to

modern life; the father in European dress, speaking French though
he still knows Arabic; and the son, an architect, doctor or lawyer,
trained in French schools, who is, or desires to be, a French citizen,
completely cut off from his ancient origins. (*Forum for the Problems
of Zionism, Jewry and the State of Israel.* Proceedings at the Jerusalem Ideological Conference. Published by the World Zionist Organization. Jerusalem, 1959, pp. 261–262.)

11

Morocco: Frozen Stampede

THE JEWISH MINORITY

Origin and Status. Of the 500,000 Jews of the Moghreb in 1951, some 225,000 lived in French Morocco, among more than 8,-000,000 Moslems, comprising about 2.4 per cent of the country's total population. Slightly outnumbered by European, predominantly French, settlers, they constituted the country's third largest group.

Morocco's Jews have a long and checkered history. They appeared in the country in successive waves, dating from the third century before the Christian era to the sixteenth century of modern times. Among the earliest inhabitants, two main strata can be distinguished. One constituted the ancient Berber tribes who embraced Judaism at the end of the Roman era and during the Byzantine rule, that is, from the third to the sixth centuries C.E. Another group were refugees from Palestine after the Temple of Jerusalem was destroyed in the first century. The most recent immigrants came from Spain in the fifteenth and sixteenth centuries. The earlier inhabitants, Berbers and Palestinians, settled in the small towns of central and southern Morocco, in the oases and mountain villages. The later arrivals from Spain, joined by those from France or Italy, settled mainly in the large cities of northern Morocco; their descendants in the seventeenth and eighteenth centuries established important businesses and maintained commercial relations with traders in all parts of the world.[1]

It is estimated that of the present Jewish population of Morocco about 45 per cent are of Arab-Berber origin, and 13 per cent Hebrew-Aramaic; 17 per cent are descendants of emigrants

from Spain and other Latin countries, and 4 per cent descendants of more recent emigrants from Germany. Over the centuries, all these successive strata of newcomers have inter-
mingled with the indigenous Moroccan Jews.[2]

Both before and after the establishment of the French Protectorate (1912), Morocco was a Sherifian state, that is to say,
a theocratic state, where the Sultan, a descendant of Mohammed, combined total spiritual and secular power. The legal
status of the country's Jewish minority has never been secured
either in Moroccan domestic legislation or in any of the treaties on which the Protectorate was based. Fundamentally, the
Jews were considered as *dhimmis*—tolerated unbelievers. In
practice, they have been treated as second-rate subjects, suffering from all sorts of discrimination. Their situation improved
under the French rule, but they remained subjects of the Sultan, unable to acquire other citizenship unless they left the
country. Deprived of rights enjoyed by either native Moslems
or French citizens, they remained socially isolated from the
Moslem population by the centuries-old tradition of scornful
toleration which is characteristic of Islam, and did not become
integrated with the Europeans either: in matters of personal
status they were under the jurisdiction of the rabbinical courts
(appointed by the Sultan from the panel of candidates submitted by the Jewish community), and in civil and criminal
matters—under the jurisdiction of the Islamic courts. The Jewish community faithfully preserved its religion, tradition and
national consciousness.

The numerical growth of Moroccan Jewry after the establishment of the French Protectorate is illustrated by the following table.[3]

Year		Number of Jews
1921	. . . .	81,000
1926	. . . .	107,600
1931	. . . .	116,950
1936	. . . .	161,942
1947	. . . .	203,339
1951	(census)	199,156

About 73 per cent lived in urban areas, where Jews constituted 9 per cent of the population (almost four times more than their percentage of the country's total population).* They were concentrated (1947) mainly in:[4]

Casablanca	86,375
Marrakesh	18,750
Fez	18,020
Meknés	15,842
Mogador	7,425
Mazagan	4,250
Rabat	14,250
Oudjda	8,000
Sefrou	6,958

The Mellah. Now as before, the special Jewish quarter, the *mellah*, remains the most distinctive feature of the Jewish life in Morocco. It is usually about a quarter of the size of the neighboring Moslem quarter, the *medina*: the houses are of the same Moorish architecture.[5] The *mellahs* have the greatest population density of all the areas of the country: three to four times as much as the most crowded Moslem slum quarters.[6]

The approach is always through the "business section," located on both sides of the narrow streets lined with tiny shops, some of them no more than holes in the walls. Business and "industrial" sections are in separate districts. Typically the Jew is a shopkeeper, but in the bigger cities, the *mellah* is a largely self-supporting urban community. It contains *souks*, or combined factories and markets, for all commodities; up one alley brassworks bang, up another carpenters turn, guiding the chisel with their big toes.

From these business "streets" run tiny alleys—*impasses*, they are called—where the people live, many of them in one-story, single-room hovels clustered round an outhouse. There is no other plumbing, and certainly no running water. The cooking is done outside, in a common courtyard used by a number of families, either over kerosene or pressure gasoline stoves, or over braziers.[7]

---

* About 12,500 Jews lived in the Spanish zone of Morocco and about 10,000 in the international zone at Tangier.

Poverty is overwhelming. Thirty-five per cent live on public charity. In Casablanca, about 65 per cent of the Jewish dead have to be buried at the expense of the community—a humiliation to which the bereaved kith and kin submit only when they are utterly destitute.[8]

The housing problem of the *mellah*, with its high birth rate and constant overcrowding, is becoming ever more critical. There was no construction in Morocco during the war and the first few years thereafter. This, coupled with the migration of a large number of Jewish families from the interior to the large cities, has resulted in appalling living conditions. Reporting early in 1955 in Paris on the condition of Moroccan Jewry, Mr. Jacques Dahan, then Secretary General of the Council of Jewish Communities of Morocco, admitted that the Government had been trying hard to remedy this state of affairs, allocating during the previous few years a billion francs (about $2,-800,000 at the then current official rate) to alleviate the housing shortage for the benefit of the Jewish population; it also encouraged private construction. "The results, however, have been very meager," Mr. Dahan said: "only a few hundred dwellings, a drop in the bucket. Moreover, the social aspect of the problem has been overlooked entirely: the high cost of construction entailed rents which the people for whom these homes were built could not afford. Thus, only some middle-class families have profited by all these building projects, while those who are economically weak have been left to rot in their slums."[9]

Before France became the protecting power in 1912, the role of the Jews in economic life was conditioned by their political subjection. Because of the danger to their lives and property, they followed callings which required no fixed locale and which permitted the accumulation of wealth in its most mobile form, money. They became money-changers, traders or artisans, entered the liberal professions, and were active in fields such as import and export, which the Moslems neglected.

Declining Economy. Throughout the decades following the establishment of the French Protectorate, when Jews were freed from the economic restrictions of the pre-1912 era, their occupational structure continued reflecting the centuries of discrimination. Thus, though about one-third of the Jewish population were gainfully employed (as against one-fourth of the Moslems), in 1947, 46.5 per cent among them were engaged in commerce; 36.1 per cent in industry; 7.6 per cent in the liberal professions and public service; and 4 per cent in fisheries, forestry and agriculture. Most of the Jewish artisans are jewelers, leather craftsmen, textile and fur workers, and ropemakers. They, and many of the Jews engaged in commerce or industry, actually constitute the Jewish proletariat of Morocco. Almost half of the Jews counted in these two latter categories are employees, and most of the self-employed own little more than their skill and a small stock of goods. In public service, the Jews fill only minor positions as office boys, copyists and clerks.[10] On the other hand, in the liberal professions they are now represented beyond and above their numerical proportion in the country. In 1956, of the 45 registered doctors of medicine of Moroccan nationality, 25 were Jews; and 28 of the 55 lawyers.[11] There is also a thin upper-class layer, composed of rich and well-to-do merchants and industrialists, who exhibit the most ostentatious luxury and make a point of mingling ever more with their European and Moroccan counterparts. But the overwhelming majority are pathetically poor and live in the disease-ridden mellah.

And what is even worse—the meager economic positions held by the Jews are being inexorably undermined. There is a steady advance of Arab competition in business and trade which used to be almost exclusively in the hands of the Jews. Whereas mellah business sections were once almost wholly Jewish, they are now mixed. One can see a number of mellah shops closed on the Arab Sabbath and open on Saturday when all the Jewish shops are closed.[12] Morocco's traditional handicraft-agrarian society is disintegrating under the impact of rising industrialism and a money economy. Jewish small tradesmen and artisans are the first victims of this new development. They find themselves squeezed out of their old occupations, and even their present miserable livelihoods are threatened. "In the eighteen to forty age bracket, large numbers of Jews are completely without occupations," related the "Record of Ten Years of Rebuilding Jewish Economic Life" published by ORT (Organization for Rehabilitation Through Training) in 1957. "The ghettos overflow with peddlers and petty merchants. Artisans ply their crafts with hand tools and primitive work methods."[13] Those familiar with the realities of the Moroccan economic life believe that what is happening is that the Jews, who have held the so-called "middle positions," are now feeling pressure from Arabs who are preparing to take over these positions not only in the *mellah*, but also outside of the *mellah* walls, where the Jews have held a good share of the white-collar jobs in banks, businesses, and in some of the government agencies, such as post offices. The Moslems, according to Alfonso Sabah, Vice-Chairman of the Zionist Organization of Morocco, at the August 1955 session of the Zionist General Council

have more and more been able to acquire an education, and the number of students in the French universities is steadily increasing. The Arab merchants today have great businesses and some of them even very considerable fortunes. . . . The Arabs have one enormous advantage over the Jews. They work from morning to night, without any overhead expenses and with very few wants. The Jews [outside of the *mellah*], on the other hand, have become used to modern methods of work and to a standard of life which obliges them to calculate a much higher margin of profit than their Arab competitors. Today the small Jewish businessman is beginning to feel this state of affairs very painfully. Moreover, the young Jew who is leaving school no longer finds a situation in commerce so easily. On the one hand, his education is insufficient for the new pace in business, while on the other hand the miserable situation of his parents does not allow him to stay longer in order to acquire a better education.[14]

As the new Arab regime consolidates, the tendency to Islamize these jobs is hardening, and the Jew—as well as the Frenchman with whom he now shares these positions—is being pushed out. Office and government workers, many of them Jews, are already being asked by their superiors to train young Arabs, who, they know, will one day replace them. This is also true of medicine, dentistry, and the law—professions which have been largely "Jewish" and which increasing numbers of Arabs are now following.[15]

The Helping Hand. "The need is so great," Maurice Carr, reported early in 1959, "that without the massive financial aid furnished by the American Joint Distribution Committee, thousands and tens of thousands of Jews would just drop dead of hunger before the week was out."[16] Observers of the Moroccan Jewish scene have only praise for the work of the Joint, which a visiting journalist described as "the fairy godmother of all," performing in Morocco the kind of function which UNRRA did in Europe after the World War II, with quite as much emphasis on rehabilitation as on relief.[17] In 1958, the Joint maintained eighteen kindergartens; its canteen program was feeding 27,000 children throughout the country.[18] It also largely financed the constructive job of the ORT, which is training young people for skilled trades and craftmanship. In 1958, ORT's boys' school in Casablanca had 680 students, of whom 580 were resident students, coming from all parts of Morocco; in the girls' school, 389 pupils were learning dressmaking, chemical laboratory work and other practical arts. ORT's apprenticeship program, initiated in 1952, had an enrollment of 1,200. In its totality, the vocational training offered by ORT is intended "to provide the most favorable conditions for the continued existence of the Jewish communities, simultaneously helping those who are leaving to prepare for a useful life in Israel. . . . Whether he stays or leaves, the one certainty for the Jew is the impossibility of continuing as in the past. . . . The vocational school, combining general knowledge with skills, is an exit from the ghetto for thousands."[19]

For years, trachoma was the *mellah's* most widespread plague, causing a high incidence of blindness. It was stopped by the heroic efforts of OSE (Society for Protection of Jewish Health). In 1956, its special dispensaries had 48,449 treatment visits from patients suffering from this disease. Now, not one Jewish child in Morocco is going blind from trachoma. In the fight against ringworm (favus), OSE's dispensaries in 1956 examined 38,448 cases, effecting 4,806 cures. The total for that year involved 92,611 patients with all types of diseases; medical treatment was given in 448,556 instances. The school hygiene program serviced 6,770 children; milk stations distributed 1,700,738 bottles of milk for mothers and children from OSE's own fluid milk processing plant. The year's budget of $450,000 was covered mainly by the Joint.[20]

Education. The field of education has been for decades fully dominated by the Alliance Israélite Universelle, which offers educational facilities for a large majority of Jewish school-age children. At an early stage, it was the policy of the Alliance to entrust religious instruction to local Jewish communities. The latter were, however, not always able to adapt their teaching methods to the changing conditions of life and to the requirements of modern pedagogy. In 1950, of 35,638 children of school age, 5,450 (15.2 per cent) still attended *chedarim* (elementary Hebrew schools), whose curriculum and methods were an antiquated counterpart of the *cheder* in Poland or Rumania of a century ago. Dozens of children were crowded into a small, dark, often smelly cell, shut off from sun and air, ten hours a day, twelve months a year, with the *melamed* (elementary Hebrew teacher) cracking the whip over them. They were taught —by repetition in unison, by rote—to recite the prayers in Hebrew, the highest achievement being the ability to read and translate a portion of the Pentateuch. By 1954, fifty-five of the former *chedarim* were closed and their 2,400 pupils transferred to normal schools.[21]

Since 1940 the Alliance has taken over the religious instruction in its schools, gradually intensifying its scope and introducing the study of Hebrew. A report published in 1955 offers insight into the functioning of this new setup:[22]

Every hour of every school day a staff of one hundred Hebrew instructors is teaching Bible (sometimes with Raschi's commentary), Hebrew language and Jewish history to students in all the Alliance schools in Morocco. From seven to ten hours a week are devoted to these subjects in the schools for boys, from five to seven hours for girls.

Shortly after World War II, the Alliance created a Hebrew Normal School in Casablanca, dedicated solely to the training of teachers in Jewish subjects for the entire Alliance network. Every year twelve to fifteen men are graduated from the Normal School, after acquiring a profound knowledge of Judaism and a solid grounding in secular subjects including literary Arabic. The course also includes a full year of specialized pedagogical training and intensive study of the Talmud. . . . The students at the Paris Normal School of the Alliance, who are being trained as teachers of secular subjects for the Alliance system, also receive a thorough Jewish education.

In 1960, the Alliance maintained 77 schools in Morocco with a total enrollment of 28,702 pupils.[23] Its educational program, which for years had been steeped in the tradition of French culture and the policy of gallicization, has in recent years been largely adapted to the spirit of Jewish national consciousness and culture, and to the new realities created by the emergence of the state of Israel.

There is, however, in many circles a strong feeling that insufficient attention is being paid in the Alliance school network to both religious education and the study of Hebrew. *Ozar Hatorah*, the Society for Youth Education in the Middle East and North Africa, founded in 1944 in New York, is maintaining in Morocco a network of thirty elementary schools, high schools and evening schools with a total enrollment of 5,834 pupils— boys and girls, and a combined program of religious and secular education. Half of the school curriculum is devoted to the study of Torah and allied subjects. In all the schools where a full-day program is conducted, students are provided with food, medical care, clothing and physical training. Hebrew teachers training institutes in Tangiers (100 students) and Sefrou (60 students) and a rabbinical seminar in Tangiers are preparing professionally qualified teachers, community leaders, and rabbis. Girls' teachers seminars in Casablanca and Tangiers have 53 students.[24] Lately, emissaries of the rigidly orthodox "Lubavitcher Rebbe" have entered the Moroccan educational scene. Their schools and Talmud Torahs have an enrollment of 1,050.[25]

A total of more than 40,000 Jewish children, equally divided between boys and girls, almost 100 per cent of school-age children, now receive education in various types of Jewish schools. This compares favorably with the educational level of the Moslem majority. Of the estimated 1,500,000 children of

school age, only 481,368 in the school year 1957–1958 were
receiving elementary education in Moslem public schools, and
72,350 in Moslem private schools; only 12,368 boys and 1,006
girls attended Moslem secondary schools in 1956–1957.[26]

The combined effort of the Joint, the Alliance, the *Ozar
Hatorah*, the ORT and the OSE during the last two decades has
considerably bettered the economic, physical, cultural and
spiritual standard of the Moroccan Jewish community. Its
evolution is in many repects reminiscent of that among the
Jewish population in Eastern Europe at the turn of the century.
The emergence of Israel introduced a source of pride and confidence in the future. Several keen observers of the Moroccan
Jewish scene speak of a "revival of Moroccan Jewry."

FACING THE FRENCH-MOROCCAN SHOWDOWN

Birth Pangs of Moroccan Nationhood. It was a small group of
French-educated Moroccan Arab intellectuals that was responsible for the formation of the nationalist *Comité d'Action
Marocaine*, aiming at bringing about, by legal methods, autonomy for their country within the framework of the French Protectorate. Their leaders were Mohammed Allal el Fassi, Ahmed
Belafrej, and Mohammed el Yazidi. They entertained some
hope for realizing their aims as the Popular Front came to
power in Paris (1936–1939). But the Blum Government cold-
shouldered their demands. The party split in 1938 into a moderate wing, the *Qaoumhyene*, headed by Hassam el-Quazzini,
which still adhered to the idea of inner reforms in cooperation
with the French authority, and the more revolutionary *His-
byéne*, whose spiritual leader was el Fassi and the actual chief—
el Yazidi. In 1944, the *Istiqlal* (Independence) party unified
both wings, under the leadership of Belafrej el Yazidi and Ben
Abd el-Djellil. Its main demand was application of the Atlantic
Charter and independence of Morocco within the Pan-Islamic
framework.[27] Istiqlal-instigated riots caused bloodshed and led
to arrests of its leaders; repression alternated with attempts at
belated partial reforms. The conflict grew and sharpened. While
the French authorities were aiming at a French-Moroccan entity
within a French Empire, the nationalists, backed by the Sultan

Mohammed ben Youssef, wanted an independent Moslem Morocco. In August 1953, the Sultan was forced to resign and was deported to Corsica and later to Madagascar. Moulay ben Arafa was proclaimed Sultan in his place.

A period of fierce struggle followed. Nationalist violence was countered by mass arrests. The Istiqlal party was banned and its newspapers suppressed. Moslem terrorists found their counterpart in vigilante groups organized by European colonists who began to take the law into their own hands. The situation grew increasingly tense and explosive. At the end of August 1955, a top level French-Moroccan conference took place at Aix-les-Bains. It resulted in a compromise providing for the removal of Sultan ben Arafa and the formation of a Moroccan Government headed by Si Bekkai, leader of the Istiqlal. In November 1955, Sultan Mohammed ben Youseff triumphantly returned to Morocco, later assuming the title of King Mohammed V. Further negotiations led, on March 3, 1956, to the abrogation of the Protectorate Treaty of 1912 and the recognition of Morocco's independence.

The Jewish Position. In the struggle between Moroccan nationalism and the French colonial rule, the Moroccan Jewish community has been for years striving to remain uncommitted, taking neither one side nor the other. However, the sympathies of the middle-aged section and those of the more prosperous Jewish merchants were on the whole with France, which stood for the *status quo*, for order and calm. Some of the younger generation, on the other hand, though French-educated, were leaning toward the Istiqlal, which symbolized for them the struggle of the underdog for a cause of liberation. Yet none of these two trends found expression in actual participation in the struggle. French sympathizers knew too well that they were exposed to Moslem vengeance in a way no Frenchman was. They lived in the *mellah*, right beside, or even enclosed by, the *medina*—both forming part of the Old Town—while the Frenchman dwelt on the other side of the hill, in the New Town. The ardent Jewish youth, who would make common cause with the Moslem nationalists, also knew that, if caught in a riot, they would as likely as not get a much harsher treatment from the

French police than their Moslem comrades. Nevertheless, when
Mahjoub ben Seddik, the leader of the illegal Moroccan
nationalist trade union movement, opened a subscription for
the relatives of the Moslem dead after the Casablanca riots of
1955, he was astonished at the amount of Jewish support.[28]

Negotiations. During the crucial period preceding the estab-
lishment of Morocco's sovereignty, it was the World Jewish
Congress that played a leading part in shaping the status of
Moroccan Jewry in the new state of Morocco.

The report submitted in August 1959 to the Fourth Plenary
Assembly of the World Jewish Congress in Stockholm, by the
directors of Congress Political and International Department,
A. L. Easterman and Dr. M. L. Perlzweig, gives a succinct account of the frequent consultations conducted in Paris, "always with the consent and approval of the French Government," with the leaders of the Moroccan Independence Movement:[29]

In January 1955, the Moroccan Independence leaders in Paris
requested a meeting with representatives of the Congress. At this
meeting, the future status and rights of the Jews of Morocco were
fully discussed. The Moroccan leaders maintained, on the close inquiries of the Congress representatives, that the aims of their movement were fully democratic, and that an independent or autonomous
Morocco would guarantee the freedom and equality of all its citizens,
irrespective of origin and faith, and would not only assure non-
discrimination, but would provide for the participation of Jews in
all branches of public administration.

In later discussions, the Moroccan leaders declared their intention,
in the event of Moroccan independence, to assure freedom of emigration for Jews to Israel and elsewhere, and to observe the Universal
Declaration of Human Rights in this respect. When, subsequently,
the Moroccan leaders conferred with the Sultan in Madagascar, they
informed the Congress representatives that the Sultan fully endorsed
the undertakings given to the Congress delegation, including the
right of emigration.

In the meantime, the situation in Morocco worsened steadily, with
increasing prospects of an outbreak of violence. In the result, the
Moroccan nationalists issued an ultimatum naming August 20th as
the fateful date for the acceptance by the French Government of

proposals for reforms, the principal features of which were the removal of the [French-installed] Sultan Moulay Ben Arafa, the appointment of a Council of the Throne, prior to the return of the Sultan Mohammed Ben Youssef, and the setting up of a Moroccan Government. Rejection of these proposals, it was openly declared, would be followed by violence on a civil war scale. This involved the clear prospect of large scale terrorism in Morocco, with the real danger that Jews might be victims of attack.

In this grave situation, the Congress representatives requested a conference with the principal Moroccan leaders. At this conference on August 9, 1955, the Congress most strongly urged that the Moroccan nationalist leaders should take special measures to protect the Jews against attack, and that this should be done, *inter alia*, by way of a clear and public directive to their supporters in Morocco.

The Moroccan leaders were asked to make such a declaration before the fateful date of August 20th so that the Moroccan population would have ample notice of the desire of the Nationalist leaders to protect Jewish life and property.

The Moroccan leaders agreed to act as requested. On August 15, Ahmed Belafrej, the Secretary-General of the Istiqlal party (later Foreign Minister and Prime Minister of Morocco), issued a statement declaring, *inter alia*:

'There is no justification for fear that in an independent Morocco Jews would suffer discrimination in any form. Jewish Moroccans will be citizens equal both in law and in fact with Moslems. They will enjoy the same rights and will be under the same obligations; their religious liberty will remain untouched. The greatest service that can be rendered them is to help them. Morocco is their country, its freedom their freedom; whoever helps Jewish Moroccans helps Moroccan independence.'

This important declaration was given widespread publicity in the Moroccan and French press, and was broadcast to the Moroccan people over the Tangier radio. In addition, the Moroccan Nationalists distributed leaflets to their followers throughout Morocco, calling on them to refrain from attacks against the Jews.

Widespread terrorism broke out throughout Morocco on August 20 and lasted several days, during which there were massacres on a large scale involving, it is estimated, several thousand persons.

The report asserts that "although there were a very small number of Jewish casualties, there was not evidence of any attack specifically directed against Jews or motivated by anti-Semitism." This is, however, hardly accurate. On August 28, the special correspondent of the London *Jewish Chronicle* reported from Casablanca that specifically anti-Jewish violence was widespread in the interior of the country. Several Jews were killed in Qued Zem. The town's *mellah*, where many Jewish houses were demolished, was evacuated; 1,500 Jews were removed from the *mellah* of Mazagan before it was sacked by Moslem mobs, and 500 were evacuated from the *mellah* of Safi. "Even though large numbers of troops have arrived from France, there is great anxiety among the quarter of a million Jews of Morocco, who feel that they are now in real danger." The Casablanca correspondent of the Parisian *Le Figaro* reported that the Moroccan "Army of Liberation" was aiming its activities "more and more" at the Jewish community, acting under the inspiration of overseas Arab radio stations, particularly the Cairo "Voice of the Arabs."[30]

Agreement. Subsequent development of the contacts between Moroccan nationalists and Jewish leaders (Meyer Toledano of Casablanca, Dreyfus-Schmidt, and World Jewish Congress representatives, Dr. Maurice Perlzweig and A. L. Easterman) is described in a report published in the *Jewish Chronicle* of September 2, 1955. They met late in August at Aix-les-Bains, behind the scenes of the Franco-Moroccan conference, and reached what was described as a "large measure of agreement":

As a gesture to the Nationalists, whose susceptibilities the Jews were anxious not to offend, the Jewish delegation, appearing officially before the French Committee of Five, breathed not a word about the many discriminations from which the Moroccan Jews suffer as second-rate subjects of a theocratic state. The Jewish spokesmen, who were greeted by the French Prime Minister, M. Edgar Faure, chairman of the Committee, as objective people, simply stated that the Jews, after 2,000 years in Morocco, consider themselves an integral part of the Moroccan people and as such want the country to be made democratic and modernized, and equal rights to be accorded to all citizens.

At the encounter with the Jews, the representatives of the progressive Moroccan Democratic Party of Independence (P.D.I.) gave assurance—in the presence of delegates of the more conservative

Istiqlal party (who remained silent)—that all Jewish disabilities
would be removed in the new Morocco.

In the wake of the agreement reached at Aix-les-Bains, responsible Moroccan Jewish leaders have abandoned their traditional attitude of mute neutrality as between the Moorish
Nationalists and the French Protectorate authorities, and have
openly declared themselves in favor of a fundamental revision
of Franco-Moroccan relations, more or less on the lines of the
Tunisian settlement. Maître Meyer Toledano, acting in his
capacity of Secretary-General of the Moroccan Central Committee of the World Jewish Congress, published an article in
the Parisian *Le Monde* entitled "The Morocco of Tomorrow,"
in which he described the Nationalist movement as "natural and
irresistible." . . . If, instead of thwarting a natural and irresistible movement, France will facilitate the political evolution of the country, the grateful Moroccan people will never be
able to contest the intangible rights of France in Morocco, the
exercise of which is essential to her role of a great world power.[31]
Maître Toledano and, before him, at Aix, the delegation led by
M. Jacques Dahan, the Secretary-General of the Council of
Jewish Communities, have thus formally arrayed Moroccan
Jewry behind the idea of a free Morocco conscious of its ties
with France.

. . . *And Its Implementation.* In the course of the negotiations
at Aix-les-Bains, the Nationalist leaders broached the matter
of the inclusion of a Jewish Minister in the next Moroccan
government. Jewish representatives pointed out, however, that
they were opposed to the creation of a special ministry for Jewish
affairs. Their attitude was that if the Nationalists would give
an "ordinary" portfolio to a Jew, it would show their genuine
desire to make a clean break with the theocratic past.

In fact, Dr. Léon Benzaquen, who had a noteworthy communal record on Jewish social welfare without political over-
tones and had been an early advocate of Jewish "integration,"
was appointed Ministre des Postes, Télégraphes et Téléphones,
a position which he retained till May 1958, when a virtually
all-Istiqlal cabinet, with no Jewish member at all, came to

power. Several other qualified Jews were placed in positions of trust in the governmental machinery. "There is no secular ministry in the administration," reported Hal Lehrman in the summer of 1958, "which does not have some Jewish personnel, often in a high place." Among these, in addition to a cabinet minister, have been a *directeur de cabinet* in the Foreign Ministry, a director of mining production and a planning expert in the National Economy Ministry, an attaché in Agriculture, a *chef de cabinet* in the P.T.T., an important official in the Interior Ministry, and the director of the important *Office des Céréales*. Jewish students, in addition, are well represented in the *Ecole Supérieure d'Administration*, the training school for future civil service élite.[32]

The report submitted to the Stockholm Assembly of the World Jewish Congress correctly stated that "from the beginning of the new Moroccan state until the present time, there has been no single instance of attacks upon Jews or of discrimination against them in respect of their civil liberties."

Istiqlal Jews. Even before Morocco's independence was proclaimed, a Jewish group known as *Mouvement National Marocain*, led by one Joe Ohana (a merchant who had contributed to Istiqlal's treasury) had merged with Istiqlal. Another Istiqlal man, Marc Sabah, who emerged as spokesman for the party's ultrapatriotic Jewish Section, a sort of Arab-Nationalist Yevsektzia, who consider themselves as Moroccan as the Moslems —some of them even more so—has, together with several Jewish and Moslem friends, established, in January 1956, a society called El Wifaq (Understanding), to promote a rapprochement between the Moslem and Jewish communities. The inaugural meeting in Rabat was attended by 1,800 persons and was addressed by the Crown Prince, Moulay Hassan,* and several members of the Cabinet. Similar gatherings were arranged in Casablanca, Meknes, and other cities. In 1958, Wifaq claimed to have chapters in twenty-seven communities. Yet its actual influence among the Jews of Morocco seems to have been rather

* It is interesting to note that at this meeting the Crown Prince declared that it was as natural for Jews to look to Jerusalem for inspiration—as it was for Moslems to look to Cairo and Mecca.

scarce. The appeal to enroll into a voluntary youth labor corps for the construction of the forty-mile "Unity Road" connecting Fez with the Mediterranean port of Alhusemas, was a manifest failure: of a crew of 10,537 which completed the road in October 1957, only 150 were Jews. Not a single Jewish youth responded to the appeal to join the newly created Royal Army. And it was reported that at the second anniversary meeting of the Wifaq's Casablanca branch in March 1958, an audience variously estimated from four to ten turned up.

Wifaq's opponents described its Jewish membership as an exclusive, highly educated group, mostly professional men who have been out of the *mellah* for years, and do not identify themselves with its inhabitants. Their identification is with the top layer of educated nationalist Moslems, who have provided the intellectual leadership of the Moroccan liberation movement. They are considered as Johnny-come-latelies to the Jewish scene, attracted by prospects of political advancement through becoming "spokesmen" for the Jewish community. Sabah himself was accused of being a slavish messenger boy of the all-powerful Ben Barka, boss of the Istiqlal's party machinery. It was stressed that instead of preaching understanding and brotherly attitude among the Moslems (a mission pitifully neglected by Wifaq's Moslem membership), the society was concentrating on converting Jews to the gospel of Moroccan nationhood; its leaders fervently advocate the study of Arabic in Jewish schools at the expense of Hebrew instruction, and have little understanding of and sympathy for the spiritual needs of the Jewish community and its rights as a legitimate ethnic and religious minority; foreign Jewish institutions (Joint, OZE, *Ozar Hatorah*) working in the country are to them "intruders" who should either get out or turn their management over to Moroccan Jews—or to the Moroccan Government; overzealous preachers of complete integration are vying with one another in proclaiming their Moroccan patriotism, and their frenzied protestations of loyalty have more than once reached the level of unedifying slavishness. A Casablanca Jewish group, at the time of the Sinai campaign, has distributed a pamphlet denouncing Israel as "an imperialist power which had stabbed our Egyptian

brothers in the back."[33] In January 1956, Dr. Nachum Goldman warned at the London Conference of the World Jewish
Congress that Jewish youth in Morocco, intoxicated with the
freedom and opportunities offered for the first time in a history
of 2,000 years, might become, as he put it, "more Istiqlal than
the Istiqlal," and forego its Jewish heritage in order to be fully
accepted as Moroccan patriots.[34]

LEAVING FOR ISRAEL

Growing Emigration Trend. Moroccan Jewry had traditionally
maintained spiritual ties with Eretz Israel. *Halukkah* collections
flourished. In the 1930's a small Zionist organization was established. But throughout the decade preceding the establishment
of the State of Israel only a small trickle of immigrants flowed
to Palestine. During the twenty-nine years of British Mandate
rule (1919–1947), when nearly half a million Jews entered the
country, merely 1,000 (.002 per cent of total immigration) came
from Morocco-Tunisia.

Their number began to rise during the first stage of the War
of Liberation. Of their own accord, hundreds of young Jews
stole their way out of Morocco to join the Israeli Army; many
laid down their lives. Organized large-scale immigration began
in the second part of 1948. In the two-year period 1948–1949,
some 8,000 left Morocco.[35] Israeli recruiting missions, financed
by the Jewish Agency, were established in the country. They
were working through the indigenous Moroccan Zionist organization *Kadimah*, which supervised the passport formalities,
assembling and transportation of the greater part of the emigrants, who—because of remote geographic location, poverty or
illiteracy—were unable to arrange matters for themselves. Recruiting offices were set up in the major centers, principally in
Casablanca and Marrakesh. From there a steady flow of information and propaganda material was distributed all over the
country, mainly through local synagogues; on Sabbath, rabbis
read it to their congregations, painting a glowing and appealing
account of life in the resurrected Jewish state. There was no
deceit in this representation, but it was, at best, one-sided: the
hard realities of a young and poor pioneering country were only

sketchily mentioned. In rural areas, the Agency recruiting personnel moved from village to village, registering candidates for immigration.

The response was not uniform. Those well off and those who felt "most French" kept aloof. Excited and enthusiastic were those who had little to lose: small shopkeepers, artisans, members of the new urban proletariat in the city and country *mellahs*. In some cases, entire villages signed up for emigration. In 1950, 4,980 left; and 7,770 in 1951. Relative relaxation of political tension brought down the emigration figure to 5,031 in 1952 and to 2,996 in 1953. The pre-independence year of 1954 saw the departure of 8,171.[36]

Selectivity. At an early stage, every Jew who registered for emigration was unquestioningly admitted to Israel. But later, a rigid selective system was introduced: the aged and the ill were excluded. The new procedure was as follows:

At some time following registration, each family was summoned to the Jewish Agency immigration office, where a *prima facie* case for *aliyah* had to be made out by undergoing exhaustive medical examination in accordance with the selectivity rules. Each family had to have at least either a father or a son not older than forty-five and not younger than eighteen capable of earning a living for all and enjoying resonably good health. The whole family was definitely rejected if there was a paralytic, lunatic, idiot or other dependent afflicted with a serious incurable or contagious disease. No attempt was made at the almost impossible task of carrying out morality probes, of weeding out thieves, prostitutes and beggars.

Maurice Carr, who witnessed the procedure of selection in Casablanca, reported in 1951:[37]

The screening process is a nerve-racking business. . . . The men, women and children arrive well-washed and in their Sabbath finery for this occasion. . . . Since birth certificates were a thing unknown until a couple of years ago, no family head admits to being above forty-five and no youth to being under eighteen. . . . Some of the rowdiest and most pathetic scenes occur when an aged and widowed mother, or elderly parents whose sons and daughters have preceded them to Israel, are turned away because the thoughtlessly drafted regulations require that a family breadwinner be on hand in the Diaspora at the time of application. The old folk weep and shout, demanding why they, who may have sons in Israel, in the Army, be penalized as against other people whose children are still in Morocco.

. . . When asked to state his trade, the breadwinner almost invariably replies, 'I can do anything,' and when further pressed, adds that he is a cobbler or a tailor or a peddler, or confesses that he has no trade. To ingratiate himself, he will give the Israelis behind the table a military salute or throw himself forward to kiss their hands.

. . . And then comes the most awesome day of judgment; the final decision is taken by a panel headed by a doctor sent over from the Israel Ministry of Health. . . . The families are not told immediately what the outcome of the selection is; but they always guess, infallibly. The rejected ones often dissolve in tears, fly into fits of rage. As I watched these scenes, and I attended a dozen such selections, I was moved as never before. It needs supreme callousness to remain dry-eyed.

Those admitted had to wait for their turn to leave—sometimes several months and even longer. This was for them a trying time. Prospective immigrants had usually sold to their Moslem neighbors all their meager possessions well in advance of actual emigration, and had to live off the proceeds of this sale. There were persistent rumors of bribery designed to gain quicker departure. When one's *tor* (place on the immigration schedule) finally arrived, the emigrants were directed to transit camps in the vicinity of Casablanca where they waited to board the ship. Some were first taken to France where they again had to wait weeks or months before leaving for Israel.

. . . *And Its Impact.* Already the first years of applying selection have markedly influenced the age scale, percentage of earners, and occupational distribution of the Moroccan immigration. Comparing its structure with that of the Jewish population of Morocco (as stated by the census of 1947) and that of immigrants from other countries, Dr. B. Gil, Director of Demographic and Social Statistics of Israel's Central Bureau of Statistical and Economic Research, summarized the results as follows:[38]

1. The total percentage of the working-age groups (fifteen to

fifty-nine years) was higher among the Moroccan [and Tunisian] immigrants (65 per cent) than that found among other African and Asian immigrants (56 per cent), and nearly equal to the percentage among European immigrants (66 per cent);

The percentage of young persons was particularly high; those aged fifteen to twenty-nine amounted to 45 per cent of the Moroccan-Tunisians, as compared with 30 per cent of the Asian and other African immigrants, or with 29 per cent of those from Europe;

On the other hand, persons aged sixty years and over accounted for only 1.6 per cent, as against 8 per cent of the Jewish population in Morocco and 6 to 7 percent of other immigrants (Asian and European).

2. Among those who immigrated in 1950–1951 the earners accounted for 36 per cent, as compared with 30 per cent among Jews in Morocco or 27 per cent among other Oriental immigrants. It approached the percentage found among European immigrants (37 per cent).

3. While among the Jews of Morocco the secondary occupations (mainly handicrafts) comprise less than one-third of male earners, this category was represented by two-thirds among the immigrants to Israel. On the other hand, the tertiary occupations which among the Moroccan Jewish population are represented by 65 per cent of all male earners (among these, commerce occupies 55 per cent), comprised merely 26 per cent among immigrants to Israel (commerce but 11 per cent).

The Writing on the Wall. The year 1955 started with a new intensification of the immigration trend. Dr. Joseph S. Schwartz, the Executive Vice-Chairman of the United Jewish Appeal, reported that "registration for emigration is so fast that Jewish officials cannot keep pace" and that 70,000 Jews in Morocco and Tunisia are eager to leave.[39] The French authorities quietly tolerated this trend. But already in the spring of 1955 they started talking of curbs. Michael Clark of *The New York Times* quoted one official saying, "We have been very liberal with the Jews, but they must not carry this thing too far."[40] Three months later, Gilbert Grandval, the new French Resident-General in Rabat, in a move to appease Moroccan nationalists, clamped on a ban on further Jewish emigration. It was only after "a dramatic talk with the Prime Minister Edgar Faure at the home of some mutual acquaintances near Cannes" that this ban was rescinded, recalled four years later Mr. Yakov Tsur, who was then Israeli Ambassador to France.[41]

There were also disturbing indications of an adverse attitude on the part of the Moroccan leaders:

The *Makhzen*, or central government, has taken no official cognizance of the departure of large numbers of Jews for Israel [reported Michael Clark]. The matter has not been alluded to in public. But the *Makhzen* is known to deplore a devolpment that deprives the Sultan of many of his subjects while at the same time increasing the strength of a country at odds with the Arabs of the Middle East.

From the Moroccan point of view, Jewish emigration also looks unpleasantly like a vote of "no confidence" in the ability of the Moslems to manage the affairs of the country with equal justice for all.[42]

Responsible Zionist leaders in the North African countries, familiar with the facts and trends of the Moroccan scene, were timely is seeing the writing on the wall. Faced with the impending prospect of Morocco's independence, a delegation representing the Zionist organization of Morocco, Tunisia, and Algeria appeared before the August 1955 session of the General Council of the World Zionist Organization in Jerusalem, to plead *periculum in mora* and to urge evacuation of the endangered Moroccan Jewish community.[43]

Alfonso Sabah, Vice-Chairman of the Zionist Organization of Morocco, bluntly put the question:

What will be the situation of the Jews of Morocco at this new juncture?

There are optimists who think that they will be able to become integrated into the Moroccan community by renouncing any relationship with the Jewries of other countries in general and that of Israel in particular. Others feel instinctively that they are witnessing a process that will necessarily have repercussions upon their own existence, but they have no clear idea how they will be affected by this evolution. Those people prefer a wait-and-see policy. They believe that they can bide their time for several months or even years and that the hour of decision has not yet come. Finally there are those who are frankly anxious and see no other way out than their immediate departure before the doors of Morocco are definitely closed.... There will be no official discrimination ... after the Jews have acquired Moroccan nationality, but ... they will be subjected to the regulations which will be enacted in matters of emigration and foreign affairs. . . . A certain anxiety prevails in Jewish circles that the future Moroccan state might be obliged, in certain delicate situations, to try and obtain the assistance of the Arab states, by following their line of conduct, as was the case in Lybia.

Without mincing words, Mr. Sabah told the hushed Council that Moroccan Jewry "turns its eyes with fervor and hope toward Israel. From there it expects the salvation. It utters only two words which are terrible in their simplicity: *Make haste!* Taking into account the difficulties of absorption in Israel which we do not underestimate and which necessarily limit the possibilities of *aliya*, we do not request a 'flying carpet' between Morocco and Israel; but we consider it our duty to ask for a monthly quota of 5,000 persons . . . [and] to alleviate the rules of selection limiting them to contagious diseases and incurable illnesses. . . . You are of course entitled to wish that emigration from Morocco should be carried through gradually and distributed over several years. But then you forget the risk that it might dry up."

This pathetic appeal for "making haste" irrespective of other considerations was emphatically endorsed by representatives from two other North African countries.

Meyer Bellity, Chairman of the Zionist Organization of Tunisia, insisted that "the whole basis of the Jewish Agency's methods must be altered as it has been proved false by the events. Economic stability [of Israel], commercial equilibrium, the laws of production and consumption cannot serve as an argument. It may be valid for any state, but it is not valid for Israel! At this moment, Israel must, unfortunately, violate the laws of economy."

Not less explicit was André Narboni, Chairman of the Zionist Federation of Algeria: "In Morocco as well as in Tunisia *aliya* is a matter of emergency. The position is the same as it was at

a certain time in the countries behind the Iron Curtain . . .
[where] it was necessary to make haste before the curtain descended, as indeed happened shortly afterward. The same holds
true for the *aliyah* from Morocco and Tunisia, and it is for this
reason that we Algerians have joined our friends from Morocco
and Tunisia in trying to arouse you to a sense of danger."

The well-informed Chairman of the Zionist Federation of
France, André Blumel, added a meaningful warning: "At present, no difficulties are being encountered in regard to *aliyah*,
either on the part of the French Government or on the part of
the local French administration [in North Africa]. . . . But tomorrow, the Jewish Agency and the Zionist Federation will no
longer have to deal and talk with the French authorities. You
will have to deal and talk with a Tunisian and Moroccan Government."

Rabbi Fingerhut of Algeria warned: "If we are denied the
opportunity of *aliyah*, we shall organize an illegal immigration
to Israel, an *Aliya Bet*, such as took place in the days of the
British Mandate. What will the nations of the world say when
they see that the Jews of North Africa have to resort to such
measures when there is a Jewish state. . . . ?"

Official Zionist and Israeli Attitude. Jewish Agency leaders
were, however, not impressed, let alone convinced, by the
unanimous appeal for urgency voiced by qualified representatives of North African Jewish communities and by their insistence that timely rescue of Moroccan Jewry must take precedence over the Agency's budgetary considerations and even over
the everyday economic interests of Israel's present population.
They were in no hurry. Said Dr. Nachum Goldman: "For me,
the economic stability of Israel . . . tops the list [of priorities],
even if it should mean that the transfer of Moroccan Jews should
take a decade or even two. It is perfectly correct that the emigration of North African Jewry must take place in Israel. But no
Zionist program provides that it must be achieved in 1955!"

The Treasurer of the Agency, Mr. G. Josephstall, denied the
rescue nature of the emigration from Morocco and agreed
merely to doubling last year's quota of 18,000. He added, however, that "if, heaven forbid, a situation should arise which

would compel immediate *aliyah* . . . we shall be obliged to resort to every absorption effort . . . and to abandon all numerical and economic considerations." The resolutions adopted by the majority of the Council merely expressed "sympathy to the Jews of Morocco in their present difficulties" and charged the Executive, "in view of the deterioration of the situation in Morocco and the demand from that country for intensified immigration . . . to adopt special measures for the organization of intensified and urgent immigration during [the Jewish year] 5,716."

Somewhat less complacent was the attitude of Israel's Parliament. At a specially convened session, the Knesset approved a resolution stating that emigration to Israel was the only practical solution to the danger facing North African Jewry. It requested the Government to present a program for financing increased immigration and absorption, and called on Jews in Israel and in the Diaspora, particularly those in the United States, to mobilize the necessary funds. Yet at the same time, Prime Minister Moshe Sharett, surveying the position of North African Jewry, averred that his government believed that the French authorities were aware of their duty to safeguard the lives and property of the Jewish minority in Morocco and of assuring their freedom to emigrate to Israel; he nevertheless admitted that this did not depend entirely on the French authorities as there might be unforeseen complications or upheavals. The Minister of Finance, Levi Eshkol, added that to finance large-scale immigration from North Africa, the amount of $210 million would be needed and that the funds derived from appeals, bonds, German reparations, etc., were mortgaged for the next six to eight years for development purposes and the integration of the present population.[44]

Protests and Projects. North African immigrants in Israel were bitterly disappointed by this attitude of the Zionist and Israeli ruling bodies. A mass demonstration, carrying national flags and banners, marched through Jerusalem to the Jewish Agency building, to demand the urgent rescue of Jews still in North Africa, increased immigration quotas, reunion of families, and abolition of the selective immigration system. A smaller protest march took place in Haifa, where the demonstrators broke into the offices of the Jewish Agency and smashed the windows before the police arrived. Newcomers from Morocco reported that the situation at home represented "constant danger." Though some Arabs had tried to reassure them by saying that the disturbances were directed solely against the French, they felt that the Arabs wanted the Jews to stay now in order to be able to buy Jewish property cheaply when they eventually would be compelled to leave the country hurriedly in the face of mounting Arab violence.[45]

The situation grew so tense that it aroused concern of non-Jewish bodies. The Immigration Subcommittee of the United States House of Representatives gave serious attention to the pressing problem of Jewish mass exodus from French Africa to Israel. In September 1955, the Committee Chairman, Congressman Francis E. Walter, asked the Secretary of State John Foster Dulles to instruct the United States delegation to the sessions of the Intergovernmental Committee for European Migration (ICEM), scheduled to open in Geneva on October 17, to urge that ways and means be found of assisting the State of Israel in the task of moving and settling the North African Jewish migrants to that country. Pointing out that a total of 200,000 Jews might desire to move to Israel within the next five to six years, and that some 80,000 Jews from North Africa had entered Israel between May 1948 and May 1955, Rep. Walter stressed that Israel was bearing the brunt of all the expenses in the moving and resettling of immigrants, and that voluntary contributions and the efforts of the Jewish Agency only partially alleviated the economic burden placed upon it. Since the ICEM's constitution authorized the committee to concern itself with refugees from areas other than Europe, the Jewish migrants from French North Africa could justifiably claim the status of refugees "fleeing their century-old abodes in fear of persecution on account of race or religious beliefs." These migrants, he cogently argued, "are not much different from refugees fleeing to escape Communist persecution; they therefore appear to be deserving of international support and assistance," and should be accorded, for humanitarian reasons, "higher priority than the migratory movements of manpower prompted solely by economic factors."

The proposals of Rep. Walter's committee called for ICEM to finance the transfer to Israel of about 200,000 Jews from North Africa over a five-year period; 75,000 would be moved in the first two years, with the United States contributing a large portion of the necessary financial means. It seemed that the U.S. Department of State favored the scheme, and a committee of ICEM experts was reported studying Rep. Walter's report. The project was, however, buried in ICEM's archives.[46]

Simultaneously, it became apparent that Moroccan nationalist leaders, while solemnly promising that the Jewish minority in independent Morocco would enjoy all rights, including the right to emigrate, were strongly opposed to the exercise of this right. In the early autumn of 1955, the Moroccan Party of Democratic Independence issued a statement declaring that "the attention of the P.D.I. has been drawn to news from various parts of Morocco according to which a large number of our compatriots of the Jewish faith are leaving or have expressed a desire to leave Morocco to settle in Israel. In the present circumstances, and at a moment when a new era is taking shape for Morocco, the P.D.I. considers this attitude as inopportune and unjustified." The communiqué urged the Jews not to emigrate, alluding to the increased *aliyah* as "an attempt to exploit the feeling of certain Jewish circles in Morocco," and contained a "solemn appeal to the compatriots of Jewish faith to recover their confidence and to serve their country to which they have been attached for thousands of years."[47]

Moroccan Jews were more frightened than reassured by this appeal to their patriotic duty. In March 1956, the Casablanca correspondent of *The New York Times* reported that "a wave of fear has swept the ancient Jewish community of Morocco." Quoting Ira Hirshman, a New York businessman on an unofficial mission of inquiry in the country, he related that "the rush to leave Morocco is such that the men responsible for Jewish emigration to Israel are overwhelmed; the dominating fear is that the Moroccans will use their newly won independence to slam the door on Jewish emigration. . . . Several small Jewish communities in the interior have vanished entirely."[48] A near stampede to get out in time developed.

Notwithstanding the obvious and imminent threat to the prospects of Jewish emigration, the 24th Zionist Congress in Jerusalem (April 24–May 7, 1956), at which the problem of Moroccan Jewry was one of the main topics in the debate, still deliberated "whether there exists the danger that the gates of egress would be shut," said S. Z. Shragai, member of the Jewish Agency Executive in charge of immigration, a year later. "The tragedy of the situation," admitted the Agency official, "is that meantime the gates have been shut in the faces of one hundred thousand potential emigrants."[49]

THE FROZEN STAMPEDE

Shutting the Gates. On June 11, 1956, the Moroccan security authorities suddenly ordered the dissolution of *Kadimah*, and closed its premises in Casablanca. Simultaneously, expulsion orders were served on twenty Israelis who had been assisting *Kadimah*. Organized emigration was banned. A bottleneck arose. The transit camp at Mazagan, near Casablanca, where most of those bound for Israel waited for transportation, housed, as usual, some 1,000 prospective emigrants. Within two months, its population had swelled to nearly 8,000. Lengthy negotiations, inaugurated through the World Jewish Congress, secured agreement at least to permit the departure of the Mazagan group, and between August 12 and September 26, all of them were allowed to leave for Israel.

But others were not. For the 50,000 to 60,000 Jews who had registered for emigration, Morocco became a forced residence. They proclaimed a fast on the day the gates of exit were closed. They have not withdrawn their applications and have not reverted to their former way of life, both because that was no longer possible and because they wished to come to Israel. As Richard Yaffe, the *Jewish Chronicle* special correspondent for North Africa, put it in August 1956, the closed offices of *Kadimah* in Casablanca's 16 Rue Lieutenant de Vaisseau Yves Gay had become "the graveyard of 50,000 hopes. . . . Piled on the floor of several offices of *Kadimah* are the files, complete with pictures, of 50,000 Moroccan Jews who have been medically examined for emigration to Israel, and accepted. Their visas were prepared. . . . And there are another 50,000 Jews who had indicated their desire to go to Israel and who were to have had medical examinations when the order came halting mass Jewish emigration. These files will now be sent to the reception camp in Marseilles for preservation, in the hope—believed in vain—that Morocco will change her mind and let the Jews go."

The prevailing mood among Moroccan Jewish organizations, reported Yaffe,

is to blame Israel for setting a quota on immigration, and those in the World Zionist Movement who thought there was still plenty of time to move those who wanted to leave North Africa. . . . Warnings were given time and again that it was later than they thought, but these were ignored. The excuses were excellent: Israel's defense needs had to come first; proper places of settlement and not *ma'-abarot* [transit camps] had to be found for new arrivals; world Jewry was not responding to the monetary appeals as it had done in the past. The debate at the World Zionist Congress was recalled with bitterness. Then, various parties debated how many should be brought over monthly and yearly from Morocco. . . . Even as the delegates debated, a decree was being promulgated halting mass Jewish emigration.[50]

"*Individual Emigration.*" The Moroccan authorities maintained that their new anti-emigration policy applied only to "organized collective emigration" of the kind sponsored by *Kadimah*. They claimed that their pre-independence pledges of guaranteeing to every Moroccan citizen the individual right to leave the country, as defined in the Universal Declaration of Human Rights, had not been affected: individual Jews could go abroad where and when they pleased. "Like all Moroccan citizens," Secretary of State of Information Abdallah Ibrahim told a press conference, "Jews are free to obtain a passport and leave Morocco." The World Jewish Congress received assurances from top government officials that Jews could have passports for the mere asking, "just like anyone else." But asked point-blank whether passports would be issued "to all Jewish applicants without any discrimination whatsoever," one of the most influential men in the new Morocco, Mehdi Ben Barka, Speaker of the National Consultative Assembly, answered edgily:[51]

There is no discrimination, except in very delicate cases where a person decides to leave Morocco permanently. That involves abandonment of nationality, which is a grave thing. We need all our human potential. We want all Moroccan patriots, whether they are Moslems or Jews, to dedicate themselves to the common task of national renovation. We expect the Jews to turn their eyes to Israel as we turn ours to Mecca, but if they want to change their nationality, that is bad.

The departure of our citizens would mean a loss of Moroccan blood. We have a true brotherhood between Moslems and Jews here. We have equality, not just verbal but actual equality. When some Jews go off, the atmosphere is spoiled for those who remain. It creates a malaise.

Theory and Practice. At frequent intervals, representatives of the World Jewish Congress have initiated further negotiations with the Moroccan authorities on facilities for individual emigration. But succeeding and increasingly serious internal political conflicts which were besetting Morocco prevented any progress in the negotiations on the exit of Moroccan Jews. In April 1958, the King dissolved the Government of Premier M'barek Bekkai following the resignation of the Istiqlal ministers who protested the lack of "fundamental democratic liberties" in the country. On May 12, he appointed a purely Istiqlal Cabinet, headed by Ahmed Belafrej, only to dismiss it in December. Abdallah Ibrahim, leader of Istiqlal's left wing, which favored stronger ties with Nasser's United Arab Republic, formed a new government on a "nonparty basis." Considerable friction and splits developed within the Istiqlal. Declaring their support of Premier Adballah Ibrahim, left wingers accused the official party leadership of "three years of weakness, negligence and grave errors" and set up an autonomous organization, the National Union of Popular Forces.

In May 1960, King Mohammed V, dismissed the leftist Premier Abdallah Ibrahim and installed a new cabinet with the participation of the middle-of-road Istiqlal members, headed by his son, Crown Prince Moulay Hassan. Country-wide communal elections held on May 29, did not bring clarification of the relative strength of the competing forces. Both sides claimed victory. The Istiqlal was far ahead in the number of smaller inland communities, where it had secured the majority of seats, but the National Union of Popular Forces had won important majorities in the heavily populated coastal industrial centers: Casablanca, Rabat, Tangiers, Safi, Mazagan, Kenitra (Port Lyautey), as well as in Fez, Meknés, Oujda, Mogador, and Larache. Inter-party struggle continues unabated.[52]

Under the circumstances, none of the warring factions—in the Government or outside of it—was prepared to deal favorably with matters concerning Jewish emigration. The issue has become a convenient weapon in the inter-party strife, each faction striving to outbid the other in barring Moroccan Jews from reaching Israel, be it on an organized or individual basis. As early as September 1956, Allal el Fassi, leader of Istiqlal's conservative wing, urged the Rabat Government to put complete stop to all Jewish emigration. Motivating this demand, he dropped the pretense—usually voiced by Moroccan nationalists—that the departure of the Jews would be prejudicial to the Moroccan economy. Instead, he cited Pan-Arab solidarity and enmity for Israel as the motives for the denial to the Jews of their right to freedom of movement. "The Arab land of Morocco," he stated, "cannot permit Zionism to use its soil as a theater of mobilization, maneuvers, and plots against the Arab land of Palestine." At the same time, strong disapproval of emigration was voiced by the King Mohammed V himself. Receiving a Jewish delegation, he declared that Jews who were thinking of leaving Morocco "showed a lack of faith in their own country."[53]

Already in August 1956, there were reports on the Moroccan and Tangier radios that the Governor of Casablanca had received orders not to issue any more exit visas to Jews. This was promptly denied; delay in issuing visas was ascribed to the fact that the issuing offices were overburdened with requests. Later, when (in February 1957) exit visas were abolished altogether, it became exceedingly difficult to obtain passports. Those who had already been to Israel or whose passports showed Israeli visas were refused extension or renewal of their documents. Applicants for a new passport were usually asked, "Are you sure you don't intend to go to Israel?" District officials were making unannounced visits to their homes to make sure that they did not try to liquidate their affairs with the intention of departing for good, but were leaving for a short business trip or as bona fide tourists. The 4,720 Jews who, according to official statistics, were (together with 8,000 Moslems) permitted to travel abroad, apparently belonged to this privileged category: only such Jews who were able to prove means of support in the countries they intended to visit were granted individual passports; no poor applicant could obtain permission. Wrote *Al Istiqlal* on October 26, 1957: "The place for indigents is not abroad but here where the government endeavors to create work for all, and is succeeding." And just one month later, Si Mohammed Laghzaoui, head of the State Security Office, admitted that the Government had been seeking to halt individual as well as mass departure for Israel. He maintained that migration to Israel was artificially stimulated by illegal Zionist groups using fear-mongering slogans offensive to Morocco, and that Israel was importing Moroccan Jews as menial laborers. Morocco, like any other country, he claimed, was entitled to prohibit emigration of its citizens to any other country when it deemed such movement undesirable; this right it certainly had in regard to Israel, with which no diplomatic relations existed; and it wanted to make sure that none of its departing citizens would bear arms against other Arab lands.[54]

This latter argument in later years developed into a major political consideration. Morocco had joined the Arab League on October 1, 1958.

Two weeks later, October 15, the evening paper *Al Ahd El Jadid* (The New Era), considered as representing the Morocco Government's official thinking, wrote: "All efforts must be deployed to wipe out Israel. It must be attacked relentlessly and exterminated." Some observers of the Middle East scene still believed at that time that, together with Tunisia's President Bourguiba, King Mohammed V, who had repeatedly voiced friendship for his Jewish subjects, would exercise a moderating influence on the League's belligerency toward Israel. This hope did not materialize. Tunisia has practically withdrawn from this Nasser-dominated body, but Morocco has increasingly identified itself with its policy.

In April 1959, the Moroccan State Security Department banned the sale or purchase of Israeli postage stamps throughout Morocco. All shops which buy and sell foreign stamps have received an order to this effect. Commenting on this measure, an official spokesman said that the stamps were a form of propaganda for Israel, "a country with which we have no relations and which we do not recognize." Five months later, the Rabat Government announced that, having in August 1959 joined the Arab Postal Union, it severed postal communication between Morocco and Israel. This step condemned the country's Jewish community to isolation from the 120,000 of their kith and kin who had settled in Israel. In August 1960, Morocco also suspended radio communication with Israel. Early in 1960, a number of Jews were called into the police headquarters in Casablanca to answer questions about correspondence they had allegedly sent by an indirect route to Israel.[55]

The Moroccan authorities are endeavoring to obliterate every trace of Jewish identity. Jewish schools have been ordered to teach the Bible in Arabic; the Jews are required to change their Hebrew names to Arabic ones and to dress their hair in the Arab manner.

In the summer of 1960, it was announced that in October, when the new school term began, Alliance schools in the larger cities, such as Casablanca, Rabat, Marrakesh, Fez, Salé, would be nationalized. This measure affected about one-third of the 31,500 pupils in the seventy-six schools of the Alliance. The Ministry of Education promised Alliance officials that Hebrew would be kept on the curriculum of the nationalized schools. But already prior to 1960, the teaching of Hebrew had been so readjusted as to be limited to the reading of the Bible, rather than conveying a knowledge of the living Hebrew language. As a result of the new move—clearly due to pressure from Cairo and the Arab League—the school program was further de-Judaized.[55a]

The Arab League session in Casablanca (September 1959) deliberated on boycott against Israel and the problem of Arab refugees. After a visit in Cairo, King Mohammed V, on January 22, 1960, joined with President Nasser in a statement pledging the continuation of "the joint struggle until Arab Palestine is liberated."[56] In line with this policy, Moroccan authorities do not issue a passport to a Jew who, they suspect, means to leave the country for good, with the intention of settling in Israel. The solemn official declarations about the right of every individual Jew to obtain a passport and leave the country remain empty words:[57]

Far down on the local administrative level, where the passports had to be handed out, officials refused outright or set up a Byzantine system of pretexts and delays, depending on the whim and digestion of the bureaucrat in charge. A well-dressed Jew, a man of obvious affairs, might occasionally obtain a passport for a trip to Paris on business or a journey for health or recreation. But if a Jew turned up with five to twelve children, all of them ragged, the bureaucrat automatically—and accurately, in most cases—concluded that their true destination was Israel, and the application went into a pigeon-hole. It needed no official document—though at least one was available—to demonstrate that this singular unanimity in the lower echelons, despite assertions to the contrary from on high, was produced by official order rather than coincidence.

When representatives of the World Jewish Congress complained to the higher Moroccan authorities over the refusal to issue passports to Jews, they were asked to furnish specific proofs of such cases. This they were, however, unable to do: most would-be emigrants, expecting a refusal, did not even dare apply, and those who did and received no satisfaction did not venture to submit their names, being afraid of administrative vengeance. "To mention the word 'passport' to a [Moroccan] government official when discussing the position of the Jews, is like a red rag to a bull," reported a *Jewish Chronicle* correspondent.[58]

Behind the Gates. To all intents and purposes, the Jewish emigration remained at a near standstill. It dropped from the 36,-

301 stampede in 1956 to 8,758 in 1957 and to a trickle of 1,803 in 1958.

The immediate result of this stoppage was dangerously increasing congestion of the *mellahs*. The 120,000 Jews who had left Morocco for Israel since 1948 represented the ultimate "surplus" of the Jewish community and considerably eased the pressure of overpopulation. When emigration was administratively sealed off, this outlet was closed, and the high birth rate in the *mellahs* quickly began swelling their teeming multitudes.

In addition, the Casablanca Jewish community was burdened by the influx of some 30,000 refugees from small towns, from villages in the mountains and in the confines of the Sahara, "driven from their ancestral homes by want and insecurity," reported Maurice Carr early in 1959. "These Jews have lost their traditional means of livelihood, since the petty trades and crafts which they and they alone used to ply are now being taken over by their evermore enterprising Moslem neighbors. If there were general prosperity, the Jews could no doubt adjust themselves to the new conditions: but in the deepening depression they have become economically displaced persons. Then again, the *malaise* caused by the bloody pogrom which stained Mazagan on August 20, 1955, still persists. The Government, to be sure, has proclaimed that Moslems and Jews are brethren, and this has had a most salutary effect. It will take many a year, though, to eradicate the widespread notion that the Jew is a tolerated infidel, an inferior creature."

In the big city of Casablanca, these uprooted Jews feel safe. Having no skills, they rarely find any work, but they survive on communal charity and on the help of the American Joint Distribution Committee. Their children have a chance to be admitted to an Alliance Israélite school or to a Talmud Torah, where, in addition to education, they receive three square meals a day.[59]

This, however, is no solution to the basic problem of their immediate future. Attempts at directing Jewish emigration from North Africa to countries other than Israel were made in 1956 when the Canadian Jewish Congress announced that the

Canadian immigration authorities had received "definite and detailed instructions" to proceed with the processing of applications for admission to Canada of Moroccan and Tunisian Jews, which the Congress presented to the authorities with a request for immediate action. Brazil, too, agreed to admit a thousand families within a two-year period. As yet, both projects did not result in a noticeable easing of the situation. During the period from July 1, 1956, through June 30, 1957, only 587 Jews have settled in South America or Canada.[60]

"ILLEGAL EMIGRATION"

Underground Railway. In his *Report from Morocco*, Hal Lehrman boldly appraised the immediate aftereffects of the ban on emigration:

Inevitably, a policy which was in effect turning Morocco into a prison for anyone yearning for Israel had two results. It raised geometrically the numbers of those who wanted to go—and it spurred the creation of an illicit apparatus to accommodate them. This reporter is not telling the Moroccan authorities anything they do not already know when he records here that, bit by bit, some semblance of an underground network was slowly developed. Moroccan Jews who had been associated with *Kadimah* when its non-Moroccan executives were expelled, were recruited into the new system; emissaries from abroad found new volunteers; way stations, relay points and ports of exit were set up—and before long a sporadic but substantial march was in progress again.

A favorite route was from what had been French Morocco to Tangier and the former Spanish Zone, thence to Gibraltar or France, and, usually, Israel. For a time, Moroccan authorities were apparently willing to shut their eyes to this movement. But eventually the operation was bound to overreach itself. The breaking point came in the Tangier area.

In the first half of 1957, several hundred Jewish families from different parts of Morocco, having months ago sold their homes in anticipation of emigration, had set out to reach Israel by way of Gibraltar. They got no farther than the southern shore of the Mediterranean, where they were stopped by the police. By July, the number of these would-be emigrants stranded in Tangier, which had since October 1956 lost its status as an "international zone" and become part of Morocco, reached 1,400. Some 400 of them succeeded in departing during August, but afterward Moroccan authorities sealed off the borders securely and made further movement impossible. Those stranded in Tangier lived on the charity of the local Jewish community and of the American Joint Distribution Committee, in a former garage and an institution for the aged. Urged to return to their former abodes, they refused, pointing out that they had nowhere to return to: their lodgings had been turned over to Moslem neighbors.[61]

The Prisoners of Tangier. This pathetic situation lasted till October 1958, when twenty-one of these "illegals," among them a few broken old men and a teen-age girl, were brought to trial on charges of "sedition and treason." They were nobly defended by a cosmopolitan team of six defense counselors: one Moslem, one French Jew, and four Spaniards. Particularly impressive was the plea made by Maître Abdelkader Benjelloun, former Moroccan Minister of Finance and leader of the P.D.I. (Democratic Party of Independence), who recalled the assurances given by the King that all Moroccans would be treated as equals, irrespective of race and religion. He read out from beginning to end the Universal Declaration of Human Rights, to which Morocco had subscribed as a member of the United Nations, and which prescribes freedom of movement for all, including those who desire to leave their native land to settle in another country.

"Do you forbid Moslems to go to Mecca?" he asked. "Why then should you forbid Jews to go to their spiritual capital? Let the people go whenever and wherever they wish. That is true democracy, and it is in the best interests of the state." He stressed, finally, that there was no law on the Moroccan statute book which made it an offense for the Jews to emigrate, and therefore the accused ought really to be the accusers, for they had been denied their elementary rights. At this point the presiding judge, a Moslem, Brahim Keddara, advised Maître Benjelloun to take before the Supreme Court in Rabat all complaints concerning Jews whose applications for passports had been rejected.

Six of the defendants were sentenced to short terms of imprisonment or fined for minor irregularities, the remaining fifteen were acquitted. The Public Prosecutor appealed against this verdict, which upheld—in theory at least—the Moroccan Jews' right to freedom of movement, and set an important precedent in Moroccan jurisprudence.[62]

Another route of escape was Tetuan, largest city in the former Spanish Zone. On October 1, 1957, Moroccan police stopped busses bearing 239 would-be Jewish emigrants—men, women, and children—on the way to nearby Ceuta, a port enclave under Spanish jurisdiction. They were forcibly returned to Tetuan, where criminal charges were entered against them. Since then, Jews who sought to cross the Moroccan-Ceuta border—something previously permitted without a passport on presentation of Moroccan identity papers—were prevented from doing so unless they left substantial guarantees that they had no intention of emigrating. This outlet, too, was sealed off.[63]

Denunciation Campaign. Simultaneously an Istiqlal-instigated campaign was launched, denouncing Jewish "illegal emigration." In November 1957, the Council of Jewish Communities in Morocco, claiming that clandestine exodus to Israel was harming the position of the country's Jewish population, decided to "take measures" against this movement. Four Moroccan Jewish leaders went to France and approached leading Jewish organizations with the plea to use their influence to stop clandestine departures, which, they said, were undermining the Jewish integration effort. The unanimous answer of all Jewish organizations was that the Moroccan Government itself was responsible for illegal emigration, by refusing to recognize the genuine and spontaneous desire of thousands of Jews to go to Israel and by neglecting to provide legal means enabling them to do so. They urged that the Government should, on humanitarian grounds, at least permit the departure of the transients stranded in Tangier and Tetuan, and facilitate the reunion of families; Moroccan immigrants in Israel sent a moving plea to King Mohammed V to let their kin join them.[64]

These appeals were of no avail, and clandestine emigration continued. In March 1959, thirteen men, twenty-six women with children, and eight old men who had sold their homes in Rabat, Casablanca and Meknés, were arrested at Oujda for trying to reach Israel—this time via Algeria. The women and children were later released, while the men remained imprisoned in Nador and were interrogated by the police three times a day in an attempt to discover the "ringleaders of a clandestine *aliyah* organization." Another group of twenty-six Jews, who were arrested in the same month of March in Eastern Morocco, were released, pending investigations into the alleged illegal immigration organization. This group was also charged with holding forged passports.

Originally, Moroccan officials professed to know nothing about either group. But in the latter half of April, the Moroccan Government, in a French-language broadcast of the Rabat Radio, announced that after Morocco had achieved independence a "clandestine emigration organization has been discovered whose activities took several forms. . . . By means of promises or pressure it exploited and deceived the good faith of many Jewish citizens." One of the methods used by the organizers, continued the statement, "consists of forming groups of Jews from various centers in order to send them to the small ports of the north, where makeshift maritime transports awaited them. . . . The Government is determined to discover the organizers of this systematic movement which in no way reflects the real opinions of a large majority of Moroccan Jews. . . . All persons detained while trying to leave the country would be returned to their homes."[65]

As this is written, the 200,000-strong Jewish minority of Morocco is in no danger of physical assault and enjoys civic and political equality which it had never known in its checkered history. Early in May 1960, eleven Jews have been elected to Chambers of Commerce and industry in Casablanca, Larache, Marrakesh, Meknés, Mogador, Fez, Tangier, Tetuan, and Zagora. They received a total of more than 7000 votes out of 90,000 cast for 261 seats in 20 different Chambers. A few weeks later, Jews actively participated in the country-wide communal elections. In Casablanca, they overwhelmingly sided with the left-wing National Union of Popular Forces, which won 43 out of 51 council seats, carried all Jewish quarters, whether its candidates were Moslems or Jewish. In two Jewish voting districts, the Union won with Moslem candidates. It backed winning Jewish candidates in two other districts with equal Moslem and Jewish population. The president of the Casablanca Jewish community, Meyer Obadia, openly sympathetic to the conservative Istiqlal, was defeated by a Jewish lawyer Meyer Toledano, who had the backing of the National Union of Popular Forces and stands for active Moslem-Jewish cooperation through political and cultural groups.[66]

At the same time, the quickly deteriorating economic position and growing national consciousness generate an increasing desire for *aliyah* to Israel. The Government's policy of preventing emigration is creating a deep sense of uneasiness, bordering on claustrophobia, among the entire Jewish community.

12

Tunisia: Leaving at Leisure

Under the French Protectorate. Tunisia has been a French protectorate since 1881. A native ruler, the Bey of Tunis, who, unlike the Sultan of neighboring Morocco, was not the religious head of the country's Moslem population, retained his title. However, his sovereignty was restricted by a French resident-general, who, in addition to being in full control of military, naval and civil affairs, also served as minister of foreign affairs for Tunisia.

The census of 1946 returned a population of 3,231,000, among which Europeans constituted 239,600 (144,000 Frenchmen, 84,900 Italians and 10,700 other Europeans); the Jewish community numbered about 105,000 in 1951.[1]

The Jews were predominantly concentrated in the urban centers: 65,000 lived in the capital city of Tunis, 6,400 in Sousse, 5,700 in Sfax, and 2,400 in Bizerte. About two-thirds (70,791) held Tunisian citizenship and were subject to Tunisian law and jurisdiction in civic matters, and to a Rabbinical court in personal matters of marriage, divorce, inheritance, and levirate marriages; about one-third (35,000) were French citizens, under the over-all jurisdiction of the French law. In Tunis, in 1946, 28.45 per cent of the Jews were gainfully employed: 46.5 per cent of this total were engaged in industry and handicraft, 33.1 per cent in commerce, and 8.9 per cent in the liberal professions.[2] In the interior of the country, especially in the isolated villages and in the mountainous regions, Jews lived actually beyond the pale of the law: they were despised and insulted, beaten, and often murdered. In the larger cities, the

French kept a watchful eye, and the local Arab population treated their Jewish neighbors with more consideration.

During the last decades, a new trend manifested itself in the life of Tunisian Jewry. In the capital, Tunis, a small but increasingly influential stratum of middle- and upper-middle bourgeoisie and professionals has arisen, striving to leave the suffocating *Hara*, to achieve a better economic position and a higher educational standard. The younger generation is energetically pursuing the quest for a better life, both economically and spiritually. Yet the *hara* is still thickly populated with paupers and has been repeatedly baited and intimidated by the rabidly anti-Jewish Moslem extremists who were profiting from the rising nationalistic wave in the country.

Tunisian National Movement. The first nationalist organization, the Destour (Constitution) party, was formed in 1920 with a modest program demanding self-rule and economic equality with the French. Fourteen years later, a group of French-educated dissident intellectuals, headed by Habib Bourguiba, founded the Neo-Destour, with a more ambitious platform encompassing not only political but also social and educational reforms. They went into every section of the country, doing social work, teaching the population to read and write, to understand political issues, to vote, to elect and remove its representatives. They succeeded in enrolling nearly 300,000 people, one-sixth of the adult population, in the party's ranks. Outlawed by the French authorities, the movement went underground, gaining ever growing popular support and assuming increasingly radical revolutionary character. Since 1950 it demanded not only wide autonomy, but also a Tunisian military force and sovereignty in judicial matters. In the process of growth, the movement split into two main currents. One was represented by a organized party which was staging meetings, demonstrations, conferences (both legal and illegal), conducting negotiations with the central and local French authorities, designed to obtain from them maximum political concessions. The other took the character of a revolutionary underground movement, applying terror not only against French officials but also against Frenchmen in general, as well as against Moslems who cooperated with the French. The official party never associated itself with these activities, but was not averse to capitalizing on their effects. French extremists reacted by counter-terror. A *New York Times* dispatch dated July 12, 1954, reported: "Counter-terrorists, thought to be Europeans, fired on two Moorish cafés in two Tunisian villages last night, killing four." It was estimated that in the first half of 1954 about one assassination per day was perpetrated by the *fellaghas* (Arab terrorists) or by the French vigilantes.

Tacit Understanding. The leaders of the Tunisian nationalist movement spared no effort to win the country's Jewish minority to their cause. In fact, many Jewish intellectuals strongly sympathized with the Neo-Destour and took an active part in its struggle. However, the overwhelming majority of the Jewish community cherished but one desire—to be left in peace. A kind of tacit understanding seems to have been reached between the Neo-Destour and Tunisian Jewish leaders that the Jewish minority would remain neutral in the Arab-French conflict and that no anti-Jewish excesses would be tolerated. On the whole, this understanding was kept by both sides. Nevertheless, now and then anti-Jewish attacks did occur, provoking near-panic among the Jews.

In 1952, authorities were preparing the evacuation of Jewish residents from the Arab quarters of Sfax and Kairouan to the European parts of these towns. Jewish shops were raided and pillaged in Medenine and Kairouan. In Tunis, the capital, Arab youths invaded the Jewish market center, threw stones and scattered merchandise. The Jews quickly organized a defense: for five wounded Jews there was an equal number of wounded Arabs. An ultranationalist underground organization, the "Black Hand," in March 1952 issued a proclamation warning that those collaborating with the "colonialists" (i.e., the French settlers) would be regarded as traitors and punished. On the other hand, two Jews were arrested in Tunis by French authorities and charged with lending financial support to the Arab nationalists and to the Arab political exiles in southern France.[3]

Aware that anti-Jewish violence would greatly compromise their cause in world public opinion, Neo-Destour leaders did

their utmost to keep their followers in hand. Moreover, when
in the spring of 1953 some Jewish business establishments suffered damage in the course of Arab-French clashes, they in-
demnified the Jewish owners for the losses incurred. Neo-
Destour leaders were also proud of the fact that when the
Germans occupied Tunisia in 1942, their emissaries went
from mosque to mosque urging the Arabs to pay no heed to German propaganda and to leave the Jews in peace.[4]

Home Rule. On April 22, 1955, the French Prime Minister,
Edgar Faure, and the Tunisian Premier, Tahar Ben Ammar,
signed a protocol outlining the terms on which France would
give her North African protectorate internal autonomy, replacing or modifying the Treaty of Bardo, which had established the French protectorate in 1881.[5] From the point of view
of Tunisian Jewry, perhaps the most essential provisions of the
agreement were the articles 15 and 16 of Chapter 13, which
enabled nationals of the two countries "freely to enter the territory of the other, stay there, or leave at any time." These provisions were reassuring to the Tunisian Jews, confronted as they
were with the hazards of an autonomous Moslem regime. To
them, their most treasured possession was an identity card, based
on the Franco-Tunisian conventions, which authorized the
holder to leave the country, with his family and belongings,
within the next ten years.[6]

As early as August 1954, Tahar Ben Ammar told Dr. Maurice
Perlzweig, political representative of the World Jewish Congress: "We have always maintained the best relations with the
Jews and there will be no room for any sort of racial discrimination in autonomous Tunisia. The Jews will enjoy all rights like
any other citizens of the country." He also promised that the
first Cabinet of autonomous Tunisia would include a Jew.[7]
He kept the promise. In September 1955, Maître Albert Bessis,
a leader in Jewish community affairs, was appointed Minister
of Reconstruction and Planning in the new all-Tunisian Government—the first Jew in many years to sit in the Cabinet of a
Moslem country. Maître Bessis interpreted his appointment as
"an affirmation of the permanent friendship of all autochthonous elements in the country," which "should eliminate the fears

of those who had expressed some apprehension about Tunisian Jewry's future." He implicitly condemned "those who sought safeguards for local [Tunisian] Jewry's status in the new constition of Tunisia."[8] The Neo-Destour organ, *As Sabah*, on March 29, 1955, stressed that the Tunisian Moslem and Jewish communities had always lived together in bonds of undying affection. In May, when Habib Bourguiba returned to Tunisia from exile, the Government announced that it would admit a number of Jewish youths to the Tunisian police force, and instructions were issued to make positions in the administration available to Jewish applicants.

In an attempt to summarize the attitude of the dominant party toward the Jewish minority, a young Tunisian writer, Albert Memmi, wrote at the end of 1955, in the *Nouvelles Juives Mondiales* of Paris:

The moderate nationalists are making a real effort toward a rapprochement [between the Moslems and Jews] for the following very good reasons: (1) they need the support of world public opinion; (2) with 500,000 to 600,000 unemployed, Tunisia finds itself in a difficult position economically and needs the presence of Jews in the liberal professions at least for decades; (3) Jews can supply the skeleton staff for the new administration; (4) despite interior difficulties, the Neo-Destour sincerely tries to establish a lay democratic state. In a lay democratic state, Jews normally have a place. Until now, there was no lay Arab state in existence. Tunisia would become a pilot experiment.

Light and Shadow. The prevailing mood among Tunisian Jews was at that time, according to a World Jewish Congress report, "one of serenity and of communal activity." It was, however, noted that certain circles "doubted that the coming reality would be as fine as the promises made during the struggle for political independence." It was also noted that Prime Minister Ben Ammar declared in an interview: "Tunisia, whose population is in its very large majority Arab and Moslem, will endeavor to strengthen the centuries-old links which unified it with other Arab countries of the Middle East, especially by cooperation in the cultural and economic field."[9] Not less disturbing was the article in the weekly *Frazazou*, a staunch supporter of the Neo-

Destour, which demanded from the newly appointed Jewish Minister, Albert Bessis, a statement condemning Zionism.[10] Considerable apprehension was caused by a diatribe in the official organ of the old Destour party, the weekly *Al Irada* (March 18, 1955), charging that the Jews had betrayed the prophet Mohammed at Medina and later also had opened the doors of North Africa to French colonialism. "From the time of the Pharaohs to that of the more recent Hitler, the peoples [of the world] have been unanimous in condemning the activities of the Jews," the article concluded.

The granting of home rule to Tunisia coincided with heavy economic recession. Several years of poor harvest, explosive growth of population, and flight of capital caused an abrupt increase in unemployment. The general depression strongly affected the Jewish community, which had been during the last few decades undergoing far-reaching structural changes. "Tunisia Faces the Future," a special issue of the authoritative series *World's Documents*, published in 1956 by *Le Monde Economique*, stressed (p. 51) that

the Jew in Tunisia has lost his position of middle man in the distributive industry—with commerce becoming more and more the privilege of a Moslem caste—and is resolutely directing his efforts toward the creative professions and scientific careers. . . . Forty-six per cent of Jewish activity in Tunisia is now of an industrial nature, with commercial activity now ranking second; ten per cent of the Jewish population is made up of intellectuals exercising liberal professions.

However, having been educated in French schools, very few Jewish intellectuals possess an adequate command of the Arabic language, which has become the official language of the courts and administration. Addressing the August 1955 session of Zionist General Council in Jerusalem, Meyer Bellity, Chairman of the Zionist Federation of Tunisia, said: "Our youth faces desolation, with no promise at all—no future, no field for its ambitions, no work. . . . They have nothing to hope for, for every place is filled. Replacement is being carried out in all fields —in law as in medicine, in trade as in agriculture and in commerce. There is no prospect of making a living anywhere. . . .

Considerable poverty prevails: there are disturbances, there is stagnation and decline, the first victims of which are the Jews. At present, the businesses and other concerns that are being founded are all Arab, and the Jews are excluded from them. If Jews with their capital try to penetrate into these companies, they are pushed aside."

Independence. The main body of the Neo-Destour party, headed by Habib Bourguiba, accepted in good faith the home rule agreed upon with the French Government. But a more extremist wing, represented by Salah Ben Youssef, clamored for complete independence. A national party congress in November 1955 endorsed Bourguiba's stand. Saleh Ben Youssef's partisans, however, continued and increased their opposition, resorting early in 1956 to outbreaks of violence. Many were arrested and imprisoned, but Ben Youssef himself escaped to Cairo and from there directed further diversionist activities, which included assaults and bombing attacks on Jews. The trend for full independence was strengthened by the granting, on March 3, 1956, of statehood to neighboring Morocco. France could not refuse Tunisia a status which it had given to Morocco. On March 20, the French Government of Guy Mollet announced the abrogation of the 1881 protectorate treaty and recognized the independence of Tunisia.

Elections to the first National Assembly of independent Tunisia took place on March 25. About 12,000 Jewish voters were included in the electoral lists. Originally it was assumed that four seats would be assigned to Jewish representatives. Later, however, it was decided not to establish a special Jewish representation, but two seats were reserved for Jews on the list of candidates of the Tunisian National Front, whose kernel was Bourguiba's Neo-Destour party. Albert Bessis and André Barouch were elected. As the oldest member of the Cabinet, Maître Bessis presided over the inaugural meeting of the Tunisian national legislature. Habib Bourguiba became Prime Minister on April 10. On July 25, 1957, the Assembly deposed the Bey and nominated Bourguiba the first President of the Tunisian Republic. In November 1959, more than 99 per cent of the 1,007,959 voters elected him to the Presidency.

Tunisification. The new Tunisian regime, headed by leaders educated in anticlerical French schools, is intent on breaking with the theocratic past and establishing Tunisia as a modern, secular and democratic state, and its egalitarian outlook is averse to any distinctive status for the Jewish minority, except in purely religious matters.

The first step in the governmental effort to remake the life of the Jewish community in accordance with the new general pattern of the country occurred in the autumn of 1957. Within the cadre of the general judicial reorganization, the Rabbinical Tribunal, which, on the basis of the decrees of November 28, 1898, and March 28, 1922, had jurisdiction in matters of personal status, was abolished. Motivating this measure, Ahmed Mestiri, Minister of Justice, said: "The Rabbinical Tribunal is a very old institution, dating from the pre-Protectorate era, and its procedures had been established in times immemorial. The Government believes that this institution, despite the services which it has rendered to the Jewish community, is obsolete. Its abolition corresponds to the wishes of a majority of our Jewish fellow citizens who are complaining about its archaic and slow procedures. . . . This reform, however audacious it may appear in the eyes of some people, is not contrary either to the Jewish religion or, as a matter of fact, to the Moslem religion."[12]

The next step affected the Jewish communal structure. Prior to the proclamation of Tunisia's independence, the Jewish community had a legal personality and was managed by an elected Community Council.

In keeping with the general policy of "integration" of the heterogeneous elements of the population prevailing in the newly independent North African Moslem states (in Tunisia it is termed "Tunisification"), the Tunisian Government in the summer of 1958 dissolved the elected community councils of the two largest Jewish communities (Tunis and Sfax) and appointed "Provisional Committees" instead. A decree promulgated on July 11, restricted the competence of the Jewish communal organizations to matters of "cult"—religion, religious services and concomitant philanthropic activities, as well as religious instruction of the children. In a speech made a few days after the promulgation of the decree, the Minister of Justice emphatically stressed the necessity of establishing understanding and good will between religious groups and equality before the law. The purpose of the decree, he stated, was to limit the field of activities of the Jewish religious associations and to eliminate anything likely to accentuate particularistic trends in the nation. The Government, he said, does not want to tolerate the existence in the Tunisian society of veritable castes, within which the citizen would be the prisoner of the surrounding atmosphere. The Minister claimed that at present the Jewish citizen, no matter where he turns and what are his activities, finds himself confronted by all sorts of organizations—social, religious, artistic, athletic—which emphasize that he is different from his Moslem compatriots.[13]

Following an intervention by representatives of the World Jewish Congress, the Government postponed the implementation of the decree, thus enabling the continuation of the usual communal activities, without any governmental interference. This situation can, however, hardly continue indefinitely. New communal statutes have to be deposited with the Government in conformity with the decree, and the problem facing the Jewish leadership is to incorporate in these statutes provisions whose wording, while remaining within the framework of the decree, would enable the communities to continue their normal activities in the fields of education, social welfare, etc.

It was reported that one of the reasons for the dismissal of the old community councils was the Government's contention that their leadership was not sufficiently "Tunisian" in character and policy, being more French than Tunisian in culture and outlook, and allegedly considering the Jews as a separate minority group with distinct political tendencies. The newly appointed leadership fully endorsed the policy of integration. At a reception President Bourguiba gave to a number of prominent Moslem and Jewish leaders, Maître Albert Bessis apologized for speaking French:[14] "For this my education is to blame. I am certain that our children and grandchildren will speak Arabic as well as French. . . . We shall rally round you, simply as citizens, without any distinction of race. We are going to work for the complete integration of both elements of the population."

Problems of Education. The first few years of Tunisian independence have already greatly affected the character of the country's Jewish educational system.

A decade ago, the number of Jewish children of school age was estimated at about 19,000. Of this total, some 16,000 were attending French public schools (including 3,000 in the five schools of the Alliance Israélite Universelle: three in Tunis, with 2,800 pupils, and one each in Sousse with 220 pupils and in Sfax with 250 pupils). About 4,000 attended the Talmud Torahs and *chedarim*, which were most common in the provinces. In the south, 930 children were receiving education in the spirit of traditional Judaism (thirty to forty hours per week).[15] In Tunis, the 14,000 or so Jewish children of school age had the choice between the Alliance schools with a curriculum including five hours per week of Hebrew education, the Moslem-Arab schools controlled by the Tunisian Ministry of National Education, and schools of the French Cultural Mission. In addition, the Jewish community has established several schools where pupils of non-Jewish schools received, twice a week, some instruction in Jewish subjects;[16] the *Ozar Hatorah* also maintains a Boarding High School for 50 students.[17] The ORT founded a net of vocational institutions (schools of two to three years, apprenticeship and pre-apprenticeship courses, accelerated for adults) with a 1956 enrollment of 2,508.* A survey conducted by the Tunisian ORT has established that, with few exceptions, all its graduates were employed in the trades they had learned in the ORT schools: "They work in large enterprises such as the railroads, Tunis transport system, or Radio Tunis; with few exceptions, they earn well above the average pay for Tunisian workers; this is true despite the gloomy economic picture, because skilled people are extremely scarce."[18]

As early as July 1956, the Paris correspondent of *The New York Times* reported that "Tunisian Jews are worried. . . .

---

* At present, some 15 per cent of students in the ORT schools are Moslems, and high government officials are among those most anxious to secure a place for their sons there. (*Jewish Chronicle*, London, May 13, 1960)

Most of them have been educated in French schools and wonder if they will be able to educate their children the same way in an increasingly Arabized country."[19] André Chouraqui, head of the Department of Education of Alliance Israélite, predicted in August 1957 that "the day is not far distant when Arabic will be [in the Alliance schools of Tunisia and Morocco] the language of instruction in all subjects," and the Jews "who until now spoke French both at home and on the street, will be obliged to change over to Arabic, and instead of being integrated into a French-speaking community will now be required to become attached to the Arab-speaking community."[20] According to the March 1959 issue of *Information*, a monthly published by the Comité Algerien d'Etudes Sociales, "the Arabization in the schools of the Alliance Israélite in Tunisia entered into a serious stage. The Arab language figures prominently in the programs of the communal schools of Tunis. Committees and various cultural groups are organizing courses of Arabic for the youth and adults."

Emigration played havoc with Jewish education in the predominantly religious smaller communities, particularly in the south, where it was directed by rabbis. Many teachers and some rabbis left and were not replaced. Such communities as Kebili (now 120 Jews), Medinine (220), and Zarzis (400), have lost their spiritual leaders and present a serious problem to the Tunisian Jewish leadership.[21] In Tunis and in the larger coastal cities, the educational system was less affected, but even there emigration has reduced the number of pupils in the Alliance schools from 4,218 in 1956 to 3,856 in 1957, to 3,607 in 1958, and to 3,591 in 1959.

Emigration. There are no exact data on the volume of Jewish emigration from Tunisia during the first two years (1948–1949) following the emergence of the state of Israel. Available statistics deal with the total influx from the three North African countries (Morocco, Algeria, Tunisia), which amounted to 24,-745 for that period. It was but from 1950 on that immigration from Tunisia was listed separately. In 1950, 3,725 arrived; 3,414 in 1951; and 2,548 in 1952. In 1953, following a relative becalming of the internal political situation, migration declined to 606.

The prospect of Tunisia's autonomy has again spurred the emigration trend. Henry Levy, the Joint Distribution Committee Director for Tunisia, told a *Jewish Chronicle* correspondent: "Before Mr. Mendès-France made his offer of autonomy to Tunisia, about 60 or 70 Jews a month had left for Israel; by June of this year the figure had been increased to 700 per month. For the first time in the history of the Tunisian community," he said, "the annual migration of the Jewish population exceeded the number of births."[22] A total of 2,651 left Tunisia for Israel in 1954. The figure swelled to 6,104 in 1955*—four times the natural increase, which in 1952 amounted to 1,624— and to 6,545 in 1956, when Tunisia achieved full independence.[23] Reporting from Paris, *The New York Times* correspondent cabled in July 1956:[24]

The Tunisian Government has given repeated assurances that Jews would be treated like other Tunisians. As in Morocco, there have been no acts of persecution. But the Tunisian Jews are worried just the same. . . . They share the same general anxieties as the Moroccans. Any move Tunisia might make toward closer relations with the Arab League countries would increase these anxieties. There is also a desire to emigrate, particularly among the poorer Jews.

Apprehension abated somewhat in 1957, when 2,618 emigrated. In 1958, 1,286 arrived in Israel, making a total of 21,492 for the nine-year period 1950–1958.[25] It is estimated that 40,000 to 45,000 Jews—almost 40 per cent of the country's Jewish population—left Tunisia during the decade 1948–1958. Of this number, some 30,000 came to Israel; the majority of the remainder went to France.

Unhampered But Frowned At. The Tunisian Government did not interfere with the emigration movement, though it regretted the departure of so many of its Jewish citizens. At times, this attitude was expressed in terms which sounded openly inimical.

---

* There were reports that the Tunisian authorities favored the cessation of the Jewish emigration from Tunisia. M. Basdevant, Deputy Director of the French Ministry for Tunisian and Moroccan Affairs, assured the representatives of the World Jewish Congress that these rumors were unfounded and the Tunisian Government did not intend to prevent Jews from emigrating if they so desired (*Congress Digest*, September 25, 1955).

In May 1956, Ben Yachne, Tunisian Secretary of State for Information, said at a press conference: "Tunisian citizens should not have their bodies in Tunisia and their hearts elsewhere." This utterance was, however, followed by an official statement promising that emigration would not be hampered. There were also isolated anti-Israel attacks, which created apprehension as to Tunisia's policy in regard to further emigration to Israel. On May 9, 1956, Radio Tunis broadcast a poem by a poet of Palestinian origin calling on young Arabs of all countries to avenge their "exiled brethren"; a government spokesman subsequently announced in the press that the poem was transmitted through an error, and that those responsible would be disciplined.[26] Another disturbing utterance came from Sadek Mokkadem, who was touring the Middle East on behalf of the Tunisian Government. He declared that Tunisia would join the Arab League and would side with the Arab states in the Palestinian question, because "Zionism represents one of the aspects of imperialism."[27] However, Habib Bourguiba himself took a different stand. In an article published in the French language *Action* in March 1956, he called for a round-table Arab-Israel conference, insisting that the conflict between the Arabs and Israel was a "cancer" endangering the whole of the Middle East; that all nations of the area should apply their energies to developing its latent riches and agree on common irrigation schemes.[28]

Tunisia joined the Arab League on October 1, 1958. President Bourguiba, however, assured the representative of the World Jewish Congress that this step meant no change in his policy: Tunisia had to join the League after Morocco had decided to do so, but the country would not be bound by the League's policies, including those relating to Jews and Israel, and if pressed, would leave that body. In fact, Tunisian representatives walked out on October 11 of the first session of the League they attended, accusing President Nasser of the United Arab Republic of trying to dominate smaller Arab countries and giving shelter to enemies of President Bourguiba. Two days later, Tunisia severed diplomatic relations with Cairo. Yet emigration is still considered unpatriotic. On July 18, 1959, the

Tunisian Minister of the Interior said angrily that "those Jews who feel more French than Tunisian or who feel Zionist, should leave the country; the Government itself would take the initiative to deport those who maintain secret contact with Zionist organizations" (all the Zionist groups in Tunisia dissolved themselves).

Although proceeding at a leisurely pace, continued migration to Israel and France accounts for a drastic numerical shrinkage of Tunisian Jewry. From a community of about 110,000 in 1948 it decreased to 63,609 by January 1959. Of this total, about 50,-000 are concentrated in Tunis; 3,200 live in Sfax (as against 5,700 in 1948); 3,000 in Sousse (6,400 in 1948); 800 in Bizerte (2,400 in 1948); 1,800 in Djerba; 1,000 in Gabes. The remaining 4,000 are scattered in smaller towns and villages.[29]

Most of the immigrants to Israel came from the interior of the country (Tunis was least represented in the emigration stream) and from economically weak segments of the Jewish community. Middle-class Jews preferred France and other countries. Of approximately 8,700 Jews who left Tunisia from February 1956 to March 1957, about 5,000 went to Israel; of the 2,624 who emigrated between March and October 1957, 1,721 chose countries other than Israel.[30]

There are no data specifically referring to re-emigration of Tunisian Jews from Israel. It can be assumed that they constituted but a small fraction of the 4,910 immigrants from Morocco, Algeria and Tunisia who left Israel during the eleven-year period 1948–1959.[31] It is known that in the years 1951 and 1954–1956, a total of 884 Jewish immigrants left Israel to return to Tunisia.[32]

13

Algeria: Integration or Emigration

Establishment of French Rule. Algeria was the first French bridgehead in North Africa. It was established without any "colonialist" designs, almost accidentally, when, in 1827, the irascible Dey of Algiers struck the French Consul with a fly whisk. To avenge her offended national prestige, France, after an unsuccessful blockade of Algiers for three years, dispatched a punitive expedition, which easily occupied the once-impregnable Kasbah of Algiers. Yet, having achieved this immediate goal, she was saddled with the problem of a vast, unruly, barren, disease- and poverty-ridden country, in a state of near-anarchy. It took some seventeen years to suppress a Holy War headed by Abd-el-Kader, and the pacification of the tribes proved to be a long, painful and costly process.

The government policy toward Algeria for years hesitated between complete integration with France and some form of local administration. In 1848, the country was proclaimed French territory; in 1851 it was included in the French customs system. Colonists, largely recruited from the unemployed in Paris, were encouraged to settle in Algeria, with state subsidies. They occupied large parts of the best arable land and established the pattern of a "plantation economy" based on numerous large parcels of land and on application of capital to mechanized cultivation, dependent on cheap unskilled labor. There are at present more than one million French (and other European) settlers in Algeria. They are fervently nationalistic and are determined at any price to maintain French domination of the country.

French administration caused far-reaching changes in the life of Algeria. Roads were built, tribal vendettas suppressed, free medical care introduced, infant mortality lowered. These reforms brought about an explosive growth of the native Moslem population: from 2,300,000 in 1856 to 8,500,000 in 1956. Economic opportunities, though increasing, were far too scant to keep pace with this enormous demographic upheaval. About 60 per cent of the entire Moslem (Arab and Berber) population is officially classified as indigent and about 40 per cent as unemployed.

The Jewish Community. Seven decades of French citizenship have spelled for the Jewish minority an era of full civic equality and have enabled them to find a place within the framework of the country. French public schools, the administration, the free professions, trade and commerce were open to them, and in some of these fields the Jews attained an enviable position. The stratification of Algerian Jewry strongly affected the level of its Jewish culture and consciousness. Those engaged in trade preserved closer ties with Jewish tradition and ways of life than the lawyers, physicians, officials, journalists and industrialists, particularly in the coastal cities, who had lost nearly all contact with Judaism.

The 130,000-strong Jewish community of Algeria is almost exclusively urban. There is a far-reaching difference between the majority living in large urban centers (Algiers, Oran, Constantine) and the smaller communities scattered in the back country. The latter, particularly in the south, are often almost indistinguishable from the Arabs. They eat the same foods, speak Arabic, their superstitions are very much alike: they are thoroughly Arabized and yet not Arabs. Their children received education in *chedarim*, Talmud Torahs, in some cases in yeshivas (in the eight principal southern communities with a Jewish population of 4,799, schools with a Hebrew and religious curriculum are attended by 1,014 children of 5–15 years of age); only a very thin layer of wealthier business men and members of liberal professions are linguistically assimilated and send their children to French public schools.[1] In the larger cities, nearly a majority of the Jewish population, including even its lowest strata, are linguistically, and, in part, also culturally assimilated: they speak French and send their children to French public schools. In the capital city of Algiers, with 30,000 Jews, there is only one Talmud Torah, attended by some 300 boys one and a half days a week (Thursday and Sunday, when French schools are closed). In the city of Oran (29,000 Jews), there is a Talmud Torah for some 325 boys; no educational facilities exist for the girls. In Tlemcen, the fourth largest city in Algeria, a modernized and renovated Talmud Torah building is empty; there are no teachers. In Ghardaïa, one of the important Jewish historical centers in Algeria, the Talmud Torah is not functioning, and there is no other Jewish school. Jewish knowledge implanted by the few existing educational institutions is very scant: the children are being taught practical precepts of Judaism, the catechism (in French), and some Hebrew reading. No schools of the Alliance Israélite Universelle exist in Algeria, since Jewish pupils attended French public schools. But the Alliance provides teachers for the Talmud Torahs.[1A]

Religious facilities in outlying districts of the country are in a sore state. At a meeting of Jewish leaders held in Algiers in November 1959, it was reported that there were no synagogues in areas of Kouba, Maison-Carrée, El-Biar and Hudia; in other parts of the country, the synagogues are all concentrated in a small number of villages, which are either too far away for the needs of the Jews in the surrounding communities or so located that the congregants are obliged to cross trouble spots in order to reach the houses of worship. Many Jews in such districts are unable to attend religious services even during the High Holy Days. Another problem discussed at the meeting was that of missionary activity among the elderly Jews of the community. It was reported that about 150 elderly Jews have secretly converted themselves to Christianity in order to receive subsidies from the Jewish Evangelization Movement, which has recently stepped up its missionary activities especially among the poorer sections of the community.[2]

Nevertheless, observers of the Algerian Jewish scene note a considerable strengthening of Jewish consciousness. Mr. Jacques Lazarus, who visited Constantine in November 1958, heard from many: "We wanted to integrate ourselves in the life of the country. We are rejected; so let us be Jews, and only Jews."[3] Mr. Henry L. Levy of the Joint also feels that Algerian Jews had "in 1940 learned a lesson . . . that as Jews they are in a vulnerable position."[4]

Legal Status. In 1865, Emperor Napoleon III promulgated a law offering French citizenship to all Algerians who would apply for it and abide by the French Civil Code. Very few Moslems, however, chose to renounce their personal status under Koranic law, including the right to polygamy. The Jews were more eager to take advantage of the offered option. Five years later, when Benjamin Cremieux was Minister of the Interior, a decree was issued which conferred French citizenship on the entire Jewish community of Algeria. The Moslems did not take amiss this *en bloc* naturalization, but the European settlers resented bitterly being put legally on a par with the Jews, whom they considered as low-class "natives." For almost three-quarters of a century, the cry, *à bas les Juifs!* (down with the Jews), was their battle cry in Algeria, which has become a hotbed of militant anti-Semitism.

In October 1940, the Vichy regime revoked the Cremieux decree and deprived the Algerian Jews of French citizenship. A succession of decrees eliminated the Jews from most occupations; a *numerus clausus* was introduced in the professions and schools; in the spring of 1942, French authorities inaugurated progressive Aryanization of Jewish enterprises. However, Messali Hadj, the "father" of the Algerian nationalist movement, refused to lend support to Nazi Germany and to approve the abrogation of the Cremieux decree; Allied landings in North Africa (November 1942) prevented the planned deportation of Jews to European death camps.

Yet, for almost a year, Vichy-minded officials, who continued to hold key positions in Algeria, were reluctant to heed President Roosevelt's appeal for the "repeal of all laws and decrees inspired by the Nazi government and Nazi ideology," and to restore the Cremieux decree. Yves C. Chatel, Governor General of Algeria, Admiral Darlan, General Giraud, have all used delaying tactics. It was not before October 21, 1943, that, under the pressure of the United States public opinion, the Cremieux decree was fully restored.

Political Struggle and Terror. The first timid demands for reforms in the interests of the native population can be traced back to 1926. A few more extreme Moslem leaders advocated full independence for Algeria, but found little response. Until 1954, Algeria was the most tranquil of all the North African countries under French control. Neither terrorist activities in neighboring Morocco and Tunisia nor the removal of the Sultan of Morocco had provoked immediate disturbance of security and order in Algeria. As long as Messali Hadj remained its unchallenged leader, the League for the Triumph of Democratic Liberties (M.T.L.D.) was opposed to the use of violence as a means of achieving its goal. But in 1954, a group of youthful dissidents, exponents of all-out terror, broke away and set up the rival National Liberation Front (F.L.N.), which launched an armed rebellion.

During the six years of this struggle, which involved on the rebels' side, according to their contention, more than 100,000 men fighting in the field (*fellaghas*), and on the French side an army of nearly half a million men, nearly 150,000 persons, both civilians and soldiers, have been killed. Indiscriminate terror practiced by the *fellaghas* was directed not only against the military personnel but also against European civilians and against such Moslems as were not ready to cooperate with the F.L.N. forces. Some extremist European Algerians retaliated by counterterrorism. On several occasions not only Moslem nationalists but also Christian and Jewish leaders of moderate opinion who had incurred their displeasure disappeared mysteriously.

The Jewish Position. In the fierce conflict between Moslem Algerian rebels and the French forces, Algerian Jews found themselves in an extremely difficult and dangerous predicament. They are native to Algeria, but their cultural background and citizenship is French. They are under constant pressure from both sides. The rebels have been exhorting them to support their cause. The minutes of the F.L.N. Congress in August 1956, dealing with "the Jewish minority," say ominously: "Algerians of Jewish origin have not as yet overcome their conscience troubles and have not chosen sides. It is to be hoped that they will follow those who have responded to the appeal of the generous motherland and have given their friendship to the revolution, asserting with pride their Algerian nationality. This view is based on experience, common sense and foresight."

On October 1, 1956, the F.L.N. appealed to the Chief Rabbi of Algeria and the members of the Consistoire Israélite, as well as to the representatives and responsible leaders of the Algerian Jewish Community, to "show the wisdom of contributing to the creation of a truly free and brotherly Algeria.[5] On lower levels, F.L.N. militants used less diplomatic language, "threatening with revenge by fire and sword," if the Jews did not comply, reported the Paris correspondent of the *Forward* in the spring of 1956. Jewish businessmen were warned of direst consequences if they refused to contribute to the National Army of Algerian Liberation. An anti-French demonstration in the city of Oran turned into anti-Jewish riots; for no special reason, an Algerian mob sacked Jewish shops and marched on the Grand Synagogue.[6] Jews were attacked in Tlemcen; in Orleansville, a synagogue and a number of Jewish-owned stores were burned. "Such is the fear-psychosis in Algeria. today," reported the Paris correspondent of the London *Jewish Chronicle* in May 1956, "that the Jews there who write to Parisian relatives, even to parents or to children, limit their letters to the briefest of generalities, and in telephone conversations they refuse to speak about anything beyond their personal health. . . . The position of the Jewish community in Algeria is perhaps even more serious than that in Morocco."[7]

In the same month of May, a hand grenade was tossed into a Jewish-owned café frequented almost entirely by Jews, in the ghetto of Constantine, injuring thirteen persons. When the following day a group of Arabs was seen to act suspiciously, as if preparing to attack another ghetto café, the Jewish customers (who, like many Algerian Jews, and virtually all the Christians, were carrying arms for self-defense) pulled out their guns. They were quicker on the trigger, so that only one of their number was hit, while six Arabs were shot dead and four were wounded. The Algerian press, and even some French newspapers, reported this clash as a "reprisal by Jewish counterterrorists." One account, which was obviously, if not deliberately, false and provocative, claimed that the "Jewish counterterrorists went to the gates of the Arab quarter of Constantine with tommy-guns and mowed down the first Arabs to come within range.[8]

Observers of the Algerian scene were inclined to believe that some of the extemist elements among the European settlers in Algeria would not be too unhappy if the existing precarious relations between Arabs and Jews deteriorated into large-scale bloodshed. The anti-Semitic Poujade movement was extending its activities to Algeria. In Oran, its emissaries were busily spreading anti-Semitic propaganda and repeatedly organizing anti-Jewish demonstrations.[9] Late in 1958, "racist circles in Constantine spread rumors that the Jews were going to abstain from voting for the new French constitution of General de Gaulle, and a pamphlet was distributed alleging that Dr. Jacob Kaplan, the Chief Rabbi of France, was an adversary of General de Gaulle and in favor of the Algerian terrorists."[10]

Economic Repercussions. Unabated political tension strongly reflects on the Jewish economic position. Jacques Lazarus, director of the North African office of the World Jewish Congress, who in March 1956 visited the Department of Oran, found the situation in Oran (30,000 Jews) and especially in Tlemcen (5,000 Jews) alarming. Arab boycott of all European establishments was singling out Jewish stores: "Jewish shopkeepers are slowly being squeezed out of the country's economy; first, through the boycott, and second, through their replacement, to an increasing extent, by Arab stores. Similarly, the liberal professions, long the exclusive domain of Europeans and Jews, are gradually taken over by the Arabs."[11]

A more optimistic picture was presented in October 1958 by Henry L. Levy, Director for Algeria of the American Joint Distribution Committee. Due to the enormous amounts of money the French Government has been pouring into the country,* to the presence of a half a million French soldiers, many of them with their families, as well as to the Sahara oil diggings, Algeria's economy is booming, he reported. The Jews share in this general prosperity: "Business is thriving, commerce is very active. Our Jews in the south have suddenly become very wealthy. . . . Tremendous sums of money are being deposited in the banks. Tremendous sums are being transferred outside the country, a lot of it to Israel. . . . Algerian Jews are no longer in need of philanthropic help from abroad. They are able to take care of their poor, to subsidize the existing institutions. In a canteen which the Joint Distribution Committee had established a few years ago in Constantine with some 250 children, only seventeen children are eating there now: fathers are earning money, there is food at home, and the children can eat at home."[12]

Between Two Loyalties. There can hardly be any doubt that Jews are fundamentally in favor of preservation of the French rule over Algeria. The Algiers correspondent of the *Jewish Chronicle* reported in December 1958 that "over 80 per cent of the Jewish population are in favor of Algerian integration with France." Benjamin Heller, the Chairman of the Federation of Algerian Jewish Communities, stated that "nobody in Algeria is more interested in seeing France maintaining her sovereignty over this territory."[13] Nevertheless, realizing the extreme explosiveness of the situation, the 1956 annual assembly of the Federation "reaffirmed the attachment of Algerian Jewry to the ideal of brotherhood of all the ethnic groups inhabiting the country" and "refused to become involved in political questions which are a matter of individual responsibility and individual conscience." The Federation uneasily "recommended to all coreligionists to be always on guard against provocation, from wherever it comes." Expressing the ardent hope that peace be re-established to permit everyone a free development in an atmosphere of understanding and fraternity," the Assembly significantly called upon the Jewish organizations ouside of

---

* "Of late we have been providing Algeria with 150 billion francs [$1 = 400 francs] annually," related Germaine Tillion in her story, *Algeria: The Realities.* New York, 1958, p. 79.

Algeria "to avoid all public statements concerning the future of North African Jewry: in the present state of affairs in North Africa, such statements could easily be interpreted in a sense contrary to the intentions of those who made them."[14]

At the same time, F.L.N. leadership was anxious not to appear in the eyes of the world as anti-Jewish and also to secure the support of Israel in the United Nations. *L'Observateur du Moyen Orient* published (September 20, 1957) an interview with Mr. Ferhat Abbas, in which the present President of the Provisional Government of Algeria said:

Israel can maintain friendly relations with France and still give us its moral support and aid in the forthcoming debate in the U.N. General Assembly. There is no contradiction in it. . . . When our independence will become a *fait accompli*, we shall not introduce any special legislation on minorities, irrespective of Israel's attitude toward the problem of Algeria. To us, everybody is equal before the law. The Jews have the same rights, the same privileges, and the same obligations. They will also have the right to emigrate, even to Israel if they so wish. Algeria is an integral part of the Arab world, but she is also part of the European continent. Who better than Israel and Algeria can effectuate the rapprochement of these so different worlds? Besides our common Semitic origin, we have many other aspects in common. Israel must not miss this opportunity: it must support us in our struggle.

In the course of the following three years, there was no open pressure on the Jewish community to endorse the F.L.N. demand for independence and to actively support it. But in February 1960, the French Federation of the F.L.N., in a communication to the Paris press, called on Algerian Jews "to affirm as Algerians your adherence to the ideals of independence" in order "to dissipate ambiguities which risk compromising our future relations." Algerian Jews, the communication warned, were "an integral part of the Algerian population" and for them "it is not a question of choosing between France and Algeria but of becoming effective citizens of your real country." In reply to this peremptory summons, the "Comité Juif Algerien d'Etudes Sociales" repeated the argument that there can be no "collective policy" of the Jewish community in regard to the country's political problems, but was outspoken in refusing to "abandon a [French] citizenship for the maintenance of which the community has always fought and to which it remains attached with a faithfulness that deserves respect." This firm and dignified stand can hardly be expected to satisfy the Algerian nationalist leaders and to relieve political tension, which was for years adversely affecting the Jewish economic position.[15] In fact, broadcasting in March 1960 over Tunis radio, the F.L.N. spokesman warned that Algerian Jews would endure the "consequences" of their hesitant attitude when "Algerian Algeria" will come into being.

Emigration. Smaller Jewish communities scattered in vulnerable villages and hamlets are progressively disappearing. Jews from the towns in the interior either migrated to the larger cities or left for Israel and France.

Immigration to Israel has been numerically small, as shown by the following table:

Year	Immigrants
1950	506
1951	272
1952	92
1953	81
1954	232
1955	507
1956	1001
1957	915
1958	187

A total of 3,583 left for Israel during the nine-year period 1950–1958. In the years 1951 and 1954–1956, the number of re-emigrants totaled 210.[16]

There are no figures on the movement of Algerian Jews to France. Being French citizens, they do not need entry visas and are not being registered. In the spring of 1956, it was reported from Paris that, fearful and uncertain about the future, several hundred Algerian Jewish families had fled to France. In Constantine, "migration, mainly to metropolitan France, has recently cut the former 14,000 Jewish population by 1,000 or 2,000." In Bone (3,500 Jews), where "there is still a strong feeling of insecurity," about sixty Jewish families left for France and Israel; but their departure has been compensated for by the arrival of Jews from the smaller localities in the area. Few departures were registered among the remaining 900 Jews of Philippeville.[17] There are now substantial colonies of Algerian, Tunisian and Moroccan Jews in all major cities of France. The influx of North Africans is substantially changing the composition of the Jewish community in France. The Sephardic element is increasing, and is now estimated at about half of the country's Jewish population. North African Jewish associations in Paris and its suburbs planned to establish an over-all *Union Israélite Nord Africaine* "to serve this new community of Paris, already numbering about 40,000, and differing in tradition and customs from Jews of French and European origin."[18]

PART FOUR

Integration in Israel

14

Problems of Integration

For decades, Jews from Oriental countries were somehow "not in the picture" of the dynamic upbuilding of Jewish Palestine. The Zionist movement had virtually bypassed the Oriental Jewish communities. Zionist activities in their midst were both sporadic and meager. Immigration trends were few and far between. Neither in absolute numbers, nor in their proportion to the total Jewish population, nor in their specific gravity did immigrants from Afro-Asian countries figure prominently in the life of the Palestine Yishuv.

European Jews of Ashkenazi origin constituted the overwhelming majority and played a leading role in the country's economic, political and spiritual life. In 1918, they numbered 33,000, or 58.9 per cent of the Yishuv. The second place was occupied by Oriental Jews, with 12,000 or 21.5 per cent. The number of Sephardic Jews, who had reached Palestine from Spain via the Balkans, North Africa or Italy, was 11,000 or 19.6 per cent of the total Jewish population. Oriental Jews were also poorly represented in the immigration stream during the following three decades. Of the 460,000 Jews who entered Palestine from 1919 to 1948, approximately 42,000—i.e., 9 per cent of the total—came from Asiatic and African countries. On the eve of World War II, the Ashkenazi element in Palestine constituted 77.5 per cent of the Yishuv, retaining this overwhelming numerical preponderance until the proclamation of the Jewish State in May 1948.[1]

The emergence of the State of Israel dramatically reversed this ratio. In 1949, 47.3 per cent of the entire immigration was of Asian or African origin. In 1950, the proportion reached 46.6 per cent; in 1951, 71.1 per cent; in 1952, 71.6 per cent; in 1954, 75.3 per cent; in 1954, 88.7 per cent; in 1955, 92.9 per cent; in 1956, 86.7 per cent. It was not before 1957 that it was reduced to 42.5 per cent of the numerically small immigration of that year, and to 43.6 per cent in 1958.[2]

Statistical Abstract of Israel for the year 1957–1958 (p. 20) gives the following table illustrating the distribution of Israel's Jewish population by major groups (the table disregards the rubrics "Other Countries" and "Not Stated") in the years 1948, 1951, and 1956:

Major Groups	1948 No.	per cent	1951 No.	per cent	1956 No.	per cent
Born in Israel*	253,414	35.5	353,220	25.5	548,273	32.8
Born in Asia and Africa	69,691	9.7	368,141	26.6	489,681	29.3
Born in Europe and America	391,229	54.8	663,039	47.9	629,501	37.9
Total	714,334	100.0	1,384,400	100.0	1,667,455	100.0

* It must be taken into consideration that a considerable percentage of those in the rubric "Born in Israel" are of Afro-Asian parentage.

There is now in the State of Israel a numerous and evident body of a "Second Israel"—the new immigrants from Asia and Africa—distinctive from the "First Israel," those who have come from the European and American countries. The latter are commonly designated as "Ashkenazim"—Jews originating from Germany and their descendants, Yiddish-speaking, with a Hebrew pronunciation different from that of the Sephardim, and with a religious ritual of their own.

Distinction must also be made between the "Oriental" and "Sephardic" immigrant groups. They are by no means identical, and it is erroneous and misleading to use these terms indiscriminately and interchangeably. The Sephardim are Jews originating from Spain (*Sepharad*), who lived in various parts of Turkey, Greece, Egypt, Italy and North Africa. They form a category by themselves and exhibit marked differences from other Oriental groups. Neither the Jews of Yemen, nor those of Iraq,

Iran, Afghanistan or Libya are Sephardim, and by far not all immigrants from North Africa, Syria and Lebanon are of Sephardic origin.[3]

The common denominator "Oriental Jews" covers a variety of heterogeneous components, with many marked differences among them. They range in color from deepest black to light brown and mulatto, and some even have the white complexion of the Latin type. Their features run the full scale from Negroid to Caucasian, with here and there an "Oriental" appearance. Yet, the common designation is not only geographical; it has also a specific sociological meaning. Despite the differences, most of them form a more or less unified sociological "bloc."[4]

The integration of the Oriental "Second Israel" into the socioeconomic, cultural and sociological pattern established by the predominantly Ashkenazi and European "First Israel" presented in itself an objectively difficult and delicate task. It has been considerably complicated by a tangle of misunderstandings and frictions, which led to the charges of willful "discrimination" against the Oriental newcomers on the part of the Ashkenazi old-timers and the Ashkenazi-dominated institutions.

Complaints of Discrimination. The Oriental immigrants themselves have been most outspoken and bitter in their criticism of the manner in which they were being treated by the Israel Government, the Jewish Agency and the European majority of the Yishuv.

They complained of deliberate discrimination, charging that the schools set up for their children were of the most primitive kind, that the food they were served in the camps was of inferior quality, and that they were left in rags, while European immigrants were treated with great consideration. Others asserted that they were assigned the most dangerous and least rewarding tasks in the army; that the Western Jewish immigrants were allotted rich land in the Plain of Esdrelon, while they were settled on the inhospitable soil of the black hills of Gilboa and Galilee and the sands of the Negev. The European Jews, they claimed, who constituted the ruling caste of the Yishuv, were looking upon them with either contempt or pity, but never

with brotherly respect. Said a North African Jew in an interview: "It is difficult for us, people from an African town, to get
anything here. We can live only among ourselves. . . . They
treat us as strangers, do not want to understand us, and try to
make us into 'slaves'. . . . Everything is closed to us."[5]

Most of the complaints were indubitably greatly exaggerated
or simply imagined. From the very first moment of their encounter with the realities of life in Israel, immigrants from
Oriental countries have been exposed to a series of psychological
shocks for which they were completely unprepared and which
have generated marked symptoms of oversensitivity, shyness
and suspicion. Many have acquired pronounced inferiority
complexes that often degenerated into persecution manias.
They were inclined to see in every shortcoming of their hard
immigrant existence the result of intentional discrimination
against them and, in every case of more successful integration
of a European, the result of clannish favoritism. Most of the
specific accusations formulated in their complaints were poorly,
if at all, substantiated.

After all this is said, however, every unbiased and keen observer of the Israeli scene is bound to recognize that if there was
no deliberate *discrimination* against the Oriental immigrants,
there undoubtedly existed considerable *prejudice* against them
on many levels of Israel's society.

Describing his own arrival, together with some 300 new immigrants, mostly from Arab countries, at a Jewish Agency
reception camp, Amos Eilon, a young journalist on the staff
of the influential Tel Aviv daily, *Haaretz*, related how a liaison
officer of the Jewish Agency's Absorption Department in charge
of placing the newcomers in tents, who had apparently classified him as an "intellectual," patronizingly told him: "All right,
we'll put you up in a good tent, so you won't have to be with
black barbarians." In the camp itself, there was strict "apart-
heid":

The Oriental communities are in one camp, on the left side of
the highway. They are variously referred to as "wild animals,"
"blacks," or "*schreckliche Menschen*" (terrible people), or "good
Jews"—all depending on the observer's mood. The Ashkenazi Jews

are in the other camp, on the right side of the highway. They are known as "the more civilized people," because they know how to use a knife and fork.

Behind the barbed-wire fence of the camp on the right, stands a Rumanian woman about forty years old, three months in the country. Her remarks are characteristic of the moods prevalent among the European immigrants. "So they brought here some more blacks. We've got enough blacks in this *ma'abarah* already." Her husband adds: "When I sold my house in Ploetsi, I wasn't told I'd have to live with Africans. The Jewish Agency should take us away from here, say, to Tel Aviv."[6]

Some observers complacently described the attitude of the average "Western" Israeli toward an "Oriental" as "good-natured prejudice," which implies no deliberate contempt or distaste. But this "good-naturedness" was too often accompanied by a truly remarkable lack of tact and sensitivity when dealing with or speaking of the Oriental Jew. There was a kind of invisible "silken curtain" between East and West. European parents have as a rule considered as a *"mésalliance"* the infrequent marriages of their children to the "blacks." To wide circles of the Israeli population the Oriental immigrant was an upstart, a human phenomenon of different and essentially inferior quality, and they were showing this attitude with a candid and almost disarming frankness.

Prejudice Among Intellectual Elite. Even among the intellectual élite of Israel there was a tendency to deny any affinity with the "blackies," to treat the Yemenites or Moroccans as belonging to an alien tribe, not "our flesh and blood." A good friend of mine, a life-long militant Zionist and outstanding young Hebrew scholar, indignantly said to me: "What have I in common with the colored horde that is invading my country? Racially most of them are of non-Jewish origin, and they belong to a completely different world culturally. Their entire mentality, their civilization—if they have any!—is not mine. And I am deadly afraid of the prospect of their numerical hegemony, which is bound to lower our cultural standard of living." Another highly cultured Israeli friend, usually clear-headed, broad-minded and generous, a fervent patriot of Jewry and Israel, gratefully acknowledging the receipt of some of my booklets dealing with repatriation of Oriental Jews to Israel (*The End of Galut Yemen; Exodus from Iraq; The Jews of Aden*), admitted that she "did not fail to feel somewhat peculiar while reading them:"

. . . You see, we here are really terribly concerned and full of anxiety about these people, and would like to help. . . . But we are horrified at what we get, as a problem, when we have to live with them here. . . . They definitely are not my kith and kin—they are not worse, but they are *different*—and I don't want to have them becoming (as they are) the dominant feature of this country, there being no white immigration to counteract their influx.

You see, you visit, for instance, as I do frequently, the offices of our Tel Aviv municipality; in the filing department I see Oriental girls working as *hanichot* (apprentices), and I feel as if I were in a zoo. Or take the ma'abarot during the recent floods: it was the most grotesque and disheartening sight in the world. Their Oriental in-mates not only refused to move a finger in order to help the volun-teers who came to evacuate them—they stood in circles around those who were carrying their scanty belongings and clapped their hands and sang "*Tipshim Ashkenazim, tipshim*" ("The Ashkenazis are fools, fools they are"). And when they were told to transfer their things into safe places, they refused, unless they were paid for this work. . . . And all the clothing amassed throughout the country for them (and you know what giving away clothing means here to-day) was found two days later all over Tel Aviv being sold by your black darlings on the black market.

Sorry, my dear, but we can't take it. Neither from the economic nor from the cultural point of view. They are of the kind to whose countries one should send missionaries in order to change matters, not people you rescue by bringing them to your own country to live with you, without having an influx of white settlers to counter-balance the black *malum necessarium*—because it means commit-ting sucide.

I published excerpts of this pathetically sincere, but disturb-ing and distressing, human document in the United States, South Africa, and Israel—together with my rather stern retort. It had considerable repercussions just because of its shocking outspokenness.

The attitude of many other Ashkenazi circles was more cautious. They paid lip service to the principle of the Ingathering of the Exiles, the oneness of the Jewish people, and the community of Jewish fate. But they, too, were acutely aware of the rising tide of immigrants from Afro-Asian countries and were feeling uneasy and apprehensive. The "menace of Levantinization" was widely discussed over the whole land. Anguished questions were passionately debated. None other than Jacob Zerubavel, head of the Jewish Agency's Department for Middle Eastern Jews, wrote in September 1951 that there are in Israel people who are afraid that newcomers from Oriental countries may "become too numerous, overwhelm the cultural values and endow us and our children with a Levantine culture. . . . The mass immigration streaming now from backward and primitive countries to the Land of Israel is apt to inundate with its flow all our achievements."[7] And as late as May 21, 1959, Dana Adams Schmidt reported in *The New York Times* that the European "old-timers" were "appalled by the low standards of achievement and public morals, and by sloppy working habits of many Oriental immigrants." They were anxiously asking: "What is going to happen when the new immigrants, still more or less isolated in ma'abarot (camps), begin to make their numerical weight felt in the life of the country? Is this to become an East European-Oriental slum?"

Also in the Kibbutzim. Nor were the Socialist *Kibbutzim* (collectivist settlements) free of prejudice in regard to youngsters from Oriental countries, placed with them by the Jewish Agency's Department for Youth Aliyah, which had been established in 1934 to care for children arriving from Germany. In 1948, 85 per cent of its wards were of European origin, but by 1956 children from Oriental communities constituted 76 per cent of the total.[8]

Describing "the general attitude of the *Kibbutzim* toward the young people from the Moslem countries, in particular to those coming from North Africa," Moshe Kol, head of the Department, in a study published in 1957 by the International Federation of Children's Communities, wrote:[9]

It is rather glibly repeated that the collective settlement is the home of all those who live in it. In practice, however, the success in infusing the feeling of being at home among the immigrant young people is not always apparent. Quite frankly, in many settlements the attitude toward these young people is not all it should be. . . . The situation in the collective settlements is far better than that obtaining in the towns and the cities in this respect. It is not sufficiently good, however, to permit us to assume that communal prejudice and other causes of mutual estrangement have been entirely uprooted. Something must be done to ensure that the [Oriental] immigrant youth are not met with unfriendly looks, or made to hear unkind remarks in the dining hall, the workshop, the fields and elsewhere.

A study by Samuel Z. Klausner of "typical group of Iraqis of mixed social backgrounds" placed for training in a *Kibbutz* in western Galilee, found that, while longing "to become part of the settlement . . . they were in fact living a social existence different from that of the settlement, meeting the veteran members only in their work roles as supervisors. To live in the city and be socially isolated would be hard enough, but to be within the tight frame of a collective settlement and not be completely accepted is like being a rejected child in the family." A year later, the study established that "each one had left the settlement on the pretext that he had to make an economic contribution to the home."[10]

Even more outspoken in his thoughtful analysis of the attitude of the young Sabra generation in a *Kibbutz* with a "pro-Marxist orientation," is Milford E. Spiro of the Department of Anthropology, University of Washington. Oriental Jews, he relates, were in this settlement "the objects of their [Sabra youth's] disdain and/or hostility."

In the high school the "Oriental students, frequently referred to as *ha-schorim* (the black ones)," are the victims of much teasing, taunting and name-calling. The severity of this aggression may be gauged by the reaction of the Oriental students to the suggestion of the high school that they be removed from their "segregated dormitory" and integrated with the other students. . . . They refused to live with the sabras and threatened to leave the school if the integration decision were implemented. Describing their year's experience in an article in the high school annual, those Oriental students wrote . . . "We do not feel part of the school. The other children laugh at us, and do not accept us as friends or comrades. . . . We feel lonely and lost."

This hostility was also extended to the adult Oriental immigrants who worked in the *Kibbutz*. Some students refused to eat at the same table with them. Equally hostile were the adult sabras. "Things were good in this country," one of them remarked, "until the *schorim* came."[11]

B. THE MELTING POT

"Primitive People." All the immigrants from non-Western countries have been labeled *anashim primitiviim* (primitive people)—a tag which is of course anything but ennobling. More often than not, it was both degrading and sneering. There were various degrees of *primitiviut* in this over-all concept. Newcomers from Iranian and Iraqi Kurdistan were, for example, considered "more primitive" than those from Turkey or Morocco. Moroccans, in turn, were themselves subdivided into the more advanced "Casablans" (from the city of Casablanca) and the more primitive *Harei Atlas* (coming from the Atlas Mountains area). These were, however, only various degrees of the same general order: they were all more or less *primitiviim*—far behind and beneath the "advanced" European majority. As such, they had to be "reformed"—"purified from the dross of Orientalism which attached itself to them against their will," as formulated by an article in the Histadrut daily *Davar* (September 29, 1950). Another article in the same paper (March 3, 1950) described the Oriental Jews as "formless material, a sort of soft dough which one can knead into anything one wants." The idea of "reforming" the *anashim primitiviim*, of "remaking" them— with the European majority as model—had been from the very beginning the dominant trend of Israel's acculturation effort: *Anu rotzim l'afoch otam l'Israelim* (We want to convert them into Israelis). The Afro-Asian newcomers were to become completely Westernized, adopt not only the dress and modes of

behavior, but also the ideals, culture and attitudes of the Western world as represented by the European old-timers. Carl Frankenstein describes this concept as "unwillingness to accept others understandingly . . . the tendency toward rigid and aggressive evaluation of everything that is 'different.' "

The official high-sounding name for this concept of reform is a term once coined by Israel Zangwill for America, "The Melting Pot"; (to indicate the urgency and tempo of this "melting" process, Israel was often described as a "pressure cooker"). Writing in the *Jerusalem Post* of May 2, 1959, an Indian Jew, wholeheartedly endorsing the idea that "the Jewish State constitutes a 'melting pot' for all the multifarious cultural forces," refused to accept it as a one-way proposition:

We cannot see that the Western cultures in Israel are in process of "melting." The belief that Western culture and civilization are, after all, superior to the "lethargic" and "drowsy" civilizations of the East, and especially of India, is still accepted by many thinking Israelis. . . . Apparently European culture itself constitutes the "melting pot," and all other cultural forces are expected to dissolve in it.

The whole concept of a "melting pot" is in itself an ideal of questionable value. It presupposes total disappearance of all the specific group characteristics, to be replaced by some uniform over-all pattern. It is likely to result in a *potpourri* rather than in a true melting pot. An incomparably more appealing and constructive form of acculturation is a selective synthesis of the most desirable features and attitudes of both Western and Oriental ingredients of Israel's population. Such a synthesis would vastly enrich the nascent culture of Israel as a whole.

Compound Jewishness. No matter how accustomed to, sometimes even integrated into, the fabric of their respective countries of origin, most Oriental immigrants were uneasy Jews in a Moslem-dominated world: isolated, feeling inferior, living under a perpetual shadow of apprehension. Israel's major magic was supposed to be the eradication of this feeling. In a Jewish State, where "all are Jews," Oriental newcomers have become Jews in a Jewish society and polity, full-fledged citizens, entitled to full equality not only before the law but also in relationship with all other ethnic ingredients of the country's multicellular population. *Mizug ha-Galuyot*, the intermingling of these ingredients and the obliteration of discriminating group distinctions is the stated policy of the Third Jewish Commonwealth.

Yet this equalizing trend has quickly been supplemented, partly even superseded, by powerful divisive forces. In addition to their new all-Jewish identity, the Oriental newcomers have imbibed a distinctive sameness. Over-all Jewishness was taken for granted and relegated to a commonplace background characteristic, increasingly superimposed by accessory symbols tending to distinguish between single groups of Jews. Being a Jew has become a compound term in Israeli society: there are Polish Jews, German Jews, Yemenite Jews, Moroccan Jews, and many more. It now makes a very great difference from which country one has come from. He is identified by this association, which is largely taking precedence over the basic notion of all-Jewish community. A North African immigrant quickly discovers that if in Morocco he was a Jew, in Israel he is a "Moroccan," singled out as such, with all the implications of this label. Most of these implications are stigmatizing.

The Oriental newcomer came to feel that influence, power and resulting privilege is overwhelmingly concentrated in one layer of Israeli society: the Europeans of Ashkenazi background, whom he derisively called vuz-vuzim (a mimicry of the often used Yiddish word "vuz"). The State and Jewish Agency officials, whom he was meeting day in, day out, in all the numerous institutions and on whom he was so much dependent in almost every aspect of his life, the *madrichim* (instructors) in his settlement, were all, or nearly all, *vuz-vuzim*. They were strangers to him, and he strongly suspected that they were making fun of him when they spoke in his presence a few words in that "secret language" of theirs, Yiddish, which he could not understand. Said Meir Bar Sheshet, a Wadi Salib *shofar*-maker and chairman of the Union of the North African Immigrants, pleading for a greater understanding of the feelings of his community: "We do not appreciate jokes at our expense, especially

in Yiddish, a language that we did not receive from Moses."
There was little use in trying to argue that these complaints were
largely generated by oversensitivity. Y. Cannon, Haifa town
councilor of Sephardic origin, pointedly observed that no one
denied the existence of a *feeling* of discrimination among the
Oriental immigrants: "That in itself is enough to make it essential to eradicate this feeling."[12]

Nor was there much use in explaining that there were valid
and objective reasons for the preponderance of the European
elements. Most of them had been the first to arrive and were
in possession of assets that were in themselves sources of power:
formal education, professional skills, special training, and—last
but not least—Zionist enthusiasm. Even those among the
Oriental immigrants who were broadminded enough to recognize these reasons, were not ready to accept the resulting state
of affairs, resented it bitterly, and clamored for a change.

The Crisis of the Family. A major element in the problem of the
Oriental communities in Israel is the crisis of the family, in particular the father-son conflict.

In their countries of origin, the family was the basic social
and economic unit, with the father wielding undisputed control and authority. But in some Oriental communities (in particular among the Iraqis and North Africans) family disorgan-
ization accompanying the process of Westernization had already started before the transfer to Israel. The father's position
was progressively weakening and his authority challenged. In
Israel, this trend became accelerated and intensified. The
father, whose age and estrangement from the new pattern of
life often prevents him from obtaining a steady and rewarding
occupation, ceases to be the mainstay of the family. The sons,
who had learned Hebrew, acquired some trade or profession,
and also greater knowledge and understanding of the outer
world of Israel's institutional bureaucracy, assume ever greater
responsibility. They become both major providers for the family budget and interpreters of Israeli realities. They increasingly
challenge the father's authority. Some fathers passively acqui-
esce, others refuse to yield, and conflicts and strife often result,

culminating in the sons' leaving the family. Most of the children do not want to work at their fathers' occupations. Moreover, "the average Oriental child finds it difficult to identify with his parents, who deviate from the social norms accepted by the dominant Ashkenazi culture."[13] Some even rejected peers in their own ethnic group and wanted only to play with Ashkenazi children, saying: "When I grow up, I am going to be an Ashkenazi."[14]

The Political Aspect. The overwhelming majority of Oriental immigrants came to Israel without any set political convictions and associations. But those arriving by boat (as did almost all North Africans) were, during the last days of the voyage, registered for settlement by the accompanying Jewish Agency personnel composed essentially of emissaries of Israeli political parties appointed on the basis of a fixed "party key" reflecting the numerical strength of these parties in the Zionist Congresses. Each of them sought (and sometimes fought) to enlist as many recruits as possible in the settlements associated with his movement: a type of *Kibbutz*, controlled by one of the Socialist parties, a religious or nonreligious *moshav*. Competition was fierce, and each emissary strived to outbid the others by presenting a glowing image of the opportunities offered by his particular type of settlement. Confused and bewildered, many immigrants surrendered to these high-pressure methods; even on the boat they were earmarked as "wards" of one or another political party, though they usually knew next to nothing of its program and activities. Those who had arrived not by boat were subjected to a similar procedure in the immigrant camps (*machanot olim*).

In the settlements they had "joined" in this peculiar way, the new immigrants have automatically become part and parcel of a powerful agricultural market-supply system: all necessary acquisitions had to be made exclusively from *Hamashbir Hamerkazi*, the supply organization of the Socialist-dominated Histadrut (General Federation of Labor); produce had to be sold only through *Tnuva*, Histadrut's marketing arm. Their settlements have thus become but a wheel in a very large and elaborate system of powerful institutions upon which they were completely dependent. Within each individual settlement, the most powerful "institution" was the madrich (instructor) delegated or sanctioned by the political party or movement to which this settlement had been "allotted." The madrich's duties included, among others, distribution of wages which the new settlers were receiving for their daily work. This enabled him to reward certain settlers by assigning to them easier duties, and the duller or harder tasks to others. This state of affairs generated resentment and charges of favoritism.

Lawrence Fellows reported in The New York Times on April 3, 1960, that fifty families of Kurds settled in Kfar Yovel on Israel's northern frontier had left the colony because "the government had, in effect, driven them away by trying to do too much for these fiercely independent people": experts were sent "to teach the Kurds how to plant their fields, manage their finances and care for their children." The result was that "the Kurds packed and left." It was only later, says Fellows, that Dr. Raanan Weitz, director of the Jewish Agency's Settlement Department, learned that the Kurds had resented the pressure against their traditional society.

The non-Ashkenazi communities of various descriptions have been traditionally underrepresented, in such bodies as determine and direct life in Israel. Till 1951 there was only one non-Ashkenazi Minister (of police) in the fifteen-member Israeli Cabinet; in 1959, when the Ashkenazi Minister of Religious Affairs resigned, he was replaced by a Sephardi Rabbi. Among the 2,083 senior civil servants, judges, administrative officials and diplomatic envoys, only 117 were in 1957 of non-Ashkenazi origin. Although half of the total police force of 6,000 is recruited from Oriental Jewish communities, only 10 per cent of the 600 officers and NCO's were of Oriental origin. Among the 21 members of the Jewish Agency Executive, there is not a single representative of the Oriental sector. Of the 120 members of the First Knesset, only 13 were of Sephardic or Oriental origin; only 8 were elected to the Second Knesset, and 11 to the Third:[15]

Party	Represented by	No. of Oriental and Sephardi Members
Mapai	40	5
Herut	15	2
The General Zionists	13	1
The Religious Bloc	11	1
Ahdut Ha'avodah	10	1
Mapam	9	1
Agudat Israel	6	All Ashkenazim
Progressives	5	All Ashkenazim
Communists	6	All Ashkenazim

In the wake of the Wadi Salib riots (see pp. 374–379), a general race started among Israel's political parties to place non-Ashkenazi candidates high on their lists for the November 1959 elections to the Fourth Knesset, reshuffling their top candidates to include people "with good Oriental names." All the parties were trying to hook Oriental voters, and their campaign orators, not sure that all the listeners were able to understand a political speech in Hebrew, were addressing them in Arabic, Persian and French. In addition, several separate Sephardi and Oriental "communal" lists were submitted. Among them were: North African Union, National Sephardi Union, National Sephardi Party, Yemenite Movement, Independents (North Africans), New Immigrants' Front, Tnuat Moledet.[16] None of them received the required minimum of one per cent of all votes and obtained not even one single Knesset seat, though in their totality they attracted at least two-thirds of the 32,000 votes which were cast for the so-called "small lists." Only 9 of the 120 members of the Fourth Knesset, elected on various party slates, are of Afro-Asian origin.

Numerous were also separate "communal" lists in the 1959 municipal elections. In Tel Aviv, three of the twelve contesting lists were "Oriental"; in Jerusalem—four of sixteen; in Ramat Gan, three of eleven. Four Yemenite lists appeared in Rehovot, three Iraqi lists in Ramat Gan, etc.[17] These municipal lists did not fare much better than those in the Knesset elections. In a few localities they succeeded in securing one or two seats, but on the whole voters belonging to the Oriental communities refused to support divisive political trends and gave their votes to the existing countrywide political parties.

15

The Problem Children

Not every group of Afro-Asian newcomers proved to be problem children—at least not to the same extent. Those from Iran and Afghanistan (38,781) have been little heard from and seem to have adjusted themselves in a quiet and inconspicuous way. To this category also belong the 35,000 Turkish Jews, the 32,000 Jews from Libya, the 36,000 Egyptian Jews, as well as the 8,000 from Syria and Lebanon, and the 4,600 from Aden. The most discussed have been for years the 60,000 Yemenites and the 130,000 Iraqis. The 150,000 belonging to North African, predominantly Moroccan, communities are still in the forefront of public interest and concern.

THE YEMENITES

Pre-State Community. There was a strong Yemenite community in Palestine long before the State of Israel was established. At the early stages of their adjustment to the new life, the Yemenites often felt the heavy hand of prejudice on quite unexpected levels of the Yishuv.

Roy Ottley, a Negro writer who had visited Palestine before the emergence of Israel, reports in his book, *No Greener Pastures*, that Haim Berman, secretary of the Histadrut (General Federation of Labor) admitted that when "Black Jews" first sought to enter the labor unions, "there were angry protests by many white Jewish workers against their admission." Only after months and months of educational work and after the Histadrut leadership "took aggressive action . . . were blacks enabled to enter the ranks as equals."[1] But this formal equality did not change much in the basic "facts of life" of the Yemenite community. Pitifully little was done to bring this large "exotic" group into the mainstream of the Yishuv's social and spiritual life. Unskilled, often illiterate and pathetically poor, they were the country's social outcasts.

The Yemenites were induced to become hired laborers on the cooperative farms. They agreed in the hope that from this stage they would ultimately rise to become independent small farmers. This hope was derived largely from the Biblical saying, "Each man under his own vine and under his own fig tree." Yet such desires were in conflict with the collectivist and cooperative trend predominant in the Zionist colonization. The Yemenites became discouraged. As early as 1921, the Council of Yemenite Laborers published a resolution saying:[2]

The situation of hundreds of Yemenite families in the settlements, who immigrated to Eretz Israel with devotion of soul and out of love for the country, and desire to work its land and to take root in it, has become worse from year to year. The yoke of oppression was put on our necks, on our women and children, degrading our honor, suppressing our spirit and filling us with bitterness. The uncertainty and unemployment increase. . . . The settlement, in the shadow of which we wanted to live, has become for us a bitter disappointment.

They took little pride in their toil as part of a *kibbutz* or *moshav* machine and started looking for other sources of income. The older generation, having no alternative, continued to work the land, but the young people went to the cities and sought other fields of endeavor. They were particularly eager to obtain white-collar positions, in the hope of attaining the social status associated with clerical pursuits. But very few succeeded in doing so. Those who failed, attributed this failure to lack of "pull" due to their belonging to an "inferior" ethnic group.

Industry, too, failed to absorb Yemenites on a permanent basis; it demanded skilled labor and often offered them work on a day-to-day basis only. In many circles, the Yemenites were regarded as the "hewers of wood and drawers of water," destined to do the coarsest, most difficult, poorly paid manual work. They produced a large percentage of domestic servants, the so-called *Ozrot Bayit*. In spite of their slenderness and rather thin legs, they proved to be good porters, and even comparatively heavy objects did not frighten them. There is the well-known Tel Aviv ditty, in which Sa'adya, the porter, tells how he was given a piano to carry on his shoulders while the *Shikozi* (the Ashkenazi in Yemenite parlance) sat on top of it. Yemenites were also janitors, bootblacks, street sweepers, garbage collectors, peddlers of soft drinks—mostly on a daily basis and at pitifully low wages, a situation which spelled unending poverty and perpetuated a low standard of living.

Another source of deep resentment was the attitude of wide circles of the population, which was all too often tinged with various nuances of prejudice. European Jews, even when sincerely praising the Yemenite immigrants as industrious, honest and patriotic, were doing so with an undertone of patronizing benevolence. Remarks to the effect that the Yemenites were childish, shiftless, averse to cleanliness, and unwilling to do steady work, were circulated with an outstanding lack of tact and insight.

Underground Associations. For years the Yemenites lived uncomplainingly on the fringes and in the slums. But beneath the seemingly resigned acceptance of their plight, a fierce determination was growing to break out of isolation, to cast their lot with such groups in the Yishuv as would be ready and willing to accept them as truly and unconditionally equal partners in a common struggle for a great cause. Hence their association with the underground organizations.

There are no statistics to show the ethnic composition of the "official" Hagana and the dissident Irgun Zvai Leumi (Jewish Military Organization) and Lechi (Fighters for Freedom). However, it is the inference of several authors, both Oriental (L. Yeshayahu, "Changes Among the Yemenites," *Beterem*, September 1947) and Ashkenazi, (Y. Gross, "Ethnic Differences of Social Change," *Megamot*, Vol. III, No. 2, 1952) that the part of the Oriental Jews in the dissident underground was much larger than their part in the Hagana.

Irgun, the largest of the dissident groups, was particularly successful in attracting Yemenites, who unhesitatingly risked their lives in the battles for Jewish freedom. They filled the British prisons, and hundreds of them spent years in the internment camps of Latrun and Central Africa. The cemeteries of Israel are dotted with the graves of Yemenite boys and girls killed in action. In the fiery ferment of underground comradship, in the tense atmosphere of sharing as brothers the dangers and triumphs of the underground struggle, social and psychological barriers were broken down. Several "Western" Irgun members married Yemenites, Abraham Shumsky believes that the Hagana

failed in mobilizing a sufficient representation of the Oriental youth because of monopolization and dominance by the middle-class culture, membership composed mainly of Ashkenazi youth, the resistance of parents and so forth. . . . In the Irgun, some of the Oriental youth found an outlet for their resentment, not only of the British and the Arabs, but also of the governing Ashkenazi institutions. . . . Participation in the Irgun was most important in raising the injured self-esteem of the Oriental boy. It gave him a feeling of belonging to and identification with a great national cause.[3]

Carl Frankenstein also stresses that "the fact that the dissident political parties—those that rejected the authority of the governing Jewish institutions in the pre-State era—were so largely recruited from the ranks of the Oriental youth, proves how much resentment and bitterness had accumulated in these groups, in part at least in consequence of the patronizing attitude of the European Jews."[4]

New Turn. The integration of the Yishuv's Yemenite sector took a new turn with the massive transfer to Israel of the entire Jewish community of Yemen: "Operation Magic Carpet," within a short period of 1949–1951, brought 48,000 Yemenite Jews. This mass influx, though magnifying the scope of the integration problem, radically changed its character and tempo.

The new arrivals came full of enthusiasm. They were deeply moved by the brotherly reception extended to them by the Government and people of Israel. A revealing insight into the mentality and high expectations with which they entered Israel

is offered by the poetry of Shabetai Ben Pinchas Mahron
Halevi, a Yemenite Jew who arrived with the Magic Carpet
operation. Here are the concluding lines of his short poem "On
Eagles' Wings":

> The aeroplane bears us like eagles of old.
> Rulers greet us in glory untold . . .
> With bread and garments they do meet us,
> With joy and blessings they do greet us,
> With mercy and kindness they entreat us,
> To share in rejoicing eternal.

In this mood of ecstasy and gratitude, the Yemenites were
ready, willing and eager to adapt themselves to the new, and to
them strange, life of Israel. The difficulties they met with were
tremendous. The twelfth-century "civilization" with which
they arrived from Yemen did not prepare them for the most
elementary requirements of modern existence. Since beds,
chairs and tables were not used in Yemen, where people sat on
palm mats and carpets and slept on the ground, the Yemenites
at first preferred to sleep under, rather than on, the cots in the
reception centers. When bed sheets were issued, they cut them
up into prayer shawls and skirts. Members of the camp staff had
to undress, climb on the beds, stretch out and pretend to sleep
to make the Yemenites understand the use of these strange
paraphernalia. Similarly, the use of toilets and toilet paper,
showers, washbasins, garbage cans, had to be demonstrated.
When forks were distributed, they did not know how to use
them, and a few even wounded themselves, so that for a time
only spoons were given them to be used for all meals.

But the Yemenites proved to be willing and capable pupils.
They learned eagerly and quickly. And they proved to be an
extremely valuable asset for the upbuilding of Israel. Their response to the demand for agricultural colonization was the best
among all immigrant groups. Constituting less than 8 per cent
of the total immigration up to the summer of 1951, they provided the human material for 57 out of 231 (25 per cent) of the
agricultural settlements established up to this date. None of
these were of the collectivist *Kibbutz* type, and most were

purely Yemenite in their composition. In "mixed" villages, the
Yemenites complained about alleged discrimination by the Section for Yemenite Immigrants established by the Jewish Agency
for Palestine and manned by Yemenite officials belonging to the
ruling Mapai party. A pamphlet, *Yemenite Jews in the State of
Israel*, published in 1950 by the Organization of Yemenite Jews
in Israel, claimed that Yemenite settlers were being allotted
houses which were in the worst condition and were situated on
the outskirts of the villages. There also were bitter complaints
against the Histadrut-controlled Labor Exchanges where "the
Yemenite worker was discriminated against and remains discriminated against to this day" and where he is "automatically
registered for work with the hoe. . . . All work yielding a
better income, in industry and even in road building, which is
relatively easier, is given to others."[5]

Somewhat later, trouble developed in another aspect of the
economic field. Yemenite inmates of the Rosh Ha'ayin immigrant camp near Petach Tiqvah, eager to escape the enforced
idleness of the camp existence, seized the offered opportunity
of doing part-time work on Petach Tiqvah's plantations. Since
they had obtained this work directly from the farmers and not
through the General Labor Exchange, however, and since they
had accepted lower wages than those established by the Histadrut, pickets were set up by organized labor along the road
leading from the camp to Petach Tiqvah, and the Yemenites
were forcibly prevented from going to work. The Yemenites
could not understand why they were being punished for their
eagerness to work on the land to start a productive life. They
strongly resented the picketing, seeing in it a selfish and discriminatory attempt by the Ashkenazi-ruled labor unions to
preserve their higher standard of life at the expense of newly arrived Oriental immigrants.

Thoroughly Integrated. Notwithstanding all these conflicts
and frictions, the Yemenites can be considered the most thoroughly integrated Jewish community in Israel, firmly rooted in
the land. They are the commonly acknowledged outstanding
success of Israel's absorption effort.

This success is due in the main to the Yemenites' own qualities, first and foremost to their boundless love for and attachment to the Holy Land. Though the Zionist movement had never conducted propaganda or educational activities among them, they are imbued with a deep-seated and genuine pioneering spirit. They never spurn any kind of work and possess the rare quality of being satisfied with their lot. Among them, complaints about the economic hardships of the country are heard much less frequently than among any other section of the population. Whenever they are asked about their living conditions, they answer: "*Baruch ha'Shem*" (Thank God). Less exclusive and self-centered than other immigrant communities, they are willing and eager to share in common effort, to help those who came to Israel after them. This spirit of national unity finds an eloquent expression in the touching simplicity of the concluding sentences of an autobiographical sketch, "A Yemenite Boy in Israel," by Zecharia Nissim, who arrived in Israel with the Magic Carpet:[6]

Those of us who came a year or two ago must instruct those who come today, and he who comes today, within six months or a year will have to help those who come after him. Thus we shall be a single people, "all Israel comrades," with no distinction between those who come from Yemen and those who come from Morocco, and those who come from Poland, and those who come from Iraq, and those who come from America. All of us together will built up a country that will be an example to the whole world. How? Through unity, love and friendship, through physical and mental effort, and none of our enemies will ever overcome us. Our family is the only one of Yemenites living among immigrants from Kurdistan who have settled in Katra. The people are good and they have found favor in my eyes. They work well and honestly and they love and respect each other. The hearts of some of them are still sore from what they suffered in the Exile as we ourselves suffered. Every Jew coming from the Exile, even if he were rich, suffered persecution, and only God delivered us from the hands of the Gentiles until we came to the shores of our homeland, the land of our fathers.

Now I will conclude with a blessing to all Israel that we succeed in striking root in our young homeland, we and all the children of Israel. Amen. So may it be His Will."

The Yemenites are strongly represented in Israel's agricultural economy. They like farming and can be found in the most remote and "wild" areas, where others are reluctant to venture. They till the soil joyously, and their colonies are examples of diligence and thrift. The climate does not affect them as it does many immigrants from other countries, especially during the summer months. The Yemenites' contribution to Israel's handicrafts is outstanding. Their unique style of embroidery, especially in women's wear, is known and appreciated both in the country and abroad. Famous also are their exquisitely wrought trinkets, bearing traditional Jewish characteristics. Under their influence, Israel's light industry, which is otherwise mostly Western, introduced elements of Oriental flavor in its production. There are as yet almost no Yemenites among the academic intelligentsia: no Yemenite physicians, lawyers, or engineers. They have penetrated into two professions only—teaching and nursing. But Yemenites are prominent as vocalists (Beracha Tsefira, Shoshana Damari, Esther Gamlielit) and dancers (the internationally famous ballet troupe Inbal).[7]

THE IRAQIS

A Community of 135,000. In 1950–1951, some 123,000 Iraqi immigrants entered Israel; together with those who had settled there before, they formed a community of 135,000.

Unlike the Yemenite and North African immigrants, the Iraqis had no inferiority complex. They have never been in a state of medieval semislavery such as that in which Jews lived for centuries in Yemen. They consider themselves a Jewish tribe of ancient and noble origin, in many respects superior to Jews from the West. Nor were they in any way backward in their education. In Baghdad alone, Jewish community schools in 1949 counted 10,772 pupils, and over 2,500 attended various private schools.

There was also no justification for the widespread notion that the Iraqi immigrants were predominantly merchants or people without skills. A Jewish Agency spokesman found it necessary to say in August 1951 that 70 per cent of them were "small tradesmen or unskilled workers" and that their occupational distribution made them unsuitable for a speedy and successful integration. Figures released by the Central Bureau of Statistics and Economic Research of Israel established that while merchants constituted 33.2 per cent of the total number of gainfully employed Iraqi immigrants, the percentage of manual workers (artisans, 27.1 per cent; unskilled workers, 6.4 per cent; service workers and the like, 8.6 per cent) totaled 42.1. In addition, 21.2 per cent of the gainfully employed were professionals (6.1 per cent) and clerical workers (15.1 per cent)—a category which is in high demand in Israel. Farmers constituted 3.1 per cent and construction workers 1.3 per cent. On the whole, there was no substantial difference in the main items of the sum total between the occupational structure of the Iraqi immigrants and that found among other immigrant groups. It is true that the percentage of gainfully employed among the Iraqi immigrants (28.3 per cent) was considerably lower than among immigrant groups which arrived during the same period. But this was due mainly to the fact that the Iraqi immigrants were a strikingly "young" community: 42.3 per cent were below sixteen years of age—too young to be put to work.

Also, it could not be said that the Iraqis came completely destitute, without any financial assets, thus representing a mere liability in terms of possible investment. Dr. Saleh Haydar, Deputy Director of the Iraqi National Bank, regarded as Iraq's leading economist, told the Arab News Agency in June 1951 that the Jews leaving Baghdad had managed to transfer to Israel or elsewhere approximately $30 million during the preceding two years.[8] The number of wealthy Iraqi immigrants was, however, limited, and they showed little inclination either to assist their needy brethren or—at least at the early stage—to invest their capital in constructive economic enterprise.

Frustrating Experience. During the first years following its total transfer to Israel, the Iraqi Jewish community felt intensely unhappy and frustrated. One of the basic traits of the Middle Eastern way of life was the paternalistic character of the state authority, which was often not only arbitrary but also "personal" and accommodating toward the governed population. In Israel, the Iraqi newcomers joined an essentially European so-

ciety, the majority of which had grown up in more or less in-
dustrialized environments typified by lack of personal contact in
relationship between the state apparatus and the citizen. In his
penetrating analysis of "The Problem of Ethnic Differences in
the Absorption of Immigrants," Carl Frankenstein speaks of
"the complex anonymity and impersonality of bureaucratic machinery and of bureaucratic thinking." This attitude was both
bewildering and dismaying to the Iraqi newcomers. As Samuel
Z. Klausner put it, their

first impression of Israel included clerks behind desks, who automatically ticked them off in that depersonalized fashion upon
which the bureaucracy depends for its efficiency. Food, clothing and
bedding waited at the end of long lines. . . . The clerk at the Labor
Exchange, who is interested only in specific information about the
immigrant, appears mechanical and inhuman, and the bill collector,
who thought that sickness in the family and unemployment were
beside the point, seems cold and brutal. The overburdened doctors
and nurses of the socialized medicine system perform their tasks
quickly, perfunctorily, and with a minimum of human contact. The
flood of immigration has been so sudden and so great that Israel
is unable to provide enough of the social workers and conscientious
teachers who can meet the immigrants as whole people. . . .
   . . . Treated as objects, they were overwhelmed by a feeling of
powerlessness and confusion: soon they accepted the role, becoming passive and dependent. We often find it reflected linguistically
when they [Iraqi immigrants] use active verbs to describe their behavior up to the point at which they boarded the plane for Israel.
Then they shift to the passive voice in telling what was done to
them and of the places to which they were sent." [9]

   Frustration soon developed into anger. Complaints that they
were being disregarded, discriminated against, and not given a
fair chance to use their capabilities, became numerous and vocal. In July 1951, a mass demonstration against "race discrimination in the Jewish State," the first of its kind, was staged by
Iraqi Jews in Tel Aviv before the Jewish Agency building. The
demonstrators claimed that they were not being given equal
treatment with the "white" Ashkenazi Jews, that they had been
relegated to a second-class category of Israeli citizenship, that
both the Government and the population in general showed a

condescending attitude toward them. In the *ma'abara* of Sa-kieh, near Tel Aviv, the Iraqi dwellers complained to the *Jewish Chronicle* correspondent that although they constituted the majority of the *ma'abara* population, they were not represented in the local committee which was monopolized by Rumanian and Tripolitanian immigrants who had arrived before them. Their European neighbors had nothing but contempt for them. When the correspondent asked a Rumanian family in a *ma'abara* how they mixed with the Iraqis, one of the women shrugged her shoulders and said: "I walk away when they are there. I am afraid to have anything to do with them. They even use knives against each other."

Iraqi spokesmen were particularly bitter in their assertions that many of the jobs for which they considered themselves suitable were going to non-Iraqis. Specific cases of highly qualified Iraqi immigrants were mentioned in the press: Shimeon Balas, who had held a high position in the Iraqi Ministry of Defense, and Kadoorie Levy, who had been a high official in the Iraqi railway system. It was argued that if they had succeeded in attaining such responsible jobs in the inimical Iraqi administration, they must have been highly qualified specialists in their respective fields, and only deliberate discrimination could have prevented the Israel Government from enlisting their services in similar positions.

A Breakthrough. Having overcome the initial passiveness caused by cold and impersonal bureaucratic reception, the Iraqi immigrants proved to be anything but modest and submissive, content to wait passively for better times. A current saying put the difference between them and the Yemenites in these terms: "A Yemenite stands in line patiently, while an Iraqi tries to get to the head of the queue." Little by little, the majority succeeded in finding their place in Israel's economy, mostly urban (there are large Iraqi communities in Tel Aviv, Jerusalem, Beersheba, Ramat Gan). Few are engaged in manual labor. Not many settled on the land. Those who did, originated in the main from the Kurdistan area where Jews had always been predominantly laborers and small farmers. Together with the immigrants from the Persian Kurdistan, they settled in four *kib-*

butzim and twenty-seven moshavim.[10] Among the professional intelligentsia, many physicians and nurses have found employment with the Kupat Holim and with various hospitals throughout the country. Iraqi engineers are at work in the Negev. El Al, the Israel airline, employs a number of Iraqi technicians and clerks. The Iraqis are well represented in banking. Their knowledge of French, English and Arabic considerably helped their penetration into this field. Some 10 per cent have found work as government officials, members of the police force, army officers and functionaries, etc.

Nevertheless, out of the 30,000 Iraqi families who arrived in 1950–1951, a hard core, comprising 5,800 families (20 per cent of the total), were still in ma'abaroth up to June 1, 1959; they have been there for six, seven, even eight years.[11]

THE NORTH AFRICANS

Latecomers. The most unhappy and bitter among the Oriental Jews in Israel have been the immigrants from North Africa— from Morocco, Algeria and Tunisia.

The overwhelming majority of the Jews in these countries had for centuries lived in a state of resigned lethargy. The Zionist movement displayed little active interest in North African Jewry and made no sustained effort to associate them with the aliyah to Palestine. Not more than 994 Jews from that area arrived in Palestine during the twenty-eight years from 1919 to 1948.

It took the trumpet call of the revival of Jewish statehood to awaken North African Jews. Jules Braunschvig, Vice President of the Alliance Israélite Universelle, found them in "an almost messianic state of mind." High officials of the French administration in Morocco spoke of "a quite irresistible tidal wave of mysticism" which had seized the entire Jewish population.[12] The Moroccans were the first sizable group of Oriental Jews to arrive immediately before and after the establishment of the Jewish state. Many who came in this turbulent period were illegal immigrants traveling along the hazardous ways of Aliyah Beth (illegal immigration). They fought well in Israel's War of Independence.

"Morocco-Sakin." Very soon a highly unfavorable composite image of a "Moroccan" developed in public opinion: all Moroccans, indeed all North Africans, were labeled as "bandits," wild people, ready and eager to "knife and steal." The term "Morocco-sakin" (knife-wielding Moroccan) obtained wide circulation. As early as 1949, an article in the independent, highly respected Tel Aviv daily *Haaretz* spoke of them as of "a people whose primitiveness is unimaginable. . . . They are completely ruled by primitive and wild passions. . . . In the living quarters of the Africans in the camps you will find dirt, card games for money, drunkenness and fornication. . . . [There is] chronic laziness and hatred of work . . . inability to absorb anything intellectual. . . . There is no hope even in regard to their children."[13] Demands were voiced for a selective system of immigration to prevent an "invasion by waves of criminals and assaulters of women from North Africa." Every North African was suspected of carrying a sheath knife and of being ready to stab at the slightest provocation.

This early image of the culturally and morally inferior and dangerous Moroccan has survived a full decade of attempts at integration. Early in 1959, the North Africans were infuriated by an article in the Histadrut daily *Davar* (January 23, 1959), illustrated with cartoons which, they felt, implied that Moroccans were prone to arak-drinking, knife-waving, playing of backgammon, and crime. Only with great difficulty did the leaders restrain their followers from anti-*Davar* demonstrations. Said one of them to Philip Gillon of the *Jerusalem Post*:[14]

What angers us is all this loose talk about our drinking arak and our girls being prostitutes. It seems that if it were cognac nobody would mind—there's something wicked about arak. And how many of us drink arak? I'd like the Committee of inquiry to get figures of who drinks most in this country—they'll find that it's not the Moroccans. And they can give figures on prostitutes and criminals as well. All this talk makes us seem like something different and worse. It's not fair.

When I first came here and I was asked where I came from, I said, "Morocco" in all innocence. Then I discovered that that was a bad thing. I started to say "France" till I realized that everybody knew that "France" meant North Africa. Now I either say "Morocco" softly, under my breath, as if I'm ashamed of it, or I say it loud and aggressively, as if I'm ready to fight about it.

We left Morocco because we were Jews, but we were never told that we would be Moroccans in Israel.

The Oriental immigrants had undoubtedly themselves contributed to the perpetuation of this hyphenated identity by choosing to live and work within their respective country groups—Moroccans with Moroccans, Yemenites with Yemenites—and marrying within their particular group. A kind of vicious circle is thus being created. As Levy Cohen, Haifa's Municipal Probation Officer put it: "Moroccan immigrants suffer from a sense of discrimination from the moment of their arrival in the country, and because of that, help create an atmosphere of prejudice which in turn convinces them even more of the discrimination."[15]

Lack of Education and Skills. More clear-headed North African immigrants admit that their inferior status in Israeli society is largely determined by their lack of education and skills. But they refuse to accept this explanation as justification. The leader of the Wadi Salib riots, Ben Haroush, exclaimed: "If I am unskilled, does that mean that I must raise a generation of porters and that persons with academic training raise a generation of professionals?" And in Beersheba, another Moroccan said to Philip Gillon: "Looking at it objectively, we know that there are questions of education. But knowing this doesn't help us. What's more, we see our youth growing up, and they are also going to be inferior to the *sabras*."[16]

It cannot be denied that a very high proportion of the North African immigrants, though emotionally most enthusiastic, arrived in Israel unprepared, both physically and spiritually, for the hard realities of a pioneering country. They suffered from two major disadvantages: lack of education and of skills in manual trades. According to Dr. Dov Joseph, Treasurer of the Jewish Agency, among the 14,567 immigrants from North Africa in 1957 and 1958 only 4 per cent had any skills, as against 18 per cent "university-trained"—physicians, engineers, pharmacists, etc.—among the 53,000 immigrants from Europe and 13,525 from Egypt who arrived during the same period.[17]

The basic trend in Moroccan Jewish life was migration from villages to larger urban centers, with all the ensuing implications of this change in their mode of life and mentality. In Israel, this process has been reversed. Most North African immigrants have been directed to *ezorei pituach* (development areas) and established in small rural settlements, where they felt abandoned and degraded because they had to do farm work. They had never been farmers at home: in the whole of Moghreb, farming, as physical labor in general, had always been a Moslem occupation; only the most primitive and backward people earned their living in agriculture. Farming was in their minds associated with a lower Moslem-Arab status, and they bitterly resented the necessity of "becoming an Arab." Said a North African immigrant: "At home, all this work was done by Arabs, by the lowest and worst of them. A Jew would be ashamed to do such work, but here we have to do it . . . it is a shame." Said another: "I do not want to do here all the things that only the Arab riffraff did in Morocco. I did not come to Israel to become like one of them."[18]

The North African immigrants were predominantly petty tradesmen and artisans—professions for which there was little demand in the new land. They were forced to seek employment as unskilled laborers, going daily to the Labor Exchanges and often finding no work. During the first seven years of statehood (1948–1955) they were placed in *machanot olim* (immigrants' camps), living largely on the Jewish Agency dole. Since 1955, under the new "ship to village" settlement policy, new immigrants were taken directly from the ships to new villages prepared in advance, or to small towns in development areas: 83 per cent of the 103,000 Moroccans who came since 1954 were sent to these areas.[19] The initial problems of housing and work were largely solved. The main destination was the Negev, where of the thirty-one new *moshavim*, twenty-seven were settled by immigrants from Moslem countries.[20]

Both in the camps and in the new villages, the Oriental settlers were fully dependent upon the large and ponderous bu-

reaucratically organized machinery of the Jewish Agency's Absorption and Settlement Departments, where responsibility
and direction were concentrated. The settlers felt lost and helpless, dominated by remote institutions, which were staffed
almost exclusively by European officials.

Split Personality. Throughout the first decade of Israel's statehood, friction and conflict have been a permanent feature in
the relationship between the North Africans and the non-
Oriental sections. Some of it must be attributed to a difference
in cultural and linguistic backgrounds. Many aspects were, however, the direct result of a shocking lack of sympathy, tact and
kindness on the part of the European majority of the Yishuv.

A significant feature of the problem of North African immigrants is their "split personality." As the report of the Wadi
Salib Investigation Committee put it, "this community had
lost its old cultural forms and systems of values, in part, even
before coming to Israel, and did not succeed in creating new
ones."[21] In Algeria, Morocco, Tunisia, many of them came in
contact with French culture, of which they adopted mainly
outward aspects, not intrinsic values. This French-European
polish enabled some of them to aspire to fairly influential positions in local administration and society. In Israel, they have
been thrown back to an inferior status, most of the positions
they were striving for being occupied by earlier settlers of East
and Central European origin. Their partial Europeanization
has become a source of inner conflict. They were never sure
which of their two component parts—the Oriental or the
Western—represented their true self. They have lost belief in
their old social and spiritual values and forms of life. Their own
inner image has been irretrievably broken, and they are longing for acceptance as Europeans. But they are not accepted
as such. A 1954 survey by the Israel Institute of Applied Social Research among some 450 families from 17 countries,
settled in an immigrant housing development on the outskirts
of Jerusalem, established that almost all of the Oriental dwellers
wanted to be close to Europeans, while the latter expressed the
desire to be close to other Europeans. Inquiring into the settlers' visits, the survey found that the Rumanians and Poles, for

instance, fulfilled their desire in visiting Europeans 93 and 97 per cent, respectively; the Iraqis only 18 per cent; the Moroccans only 6 per cent. Moreover, of the 367 answers to the question, "Which of the seventeen groups did they most dislike?" 143 named the Moroccans (the Iraqis occupied second place with 96 answers, the Yemenites last, with 9).[22] Said a Moroccan bitterly: "First they destroyed our old life, and now they do not allow us to do anything else. Everything is closed to us."[23]

"*Casablan.*" A revealing and disturbing insight into the tortured mentality of a Moroccan youth is offered in a three-act play, *Casablan*, by Yigal Mossinsohn, staged in the autumn of 1954 by the Tel Aviv Chamber Theater.

Its central character is Siman-Tov, a young immigrant from Morocco, who joined the Israeli Army during the War of Independence and fought bravely in the Negev, where he distinguished himself by rescuing many of his comrades from danger. His fellow fighters affectionately called him "Casablan," after his birthplace, Casablanca.

Then the war was over. The wartime camaraderie was also over. All of a sudden, the proud and sensitive young man found himself alone, almost ostracized by his former friends; even those who did manifest casual friendly interest in his welfare did so in a patronizing way, blandly overlooking the deeper emotions and motives which underlie his complex personality. The name, "Casablan," which used to be an expression of informal affection, has become a kind of stigma: he is from Casablanca, a "Moroccan."

Casablan is both hurt and indignant. He develops an acute feeling of inferiority, a feeling which he is desperately trying to overcome by adopting an overbearing and bullying attitude toward everybody and everything. He refuses to accept Israel's realities as long as he is not treated as an equal. Unhappy and apprehensive, he is often violent in his reactions. This behavior is but a pathetic attempt at compensation for the frustrating impact of his former friends' aloofness. But it creates for him the reputation of a "bad boy." And when a municipal officer is found stabbed, Siman-Tov finds himself charged with the crime; this maladjusted, vehement Casablan appears as the

most obvious suspect. Finally, another, least likely, character
turns out to be the real culprit. Casablan is proven innocent,
curtain comes down with a happy-ending rapprochement
among the different "tribes" of Israel.

What the playwright apparently tried to convey to his audience was that Casablan is not just a maladjusted young man
born in the Moroccan town of Casablanca, but a common, al-
beit not universal, feature in Israel's social fabric. Outwardly
emotional, he longs for stability. Violent on the surface, he is
in fact sensitive and yearning for the spiritual security of recognition. What he desperately wants, is to "belong" to the community of Israel. He is off balance only because this society is
not receptive, and he feels lonely, frustrated, and bitter. Nothing is fundamentally wrong with him, either individually as Siman-Tov, or collectively as a "Casablan." A great deal is wrong,
however, with Israeli society, which was eager to accept and to
praise him during the War of Independence—as long as his
bravery and eventually his blood was needed—and which in
normal times does not afford him a place of equality and dignity.
A great deal is wrong with a state of affairs where a "Casablan" is
a "natural" suspect whenever a crime of violence occurs.

Absorption and Re-emigration. In 1948–1959, North Africans
constituted 20.7 per cent of all immigrants. About one quarter
(24.8 per cent) of them went to agricultural settlements. Of the
251 *moshavim* set up in the first decade of statehood, 82 were
settled by newcomers from North Africa. Raanan Weitz, Director of the Jewish Agency Settlement Department, believes
that "generally, the percentage of North African immigrants
who made good, medium, and substandard settlers was the
same as for other immigrant groups." Nevertheless, as late as
June 1, 1959, the 5,990 North African families still constituted
the largest group among the 18,960 hard-core families in the
ma'abaroth (next came the 5,800 families from Iraq).[24]

Difficulties of economic absorption and of social integration
led to sizable re-emigration. Data put at the disposal of this
writer by the Immigration Department of the Jewish Agency
indicate that the largest number had left Israel in 1949 when
1,010 re-emigrants of Tunisian, Algerian and Moroccan origin

embarked in Haifa. Further rate of re-emigration was as follows:[25]

Year	Re-emigrants
1950	415
1951	636
1952	854
1953	883
1954	323
1955	96
1956	310
1957	200
1958	180

16

The Alarm Signal

"Chain of Violence." The long pent-up tension among the North African immigrants erupted on July 8 and 9, 1959, in the slum quarters of Wadi Salib in Haifa, populated almost exclusively by North Africans. After a Moroccan drunkard, violently resisting arrest, had been wounded in a café by a police bullet, about two hundred North Africans demonstrated before police headquarters, wrecked the café, overturned cars, etc. Thirteen policemen and several demonstrators were injured and twenty-two participants were arrested. The Wadi Salib riots were followed by similar disturbances connected with a dispute on work quotas in the new town of Migdal Ha'emek in Galilee, and an outbreak of hooliganism in Beersheba. Fresh disturbances broke out in Wadi Salib on July 31, when a Mapai meeting was interfered with by a North African group. The Jerusalem *Post* called it a "chain of violence."

The Israeli press duly appraised the significance of the Wadi Salib events. *Haboker* (July 11) wrote that the riots were alarming evidence of accumulated anger that had been seeking an outlet, and "if we fail to tackle the problem wisely, we shall be in for trouble." *Maariv* (July 12,) also stressed that Wadi Salib was "an alarm signal for all of us," while *Yediot Aharanot* reminded the Ashkenazim that after all they were a minority in the country and the only reason they held sway was because the non-Ashkenazi sector had not produced a leader of stature to guide them to the position they deserve; that being so, the Ashkenazi leaders should take advantage of the present breathing-space and consider what should be done to lessen the gap between them and the Sephardi-Oriental community, both for the general and for their own good.

Soul-Searching. There was considerable soul-searching at the July 13 session of the Israeli Parliament.[1] David Hacohen, one of the leaders of the ruling Mapai party, tried to minimize the significance of the Wadi Salib outbreak, insisting that it was caused by "drunkards and habitual troublemakers," and that "discrimination was not as widespread as had been claimed." But another Mapai Knesset member, of Oriental origin, Yisrael Yeshayahu, admitted that "while the progress made in welding together the different ethnic groups had been remarkable, not enough had been done to raise the living standard of immigrants from North Africa and Asia to that of immigrants from Europe. Moreover, preference was often given to the European where the Oriental, if anyone, should be helped along."

Yerahmiel Assa of the leftist *Ahdut Ha'Avoda* said: "We must ask ourselves whether we have done everything possible to break down the 'ghetto walls' dividing the different communities and separating the Oriental Jews from the rest of the nation, and to raise their standard of living." The Mapam speaker, Hanan Rubin, insisted that "the fusing of the different ethnic communities will not be accomplished with sermons. . . . There will be no fusion so long as there are two standards of living." In similar vein spoke the Herut Deputy, Arye Ben-Eliezer, and Israel Rokach of the General Zionists.

The Herut and General Zionists Knesset groups demanded the establishment of a parliamentary investigation committee. The Israel Government has instead appointed a five-member Inquiry Committee, headed by a District Court judge, which held seventeen public hearings, heard forty-two witnesses, and submitted a 22-page report on August 19.

Anti-Mapai Trend. A marked feature of the Wadi Salib riots seems to have been resentment against the ruling Mapai party and the Mapai-controlled Histadrut (General Federation of Labor), which, it was claimed, exercise undue domination in the employment field. Ernest Touitou, former secretary of the Union of Algerian Immigrants, which is sponsored by the Zion-

ist Federation of Algeria, reported in the August-September issue of *Information*, published in Algiers by the *Comité Juif
Algerien d'Etudes Sociales*, that the Wadi Salib rioters "had
attacked the offices of the Mapai party, which is the party in
power, the offices of the Histadrut, the offices of the 'politicized'
Labor Exchanges, which distribute work as the feel fit." Giving
evidence in a "tense and hushed courtroom," Moshe Cabal, one
of the Wadi Salib dwellers, related that last year, just before the
High Holy Days, he had obtained a temporary job at the Palestine Electric Corporation and "begged to be kept on. I was told
to say that I'm a [Mapai] party member. I lied that Nathan
Lahav (the local Mapai Secretary) had recommended me because I had been active for Mapai." His story, however, had
been checked, he said, and he was discharged. Officials of the
Histadrut-controlled labor exchanges ridiculed the Moroccan
immigrants for having many children "whom you can't feed."
Another witness, the leader of the North African Immigrants
Association (*Likud Tsefon Africa*), David Ben-Haroush, stated
that when he and his friends had been planning to set up this
organization, they first "kept it secret, for fear of Mapai
strong-arm men who see to it that only their men are in control." Mapai and other parties, he said, had tried to buy off
Likud leaders, including himself, before the Histadrut elections,
but had failed "to corrupt us." The witness insisted that the
North African community had no representatives in Histadrut
bodies, and "freedom of speech is not enough to make a living."
When the Haifa Mayor, Abba Koushi, a prominent Mapai
leader, proceeded to establish a commission to "hear our problems," Ben-Haroush said, "only those toeing the line of Mapai
were invited." Asked by committee members whether these
men did not have any influence among the North African community, the witness answered: "They aren't fit for it. They
joined the [Mapai] party but do nothing for their own people
in it." The Mapai, Ben-Haroush further charged, wanted to
open a branch in Wadi Salib and its supporters tried to influence him and his friends to join. He had no party affiliations
and had none even today, but was persuaded to attend the first
meeting "in the interests of my community." But he noted that

representatives from Europe, not all of them even residents of the Wadi Salib quarter, were chosen as committee members, together with some Oriental Jews who were favored by Mapai. When he and his friends saw that his name was not on the list, they left.

Ben-Haroush's attitude and reaction must be viewed in the light of an autobiographical account of his personal twelve-year experience in the country as recorded by the Inquiry Committee:

He came to Palestine illegally in 1947, at the age of twenty-four, with other young men from Morocco, and was deported by the British to Cyprus. He first experienced a feeling of being discriminated against, in favor of newcomers from Europe, while being held in the Cyprus detention camp. He served in the army and was demobilized in November 1948. Afterward, he charged, the best houses in Wadi Salib had been turned over by the Hagana to the European immigrants. He had joined the police, but was employed only on guard duties, which offered little prospect of promotion and on which only elderly constables from Europe were employed. The State Development Authority, the Haifa city administration, the *Hameshakem* welfare organization for the aged, the Jewish Agency,—all favored European immigrants, he claimed. When, with a loan from the Defense Ministry, he set up a café in Wadi Salib which eventually failed, only men from North Africa, never from Europe, patronized it, he said.[2]

The Committee Report. There was in the beginning a determined attempt by the ruling parties to imply that the opposition had a hand in whipping up the passions in Wadi Salib. However, the report of the Inquiry Committee unequivocally refuted "suggestions that the Likud was supported by certain public or political bodies who were interested in agitation and outbreaks."[3]

It cannot be said that the report, which is on the whole rather complacent, had added greatly to the understanding of the problem of Oriental communities in Israel, let alone to its solution. It contained, however, some meaningful admissions.

Acknowledging that "certain portions of this [Wadi Salib]

community feel sometimes very strongly that they are suffering from discrimination and inequality," the Committee also recognized that "the background which provided a fertile ground for agitation is much wider and exists among different parts of the North African community . . . there exists a deep feeling that the discrimination is deliberate." ". . . It is natural," continued the report, "that feelings are particularly noticeable among those groups which have not been fully absorbed. But it seems that even among those sections of this community which have succeeded in finding their place, and they are by no means a small group, there is a feeling of identification with the sense of inequality and discrimination."

The Committee had no doubt that "there is absolutely no deliberate discrimination on the part of public and state institutions . . . where planning and policy are evolved." It admitted, however, that "on the lower levels there are in fact situations of inequality and discrimination" and expressed its "regret that numerous and various sections of the settled Israel public still have many prejudices."[4]

These are important admissions. The Committee recognized that the Wadi Salib events were not of merely local nature: their background was nation-wide—and not only among the maladjusted slum-dwellers but also in the midst of those who "have succeeded in finding their place." They must be therefore viewed as not merely an economic, but as a deep-seated social and psychological problem as well. Noteworthy also is the Committee's attribution of responsibility for this state of affairs. Nobody had ever claimed that there was any "deliberate discrimination" on the higher planning and policy-making level. But it is precisely "on the lower levels" that the Oriental immigrant is meeting the state and Jewish Agency authorities and is experiencing "situations of inequality and discrimination." It is on the basis of such experience, strengthened by contacts with "numerous and various sections of the settled Israeli public [which] still have many prejudices," that he felt the stigma of being a second-class citizen, an unwanted and slighted intruder.

The Wadi Salib riots and the committee report have stirred

up both public and government to a heightened awareness of the difficulties encountered by Oriental immigrants. The Government hastened to introduce a number of reforms designed to meet the most pressing of these difficulties: a system of family allowances for those with four children and more; work guarantees and increase in basic salaries; building of new and more commodious dwellings. These measures have undoubtedly contributed to a notable abatement of tension. Yet, as late as April 4, 1960, Lawrence Fellows reported in *The New York Times* that "the people of Wadi Salib are still hard-pressed for regular work and decent housing . . . /and/ suspect that they are being treated as second class citizens by a society that is essentially European in character."

17

The Great Integration Effort

Type of Rural Settlement. Mizug ha'Galuyot, the intermingling of heterogeneous ethnic groups, is the avowed aim of Israel's settlement planning. Accordingly, the Oriental newcomers had been frequently settled together with East European immigrants. It was expected that, living and working together, settlers with different backgrounds would learn from each other, would be forced to speak Hebrew as a common language, would undergo a process of mutual adaptation.

It soon became apparent that this settlement policy, however logical and patriotic, was generating tensions and conflicts between groups thrown together in a haphazard manner. As late as January 8, 1960, the Jerusalem *Post* reported "violent outbursts of fissions and feuds" in the fertile plain of Lachish:

> In Beit Shikma, inhabited by immigrants from Morocco and Tripoli (with a few "neutrals" from Persia and Tunis), Yom Kippur a year ago ended, not in *Neila*, but in the arrest of a score of men. Three revolvers and a rifle were fired instead of the shofar sounding; two men were taken to the hospital. Here the trouble apparently arose because 45 families from Morocco had been brought to a village containing 35 Tripolitanian families and had outvoted them in the village elections.... In prosperous Noga, the pride of Lachish, settlers from Iraq and Persia are periodically at each other's throats, with the "neutral" Kurds trying to hold the balance between them.

However, even in settlements inhabited by immigrants from the same country, violent conflicts are frequent.

In the prosperous village of Rahava, in the Lachish development area, which is inhabited entirely by settlers from Kurdistan, a riot broke out between members of the Levi and Rachamani clans. Twenty-five men went to jail and three to the hospital as a result of a dispute over 4½ *dunams* of land. There is serious talk of the sixteen "neutral" families abandoning the fruits of all their hard work because they can no longer bear the strain of the feud. At the all-Yemenite colony of Zavdiel, the settlers are split into three clans which are constantly at loggerheads. In Menuha, there is a clan feud between Kurds. These divisions are not confined to Lachish: in Zecharya, in the Judaean mountains, such a village split ended in a killing because of a strayed donkey. It seems that "communal homogeneity" is in itself no guarantee of harmony.[1]

Nevertheless, at present, the prevalent type of agricultural settlement is the one based on geographical ("communal") origin of its members who share certain broad cultural and linguistic characteristics. This concession to expediency has been strongly criticized as "a grave danger to the process of integration," which "puts off integration and crystallizes 'communal' divisions, a 'communal' settlement of which all members belonging to the same [ethnic] community, sometimes to the same family group, is bound to perpetuate *Galut* values and standards of organization."[2]

Abraham Ziegel, Director of the Jewish Agency's Absorption Department, insists, however, that "integration is not a quick process; it will take a long time." The Department had tried out various methods of distribution of the settlers: "But we were not successful. Immigrants of different origin have no common language. Their customs are different. They are not even in accord as to praying in the same synagogue. . . . This week, a Yemenite came to see us from Rosh Pina where an entire group of Yemenites had lived some time ago. Now, only his family remained, and he demands to be transferred to a settlement where he would be together with other Yemenites."[3]

Socioeconomic Changes. The background and the present structure of single Jewish ethnic groups in Israel is indicated by an instructive table in Professor Arieh Tartakower's study, *Jewish Society:*[4]

Occupational Structure of
Various Jewish Groups Abroad and in Israel

Occupations (1954)	Among natives of Europe and America		Among natives of Asia and Africa	
	Abroad	In Israel	Abroad	In Israel
Agriculture	2.1	10.3	2.0	30.8
Industry and handicraft	31.8	29.1	39.0	17.8
Building and construction	6.2	19.5	7.4	27.1
Communications	2.4	3.4	2.9	1.8
Total physical work	42.5	62.3	51.3	77.5
Commerce	33.2	13.1	31.3	8.1
Professionals and technicians	7.0	5.5	3.5	2.6
Officials	11.6	10.8	8.9	5.8
Others	5.7	8.3	5.9	6.0
Total nonphysical work	57.5	37.7	48.7	22.5
Grand total	100.0	100.0	100.0	100.0

The occupational structure of the European-American and Afro-Asian groups "abroad," i.e., in the countries of their origin prior to their settlement in Israel, is strikingly similar, particularly in regard to agriculture and commerce. The picture changes spectacularly when we analyze their occupations in Israel.

The ratio of those engaged in commerce declined among both groups: almost to one-third (from 33 per cent to 13.1 per cent) among Israelis of European-American birth, and almost to one-fourth (from 31.3 per cent to 8.1 per cent) among those born in Asia and Africa. But even more drastic is the difference in regard to agriculture: the share of the European-American group increased fivefold (from 2 to over 10 per cent) while the increase among natives of Asia and Africa is fifteenfold (from 2 per cent in their countries of origin to over 30 per cent in Israel.

More specific is the following table based on the *Statistical Abstract of Israel* for 1957/1958 (p. 302):

Of every 100 Jewish persons employed in agriculture in Israel at the end of 1957 there were:

	Per cent
Natives of Israel	16.2
Veterans* born in Asia and Africa	5.0
Veterans born in Europe and America	20.7
New Immigrants† born in Asia and Africa	37.3
New immigrants born in Europe and America	20.8
Total	100.0

* "Veteran": An immigrant who came to Israel before 1948.
† "New immigrant": An immigrant who came to Israel in 1948 or later.

The Afro-Asian group (both "veterans" and new immigrants) constitutes 42.3 per cent of the country's farming population, considerably exceeding its ratio in the general population (29.3 per cent). The new immigrants and "veterans" of the European-American group are represented by 41.5 per cent, only slightly in excess of their proportion in the general population (37.9 per cent). The latter are, on the other hand, overwhelmingly prevalent in industry and handicraft: 65.5 per cent of those employed in this branch of Israel's economy—while both "veterans" and new immigrants from Asia and Africa constitute only 21 per cent. Still more pronounced is the discrepancy in commerce and banking: 60.3 per cent for the European-Americans and 20.9 per cent for Afro-Asians. It is truly striking among government officials and white-collar workers generally: both immigrants and "veterans" from Asia and Africa constitute only 15.9 per cent (almost half their percentage in the country's population), while those of the European-American group are represented by 60.2 per cent.

Economic stratification is reflected in the far-reaching differences in the financial status. A recent survey of family savings in 1957–1958, prepared by the Bank of Israel, showed that veteran inhabitants of European or American origin had an average yearly income of I£3,716, while those of Asian or African origin earned a yearly average of I£2,746. Arranged chronologically, this difference is illustrated by the following table:[5]

Yearly earnings of immigrants who arrived between 1948 and 1954		Yearly earnings of immigrants who arrived after 1955	
From Europe and America	From Asia and Africa	From Europe and America	From Asia and Africa
I£2,914	I£2,088	I£1,707	I£1,418

Even more striking is the discrepancy in the distribution of loans to middle-class new immigrants granted by the Bank Leumi Le Israel in cooperation with the Jewish Agency. Data put at the author's disposal by Dr. J. Foerder indicate that of the 1,218 individual loans amounting to I£2,917,000, only 184 amounting to I£474,000 were accorded to immigrants from Afro-Asian countries, while new immigrants from Eastern Europe received I£2,048,000.

The Histadrut. It is commonly acknowledged that the Histadrut possesses great possibilities of fostering the integration of Afro-Asian immigrants.

During the last two decades, its Sephardi and Oriental membership has increased considerably. It amounted to 4,796 (7.2 per cent of the total membership) in 1939, to 15,493 (12.3 per cent) in 1947, and to 250,000 in 1959 (36.5 per cent of the total). A special Department for Oriental Jews had been established within the Histadrut's Executive Committee, headed and staffed by officials of Oriental origin. At the session of the Histadrut Council in September 1950, Pinchas Lavon, General Secretary of the Federation, stressed the urgent necessity of "molding equal standards of citizenship and fellowship for all members of the Histadrut, of all communities":

It is our duty to enlist dozens and hundreds of members of Oriental communities into the service of the Histadrut administrative machinery. It is intolerable to go on with the present state of things, where a member of the Histadrut from Oriental countries needs the services of an interpreter to make his representations understood by the Histadrut official. . . . The immigrant must confer with members who understand his language, linguistic and mental, and his concepts. He should not feel himself a "client" of the "white" departments of the Histadrut. We must make a very special effort to train a cadre of Histadrut leaders from among these tribes and sections.

The late Abraham Abbas, who came from Syria with the Youth Aliyah and has advanced to a position of leadership both among Oriental Jews and in the Ahdut Ha'Avoda labor party, a constituent of the Histadrut (he was elected to the Third Knesset), subjected to stern criticism the implementation of the policy announced by the Histadrut's Secretary General. Quoting Lavon's statement, he asked:[6]

What were the results of that new policy which was termed "integration"? The machinery of the Executive Committee has since been considerably expanded and enlarged by many hundreds of new officials. But how many officers of Oriental communities have been so integrated? Little more than a handful, perhaps ten, perhaps less than ten. What happened to integration in the Trades Union Department? How many Oriental Jewish officials have been enrolled for service in the Culture and Information Center with a staff of hundreds, or in the extensive machinery of the *Mo'etzet Hapo'alot*, or in the school for the training of Histadrut leaders, or in the Organization Department, or in any of the other numerous departments? What is the share of the Oriental communities in the secretariats of the Labor Councils of the large towns, or in the Boards of Directors of the Histadrut's Economic Corporations—*Solel Boneh, Koor, Tnuvah, Hamashbir Hamerkazi, Mish'an,* or Workers' Bank?

If we turn from these to the political organs of the Histadrut, we must strike an equally sad balance sheet. A year ago the governing institutions of the Histadrut were elected by a Conference of the Histadrut convened for the first time after seven years. An Executive Committee and a Central Committee were elected. Was the substantial change in the structure of the Histadrut reflected in the composition of these bodies? Mapai is represented by nine members on the Central Committee, but not one of these is of the Oriental communities. The smaller splinter parties with only one or two representatives are, on the face of it, perhaps less blameworthy."

"There are now," Abbas continued his indictment, "over ninety members in the Executive Committee of the Histadrut, almost double its former composition." Among them

Mapai is represented by 55 members, of whom 5 are Oriental;

Ahdut Ha'Avoda is represented by 13 members, of whom 3 are Oriental;

Mapam is represented by 12 members, not one of them Oriental;

The Oved Hazioni and Oved Hadati parties have not a single Oriental Jew in their respective delegations.

"Is this the way to implement the policy of integration and equality, so often and so loudly proclaimed by the majority in the Histadrut?" asked Abbas. "Those who presume to justify the blatant inequality on the ground that there are no qualified candidates for Executive and Central Committee membership among Oriental Jews simply distort the truth, I will adduce several illustrations from my own personal experience to prove the potential of competence and ability among leaders of Oriental communities that could be tapped with advantage, if only such potential leaders are properly guided and instructed, and if they are left immune from the troubled waters of day-to-day petty politics."[7]

As against these accusations, the Histradrut leadership points out its latest "attempts to foster and create cadres of leadership" among the Oriental workers and "the high proportion of secretaries from the new communities among the workers' councils": 21 of 68 of these are now Oriental immigrants; 494 out of 1,362 are elected members of the councils, and of the 535 workers' representatives on productivity committees, no less than 232, or 44 per cent, come from Oriental countries.[8]

The Hebrew Language. One way or the other, Hebrew served as the Esperanto of the Ingathering of the Exiles, the only common language for people from the four corners of the world. New immigrants from European countries, from Rumania and Poland, were not under immediate compulsion to learn it: they knew that with Yiddish they could get along in Israel sometimes better than with Hebrew. No such easy way out was available to the newcomers from the Orient. Most of the males (but only a small minority of the women) spoke and read Hebrew when they arrived in Israel. Those who did not, had to learn the language to be able to express themselves on the simplest matters of everyday life. Few did it systematically or out of conviction. Dr. S. W. Eisenstadt quotes a Jew from Tunisia saying angrily: "Why should I study Hebrew? What do you take me for? A fool or just a Zionist? Perhaps I will learn Yiddish. That may be worthwhile!"[9] The only exception were the Yemenites, who studied "the Holy Tongue" with almost religious fervor, because, as they put it, "this is our speech, the speech of our country and our Homeland."[10] But even those who learned Hebrew fairly well are far away from being always at ease with it. Only few in the settlements receive a Hebrew newspaper. Almost each home has a radio, but the most popular programs are those broadcast in Arabic.

The Hebrew School. The Hebrew school has done a magnificent job of wiping out illiteracy and cultural disparities among its motley student body. A report by the Israel Ministry of Education, published in *Davar* of August 28, 1959, states that of the 476,000 children enrolled in the year 5719 (1959) in all institutions of learning (kindergartens, elementary schools, intermediate schools, trade and farm schools), 226,000, or over 47 per cent, were of Oriental origin. Though kindergartens were unknown in most of the countries they came from, 15,000 four-year-olds and 25,000 five-year-olds were attending kindergartens in Israel. In the eighth-grade elementary schools, 172,000 children of Afro-Asian parents were enrolled—nearly half of the total student body; and 14,000 attended the afternoon intermediate, as well as trade and farm schools.

These are impressive figures, of which Israel's educational system has every reason to be proud. There is, however, ample authoritative evidence that much is far from bright behind this statistically correct façade: there is a sad background of far-reaching disparity in educational opportunities and achievements between the Oriental and non-Oriental pupils.

It begins first of all in the kindergarten, where the Western children start off with an advantage over those from Oriental homes. The former have had a start with certain educational advantages received from their parents and show a greater aptitude to learning. The result is the insoluble problem for educationists, and often a reluctance on the part of Western parents

to send their children to schools where there are a large number
of Oriental children—not so much because they object to the
latter, but because, they argue, their own children are kept back
by those more backward, who set the pace of the classes' progress. In some cases there is in force a tacit understanding by
which every group "knows its place" and "its school."

De facto segregation is also widespread in the elementary
schools. "Although there is no deliberate policy of school segregation," relates Abraham Shumsky, "many schools are in
fact segregated or semi-segregated."[11] In 14 of the 28 primary
schools in Tel Aviv there were not more than 10 per cent of
Ashkenazi pupils, so that in 50 per cent of the schools the pupils
had no opportunity to associate with children of the other ethnic
group.[12] In planning school zoning, the educational authorities
simply followed the actual geographic distribution of the Ashkenazi (usually living in better parts of the city) and Oriental
(living predominantly in the poorer quarters) population:
"The children residing on the 'wrong side of the tracks'—many
Orientals—went to one school, while the children on the 'right
side'—mainly Ashkenazim—went to the other." In Jerusalem,
the degree of school segregation also appears to be high.[13]

The Scholastic Record. Another dismaying aspect of the Oriental children's position in the primary schools is their scholastic record.

In a monograph based on a series of surveys and studies carried out by the Henrietta Szold Institute in 1955–1957, Dr.
Moshe Smilansky established "the fact of frequent scholastic
failure" of elementary school children whose parents came
to Israel from underdeveloped areas. In the lower elementary
grades they had "great difficulty in learning to read," and thereafter, in the higher grades, were showing "inability to achieve
good progress generally in most of the school subjects." This
accounted for "the relatively low number of these children who
reach the level of secondary education, although about one half
of the primary school children are of Oriental origin, they constitute only 32 per cent of those graduating."[14]

There is nothing wrong with their intelligence or perceptive-
ness. Gina Ortar, a social psychologist who had administered

the Wechsler Intelligence Scale for Children to children of European and Oriental parentage, came to the conclusion that the latter's weakness of the power of abstraction was "not a deficiency inherent in members of Oriental groups," but something which depends on the environment, and therefore can be changed.[15] But the great majority of new Afro-Asian immigrants had left the countries of their birth practically destitute, and in Israel they usually live in crowded dwellings. A study of the Tel Aviv school system showed that nonpromotion and overcrowded living quarters are closely related.[16]

Room density	Average nonpromotion (per cent)
2.1 to 2.7	4.8
2.8 to 3.6	9.4
3.7 to 6.2	17.1

Children in overcrowded homes have no opportunity of following the normal Israeli curriculum which involves homework with the help of parents or older members of the family. Deprived of this opportunity, a child is unable to keep in step with the more fortunate pupils coming from families of European origin. Feeling that he is prevented from attaining the required scholastic level, the pupil is frustrated, develops an inferiority complex, and is inclined to play truant: it is estimated that 15 to 20 per cent of Oriental immigrant children do not attend school regularly.

Testifying in July 1959 before the Wadi Salib Inquiry Commission, Abraham Danino, teacher at an elementary school in Tirat Hacarmel, said that children of immigrants from Moslem countries accounted for 90 per cent of those who had left elementary school without completing their education: "Thousands of them drop out and cannot find work. Up to the age of thirteen, some 8 per cent of the total number of children drop out each year. A survey has shown that thousands of children leave school prematurely and the educational authorities lose sight of them."

The witness cited "lack of inclination to learn, overcrowding at home, and the parents' lack of means to care for their children as main reasons why children quit school. . . . After leaving school, children of twelve turn to occupations that offer no hope of advancement, like running errands." Of 104 children of this kind of whom the witness had kept track, all but one were from North Africa: "That imparts a communal character to this problem; two years ago it was found that of 2,000 young people looking for work at the Youth Labor Exchange, 1,800 were from North Africa.[17] Children of North African origin, according to Avner Amiel, Coordinator of the Jerusalem Municipality's Youth Club Division of the Social Welfare Department, are at the start anxious and eager to learn, "but they are met by barriers on every side. They are crushed by poverty, and many a talented boy is lost to the state simply because he must make a living hawking papers."[18]

Another potent reason for the low ratio of promotion among the Oriental pupils is the elementary schools' curriculum which was "compiled thirty years ago by Ashkenazi teachers and was adapted to the abilities and characteristics of the Ashkenazi child."[19] The schools are almost entirely staffed by European Jews. In 1955–1956, of a total of 13,927 teachers only 9.5 per cent were of Asian and 3.4 per cent of African origin.[20] The Ashkenazi teaching personnel, says Samuel Z. Klausner, are conveying to their pupils "a Hebrew-Zionist literature reflecting the experience of East European Jews and a history made of European Jewish metal, cast in a mold of European nationalism.[21] In an elementary school serving three of the villages in the Taanach region which is settled by immigrants from Kurdistan, Persia and Turkey, Rahel Zabari heard pupils in the Class VI, a grade composed entirely of children who hailed from Islamic lands, singing the hymn "Avinu Malkenu" in the traditional melody of Eastern Europe. The children were "directed by a man wearing a skullcap and who appeared in every detail of dress and manner to be a typical East European Jew."[22]

The Haifa Municipal Probation Officer, Levi Cohen, stressed that children who fail to finish elementary school are more difficult to place in jobs, and this adds to the sense of injury the children and their parents feel. As a result, 80 per cent of Haifa's delinquent boys (nine to sixteen) and girls (nine to eighteen) are from the Oriental communities, about 50 per cent from North Africa. While juvenile delinquency had in the past affected the fourteen to fifteen age group only, it now had moved forward to the nine to twelve group, most of the offenses being those against property.[23]

Secondary Education. Admittedly inadequate is the state of secondary education. Unlike the elementary schools which are fully maintained by the state, secondary schools receive only an insignificant government subsidy and are almost completely self-supporting. Their tuition fees are therefore very high: they now average 500 Israeli pounds a year, which means that only well-off families can afford to send their children to a high school. According to official data, of the 28,000 pupils who had left the elementary schools in 1958, 11,000—less than two-fifths —were going on to secondary schools.[24] Jews of European origin have brought with them the tradition that the child must continue his studies after elementary school. Parents often incur heavy burdens, and sometimes real deprivations, in order to enable their children to continue their education. This is a long way from being usual with parents of Oriental background. In their respective countries of origin, they were not in the habit of sending their children to secondary school. It is quite natural for them to make the child start working immediatcly on the outside, or to help the father in his shop, once elementary school is finished. It is true that of the 11,000 who finished elementary school and were to enter secondary schools in 1959, 4,000 were of Oriental origin. But the following three tables show that an alarmingly increasing ratio of Oriental children who started their secondary education drop out in the higher classes:[25]

TABLE 1: Distribution of secondary school population by classes (of schools) and countries of origin

Form	Oriental Jewish Students (per cent)
9	15.8
10	13.5
11	9.8
12	7.8

TABLE 2: Distribution of vocational school population by classes
(of schools) and countries of origin

Form	Total Number of Students	Students of Oriental Jewish Communities (per cent)
9	2,196	29.7
10	1,414	25.5
11	1,141	20.4
12	456	11.8

TABLE 3: Distribution of Agricultural school population

Form	Total Number of Students	Students of Oriental Jewish Communities (per cent)
9	1,285	33.9
10	968	26.4
11	694	22.3
12	380	11.6

Increasing over-all pressure for admission to secondary
schools, leading to stricter selection, is also operating against
the less prepared children of Oriental families. In 1955, when
Orientals accounted for about 40 per cent of Israel's Jewish
population, they constituted less than 5 per cent in the secondary school population.

Reforms. Lately, far-reaching reforms have been introduced to
remedy this state of affairs. In August 1959, the Ministry of
Education announced that tuition fees had been revised in accordance with a sliding scale for the benefit of lower-income
groups, and that the scope of scholarships for the needy had
been considerably enlarged. "There is now not a pupil suited to
undergo secondary education who is unable to do so for financial
reasons," declared Ya'acov Sarid, Deputy Director General of
the Ministry. Out of the 19,000 scholarships given jointly by the
Ministry of Education and the Jewish Agency to children of
new immigrants, over 70 per cent are now going to children of
Oriental parents.[26] In Jerusalem, the municipality's Department of Education has lowered the scholarship requirements

for those pupils of Oriental communities who live in poor home conditions. For instance, Ashkenazi pupils must obtain 80 per cent in the qualifying examinations, while pupils of the Oriental communities must obtain only 70 per cent; in some cases, when the pupil shows promise in several subjects, the percentage is lowered to 60. These concessions were made because it was felt that if such pupils had had better home conditions—often a family of ten lives in one or two rooms—their marks would have been higher.[27]

In the aforementioned testimony, Abraham Danino insisted, however, that what was needed for children who showed aptitude, but were unable to pay tuition, was not scholarships that covered only part of the expenses involved, but free secondary education. Essential also was a system of "trade schools on a lower level to absorb children that cannot keep up with their studies in the top classes of the elementary school"; such vocational schools could supply the country with desperately needed skilled tradesmen.

A healthy evolution in this direction seems to be taking place. In August 1959, the Minister of Labor stressed that while formerly Afro-Asian immigrant youth had been unwilling to attend vocational schools maintained by ORT, Hadassah, WIZO, and Histadrut, they now constitute about 40 per cent of these schools' total enrollment, and 70 per cent of students in the trade courses for adults: there is at present lack of vacancies.[28]

Higher Education. It is in the field of higher education that Oriental students fare worst. In 1956–1957, only 6 per cent of the student body of the Hebrew University were of Asian and African origin; in 1957–1958, this percentage dropped to 5.3. Among the 436 first-year students of the Haifa Technion in the year 1957–1958, only 14 were of Iraqi, Turkish, Egyptian, and North African origin. Even assuming that a certain proportion of the Israeli-born students were of Afro-Asian origin, the overall picture remains dismaying.[29]

Summarizing the "troubling situation" in the field of education, the report of the Committee investigating the Wadi Salib riots cautiously but unequivocally stated that "the number of students from among the Oriental immigrants in the post-primary educational institutions, and even more in the institutions of higher learning, bears no relation to their relative weight in the population. As a result, these communities are not adequately represented in positions demanding technical and higher education." "We do not think," the report went on to say, "that this is because of a lack of ability or intelligence [of the Oriental students], but is a result of objective factors."[30]

The Army. A powerful means of integration is the Army. Most young men enter the Army at the age of eighteen, and serve for two and a half years. It is for them a true melting pot, offering the youth of different ethnic communities a unique opportunity of sharing the same mode of life and cooperating in a common effort. They all wear the same uniform, all have to react to similar symbols and to partake of similar experiences—thus inculcating a new sense of social cohesion, of belonging to a common sociocultural pattern. Colonel Aharon Ze'ev, education officer of the Israeli Army, reported that since 1948 the Army had maintained teams of "absorption officers" who spoke the language of the newcomers and helped them in their orientation. The Army taught its men not only Hebrew but also the history of the country, of the Jewish people, and of the various Jewish communities that today make up the population of Israel. It also provided elementary schooling where it was lacking. Some 3,000 men a year acquire a trade during their army service.[31] Noting "with great satisfaction" that "the Defense Army of Israel is also making a tremendous contribution to the fusing of immigrants," the Wadi Salib Inquiry Committee stressed in its report that "in all stages of the inquiry the Army received only favorable mention: all those who spoke of discrimination and inequality—and among them were those who did so with great emphasis—clearly stated that in the army there is no feeling of discrimination and no inequality whatsoever."[32]

However, averring in his searching study, *The Clash of Cultures in Israel*, that the Army "professes and attempts to practice the principle of equality of opportunity for everyone, regardless of ethnic or class origin," Abraham Shumsky observes that "its success is limited" by the lack of "awareness of the existence of ethnic tensions or of the potential of the Army for alleviating those tensions." The Oriental youth feels acutely that "they live in a world which is ruled by the Ashkenazi." In the Army, where the officer corps is overwhelmingly Ashkenazi and which is based on strictest hierarchy, subordination, emphasis of status symbols, and privileges for the higher ranks, an Oriental private is confronted with a pronounced manifestation of Ashkenazi predominance. Trying to be objective and scientific, the Army commands soldiers for officers' schools on the basis of psychotechnical examinations and intelligence tests. These tests, being culturally loaded, actually discriminate against the lower-class Orientals and deprive them of a fair chance of competing with the Ashkenazim. Mere technical equality is for the most part inadequate for the stupendous task of instilling in the Oriental youth the feeling of "belonging" and of being given not merely token and formal "full rights," but also a real opportunity to make use of them.[33]

Israelization. As of now, the "Israelization" of the Oriental immigrants has had but partial and limited success. They have adopted new clothing, have mastered Hebrew and some new skills; they live in a new kind of community. But in more than one respect, their old customs, notions and ways of life have persisted and in some instances become even more deeply ingrained. They are no longer the same as they were before, yet they have not become truly integrated Israelis.

Holidays and family events (a birth or marriage) are generally celebrated as of old, in a religious-traditional manner, and not in accordance with the more secular and informal Israeli pattern. They avail themselves willingly of the services of the national health institutions, with their doctors and nurses, vaccinations, pills, and hospitalization. Yet many still consult more traditional medical practitioners: the village rabbi and a local rabbi-healer. When a baby is ill, it is brought to the clinic, but it also wears an amulet around its neck.

On the whole, immigrants from Afro-Asian countries continue to eat the food they had eaten in their respective home countries, only in much different proportions. They have not adopted new foods: milk or cheese products, a basic part of the general Israeli diet, is usually not included in their menu. They also eat little fish, but more *cuscous* (a traditional doughy mixture) and more vegetables than before. At the Third Convention of Scientific Societies held in Haifa in October 1959, Dr. Sara Bavly, Principal of the Israeli Ministry of Education's College of Home Economics and Nutrition, insisted that dietary habits of the various communities should be preserved, provided that certain vitamin deficiencies in some Oriental diets are repaired by appetizing additions. In Dr. Bavly's view, traditional diets had great psychological importance, because they help communities maintain pride in their past and a feeling of being at home; they also made housewives proud of their cookery. "We should not strive toward a unified Israel diet," Dr. Bavly said, "but rather encourage women of various communities to learn from each other to introduce variety."[34]

The Marriage Pattern. The overwhelming majority of the Israel population still marry within the same ethnic group. *Statistical Yearbook of Israel* for 1953–1954 and 1954–1955 reveals that 80 per cent of the bridegrooms born in Europe and America married women from the same continents. The corresponding percentage for European and American brides is almost 90. Among males born in Asia and Africa this percentage is even higher, but not among Asian and African women, who marry Ashkenazi men more frequently than Oriental men marry Ashkenazi women. Taking the related groups as a whole—those of European and American birth together with Ashkenazim born in Israel, and those of Afro-Asian birth together with Orientals born in Israel—we find that 10.1 per cent of the first group married women of different origin, as against 8.4 per cent of the second. In the case of brides, the difference is more pronounced: 6.1 per cent European-American brides married husbands of Afro-Asian origin, whereas 13.5 per cent of the Afro-Asian brides married "non-Oriental" husbands.

The following table, based on *Statistical Abstract of Israel,* 1956–1957, illustrates the development of intercommunal marriages for the period 1952–1955:

Marriages by Community of Bridegroom and Bride

Community	1952	Per Cent	1953	Per Cent	1954	Per Cent	1955	Per Cent
Ashkenazi with Ashkenazi	8,157	54.1	7,243	52.1	6,656	51.2	6,466	48.4
Oriental with Oriental	5,571	36.9	5,292	38.1	4,943	38.0	5,301	39.7
Ashkenazi (m.) with Oriental (f.)	843	5.6	889	6.3	983	7.1	1,001	7.5
Oriental (m.) with Ashkenazi (f.)	511	3.4	485	3.5	484	3.7	581	4.4
Totals	15,082	100.0	13,909	100.0	13,006	100.0	13,349	100.0

It can be seen that the ratio of "mixed marriages" has increased from 9 per cent in 1952 to 12 per cent in 1955. But homogamous marriages are still overwhelmingly prevalent among the Oriental groups. Optimistically asserting at the Third Convention of Scientific Societies in Haifa (October 1959) that "the number of marriages between the various communities in Israel is increasing at a much greater rate than is generally believed," Prof. Elisheva Goldschmidt admitted that this was true "especially with partners from the smaller ethnic groups, such as the German immigrants, where the choice of partners was relatively small inside the 'tribe'; the large Iraqi community, on the other hand, still tended to marry 'within.' "[35]

Analyzing, on the basis of unpublished data supplied by the Central Bureau of Statistics, Government of Israel, the problem whether heterogamous marriages are successful and enduring, Dr. H. S. Halevi comes to the conclusion that "there is reason to suppose that in such cases more couples have to separate after certain 'trial' period of common life than in instances where both spouses come from a similar background."[36]

BALANCE SHEET AND OUTLOOK

Appreciable and encouraging strides have been made in the last decade on the way to a full and harmonious integration of the "Second Israel." But the amount of "unfinished business" is still overwhelming. The three major forces, which are involved in *mizug galuyot*—the school, the Army, the Histadrut— are all, in different ways and to a different extent, cooperating in the great effort to mold Israel's heterogeneous elements into one nation. What is apparently lacking in the effort of all these, predominantly Ashkenazi, bodies, and what is largely frustrating their effectiveness, is the precious—and in this field, decisive —quality of genuine consideration and warmth toward those non-Ashkenazi elements whom they are striving to integrate.

Some three decades ago, the Hebrew poet Saul Tshernichovsky wrote a poem called "The Ingathering of the Exiles," two lines of which have now become a byword:

> We were united before your mountains,
> Brother to brother, hand to hand.

Quoting this verse in his study, Abraham Shumsky says: "The Ashkenazim have met their Oriental brothers with economic assistance, and with some patronizing, perhaps fatherly, love. They have failed, however, to extend to them the brotherly hand of equal respect. That this brotherly hand may be extended is the hope to which my study is dedicated."

It is also the hope in which this chapter is written.

Notes

The following abbreviations are used in the notes:
DNB—Jewish Telegraphic Agency Daily News Bulletin
Digest—The Jewish Agency's Digest of Press and Events

INTRODUCTION

1. Cleland, W. Wendel. "Islam's Attitude Toward Minority Groups," in *Islam and the Middle Eastern World*, Washington, 1951, p. 163.
2. Rondot, Pierre. "Islam, Christianity, and the Modern State," in *Middle Eastern Affairs*, November 1954, p. 341. See also: Rondot, P. "Les Chrétiens d'Orient," in *Cahiers de l'Afrique et l'Asie*, No. IV, Paris, 1944; and Rondot, P. "Le Liban et les foyers chrétiens en Orient," in *Politique Etrangère*, XXII, Paris, 1957.
3. Hourani, A. H. *Minorities in the Arab World*, London, 1947, pp. 12–13.
4. Rondot, P. loc. cit., pp. 342–343.
5. Stafford, A. S. *The Tragedy of the Assyrians*, London, 1935, pp. 174–177.
6. Parliamentary Debates. House of Commons. Official Report. June 17, 1948.
7. Zevi, Tula. "The Modern Pharaoh. Religious Minorities under Nasser," in *The American Jewish Outlook*, Pittsburgh, April 24, 1959.
8. *The New York Times*, January 27, 1959. Also: *The Lebanese American Journal*, October 17, 1959.
9. Albright, F. W. "Japhet in the Tents of Shem," in *Asia*, December 1942.
10. Political Intelligence Centre Middle East. *Fortnightly Summary*, May 16, 1944.
11. *Osservatore Romano*, July 6, 1946.
12. *Al-Islaah*, New York, April 14, 1950.
13. Wilbur, Donald K. *Iran, Past and Present*. Princeton, 1958, pp. 164–165.
14. *The New York Times*, December 10, 1933.
15. Vertanes, Charles. "Lo, a Dispersed People Returns to Its Homeland," in *Land and Life*, New York, March 1947.
16. *The New Beth Naharem*, May–June 1946, March–April 1947.
17. *New York Herald-Tribune*, November 11 and 19, 1947.
18. Zeidner, Robert F. "Kurdish Nationalism and the New Iraq Government," in *Middle Eastern Affairs*, January 1959.

CHAPTER 1

1. *Digest*, October 6, 1950.
2. *Ibid.*, January 5, 1950.
3. *The Jewish Encyclopaedia*, Vol. XII, New York-London 1906, p. 592.
4. *Bulletin de l'Alliance Israélite Universelle*, 1910.
5. Rihani, Ameen. *Arabian Peak and Desert. Travels in Al Yaman*, Boston and New York, 1930, p. 186.
6. Von Weisl, Wolfgang. *Zwischen dem Teufel and dem Roten Meer*, Leipzig, 1928, pp. 191, 195

7. Farago, Ladislas. *The Riddle of Arabia*, London, 1939, p. 170.
8. Quoted in: General Edouard Bremond, *Yemen et Saoudia. L'Arabie Actuelle*, Paris, 1937, p. 71.
9. *1949 Britannica Book of the Year*, Chicago, 1949, p. 777.
10. Feldman, Yoshua. *The Yemenite Jews*, London, 1913, p. 17.
11. *J.D.C. Review*, April 1948.
12. Scott, Hugh. *In the High Yemen*, London, 1942, p. 138.
13. Wyman Bury, G. *Arabia Infelix, or the Turks in Yamen*, London, 1915, pp. 147–148.
14. Scott, *op. cit.*, p. 198.
15. *Ibid.*, pp. 198–199, 135.
16. Farago, *op. cit.*, p. 271.
17. Scott, *op. cit.*, p. 198.
18. Ben Zvi, Itzhak, *The Exiled and the Redeemed*, Philadelphia, 1957, p. 23.
19. Preface to *From the Land of Sheba* by S. D. Goiteen. Tales of the Jews of Yemen, New York, 1947, p. 9; Braver, A. J. "Hostages in Arab Lands," in *Haaretz*, December 26, 1947.
20. Niebuhr, Garsten. *Reisebeschreibungen*, vol. 1, p. 422 ff.
21. Saphir, Jacob. *Even Sappir*, Lyck, 1866, p. 52.
22. Joint Foreign Committee. Memorandum by the Secretary. *The Jews of Yemen 1863–1926*, London, 1928.
23. *Bulletin de l'Alliance Israélite Universelle*, 1910.
24. Bury, *op. cit.*, p. 16.
25. Feldman, *op. cit.*, p. 19.
26. The description of the Jewish status in Yemen is based on data contained in the previously quoted studies by Hugh Scott, Ladislas Farago, G. Wyman Bury, Ahmed Rihani, Yoshua Feldman, as well as: Hans Helfritz, *Land Without Shade*, London, 1935; and *Memorandum on the Position of the Jewish Communities in the Oriental Countries*, submitted to the Anglo-American Committee of Inquiry by the Jewish Agency for Palestine, Jerusalem, March 1946.
27. Helfritz, *op. cit.*, p. 249.
28. Bury, *op. cit.*, pp. 147–148.
29. Rihani, *op. cit.*, pp. 186–187.
30. Farago, *op. cit.*, p. 266.
31. Bury, *op. cit.*, p. 74; Scott, *op. cit.*, p. 134.
32. *Universal Jewish Encyclopedia*, Vol. X, New York, 1943, pp. 591–592.
33. Feldman, *op. cit.*, pp. 19, 21, 25, 27; *Yetziat Teyman (The Exodus from Yemen)*, Jerusalem, 1951, *passim*.
34. Yavnieli, S. "The Journey to Yemen—1910," in *Jewish Frontier*, December 1949; *Idem: Massa le'Teyman (A Voyage to Yemen)*, Tel Aviv, 1951.
35. *Palestine Post*, Jerusalem, November 8, 1949.
36. *Yalkut ha 'Misrakh ha 'Tikhon*, Jerusalem, November–December 1949, p. 6.
37. Jewish Agency for Palestine. Immigration Department. *Shnat Aliyah (A Year of Immigration)*, Jerusalem, 1949, p. 11.
38. *Statistical Bulletin of Israel*, Jerusalem, Vol. 1, July 1949, p. 10.
39. *Annual Report on Aden of the Year 1946*, London, 1948, p. 11.
40. Report of Dr. Gertz Beigel re Six Months' Work among Yemenite Refugees in Aden, July 23, 1946.
41. Bentwich, Norman. "Aden After the Riots," in *Commentary*, May 1948.
42. *Colonial* No. 233, pp. 5, 17, 30.
43. *J.D.C. Review*, April 1948.
44. Barer, Shlomo. *The Magic Carpet*, New York, 1952, pp. 12–13.
45. Martin, Edward T. *I Flew Them Home*, New York, 1959, pp. 32–33, 38.
46. Barer, *op. cit.*, p. 11.

47. Martin, op. cit., pp. 32–33.
48. *The New York Times*, June 24, 1950.
49. Martin, op. cit., pp. 32–33.
50. Resner, Lawrence. *Eternal Stranger*, New York, 1951, p. 194.
51. *Jewish Herald*, April 1, 1949.
52. *New York Herald Tribune*, March 19, 1949.
53. *DNB*, May 30, 1939.
54. Mission to Aden. Report of Dr. A. Leon Kubowitzky to the Executive Committee of the World Jewish Congress, Tel Aviv, April 24, 1949.
55. Vainstein, J. "The Magic Carpet. The End of the Yemen Golah," in *Iggeret Lagolah*, Jerusalem, January 1950.
56. *Ibid.*
57. Barer, op. cit., pp. 147–148.
58. *Ibid.*, p. 159, 145.
59. *Ibid.*, pp. 160–161, 178.
60. Nissim, Zecharia. "A Yemenite Boy in Israel" in *Sound the Great Trumpet*, M. Z. Frank (ed.), New York, 1955, pp. 374–375.
61. Barer, op cit., p. 184,
62. *New York Herald Tribune*, November 7, 1949.
63. Nissim, loc. cit., pp. 375–376.
64. *Digest*, November 18, 1949.
65. Barer, op. cit., p. 183.
66. *Ibid.*, pp. 154–156, 187–190, 194.
67. *Digest*, November 18, 1949.
68. Zadok, Joseph. *B'Saarot Teyman, Megilat Marbar Haksamim*, Tel Aviv, 1955, p. 232.
69. Barer, op. cit., pp. 199–200.
70. Zadok, op. cit., p. 232.
71. Barer, op. cit., pp. 204–206.
72. *Ibid.*, pp. 203–204; Vainstein, loc. cit., p. 22.
73. Barer, op. cit., pp. 40–41.
74. Nissim, loc. cit., p. 376.
75. Resner, op. cit., pp. 194–195.
76. Barer, op. cit., pp. 40–41.
77. *Ibid.*, p. 140.
78. Zadok, op. cit., pp. 59–73; Barer, op. cit., pp. 200–202.
79. Zadok, op. cit., p. 232; Barer, op. cit., pp. 200–203.
80. Zadok, op. cit., p. 232.
81. *Jewish Chronicle*, September 29, 1950; Barer, op. cit., p. 225.
82. Data supplied by the Immigration Department of the Jewish Agency.
83. *Israel Reports*, vol. V, March 1950.
83a. Simon Federbush, ed. *World Jewry Today*, New York, 1959, p. 374.
84. B. W. Seager, "The Yemen," in *Royal Central Asian Journal*, July–October 1955.
85. Barer, op. cit., p. 92.
86. *Israel Digest*, Jerusalem, May 15, 1959.

CHAPTER 2

1. Yaish, B. J. *History of the Jews of Aden* (unpublished) and *Modern History of the Jews of Aden* (unpublished); also *Palestine Post*, December 12, 1947.
2. Colonial Office. *Annual Report on Aden for the Year 1946*, London, 1948, p. 12.
3. Bentwich, Norman. "Aden After the Riots" in *Commentary*, May 1948.

4. Yaish, op. cit.; Bentwich, loc. cit.
5. Yaish, op. cit.; Palestine Post, December 12, 1947.
6. Hickinbotham, Sir Tom. Aden, London, 1958, pp. 82–83.
7. A.T. The Disaster of the Jews of Aden. Memorandum dated Aden, December 13, 1947.
8. Colonial Office. Report of the Commission of Inquiry into Disturbances in Aden in December 1947, London, 1948, Colonial N233, pp. 6–7.
9. Ibid., p. 7.
10. Colonial N233, passim.
11. Ibid., pp. 24–25.
12. Ibid., p. 24.
13. Jewish Chronicle, London, January 14, 1949.
14. Digest, May 6, 1949.
15. J.D.C. Review, July 1949.
16. Data supplied by the Jewish Agency's Department of Immigration.
17. Digest, December 23, 1949.
18. Hickinbotham, Sir Tom, op. cit., p. 87.
19. Institute of Jewish Affairs. The Jewish Communities of the World, New York, 1959, p. 41.
20. Jewish Chronicle, London, November 7 and 11; December 5, 1958.
21. Mack, A. J. "Jewish Life in Aden," in Jewish Chronicle, February 12, 1959.
22. Colonial Office. Annual Report on Aden for the Year 1946, p. 4.
23. Report by Dr. Leon Kubowitzky. In the files of the World Jewish Congress.
24. Hickinbotham, Sir Tom. op. cit., p. 51.
25. Yalkut ha-Misrakh ha-Tikhon, Jerusalem, January–February, 1950.
26. Ingrams, W. H. Report on the Social, Economic and Political Conditions of the Hadramaut, Aden Protectorate, London, 1946; Ingrams, W. H. Arabia and the Isles, London, 1944; Stark, Freya. The Southern Gates of Arabia, London, 1936; Stark, Freya. A Winter in Arabia, London, 1940; Stark, Freya. Seen in the Hadramaut, London, 1938; Philby, H. St. J. B. The Empty Quarter, London, 1933; Thompson, G. Carton. The Tombs and Moon Temple of Hureidha (Hadramaut), London, 1944; Helferitz, H. Geheimnis um Schobua: Unter südarabischen Beduinen ins Land der Säbaer, Berlin, 1948; Van der Meulen, D. Aden to the Hadramaut, London, 1947.
27. Ashkenazi, Touvia. "The Jews of South Arabia," in New Palestine, June 21, 1945; Prof. Nahum Slouschz, "Jewish Nomads in Arabia," distributed by the Youth Department of the Zionist Organization, May 1945; S.B.A. "Jews of the Hadramaut" in Palestine Post, January 6, 1945.
28. Barer, Shlomo. The Magic Carpet, New York, 1952, p. 87.
29. Iggeret la'Askan ha'Zioni, Jerusalem, March 3, 1950.
30. Palestine Post, August 26, 1950; DNB, August 29, 1950.

CHAPTER 3

1. Lurie, Jesse Zel, "The Jews of Iraq," in Jewish Digest, New York, July 1941.
1a. The Travels of Rabbi David d'Beth Hillel from Jerusalem through Arabia, Koordistan, part of Persia, and India to Madras, 1832, pp. 44–70.
2. Coke, Richard. The Heart of the Middle East, London, 1925, p. 203.
3. Main, Ernest. Iraq, From Mandate to Independence, London, 1953, p. 153.
4. Harris, George L., and others. Iraq, Its People, Its Society, Its Culture. New Haven, 1958, p. 4.
5. Published in Al-Waqaii al Iraqiya, Baghdad, No. 989, June 1, 1931.
6. Official Journal, Baghdad, 1931, pp. 2057, 2177.
7. League of Nations. Document C 444, 1932, VI.

8. Stafford, A. S. *The Tragedy of the Assyrians*, London, 1935, pp. 174–77; Kirk, George E., in his *Short History of the Middle East from the Rise of Islam to Modern Times*, Washington, 1949, says: "Young King Ghazi openly displayed his approval of the part played by Iraqi troops in this discreditable affair, decorated the colors of the regiments involved, and conferred on their Kurdish commanding officer Bakir Sidki the title of pasha. He thereby won immense popularity." (p. 178).
9. Davis, Helen Miller. *Constitutions, Electoral Laws, Treaties of States in the Near and Middle East*, Durham, N.C., 1947, pp. 107 ff.
10. Hourani, A. H. *Minorities in the Arab World*, London, 1947, p. 104.
11. "Paper on the Situation of Iraqi Jewry" in: The Jewish Agency for Palestine. *The Jewish Case Before the Anglo-American Committee of Inquiry*, Jerusalem, 1947, p. 408.
12. Lurie, *loc. cit.*
13. Hourani, A. H. *op. cit.*, p. 104.
14. Lurie, *loc cit.*
15. *Congress Weekly*, February 15, 1946.
16. *Yalkut ha'Misrakh ha'Tikhon*, Jerusalem, November–December 1949.
17. Anglo-American Committee of Inquiry, Hearing at Mena House, Cairo, March 5, 1946, p. 4; Crum, Bartley C. *Behind the Silken Curtain. A Personal Account of Anglo-American Diplomacy in Palestine and the Middle East*, New York, 1947, p. 151.
18. Crum, B. C., *op. cit.*, p. 247.
19. *The New York Times*, July 18, 1937.
20. Habas, Braha. *Achim Krovim Nidachim*, Tel Aviv, 1945, p. 46.
21. *Ruz al-Yusuf*, Cairo, 1948, No. 1060.
22. *The New York Times*, July 12 and 15, 1948.
23. *Al Ahram*, Cairo, July 28, 1948; *Al Yom*, Beirut, September 30, 1948; *Barada*, Beirut, August 28, 1948.
24. *Al Ahram*, October 19, 1948; *Le Combat*, Paris, October 20, 1948.
25. *Jewish Chronicle*, June 23, 1950.
25a.*Ruz al-Yusuf*, 1948, No. 1060.
26. *Al-Amal*, Beirut, October 31, 1948.
27. *Al-Zaman*, Cairo, August 10, 1948.
28. *Al-Liva al Istiklal*, Baghdad, April 26, 1949.
29. See full list, with indication of Arab press sources, in *The Jews of Iraq* by this author, released by the Research Department of the Jewish Agency for Palestine, New York, 1949, Appendix, pp. xiv–xix. By the end of 1949, the number of Jews sentenced to three to ten years in prison amounted to 1,450. Cf. *Igeret l'Askan ha-Zioni*, Jerusalem, March 30, 1950.
30. *The New York Times*, February 7, 1950.
31. *New York Herald Tribune*, November 21, 1949.
32. *The New York Times*, February 7, 1950.
33. *Ibid.*, February 14, 1950.
34. *Jewish Chronicle*, London, March 24, 1950.
35. *Ibid.*
36. The full text of the Law appeared in: Institute of Jewish Affairs, *Current Events in Jewish Life*, New York, January–March 1950.
37. *Digest*, March 17, 1950; *Middle Eastern Affairs*, New York, March, 1950.
38. *Jewish Chronicle*, March 24, 1950.
39. *Ibid.*, May 26, 1950.
40. *Ibid.*
41. *The New York Times*, May 20, 1950.
42. *Jewish Chronicle*, London, May 26, 1950.
43. *Ibid.*

44. *The New York Times*, January 20, 1951; *Davar*, Tel Aviv, January 19, 1951; New York Herald Tribune, June 27, 1951.
45. *The New York Times*, October 30, 1950.
46. *Jewish Chronicle*, June 23, 1950.
47. *Ibid.*, March 31; April 28, 1950.
48. *Ibid.*, March 24, 1950; *The New York Times*, May 22, 1950.
49. *Jewish Chronicle*, April 28, 1950.
50. Resner, Lawrence. *Eternal Stranger*, New York, 1951, p. 150.
51. *Digest*, June 2, 1950.
52. *Jewish Chronicle*, March 24 and 31; May 26; June 2 and 9, 1950.
53. Resner, *op. cit.*, pp. 150–151.
54. Jewish Agency for Palestine. Immigration Department, Jerusalem Statistical Office. *Sikumei Aliya*. November–December 1950.
55. *The New York Times*, October 30, 1950.
56. *Ibid.*
57. *Mideast Mirror*, Cairo, July 1, 1950.
58. *DNB*, June 6, 1951.
59. *Davar*, March 29, 1951.
60. *Ibid.*, June 22, 1951.
61. *DNB*, April 12, 1951.
62. *Digest*, January 12, 1951.
63. *Ibid.*, January 26; February 2, 1951.
64. *Ibid.*, February 9, 1951.
65. *Jewish Chronicle*, February 2, 1951.
66. *DNB*, February 6, 1951.
67. *Sikumei Aliya*, January–February 1951.
68. Jewish Agency for Palestine. Aliyah Department. *Dapei Aliyah*, Jerusalem, 1952. *The Jewish Chronicle*, March 30, 1951, reported that by a new decree "the original time limit of March 9 for prospective emigrants to register has now been indefinitely deferred." In fact, many more Iraqi Jews emigrated in 1950–1951 than the 104,630 who registered till March 9.
69. *Jewish Chronicle*, March 25, 1951.
70. *Sikumei Aliya*, March–May 1951.
71. *The New York Times*, June 3, 1951; *Sikumei Aliyah*, June 1951.
72. *Digest*, July 6, 1951; *Sikumei Aliya*, December 1951.
73. *Digest*, August 17, 1951.
74. *Jewish Chronicle*, August 17, 1951.
75. *Sikumei Aliyah*, December 1951; December 1952.
76. Data supplied by the Immigration Department of the Jewish Agency.
77. *Idem.*
78. *The New York Times*, June 30, 1951.
79. *Official Government Gazette*, Baghdad no. 2938, March 10, 1951.
80. *Ibid.*, no. 2393, March 10, 1951.
81. *DNB*, March 15, 1951.
82. *Divrei ha-Knesset*, Jerusalem, vol. 3, March 19, 1951.
83. Quoted in *Mideast Mirror*, March 17, 1951.
84. Full text in *Al-Shaab*, Baghdad, March 21, 1951.
85. *Jewish Chronicle*, March 30, 1951.
86. *Ibid.*
87. *Mideast Mirror*, Cairo, March 24, 1951.
88. *Divrei ha-Knesset*, vol. 3, March 19, 1951.
89. *Digest*, April 6, 1951.
90. *Jewish Chronicle*, July 18, 1951.
91. *Jerusalem Post*, December 5, 1952.
92. *Ibid.*, October 9, 1952.

93. *The Israel Digest*, Jerusalem, November 28, 1958.
94. Harris, George L., and others, op. cit., p. 44.
95. *Israelitisches Wochenblatt*, Zurich, November 13, 1959.
96. *Times*, London, March 27, 1951.
97. *Der Spiegel*, Hanover, May 2, 1951; *Davar*, March 29, 1951.
98. *Jewish Chronicle*, June 6, 1951.
99. DNB, June 12, 1951; *Der Spiegel*, loc. cit.
100. *Jewish Chronicle*, December 7, 1951.
101. *World Jewry*, London, April 1958; *Jewish Chronicle*, July 18, 1958.
102. *Israelitisches Wochenblatt*, November 13, 1959; DNB, January 25, 1960.

CHAPTER 4

1. Slouschz, Nahum. *Travels in North Africa*, Philadelphia 1927, pp. 11, 33, 107–108, 203, 215–216, 223–224.
2. *The Universal Jewish Encyclopedia*, Vol. III, New York, 1942, p. 45.
3. *Annual Report of the United Nations Commissioner in Libya*, prepared in consultation with the Council for Libya. General Assembly. Official Records: Fifth Session. Supplement N15 (A/1340). Lake Success, N.Y., 1950, Annex XXVIII, p. 103.
4. Kimche, Jon. "Tripolitanian Jewry–Inexorable Decline," in *Jewish Chronicle*, London, March 19, 1948.
5. Kimche, Jon. "The Oldest Jewish Underground," in *Jewish Chronicle*, March 26, 1948.
6. Steiner, M. J. *Inside Pan-Arabia*, Chicago 1947, pp. 152–154.
7. Italian-Jewish Representative Committee (affiliated with the World Jewish Congress). *Memorandum on the Jews in Italy and Libya. Idem, Report on the Situation of the Jewish Communities of Libya and Suggestions for Emergency and Permanent Measures to Be Taken upon Allied Occupation*, New York, 1943.
8. *American Jewish Yearbook*, New York, Vol. XLIII, p. 20.
9. Rabinowitz, L.: "Liberation in North Africa," in *Menorah Journal*, April–June 1945, p. 117, 119, 122.
10. Letter of Rabbi L. Rabinowitz to the President of the World Jewish Congress, dated April 14, 1943; CMD 6589. *War Office, British Military Administration of Occupied Territories in Africa During the Years 1941–1943*, London, January 1945, p. 23; *American Jewish Yearbook*, Vol. XLV, p. 293.
11. Reports of the Jewish Community Council of Tripolitania and Cyrenaica to the World Jewish Congress.
12. *American Jewish Yearbook*, Vol. XLV, pp. 293–294.
13. Report of the Jewish Community Council to the World Jewish Congress.
14. Communita Israelitica della Tripolitania. *I'Tumulti Antiebraci in Tripolitania (4, 5, 6, e 7 Novembre, 1945)*, Tripoli, 1946, pp. 4–5.
15. *The New York Times*, November 14, 1945.
16. *Ibid.*, November 11 and 13, 1945.
17. "Anti-Jewish Riots in Tripolitania" in *The Jewish Case Before the Anglo-American Committee of Inquiry on Palestine*, as presented by the Jewish Agency for Palestine, Jerusalem, 1947, p. 395.
18. Communita Israelitica della Tripolitania, op. cit., pp. 6, 31; "Jews in Moslem Countries," in *J.D.C. Review*, May 1948.
19. *The New York Times*, November 13, 1945; May 14, 1946.
20. *Report on the Jewish Community of Tripolitania*, London, January 1949.
21. *Corriere di Tripoli*, November 8, 1945.
22. *The New York Times*, November 17, 1945.

23. ONA (Overseas News Agency), New York, November 26, 1945.
24. *The New York Times*, November 16, 1945.
25. ONA, November 28, 1945.
26. "Libyan Jewry: Accord With Moslems?" in *Jewish Chronicle*, March 12, 1948. Also: *DNB*, April 16, 1948.
27. Stafford, F. E. "The Ex-Italian Colonies," in *International Affairs*, January 1949, p. 33.
28. *DNB*, April 18, 1948.
29. *The New York Times*, June 13, 1946.
30. *Les Cahiers de l'Alliance Israélite Universelle*, Paris, June–July 1948.
31. *DNB*, June 14, 1946; *New York Herald Tribune*, June 14 and 15, 1948; *Les Cahiers de l'Alliance Israélite Universelle*, October 1948.
32. Segal, J. B. "Tripolitania, 1943–1949," in *Jewish Chronicle*, February 11, 1949.
33. *Jewish Chronicle*, March 19, 1948.
34. *Independent Jewish Press Service*, December 7, 1945.
35. ONA, November 26, 1945.
36. *The New York Times*, May 14, 1946.
37. *Les Cahiers de l'Alliance Israélite Universelle*, October 1948.
38. *DNB*, August 2, 1948.
39. *Jewish Chronicle*, January 14, 1949.
40. *Yalkut ha'Misrakh ha'Tikhon*, Jerusalem, May–June 1950.
41. Survey of Immigration and Activities of the Immigration Department submitted to the General Zionist Council, Jerusalem, April 1950 (later referred to as *Survey*.)
42. *DNB*, March 31, 1949.
43. *The New York Times*, April 6, 1949.
44. *Survey*
45. Report of Dr. M. Perlzweig. (In the files of the World Jewish Congress.)
46. *Yalkut ha 'Misrakh ha 'Tikhon*, July–August 1949; May–June 1950.
47. *The New York Times*, August 28, 1950.
48. *Jewish Chronicle*, August 26, 1949; *The New York Times*, August 28, 1950.
49. *Yalkut ha 'Misrakh ha 'Tikhon*, May–June 1950.
50. *Jewish Chronicle*, August 11, 1950.
51. *Sikumei Aliyah*, January–September 1950.
52. Resner, Lawrence. *Eternal Stranger*, New York, 1951, pp. 101–102.
53. *DNB*, October 11, 1949.
54. *Congress Digest*, New York, December 1, 1949.
55. Data supplied by the Immigration Department of the Jewish Agency (Jerusalem).
56. *Alliance Review*, New York, February 1955.
57. *Corriere di Tripoli*, January 6, 1959.
58. In the files of the World Jewish Congress.

CHAPTER 5

1. Hourani, A. H. *Syria and Lebanon. A Political Essay*, London-New York-Toronto, 1947, pp. 20, 62–63.
2. Steiner, M. I. *Inside Pan-Arabia*, Chicago, 1947, p. 82.
3. *Ibid.*, p. 85.
4. Davis, Kingley. "Population Analysis," in *The Republic of Syria*, ed. by Raphael Patai, New Haven, Human Relations Files Vol. I, 1956, p. 56.
5. *American Jewish Yearbook*, vol. XXXVIII, pp. 265–266.
6. MacCallam, Elizabeth P. *The Nationalist Crusade in Syria*, New York, 1928, p. 63.

7. *Daily Intelligence Summary*, Washington, D. C., April 28, 1945.
8. "Jews in Moslem Countries," in *J.D.C. Review*, April 1948.
9. *DNB*, March 26, 1946.
10. *Hechayal*, Jerusalem, March 20, 1946.
11. *Jewish Chronicle*, November 11, 1947.
12. Landshut, S. *Jewish Communities in the Moslem Countries of the Middle East*, London, 1950, p. 57.
13. *New York Herald Tribune*, April 14, 1947.
14. *Jewish Chronicle*, London, February 11, 1949.
15. Memorandum to the World Jewish Congress by Abraham Abbas, August 1948.
16. *Jewish Chronicle*, July 11, 1947.
17. *Les Cahiers de l'Alliance Israélite Universelle*, Paris, February–March 1947.
18. *New York Herald Tribune*, November 11, 1945.
19. *Les Cahiers de l'Alliance Israélite Universelle*, February–March 1947.
20. W(orld) J(ewish) C(ongress) *Information Bulletin*, New York, May 1946.
21. *Memorandum on the Position of the Jewish Communities in the Oriental Countries*, submitted to the Anglo-American Committee of Inquiry by the Jewish Agency for Palestine, Jerusalem, March 1946.
22. *Jewish Herald*, Johannesburg, April 18, 1946; *Hed Ha-Misrach*, Jerusalem, March 23, 1946.
23. *Hed Ha-Misrach*, March 1, 1946.
24. *DNB*, July 28, 1946.
25. *Ibid.*, September 5, 1946.
26. Bigart, Homer. "Jews of Syria Face Death for Aid to Zionists," in the *New York Herald Tribune*, March 25, 1947.
27. Crum, Bartley C. *Behind the Silken Curtain. A Personal Account of Anglo-American Diplomacy in Palestine and the Middle East*, New York, 1947, p. 239.
28. Reports on the files of the World Jewish Congress.
29. *Digest*, December 28, 1947.
30. *P.M.*, New York, January 18, 1948.
31. *Digest*, December 28, 1947.
32. In the files of the World Jewish Congress.
33. *Jewish Chronicle*, March 26, 1948.
34. *New York Herald Tribune*, April 14, 1947.
35. *Times*, London, October 3, 1948.
36. *Al Hayat*, Beirut, December 20, 1947.
37. *Jewish Chronicle*, October 15, 1948.
38. *DNB*, May 22, 1947.
39. *DNB*, January 16, 1948.
40. *Palestine Post*, Jerusalem, December 24, 1948.
41. *The New York Times*, August 7 and 10, 1949.
42. *Jewish Chronicle*, September 30, 1949.
43. *Ibid.*, September 23, 1949.
44. *DNB*, September 16, 1949.
45. *The New York Times*, December 30, 1949.
46. *Jewish Chronicle*, May 12 and June 2, 1950.
47. *DNB*, November 6, 1950.
48. *Jerusalem Post*, November 17, 1959.
49. Data supplied by the Immigration Department of the Jewish Agency, Jerusalem.
50. *American Jewish Yearbook*, Vol. LIX, pp. 399–400.
51. *Jewish Chronicle*, October 10, 1959.

52. Data supplied by the *Ozar Hatorah*, New York.
53. *Jerusalem Post*, September 25, 1959.

CHAPTER 6

1. Stein, Leonard. *Syria*, London, 1926, pp. 15–16.
2. *Economic Organization of Syria*, ed. by Sa'id B. Himadeh. American University of Beirut Publications, Beirut 1936, p. 409.
3. *Les Cahiers de l'Alliance Israélite Universelle*, Paris, October–November, 1947.
4. Report of the Jewish Community Council of Beirut to the World Jewish Congress, June 1947.
5. Rondot, Pierre, *Les Institutions Politiques de l'Orient Contemporain*, Paris, 1947, pp. 28–29.
6. *Times* (London), October 10, 1938.
7. *American Jewish Yearbook*, Vol. XL, p. 337.
8. *Universal Jewish Encyclopedia*, Vol. X, p. 136.
9. Awad, Joseph. "In the Lebanon Today," in *Al Hoda*, New York, January 4–5, 1949.
10. *Daily Mail*, London, November 6, 1945.
11. *Memorandum on the Position of the Jewish Communities in the Oriental Countries*, submitted to the Anglo-American Committee of Inquiry by the Jewish Agency for Palestine, Jerusalem, March 1946.
12. *DNB*, May 10, 1946.
13. *Chicago Tribune*, October 21, 1946.
14. *Al Diyar*, Beirut, October 15 and 17, 1945; *Al Alam al-Israeli*, Beirut, November 30, 1945.
15. *The New York Times*, October 15, 1946.
16. Report of the Beirut Jewish Community Council to the World Jewish Congress, June 23, 1947.
17. *Chicago Tribune*, December 23, 1947.
18. "Lebanese Jewry in Isolation," in *Midstream*, Winter 1958.
19. *Les Cahiers de l'Alliance Israélite Universelle*, February–March, 1948.
20. Report of the Beirut Jewish Community Council.
21. *DNB*, June 4, 1948.
22. Quoted in *L'Orient*, Beirut, January 13, 1948.
23. *Al Zaman*, Beirut, January 13, 1948.
24. *Sida al-Ahwal*, Beirut, January 13, 1948; *Al Diyar*, January 13, 1948. In October 1948, an official Lebanese announcement denied the reports that the governments of Syria and Lebanon had agreed to return to Syria those Syrian Jews who fled to Lebanon (*Saut al-Ahrar*, Beirut, October 24, 1948).
25. *Digest*, December 28, 1947.
26. *Al Hoda*, January 4–5, 1949.
27. *Telegraph*, Beirut, January 12, 1948.
28. *Al Diyar*, January 12, 1948.
29. *The New York Times*, May 26 and July 28, 1948.
30. *Al Beyraq* and *L'Orient* (Beirut), January 13, 1948.
31. *New York Post*, April 17, 1948.
32. Awad, Joseph E., *loc. cit.*
33. "Israel and its Minorities" in *Palestine*, New York, December 1948–January 1949.
34. *Jewish Chronicle*, London, August 19, 1949.
35. *Digest*, September 16, 1949; *Jewish Chronicle*, August 19, 1949.
36. *Palestine Post*, Jerusalem, May 8, 1949.
37. *DNB*, December 30, 1949; February 23, 1950.

38. *Jewish Chronicle*, March 10, 1950.
39. *DNB*, July 11 and 31, 1950.
40. *Jewish Affairs*, New York, September–October 1950.
41. "Position of the Jews in Lebanon," in *Jewish Chronicle*, November 5, 1952.
42. "Lebanese Jewry in Isolation," in *Midstream*, Winter 1958.
43. Institute of Jewish Affairs. *The Institute Annual 1956*, New York, 1957, pp. 428–429.
44. *Midstream, op. cit.*
45. *Les Cahiers de l'Alliance Israélite Universelle*, July-August 1959.
46. *The New York Times*, August 7, 1959.
47. *Jewish Chronicle*, November 11, 1958.
48. Quoted in *DNB*, November 11, 1959.
49. *Jewish Chronicle*, October 19, 1959.

CHAPTER 7

1. Leven, N. *Fifty Years of History—Alliance Israélite Universelle*, Paris, 1910, pp. 124–126.
2. World Jewish Congress. *The Treatment of Jews in Egypt and Iraq*, New York, 1948, p. 11.
3. Jewish Agency for Palestine. *Memorandum on the Position of the Jewish Communities in the Oriental Countries*, submitted to the Anglo-American Committee of Inquiry, Jerusalem, March 1946.
4. *Supplement du Journal Officiel*, Cairo, No. 74, August 11, 1947.
5. *Journal Officiel, Numéro Extraordinaire* (64), May 30, 1948.
6. *Journal Officiel, Numéro Extraordinaire* (102), July 21, 1948.
7. *Journal d'Egypte*, October 21 and 27, 1948.
8. *Progrès Egyptien*, November 9; *Bourse Egyptienne*, November 13 and 22; *Journal d'Egypte*, November 25, 1948.
9. *Progrès Egyptien*, December 2; *Journal d'Egypte*, December 16, *Bourse Egyptienne*, December 21, 1948.
10. *Bourse Egyptienne*, January 5 and 19; *Progrès Egyptien*, January 24 and 29, 1949.
11. *Progrès Egyptien*, February 28, 1949.
12. *Journal Officiel*, No. 146, September 30, 1948.
13. *Journal Officiel*, No. 124, August 28, 1948.
14. *Al Ahram*, Cairo, May 14–16 and 19, 1948; *The New York Times*, May 16, 1948.
15. *The New York Times*, June 21, 1948; *Al Ahram*, June 23, 1948.
16. *The New York Times*, July 24 and August 2, 1948.
17. Ibid., September 24, 1948; *New York Herald Tribune*, September 23, 1948; *Al Zaman*, Cairo, September 23, 1948.
18. *The New York Times*, May 16, 1948.
19. *Journal Officiel, Numéro Extraordinaire* (61), May 26, 1948.
20. *Journal Officiel, Numéro Extraordinaire* (146), September 26, 1948.
21. Ibid., Numéro Extraordinaire (63), May 28, 1948, and Numéro Extraordinaire (64), May 30, 1948.
22. Data supplied by the Immigration Department of the Jewish Agency, Jerusalem.
23. *The New York Times*, August 2, 1948.
24. Data supplied by the Immigration Dept. of the Jewish Agency.
25. *Digest*, September 25, 1953.
26. *Jewish Chronicle*, London, October 15 and 22, 1954.
27. Data supplied by the Immigration Department of the Jewish Agency.
28. *Congress Digest*, New York, October 25, 1954.

29. *Jewish Chronicle*, December 17, 1954.
30. Institute of Jewish Affairs. *The Institute Annual 1956*, New York 1957, pp. 414–418, 421, 422.
31. *Ibid.*, pp. 425–426.
32. *Ibid.*, pp. 218–419.
33. Data supplied by the Immigration Dept. of the Jewish Agency.
34. *The New York Times*, November 29, December 4, 1956.
35. *Journal Officiel*, No. 68–bis "A," November 1, 1956.
36. *Ibid.*, Numéro Extraordinaire (90 "A"), November 8, 1956.
37. Statement of the European Branch of the World Jewish Congress, March 10, 1957.
38. *New York Journal American*, December 21, 1956.
39. *New York Post*, January 8, 1957.
40. Spark, Fred. "Egypt's Shadowy Persecution Ousts Jews," in *New York World Telegram and Sun*, December 27, 1956.
41. Institute of Jewish Affairs. *Egypt in September 1957*, New York, 1958, p. 6.
42. *Alliance Review*, April 1957.
43. *Jewish Chronicle*, November 20, 1959.
44. *Ibid.*, October 31, December 19, 1958.
45. *The New York Times*, October 20, 1959; *Daily Hebrew Journal*, Toronto, November 13, 1959.
46. *Daily Hebrew Journal*, February 4, 1959.
47. *Jewish Chronicle*, October 31, 1958; November 20, 1959.
48. *New York Herald Tribune*, December 20, 1959; *Jewish Chronicle*, January 22, 1960.
49. *The New York Times*, November 19, 1959.
50. *Jewish Chronicle*, January 2, April 22, 1960; *Daily Hebrew Journal*, June 25, 1959; *Jewish News*, Newark, April 24, 1959.
51. *Daily Hebrew Journal*, October 15, 1959.
52. *Ibid.*, January 30, 1959; *Jewish Chronicle*, January 22, 1960; *Congress Digest*, January 1959.

CHAPTER 8

1. For the history of the Jews in Turkey see: Abraham Galante, *Histoire des Juifs d'Istanbul*, Istanbul 1941; *Idem, Les Juifs d'Izmir* (Smyrne), Istanbul, 1937.
2. Ward, Barbara. *Turkey*, London, 1942, p. 20. Ekrem, Selma. *Turkey: Old and New*, New York, 1947, pp. 32–33.
3. *Zeitschrift für Demographie und Statistik der Juden*, Berlin, 1908.
4. *Bulletin de l'Alliance Israélite Universelle*, Paris 1904, p. 168.
5. Jackh, Ernest. *The Rising Crescent. Turkey Yesterday, Today, Tomorrow.* New York, 1944, p. 93.
6. Wischnitzer, Mark. *Die Juden in der Welt*, Berlin, 1935, pp. 246–247.
7. *The Universal Jewish Encyclopedia*, Vol. X, p. 328.
8. Wischnitzer, M. *op. cit.*, pp. 246–247; *Palestine Post*, February 20, 1949.
9. *Haaretz*, Tel Aviv, October 29, 1947.
10. Institute of Jewish Affairs. *Were the Minorities Treaties a Failure?*, New York, 1943, p. 81.
11. *Le Temps*, Paris, October 10, 1925.
12. *Ibid.*, October 31, 1925, and January 9, 1926.
13. *Ibid.*, June 2, 1926.
14. Institute of Jewish Affairs, *op. cit.*, p. 81.
15. *Ibid.*, p. 235.
16. *American Jewish Yearbook*, Vol. XL, p. 336.

17. Wischnitzer, M. *op. cit.*, p. 109.
18. *DNB*, August 25, 1950.
19. Camber, Éric. "La Situation des Juifs de Turquie," in *Evidences*, Paris, November 1949.
20. Lestschinsky, Jacob. *Jews in Moslem Lands*, New York, 1946, p. 10.
21. *American Jewish Yearbook*, Vol. XXXIX, p. 493; Vol. XLI, p. 372; Vol. XLII, p. 440.
22. *Jewish Chronicle*, January 27, 1950.
23. "Turkish Jewry: A Declining Community" in *South African Jewish Times*, Johannesburg, November 4, 1949.
24. *The New York Times*, May 27, 1948; May 14, 1948.
25. *DNB*, July 18, 1949.
26. *DNB*, January 25, 1950.
27. *Jewish Standard*, London, September 9, 1948.
28. Webster, Donald E. *The Turkey of Ataturk; Social Process in the Turkish Reformation*, Philadelphia, 1939, pp. 280–281.
29. The Zionist Organization and the Jewish Agency for Palestine. *Reports of the Executive Submitted to the Twenty-Second Zionist Congress at Basle*, Jerusalem, 1946, pp. 165–170. Also: *Report on Immigration via Turkey to Palestine* by Ch. Barlas, dated December 18, 1943 (unpublished).
30. Ward, Barbara. *op. cit.*, 83–84.
31. Webster, D. E. *op. cit.*, pp. 280–281.
32. Turkish *Official Gazette*, No. 5255, November 12, 1941.
33. Gunther, John. *D Day*, New York, 1944, p. 194.
34. *The New International Yearbook for the Year 1943*, New York and London, 1944, p. 648.
35. *The New York Times*, September 11, 1943. Also: Kalendrian, Vahan H. "The Legal System of the Republic of Turkey and its Administration with Particular Stress on Taxation Affecting Domestic and Foreign Interests," in Foreign Law Association, *Proceedings*, No. 251, February 1944, p. 21.
36. *Der Neue Tag*, Prague, January 18, 1943.
37. Gunther, J. *op. cit.*, p. 194.
38. Decree No. 2/19 288, January 12, 1943, Turkish *Official Gazette*, No. 5302.
39. Gunther, J. *op cit.*, p. 195.
40. In the files of the World Jewish Congress.
41. *Donau Zeitung*, Belgrade, January 26, 1943.
42. *The New International Yearbook*, p. 651.
43. *American Jewish Yearbook*, Vol. XLVIV, p. 438.
44. *Palestine Post*, February 2, 1949.
45. *Jewish Chronicle*, June 2, 1950.
46. *Palestine Economist*, Jerusalem, July-August 1948.
47. *Report of the Executive Submitted to the Twenty-Second Zionist Congress at Basle*, p. 192.
48. *The New York Times*, October 21, 1948.
49. *Jewish Herald*, Johannesburg, November 21, 1948.
50. *Jewish Chronicle* and *Jewish Standard*, December 24, 1948.
51. *The New York Times*, November 2 and 12, 1948.
52. *Jewish Chronicle* and *Jewish Herald*, December 24, 1948; *Jewish Herald*, November 5, 1948.
53. *The New York Times*, November 12, 1948; *Jewish Chronicle*, December 3, 1948 and February 3, 1949; *Jewish Herald*, December 31, 1948.
54. *Jewish Herald*, December 17, 1948; *Jewish Chronicle*, December 3, 1948, January 7 and February 11, 1949.
55. *Jewish Chronicle*, February 4 and 11, 1949.
56. *Ibid.*, February 18, 1949.

57. *Survey of the Activities of the Jewish Agency's Immigration Department*, submitted to the Zionist General Council, Jerusalem, April 1950.
58. Lewis, Geoffrey. *Turkey*, New York, 1955, pp. 158–159.
59. Data supplied by the Immigration Department of the Jewish Agency, Jerusalem.
60. *Idem*.
61. *Davar*, Tel Aviv, October 14, 1955.
62. *Jewish Chronicle*, October 14, 1955.
63. *Ibid.*, January 16, 1959.
64. *Alliance Review*, New York, November–December 1950.
65. *Ibid.*; *Jewish Chronicle*, January 16, 1959.
66. *Alliance Review*, April 1957.
67. Lewis, G. *op. cit.*, pp. 156–157.
68. *Alliance Review*, April 1957.

CHAPTER 9

1. Fischel, Walter. "The Jews of Kurdistan a Hundred Years Ago," in *Jewish Social Studies*, July 1943, pp. 222–223.
2. Goldzieher, T. *Vorlesungen Über den Islam*, Heidelberg 1925, pp. 323 ff.
3. Perkins, J. "Journal of a Tour from Oromias to Mosul Through the Koordish Mountains," in *Journal of the American Oriental Society*, Vol. II, 1851, p. 270.
4. Peterman, M. *Reisen in Orient*, Leipzig, 1861, Vol. II, pp. 175–176.
5. Groseclose, Elgin. *Introduction to Iran*, New York, 1947, p. 58.
6. Curzon, G. W. *Persia and the Persian Question*, Vol. II, London, 1892, pp. 510–511.
7. Groseclose, E. *op. cit.*, p. 58.
8. Adler, Cyrus, and Margalith, Aaron M. *With Firmness in the Right*; American Diplomatic Action Affecting Jews, 1840–1945. Published by the American Jewish Committee, New York, 1946, pp. 9–10.
9. Fischel, W. *op. cit.*, pp. 224–225.
10. *The Travels of Rabbi David d'Beth Hillel from Jerusalem through Arabia, Koordistan, part of Persia and India to Madras*, 1832, pp. 85–86.
11. Peterman, M. *op. cit.*, pp. 175–176.
12. Emanuelson, Abraham. *The Remnant of the Jews*, New York, 1939, pp. 32–34; Report of Dr. I. Kleinbaum, Jewish Agency Representative in Teheran, dated May 19, 1946; Fischel, Walter J. "Secret Jews of Persia, A Century-Old Marrano Community in Asia," in *Commentary*, New York, January 1949; Sholami, Judah. "The Marranos of Mash-Had," in *The Jewish Frontier*, New York, October 1945.
13. Richter, J. *History of the Protestant Mission of the Near East*, New York 1910, pp. 326 ff., and 390–411.
14. Report of the Teheran Committee of the World Jewish Congress, February 18, 1947.
15. Quoted by Fischel in *Jewish Social Studies*, New York, April 1950, p. 156.
16. Wilson, S. G. *Bahaism and Its Claims*, London, 1915, pp. 51, 201.
17. Report of the Teheran Committee of the World Jewish Congress.
18. Fischel, Walter J. "The Jews of Persia 1795–1940," in *Jewish Social Studies*, April 1950, p. 211.
19. Greenfield, T. *Die Verfassung von Persien*, Berlin, 1904, pp. 32, 76.
20. Sikes, E. *Persia and its People*, London 1911, p. 128.
21. *Universal Jewish Encyclopedia*, Vol. VIII, New York, 1942, pp. 464–465.

22. *American Jewish Philanthropy and Jews Overseas.* The Institute on Overseas Studies of the Council of Jewish Federations and Welfare Funds, New York, 1948, p. 12.
23. *The Palestine Year Book,* Vol. III, New York, 1947–1948, p. 77.
24. Landshut, S. *Jewish Communities in the Moslem Countries in the Middle East;* a survey, London, 1950, p. 63.
25. Jaffe, Jean. "Persian Jewry—Shadow of the Ancient Glory," quoted in *Alliance Review,* New York, June 1952.
26. Haas, William S. *Iran,* New York, 1946, p. 72.
27. *Les Cahiers de l'Alliance Israélite Universelle,* Paris, February–March 1947 (later referred to as Cahiers).
28. Millspaugh, Arthur C. *Americans in Persia,* Washington, D. C., 1946, p. 8.
29. *Christian Science Monitor,* Boston, November 11, 1948.
30. New York *Herald Tribune,* November 19, 1947.
31. Curzon, G. N. *op. cit.,* Vol. II, pp. 510–511.
32. "Report of the Economic Committee," in *Bulletin of Bank Melli,* Teheran, February–March 1945.
33. Office of Jewish Information, *OJI Items,* New York, April 5, 1946.
34. American Joint Distribution Committee (AJDC). *Thirteenth Annual Country Directors Conference,* Geneva, October 27–30, 1958, p. 38 (later referred to as AJDC Conference).
35. *ORT Yearbook 1957.* New York, 1958, p. 18.
36. "The Jewish Community of Isfahan (Iran). From a report of a former student of the Ecole Normale Israélite of the Alliance." *Bulletin of the Alliance,* 1948, No. 10.
37. *Yalkut ha-Misrakh ha-Tikhon,* Jerusalem, November–December 1949.
38. Roosevelt, Eleanor. "Picture of Poverty," in St. Louis *Post Dispatch,* March 26, 1959.
39. *Cahiers,* February–March 1947.
40. *Ibid.,* June–July 1947.
41. Cuenca, Andre. "Educational Conditions Among Iranian Jews," in *Alliance Review,* June 1953. Also: *Alliance Review,* April 1957.
42. Rosen, Leon. "Les Ecoles de l'Alliance en Iran," in *Cahiers,* December 1957.
43. Vreeland, Herbert H. (ed.) *Iran,* New Haven, 1957, p. 203.
44. *Ozar Hatorah in the Middle East and North Africa. Facts and Figures,* New York, 1959.
45. *Alliance Review,* December 1957.
46. Rosen, Leon. "Les Ecoles de l'Alliance en Iran," in *Cahiers,* September–October 1959.
47. *AJDC Conference,* pp. 32–33.
48. *Ibid.,* pp. 33–36.
49. Jacobs, Arthur L. "Rehabilitating an Entire Community," in *The Day—Jewish Journal,* October 16, 1957.
50. In the files of the World Jewish Congress, New York.
51. *ORT Yearbook 1957,* pp. 19–20.
52. In the files of the World Jewish Congress, New York.
53. Report of the Teheran Committee of the World Jewish Congress. Also: Cuenca, André. "Le Judaisme Iranien," in *Cahiers,* February–March 1944.
54. *AJDC Conference,* pp. 36–37.
55. Kermanian, M. *Les Juifs de l'Iran.* Rapport à la 3-e Assemblée Générale de World Jewish Congress, 4–11 Aout, Genève, 1953.
56. Letter of M. Kermanian to the World Jewish Congress, New York, dated October 11, 1953.
57. The Zionist Organization and the Jewish Agency for Palestine. *Reports of*

the Executive Submitted to the 22nd Zionist Congress at Basle, Jerusalem 1946, pp. 172–173.

58. Christian Science Monitor, Boston, November 3, 1948.
59. Statement made on May 7, 1943, by the Foreign Vice Commissar of the U.S.S.R.; also statement by the British India Office in The New York Times, January 25, 1943.
60. The New York Times, May 2, 1950; JDC Digest, New York, November 1950.
61. The New York Times, October 5, 1950.
62. Thon, Hannah. "Olei Paras b'Yerusholaim," in Yalkut ha-Misrakh ha-Tikhon, Jerusalem, March–April 1950, pp. 40–43.
63. Data supplied by the Immigration Department of the Jewish Agency, Jerusalem.
64. Letter of Moussa Kermanian, editor, Alame Yahoud (Teheran), to the World Jewish Congress Executive, dated October 30, 1954.
65. Statement by Moussa Kermanian to the World Jewish Congress Office in Israel (report of Dr. L. Bernstein to the World Jewish Congress Executive in New York, dated December 12, 1955).
66. Jacobs, Arthur L. "A Visit with the Jewish Community in Iran," in The Day—Jewish Journal, December 8, 1957.
67. South African Jewish Times, Johannesburg, April 4, 1958.
68. Vreeland, H. H., loc. cit.
69. Institute of Jewish Affairs. Jewish Communities of the World, New York, 1959, p. 44.
70. Wilbur, Donald R., ed. The Middle East; a Political and Economic Survey (3rd edition), New York, 1958, p. 107.

CHAPTER 10

1. Wolff, Joseph. Researches and Missionary Labours, London 1937, p. 225.
2. Emanuelson, Abraham. The Remnant of the Jews, New York, 1939, p. 48.
3. Ben Zvi, Itzhak. The Exiled and the Redeemed, Philadelphia, 1957, p. 204.
4. Brauer, Erich. "The Jews of Afghanistan. An Anthropological Report," in Jewish Social Studies, New York, Vol. IV, No. 2, April 1942, p. 121.
5. Benjamin II, Eight Years in Asia and Africa, Hanover, 1859, p. 157.
6. Discussion held on January 15, 1948, between Mr. I. Ben-Zvi and Mr. Borochov from Bokhara regarding situation of Jews in Pakistan and Afghanistan (in the files of the World Jewish Congress, New York).
7. Jewish Chronicle, Supplement, London, March 26, 1947.
8. In the files of the World Jewish Congress, New York.
8a. Yalkut ha-Misrakh ha-Tikhon, Jerusalem, January–February, 1950.
9. Brauer, op. cit., pp. 134–135.
9a. Yalkut, loc. cit.
10. Dollot, R. L'Afghanistan, Paris, 1937, p. 219.
11. Brauer, op. cit., pp. 133–134; Emanuelson, op. cit., p. 47.
12. Brauer, op. cit., pp. 124–125.
13. Ibid., pp. 126, 123.
14. In the files of the World Jewish Congress, New York.
15. Brauer, op. cit., p. 138.
16. Yalkut ha-Misrakh ha-Tikhon, November–December 1949.
17. Jewish Chronicle, London, April 19, 1946.
18. The Jewish Standard, London, July 30, 1948.
19. India Today, New York, November 1947.
20. Yalkut ha-Misrakh ha-Tikhon, November–December 1949.

21. *Jewish Affairs*, New York, August–September 1950; *Digest*, November 11, 1949.
22. *Sikumei Aliyah, Jerusalem*, January–August 1950.
23. *Congress Digest*, New York, February 20, 1950.
24. *Ibid.*, November 17, 1950.
25. Institute of Jewish Affairs. *The Jewish Communities of the World*, New York, 1959, p. 41.

CHAPTER 11

1. Chouraqui, André. *La Condition Juridique de l'Israélite Marocain*, Paris 1950, pp. 31–32. *Idem: Marche Vers l'Occident. Les Juifs de l'Afrique du Nord*, Paris, 1952, p. 136.
2. Eisenbeth, Maurice. *Les Juifs de l'Afrique du Nord. Démographie et Onomastique*, Alger, 1936, pp. 72–73.
3. Chouraqui, André. *Condition* . . . p. 35–36; *Idem: Marche* . . . p. 163.
4. *Idem: Condition* . . . pp. 212–213.
5. Young, Wayland. "Position of Moroccan Jewry," in *Jewish Chronicle*, August 19, 1955.
6. Chouraqui, André. *Condition* . . . p. 34.
7. Yaffe, Richard. "Fate of Moroccan Jewry. Danger of Economic Strangulation," in *Jewish Chronicle*, August 31, 1956.
8. Carr, Maurice. "Jewish Exodus from Bled," in *Jerusalem Post*, February 6, 1959.
9. *Alliance Review*, February 1955.
10. Chouraqui, André. *Condition* . . . pp. 37–41.
11. *Jewish Chronicle*, June 22, 1956.
12. Yaffe, R. *loc. cit.*
13. ORT. *Record of Ten Years of Rebuilding Jewish Economic Life*, New York, 1957, p. 29.
14. *Session of the Zionist General Council*, August 23–31, 1955. Addresses, Debates, Resolutions. Jerusalem, 1957, p. 55.
15. Yaffe, R. *loc. cit.*
16. Carr, M. *loc. cit.*
17. Kessler, David. "The Jewish Position in Morocco," in *Jewish Chronicle*, July 18, 1958.
18. American Jewish Joint Distribution Committee. *Thirteenth Annual Country Directors Conference*, Geneva, October 27–30, 1958, pp. 17–18.
19. ORT, *op. cit.*, p. 25.
20. *OSE Newsletter*, November–December, 1957.
21. S. S. "Preserving the Jewish Spirit" in *Alliance Review*, February–March 1950; Institute of Jewish Affairs. *Current Events in Jewish Life*, New York, January–March 1950; Braunschwig, Jules. "Orthodox or Hassid?" in *Alliance Review*, January 1953; Lehrman, Hal. "Moroccan Jews Enter the 20th Century," in *Commentary*, New York, August 1954.
22. S. S., *loc. cit.*
23. *Cahiers de l'Alliance Israélite Universelle*, Paris, January 1960.
24. *Ozar Hathorah in the Middle East and North Africa. Facts and Figures*, New York, 1959.
25. Institute of Jewish Affairs. *The Jewish Communities in the World*, New York, 1958, pp. 5–6.
26. Royaume de Maroc. Ministère de l'Education Nationale de la Jeunesse et des Sports. *Le Mouvement Educatif au Maroc Durant l'Année Scolaire 1957–1958*. Rapport soumis à la XXI-e Conference Internationale de

l'Instruction Publique (July 7–16, 1958, Genève), p. 5; Royaume du Maroc. Ministère de l'Education Nationale de la Jeunesse et des Sports. *Education Secondaire Musulman.* Rabat, October 1947, p. 9.

27. Taillard, F. *Le Nationalisme Marocain*, Paris, 1947, pp. 10 ff.
28. Young, W. *loc. cit.*
29. *World Jewry*, London, September 1959.
30. Quoted in *Jewish Chronicle*, September 30, 1955.
31. Quoted in *Jewish Chronicle*, September 9, 1955.
32. Lehrman, Hal. "Report from Morocco," in *Midstream*, Summer 1958.
33. *Ibid.*
34. Institute of Jewish Affairs. *The Institute Annual 1956.* New York, 1956, p. 458.
35. Gil, B. "The Selectivity of the North African Aliyah," in *Alliance Review*, February 1955.
36. Data supplied by the Immigration Department of the Jewish Agency, Jerusalem.
37. Carr, Maurice. "The Human Side," in *Israel Youth Horizon*, Jerusalem, December 1951.
38. Gil, B., *loc. cit.*
39. *Jewish Chronicle*, March 4, 1955.
40. *The New York Times*, April 18, 1955.
41. *Jerusalem Post*, July 6, 1959.
42. *The New York Times*, April 18, 1955.
43. *Session of the Zionist General Council*, pp. 42–43, 53–59, 283.
44. *Jewish Chronicle*, September 9, 1955.
45. *Ibid.*, August 26 and 19, 1955.
46. *Ibid.*, September 30, 1955; *Congress Weekly*, New York, October 10, 1955.
47. *Jewish Chronicle*, September 16, 1955.
48. *The New York Times*, March 11, 1956.
49. *Session of the General Zionist Council*, July 10–23, 1957. Addresses, Debates, Resolutions. Jerusalem 1958, p. 120.
50. Yaffe, Richard. "Moroccan Jewry's Fate," in *Jewish Chronicle*, August 10, 1956.
51. Carr, Maurice. "Report From Morocco," in *Jerusalem Post*, February 2, 1959.
52. *The New York Times*, May 20, 27, 31, 1960.
53. *Jewish Chronicle*, September 7 and 21, 1956.
54. *American Jewish Year Book*, Vol. LIX, pp. 359–61.
55. *Jewish Chronicle*, April 10, October 9, 1959; January 8, 1960.
55a. *Israelitisches Wochenblatt*, Zurich, March 25, 1960; *Jewish Chronicle*, London, July 1 and 8, 1960.
56. *Near East Report*, Washington D. C., February 1, 1960.
57. Lehrman, Hal. "Report from Morocco," *loc. cit.*
58. Kessler, David. "The Jewish Position in Morocco," *loc. cit.*
59. Carr, Maurice. "Jewish Exodus from Bled," *loc. cit.*
60. *The New York Times*, September 14, 1956; *American Jewish Yearbook*, Vol. LIX, p. 359.
61. Carr, Maurice. "The Prisoners of Tangiers," in *Jewish Chronicle*, March 13, 1959.
62. *Ibid.*
63. *American Jewish Yearbook*, Vol. LIX, pp. 359, 360.
64. *Ibid.*, p. 361.
65. *The New York Times*, March 27, April 2 and 8, 1959; *Jewish Chronicle*, April 3 and 10, 1959; *Daily Hebrew Journal*, Toronto, April 20, 1959.
66. *Jewish Chronicle*, May 13, 1960; *The New York Times*, June 5, 1960.

CHAPTER 12

1. Chouraqui, André. *Marche Vers l'Occident. Les Juifs d'Afrique du Nord.* Paris 1952, pp. 147, 152.
2. *Ibid.,* pp. 237, 238, 240.
3. Institute of Jewish Affairs. *Current Events in Jewish Life,* January–March 1952.
4. *Ibid.,* April–September 1954.
5. *The New York Times,* April 23, 1955.
6. *Jewish Chronicle,* July 29, 1955.
7. *Current Events in Jewish Life,* April–September 1954.
8. *Jewish Chronicle,* September 16 and 30, 1955.
9. *Current Events in Jewish Life,* April–September 1954.
10. *Congress Weekly,* October 10, 1955.
11. *Session of the Zionist General Council,* August 23–31, 1955. Addresses, Debates, Resolutions. Jerusalem, 1956, p. 59.
12. Report to the World Jewish Congress, New York, by Jacques Lazarus, Algiers, dated October 14, 1957.
13. *Information Juive,* Algiers, August–September 1958.
14. *World Jewry,* London, March 1959.
15. *Current Events in Jewish Life,* January–March 1956.
16. *Congress Digest,* November 10, 1956.
17. *Ozar Hatorah in the Middle East and North Africa,* New York 1959.
18. *ORT Yearbook 1957.* New York 1958, pp. 13–15.
19. *The New York Times,* July 22, 1956.
20. Chouraqui, André. "North African Jewry" in *Forum for the Problems of Zionism, Jewry and the State of Israel.* Proceedings of the Jerusalem Ideological Conference, Jerusalem 1959, p. 259.
21. *Congress Digest,* November 10, 1956.
22. *Jewish Chronicle,* September 16, 1955.
23. *Ibid.; Nir Hakvuza,* Tel Aviv 1955, p. 614.
24. *The New York Times,* July 22, 1956.
25. Data supplied by the Immigration Department of the Jewish Agency, Jerusalem.
26. ZINS (Zionist Information Service), New York, May 25, 1956.
27. Institute of Jewish Affairs. *The Institute Annual 1958,* p. 443.
28. ZINS, March 25, 1956.
29. *Information Juive,* Algiers, March 1959.
30. Report to the World Jewish Congress dated "end of September 1957."
31. Data supplied by the Immigration Department of the Jewish Agency, Jerusalem.
32. The Central Bureau of Statistics. *Statistical Abstract of Israel,* Jerusalem, 1957, p. 40.

CHAPTER 13

1. *Information,* Algiers, March 1960.
1a. American Joint Distribution Committee. *Thirteenth Annual Country Directors Conference,* Geneva, October 27–30, 1958. Report by Henry L. Levy, Director for Algeria, pp. 29–30.
2. DNB, November 23, 1959.
3. Report by Jacques Lazarus to the World Jewish Congress, dated November 11, 1958.
4. Report by Henry L. Levy, *loc. cit.,* pp. 30–31.

5. *Assises du Judaisme Algérien*, 12–13 Mars 1958, Alger 1958, p. 12.
6. *Forward*, New York, March 27, May 24, 1956.
7. *Jewish Chronicle*, May 18, 1956.
8. *Ibid.*
9. *Congress Record*, New York, March 25, 1958.
10. *Ibid.*, December 12, 1958.
11. *Ibid.*, May 18, 1956.
12. Report by Henry L. Levy, *loc. cit.*, pp. 29–30.
13. *Jewish Chronicle*, December 12 and 19, 1958.
14. *Congress Record*, June 25, 1956.
15. *DNB* and *Bulletin Juif d'Information*, Paris, February 24, 1960.
16. The Central Bureau of Statistics. *Statistical Abstract of Israel 1956/57*, Jerusalem 1957, p. 40.
17. *Congress Digest*, New York, March 1958.
18. *American Jewish Yearbook LIX*, p. 249.

CHAPTER 14

1. Patai, Raphael. *Israel Between East and West*, Philadelphia, 1953, pp. 63, 66.
2. *Facts and Figures in Israel*, Jerusalem, March 1959.
3. Eisenstadt, S. N. *The Absorption of Immigration. A Sociological Study*, Jerusalem, 1952, p. 90.
4. *Ibid.*, p. 91.
5. *Ibid.*, p. 156.
6. Eilon, Amos. "The Other Israel," in *Sound the Great Trumpet*, ed. by M. Z. Frank, New York, 1953, pp. 365, 369–370.
7. Zerubavel, Y. "The Central Problem," in *Yalkut ha-Misrakh ha-Tikhon*, Jerusalem, August–September 1951.
8. Ravid, Moshe. *Youth Aliyah in Figures During a Quarter of a Century* (mimeographed), Jerusalem, 1959.
9. Kol, Moshe. *Youth Aliyah; Past, Present and Future*, Jerusalem, 1957, pp. 60–61.
10. Klausner, Samuel. "Immigrant Absorption and Social Tension in Israel. A Case Study of Iraqi Jewish Immigrants," in *The Middle East Journal*, Washington D. C., Summer 1953, p. 286.
11. Spiro, Melford E. "The Sabras and Zionism; A Study in Personality and Ideology," in *Social Problems*, Brooklyn, Fall 1957, pp. 101–102.
12. *Jerusalem Post*, July 30, 1959.
13. Shumsky, Abraham. *The Clash of Cultures in Israel*, New York, 1955, p. 15.
14. Sapir, R. "A Home," in *Megamot*, Vol. III, No. 1, 1951.
15. Abbas, Abraham, M. K. *From Ingathering to Integration*, Jerusalem, 1959, pp. 17, 18, 26.
16. *Jerusalem Post*, October 2, 1959.
17. *Ibid.*

CHAPTER 15

1. Ottley, Roy. *No Greener Pastures*, New York, 1951, p. 208.
2. Quoted by Patai, *op cit.*, p. 198.
3. Shumsky, A. *op. cit.*, p. 86.
4. Frankenstein, Carl. "The Problem of Ethnic Differences in the Absorption of Immigrants," in *Between Past and Future. Essays and Studies on Aspects of Immigrant Absorption in Israel*, Jerusalem, 1953, p. 16.

5. Patai, *op. cit.*, p. 203–205.
6. Nissim, Zecharia. "A Yemenite Boy in Israel," in *Sound the Great Trumpet*, p. 308.
7. Remba, Isaak. "The Yemenite Jews of Israel," in *Congress Weekly*, February 16, 1953.
8. *The New York Times*, June 30, 1951.
9. Klausner, *op. cit.*, p. 287.
10. Communicated by Alex Weingrod, Settlement Department of the Jewish Agency, Jerusalem.
11. "À Propos de Discrimination," in *La Tribune Sioniste*, Brussels, August 31, 1959.
12. *Alliance Review*, November–December 1949.
13. Gelblum, Arye. "The Truth About the Human Material," in *Haaretz*, Jerusalem, April 22, 1949.
14. Gillon, Philip. "Beersheba: After the Storm," in *Jerusalem Post*, July 24, 1959.
15. *Jerusalem Post*, July 29, 1959.
16. *Ibid.*, July 24, 1959.
17. *Daily Hebrew Journal*, Toronto, September 8, 1959.
18. Eisenstadt, *op. cit.*, pp. 16, 20.
19. Statement by Moshe Braginski, head of the Absorption Department, Jewish Agency Jerusalem in *DNB*, August 11, 1959.
20. Communicated by Alex Weingrod, Jerusalem.
21. *Jerusalem Post*, August 20, 1959.
22. Shuval, Judith. "Emerging Social Relationship in a Heterogeneous Immigrants' Community," Jerusalem, 1954, p. 91.
23. Eisenstadt, *op cit.*, p. 156.
24. *Daily Hebrew Journal*, September 8, 1959; *DNB*, August 21, 1959; *La Tribune Sioniste*, August 31, 1959.
25. Data supplied by the Immigration Department of the Jewish Agency, Jerusalem.

CHAPTER 16

1. *Jerusalem Post*, July 14, 1959.
2. *Ibid.*, July 28 and 27, 1959.
3. Report of the Inquiry Committee. *Jerusalem Post*, August 20, 1959.
4. *Ibid.*

CHAPTER 17

1. Gillon, Philip. "Feuding Mars Village Edens," in *Jerusalem Post*, January 8, 1960.
2. Abbas, *op. cit.*, pp. 9–10.
3. *La Tribune Sioniste*, August 31, 1959.
4. Tartakower, Arieh. *Jewish Society*, Tel Aviv and Jerusalem 5719, (Hebrew), p. 100.
5. B'ari, Shmuel. "Israel's Problem of Integration," in *New Outlook*, New York, October 1959.
6. Abbas, *op. cit.*, pp. 28–31.
7. *Ibid.*
8. Josephsthal, Senta. "Welcoming the Oriental Newcomer," in *Jewish Frontier*, New York, December 1959.
9. Eisenstadt, *op. cit.*, p. 91.

10. Eilon, *loc. cit.*, pp. 392–393.
11. Shumsky, *op. cit.*, p. 91.
12. Enoch, D. "Non-Promotion in Elementary Schools in Tel Aviv," in *Megamot*, Vol. II, No. 1, 1950.
13. Shumsky, *op. cit.*, pp. 92–93.
14. Smilansky, Moshe. *The Social Implications of the Educational Structure in Israel* (Hebrew), Jerusalem 1957.
15. Ortar, Gina. "A Comparative Analysis of the Structure of Intelligence in Various Ethnic Groups," in Frankenstein, Carl, (ed.). *Between Past and Future*, p. 289.
16. Enoch, D. "Elementary School Graduation in Tel Aviv," in *Megamot*, Vol. IV, No. 1, 1952.
17. *Jerusalem Post*, July 29, 1959.
18. *Ibid.*, September 25, 1959.
19. Klausner, *loc. cit.*, p. 290.
20. Abbas, *op. cit.*, p. 171.
21. Klausner, *loc. cit.*, p. 290.
22. Zabari, Rahel. "Our Schools: The Crucible of Integration," in *Jewish Frontier*, December 1959.
23. *Jerusalem Post*, July 29, 1959.
24. *Davar*, Tel Aviv, August 28, 1959.
25. Abbas, *op. cit.*, p. 14.
26. *DNB*, August 11, 1959.
27. *Israel Digest*, Jerusalem, September 4, 1959.
28. *Davar*, August 28, 1959.
29. Abbas, *op. cit.*, pp. 16–17.
30. *Jerusalem Post*, August 20, 1959.
31. *Israel Digest*, August 21, 1959.
32. *Jerusalem Post*, August 20, 1959.
33. Shumsky, *op. cit.*, pp. 77–79.
34. *Jerusalem Post*, October 20, 1959.
35. *Ibid.*
36. Halevi, H. S. "Divorce in Israel," in *Population Studies*, November 1956, pp. 186–188.

Index